Lecture Notes in Computer Science 14516

Founding Editors

Gerhard Goos
Juris Hartmanis

The series Lecture Notes in Computer Science (LNCS), including its subseries Lecture Notes in Artificial Intelligence (LNAI) and Lecture Notes in Bioinformatics (LNBI), has established itself as a medium for the publication of new developments in computer science and information technology research, teaching, and education.

LNCS enjoys close cooperation with the computer science R & D community, the series counts many renowned academics among its volume editors and paper authors, and collaborates with prestigious societies. Its mission is to serve this international community by providing an invaluable service, mainly focused on the publication of conference and workshop proceedings and postproceedings. LNCS commenced publication in 1973.

Shelly Sachdeva · Yutaka Watanobe
Editors

Big Data Analytics in Astronomy, Science, and Engineering

11th International Conference on Big Data Analytics, BDA 2023
Aizu, Japan, December 5–7, 2023
Proceedings

 Springer

Editors
Shelly Sachdeva 🆔
Department of Computer Science
and Engineering
National Institute of Technology Delhi
New Delhi, Delhi, India

Yutaka Watanobe 🆔
Information Systems Laboratory, Department
of Computer Science and Engineering
University of Aizu
Aizu-Wakamatsu, Fukushima, Japan

ISSN 0302-9743   ISSN 1611-3349 (electronic)
Lecture Notes in Computer Science
ISBN 978-3-031-58501-2   ISBN 978-3-031-58502-9 (eBook)
https://doi.org/10.1007/978-3-031-58502-9

This Springer imprint is published by the registered company Springer Nature Switzerland AG
The registered company address is: Gewerbestrasse 11, 6330 Cham, Switzerland

Paper in this product is recyclable.

Preface

The volume of data managed by computer systems continues to grow with time. It has increased many fold in recent times. It is due to advances in networking technologies, storage systems, mobile and cloud computing adoption, and the wide deployment of sensors for data collection. As a result, five attributes of data pose new challenges: volume, variety, velocity, veracity, and value. To make sense of emerging big data to support decision-making, the field of Big Data Analytics has emerged as a key research and study area for the industry and other organizations. Numerous big data analytics applications are found in several diverse fields, such as e-commerce, finance, healthcare, education, e-governance, media and entertainment, security and surveillance, smart cities, telecommunications, agriculture, astronomy, and transportation.

Big data analysis raises several challenges, such as processing extremely large volumes of data, processing data in real-time, and dealing with complex, uncertain, heterogeneous, and streaming data, which are often stored in multiple remote storage systems. New big data analysis solutions must be devised to address these challenges by drawing expertise from several fields, such as big data processing, data mining, database systems, statistics, machine learning, and artificial intelligence. Additionally, it is crucial to develop data analysis systems for new applications, including time-domain astronomy, social media analysis, and vehicular networks. Additionally, it is vital to support using big data analysis techniques in artificial intelligence and related fields.

The eleventh International Conference on Big Data Analytics (BDA) was held on December 5–7, 2023. It was held jointly by the University of Aizu, Japan, the Indian Institute of Technology, Delhi (IITD), and the National Institute of Technology, Delhi. These proceedings include 19 peer-reviewed research papers, and contributions by keynote speakers, and invited speakers. This year's program covers a wide range of topics related to big data analytics on themes such as: Data Management for Data Centres and Transactions, Data Science and Applications, Data Visualization, Cyber Systems, and Information Security.

Research papers, keynote speeches, and invited talks presented at the conference are expected to encourage research on big data analytics and stimulate the development of innovative solutions and their adoption in the industry.

The conference received 55 submissions. The Program Committee (PC) was comprised of researchers from academia and industry from many different countries. Each submission was reviewed by at least two, and at most by three Program Committee members, and was discussed by PC chairs before taking the decision. The Program Committee selected 19 full papers based on the above review process. The overall acceptance rate was 34%.

We want to extend our sincere thanks to the members of the Program Committee and external reviewers for their time, energy, and expertise in supporting BDA 2023.

Additionally, we would like to thank all the authors who considered BDA 2023 to be the forum to publish their research contributions. The Steering Committee and the Organizing Committee deserve praise for their support. Several individuals contributed to the success of the conference. We thank Marcin Paprzycki, Srinath Srinivasa, Ponnurangam Kumaraguru, HV Jagadish, and Huzur Saran for their insightful suggestions. We also thank all the keynote speakers and invited speakers. We want to thank the sponsoring organizations, including the Indian Institute of Information Technology, Delhi (IITD), India, the University of Aizu, Japan, and the Department of Computer Science at the National Institute of Technology, Delhi (NITD), as they deserve praise for the support they provided.

The conference received valuable support from the University of Aizu, IIT Delhi, and NIT Delhi for hosting and organizing it. At the same instance, thanks are also extended to the faculty, staff members, and student volunteers of the Department of Computer Science at the University of Aizu, IIT Delhi, and NIT Delhi for their constant cooperation and support.

December 2023   Shelly Sachdeva
                                                                                    Yutaka Watanobe

Organization

BDA 2023 was organized by University of Aizu, Japan, Indian Institute of Technology, Delhi (IITD) and National Institute of Technology, Delhi, (NITD), India.

Chief Patrons

Ajay K. Sharma	NIT Delhi, India
Qiangfu Zhao	University of Aizu, Japan

General Chair

Shelly Sachdeva	NIT Delhi, India

Steering Committee

Subhash Bhalla (Co-chair)	University of Aizu, Japan
Srinath Srinivasa	IIIT Bangalore, India
Huzur Saran (Co-chair)	IIT Delhi, India
Prem Kalra	IIT Delhi, India
H. V. Jagadish	University of Michigan, USA
Divyakant Agrawal	University of California at Santa Barbara, USA
Arun Agarwal	University of Hyderabad, India
Nadia Berthouze	UCL, UK
Cyrus Shahabi	University of Southern California, USA

Patron

Geeta Sikka	NIT Delhi, India

Program Committee Chairs

Shelly Sachdeva   NIT Delhi, India
Yutaka Watanobe   University of Aizu, Japan

Organizing Chair

Shelly Sachdeva   NIT Delhi, India

Publication Chair

Subhash Bhalla   University of Aizu, Japan

Convenors

D. Vaithiyanathan   NIT Delhi, India
Shivani Batra   Flexera, India

Tutorial Chair

Punam Bedi   Delhi University, India

Publicity Chairs

Rahul Katarya   DTU Delhi, India
Chandra Prakash   NIT Delhi, India
Baljit Kaur   NIT Delhi, India

Executive Members

Rashmi Prabhakar Sarode   Indian Institute of Technology, Madras, India
Rishav Singh   NIT Delhi, India
S. Kikuchi   Institute of Physical and Chemical Research,
                                  RIKEN, Japan

Program Committee

D. Agrawal	University of California, USA
F. Andres	National Institute of Informatics, Tokyo, Japan
Nadia Bianchi-Berthouze	University College London, UK
S. Selvakumar	IIIT, Una, India
Paolo Bottoni	University of Rome, Italy
L. Capretz	Western University, Canada
M. Capretz	Western University, Canada
Richard Chbeir	Pau University, France
Punam Bedi	University of Delhi, India
Pratul Dublish	Microsoft Research, USA
William I. Grosky	University of Michigan-Dearborn, USA
Jens Herder	University of Applied Sciences, Dusseldorf, Germany
Masahito Hirakawa	Shimane University, Japan
Qun Jin	Waseda University, Tokyo, Japan
Srinath Srinavasa	IIIT Bangalore, India
Akhil Kumar	Pennsylvania State University, USA
Siddhartha Asthana	AI Garage Mastercard, India
Jianhua Ma	Hosei University, Tokyo, Japan
Shivani Batra	Flexera, India
K. Myszkowski	Max-Planck-Institut für Informatik, Germany
T. Nishida	Kyoto University, Japan
Saroj Kaushik	IIT Delhi, India
Prabhat Manocha	IBM Gurgaon, India
Harsh Verma	NIT Jalandhar, India
Kavita Pandey	JIIT Noida, India
Ashish Kumar Tripathi	Malaviya National Institute of Technology Jaipur, India
Prakash Srivastava	IIET Group of Institutions, India
Rahul Katarya	DTU, Delhi, India
Mark Sifer	University of Wollongong, Australia
Neeraj Goel	IIT Ropar, India
Tanmoy Chakraborty	IIT Delhi, India

Sponsoring Institutions

National Institute of Technology, Delhi, India
Indian Institute of Technology, Delhi, India
University of Aizu, Japan

Contents

Data Science and Applications

Cyber Systems and Information Security

Data Management and Visualization

AI-Based Assistance for Management of Oral Community Knowledge in Low-Resource and Colloquial Kannada Language

M. Aparna[1]([✉]) [iD], Sharath Srivatsa[1] [iD], G. Sai Madhavan[1] [iD], T. B. Dinesh[2] [iD], and Srinath Srinivasa[1] [iD]

[1] International Institute of Information Technology, 26/C, Electronics City Phase 1, Bangalore, Karnataka, India
{aparna.m,sharath.srivatsa,g.saimadhavan,sri}@iiitb.ac.in
[2] iruWay Rural Research Lab, Janastu, Durgadahalli, Tumkur Dist., India
dinesh@janastu.org

Abstract. Knowledge in rural communities is largely created, preserved, and is transferred verbally, and it is limited. This information is valuable to these communities, and managing and making it available digitally with state-of-the-art approaches enriches awareness and collective knowledge of people of these communities. The large amounts of data and information produced on the Internet are inaccessible to the population in these rural communities due to factors like lack of infrastructure, connectivity, and limited literacy. Knowledge internal to rural communities is also not conserved and made available in any global Big Data information systems. Artificial Intelligence (AI) technologies such as Automatic Speech Recognition (ASR) and Natural Language Processing (NLP) provide substantial assistance when vast quantities of data, like Big Data, are available to build solutions. In the case of low-resource languages like Kannada and rural colloquial dialects, publicly available corpora are significantly less. Building state-of-the-art AI solutions is challenging in this context, and we address this problem in this work. Knowledge management in rural communities requires a low-cost and efficient approach that social workers can use. This paper proposes an architecture for oral knowledge management for rural communities speaking colloquial Kannada. The proposed architecture has an interface for oral knowledge retrieval using text processing on transcripts generated from the smallest state-of-the-art ASR model. We propose three interfaces to search for content: an n-gram based fuzzy search to search for texts in audios, the most frequent entities search based on the Kannada Named Entity Recognition (NER) model, and question-answering with Large Language Model (LLM) using a community knowledge vector store.

Keywords: Community Knowledge Management · Low-resource Languages · Automatic Speech Recognition · Keyword Search · Named Entity Recognition · Large Language Model · Big Data

This work was supported by the *Mphasis F1 Foundation*.

1   Introduction

The rapid advancement of digitization has congregated data from diverse and heterogeneous sources. The amount of data created by the Internet daily is estimated to be 328.77 million terabytes [6]. Platforms for video sharing, social media, gaming, and web browsing make up most of the internet traffic [6]. These information modalities are complex to use for rural communities in India due to low literacy levels and limited communication infrastructure. Even with programs such as Digital India, which aims at integrating the advancements in information technology in various development schemes for digital empowerment of the country, digital literacy remains a goal to achieve[1].

The diverse language culture of rural India and obstacles like poverty and limited (digital) literacy make it hard to consume knowledge and information on the web. The most beneficial digital content for rural communities is the rich indigenous knowledge created by the region's people. Collective community knowledge is discrete, vocal, un-codified, and valuable to rural social community members. It is vital to preserve and effectively disseminate this knowledge for social wellness. Searchable access to this indigenous knowledge benefits members and non-members of the community. Due to low literacy levels and limited infrastructure, documenting data relevant to these lesser-known communities is complex and usually least prioritized. Audio and other vocal modalities are an effective medium in this scenario as they are economical to create and convenient to use by listening. It is also to be noted that audio data contributes the least to internet traffic [6]. Members in several rural communities often resort to means of vocal communication such as storytelling, songs, and speeches to share and pass down knowledge of tacit, implicit, or explicit nature. Such content is frequently collected by non-governmental organizations (NGOs) and volunteers in rural areas as recorded audio content since it is easy and low-cost. On-demand access to this content can be helpful to even marginally literate community members as they can listen to and understand it. Considering limited literacy in the audience and audio being an easy and less expensive medium, simple and convenient searchable access to informational audio with that to collective community knowledge is of much importance.

An AI-based Big Data architecture can arrange audio content, handle search queries, and present the results. The main challenges in building such a solution with low cost and low maintenance are using vernacular language in the audio, noisy audio contents, and less or minimal available corpus. In this work, we use Kannada language audios collected by the organization Namma Halli Radio[2] in villages of *Tumakuru* region of Karnataka. The audio contents include conversations, interviews, songs, and other interactions with the village population, primarily using a dialect of Kannada spoken around the *Tumakuru* region. This dialect represents the variation from the literary Kannada in this study. We have

---

[1] https://www.statista.com/statistics/1232343/internet-literacy-index-by-category-india/.

[2] https://blog.janastu.org/covid-19-campaign-namma-halli-radio/.

processed and used this radio channel's recordings to realize the architecture's components.

Recording experiences, opinions, and knowledge of rural populations in audio form can give us a few hours of speech data. Acquiring more audio hours is not possible in the case of small communities, and this further complicates the task of building an ASR model for a colloquial variety of languages. Recent studies on language varieties in building an ASR model, such as Aksënova et al. [1], used a fine-tuning corpus of accented speech of roughly 45 h of data. Achieving this scale of speech data is infeasible for social workers and volunteers who work on collecting the speech corpus. Since the communities are (digitally) ignored and underrepresented, even a knowledge management solution in this scenario needs to be low-cost. In this study, we make the best use of the available corpus by fine-tuning a small ASR model to create a transcripts corpus, which is used to implement knowledge management functionalities by keyword search, entity search, and question-answering LLM.

The functionalities of user interfaces are built using the transcripts corpus of audio contents that tackle the critical problems for community knowledge management: oral knowledge, low-resource, and diglossia[3]. A language is diglossic if the formal or literary version of the language is dissimilar to the colloquial or spoken version. In Kannada, regional dialects such as Bangalore Kannada, Mysore Kannada, Dharwad Kannada, and Mangalore Kannada exist and each of them represents the dialect being spoken in the respective regions. The state-of-the-art multi-lingual model is fine-tuned with Namma Halli Radio audio corpus to be used in real-time to ingest new audio files by creating transcripts and to convert speech queries to text in the user interface. The challenge of diglossia is mitigated by fine-tuning the model on the vernacular corpus. The fine-tuning annotations corpus is created from a sample of audio using a very low WER commercial ASR model and manually correcting the errors to get the best annotations corpus. Fine-tuning small multi-lingual ASR models can be achieved using low-cost computing resources and is easy to manage and enhance. In contrast, fine-tuning large multi-lingual ASR models requires expensive computing resources, a large corpus, and difficulty maintaining. Building and maintaining large models is hard even though we get very low WER. To make available a low-cost solution, we have fine-tuned a small multi-lingual ASR model with a WER of around 60%, which is not very high, which means transcripts contain words with errors in spelling, to create a transcripts corpus and propose the following components that achieve Knowledge Management using transcripts with word errors:

1. N-gram fuzzy search
2. Entity search recommendations using a Kannada Named Entity Recognition model built using Active Learning technique
3. Knowledge retrieval using a Question-Answering Large Language Model along with a community knowledge vector store

Keyword searching in the transcripts is achieved using an n-gram fuzzy matching. The matching is fuzzy to overcome word errors in the transcripts and

---

[3] http://lisindia.ciil.org/Kannada/Kannada.html.

show the best search results to the user. The Kannada Named Entity Recognition model is built using the Active Learning (AL) technique. The entities identified by the NER model in the transcripts, spelling corrected when needed, are shown in the user interface for the user to use as a search term. The audio transcripts corpus can also be used to build a community knowledge vector store containing embeddings corresponding to the corpus, which can be utilized by a Large Language Model (LLM) for generating accurate answers for any query posed by the user that is relevant to the community context. An oral interface can be enabled using the ASR model, which converts voice search content to text, passed to the components.

2 Related Work

Knowledge management system for audio content requires an efficient pipeline for recording, storing, sharing, and retrieving data. Many models using the deep learning approach for Automatic Speech Recognition (ASR) and Speech to Text (STT) have been proposed. Baevski et al. (2020) [3] proposed Wav2Vec 2.0, which included a self-supervised pre-training approach that performed better than existing semi-supervised methods. This was improved as Wav2Vec-U, a framework for unsupervised learning presented by Baevski et al. (2021) [2] which was also used for experimenting on low-resource languages. Radford et al. [15] came up with the Whisper speech recognition model which used 680,000 h of labeled audio data for weakly supervised pre-training to achieve better results without requiring any self-supervision technique. Being a multilingual model, Whisper supports 96 languages. Massively Multilingual Speech (MMS) project proposed by Pratap et al. [14] includes a single multilingual ASR model for 1107 languages. Compared to Whisper, MMS performed with Word Error Rate (WER) reduced by more than half on 54 languages of the FLEURS benchmark even though it was trained on a smaller labeled data.

A survey by Najafabadi et al. [12] summarises the application of architectures and algorithms of deep learning techniques to big data analytics. This study also discusses how adapting to deep learning methods is challenged by different characteristics of big data such as high dimensionality, scalability of deep learning models, and standards for extracting good data representations. Zhang et al. [20] surveyed and presented different categories of big data deep learning models. It also addresses the challenges of combining the paradigms of big data and deep learning. This study emphasizes challenges such as constraints for storing high volumes of data and for model training in terms of memory and computational resources such as CPU clusters and GPU. Another challenge is the type of data being processed, multi-modal inputs, or complex data such as audio and videos. Complex and multi-modal deep learning models perform effective feature engineering when provided with a large quantity of data for learning. This requirement is hard to meet in the case of low-resource domains and lesser computational architectures. Noisy or incomplete data is seen as another challenge, for which feature engineering is complicated and very few reliable models for processing such data have been proposed. Various issues, challenges, and applications of big data analytics involving various forms of data including audio were discussed by Verma et al. [16]. This study defines audio analytics as the extraction of meaning and information from audio for analysis. Different application areas of audio analytics are also covered.

Many studies have focused on the storage, processing, and retrieval of audio content using a big data architecture. A solution for managing and analyzing large volumes of environmental acoustic data was proposed by Zhang et al. [19]. The framework included efficient, accurate, and cost-effective methods for data collection, storage, and analysis and processed data initially 24 TB of size and growing. Goodman et al. [7] discusses the development of a publicly searchable database for radio materials and techniques used by the Radio Preservation Task Force of the Library of Congress's National Recording Preservation Board for the same. The project combined metadata on 2,500 unique collections and also sheds light on various technical, social, and ethical challenges faced. A framework for knowledge extraction from radio content was proposed by Vryzas et al. [17]. The proposed framework also included a supervised model for speaker classification of 24 known speakers and a web application for live production and streaming of radio. Recently, a method for selecting audio learning resources based on the big data of education was proposed by Wang et al. [18].

Natural Language Processing (NLP) in Indian languages is a fast-growing area of research. Due to the lack of a monolingual model in Kannada, we use multilingual models whose pre-training corpus includes Kannada text. IndicBERT [8] is a multilingual model trained on 12 Indian languages. Multilingual BERT ($mBERT$) [5] model is pre-trained for the top 104 languages in the world, including more than 8 Indian languages. Wikipedia corpus is used for training mBERT. IndicNER [11] is a model for Named Entity Recognition in Indian languages, fine-tuned on Naamapadam [11] dataset. F1-scores of IndicNER is reported to be more than 80 in the case of 7 languages out of 9 Indian languages.

3   Approach

This paper presents an approach for AI-based audio assistance for rural community audiences in colloquial and low-resource Kannada language. Knowledge is communicated orally in the majority of Indian villages. Storytelling, songs, and speeches are the leading methods of sharing expertise. Knowledge and intelligence in such communities contain elements of native culture and demographics, contain a narrative, and are often arranged in chronological order. Examples of such expertise can include knowing essential flora such as medicinal plants that are native to the region, awareness about the endangered fauna in the surroundings, being aware of important events in local history, and a grasp of unique artisanal forms and folk art. Effective knowledge management is vital as most knowledge is not documented or accessible online. Figure 1 shows the proposed architecture.

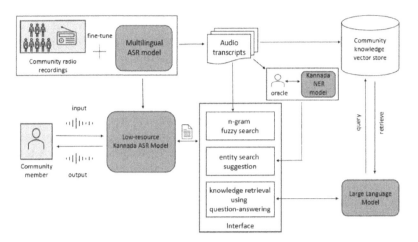

Fig. 1. Proposed approach

Using the recorded audio files from Namma Halli radio, a Kannada Automatic Speech Recognition (ASR) model is built by fine-tuning the smallest variant of popular multilingual ASR models. The smaller variant is chosen considering the trade-off between achieving the least Word Error Rate (WER) using a large ASR model with billions of parameters fine-tuned on a large training set and utilizing the available limited audio corpus to obtain an economically optimized ASR model using minimal resources and time. Hence, the transcripts acquired using our Kannada ASR model can have minor transcription errors in words that can be managed or manually corrected. This transcripts corpus supports multiple other components of the proposed architecture. Any new recording from Namma Halli radio can be transcribed using the Kannada ASR model and added to the transcripts corpus.

A user interacts with the system using voice as the medium, which is converted into text by the Kannada ASR model. The Kannada ASR model receives audio inputs from the user and passes the text form of the input audio to the interface. The interface provides n-gram fuzzy search, entity search, and question-answering functionalities using the transcripts of the audio corpus. To achieve a search of input n-gram, we propose an n-gram fuzzy search to overcome the spelling errors in the transcripts corpus by matching the search text with the corresponding length of n-grams in the transcripts corpus based on Levenshtein Distance [9].

The entities in the corpus are retrieved from the NER model built using Active Learning. The most frequent entity names are shown in the interface as suggestions to search for the user. This can be beneficial as it provides suggestions regarding the entities of interest to the community and can be a good starting point for an external user who wants to explore the community. We propose a knowledge retrieval component for easy access and querying purposes built with a vector database of the embedding representations of the transcripts corpus. An LLM can query and retrieve from the vector database, treating it as an external knowledge source for any query specific to the community and providing accurate answers related to the community. Implementation of knowledge retrieval using question-answering model and the voice interface components is part of the ongoing work. However, we briefly discuss them here to provide an overall picture of the proposed architecture. The following sub-sections contain details of these components.

3.1   Low-Resource ASR Model

Speech Recognition is an essential step in our approach. The goal is to use ASR models to generate transcripts for the limited audio corpus in an economically optimal method and use them to build knowledge management functionalities. Figure 2 shows the approach to building a low-resource ASR model. As the first step, the available audio files are cleaned using the Audacity tool[4]. The audio cleaning process involved background noise reduction, removal of noise by non-speakers and additional noise such as horns and bird chirps using spectrograms, using low pass filters to remove mic disturbances and negligible sounds, using high pass filters to remove echo and large frequencies, using vocal isolation to remove any music in background and amplification of low volume voices.

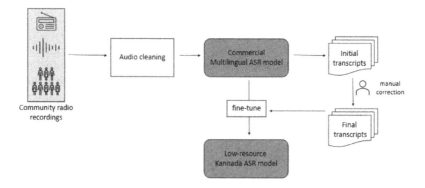

Fig. 2. Fine-tuning approach for Kannada ASR

A critical challenge for ASR in low-resource languages is achieving the least possible Word Error Rate (WER). WER quantifies the dissimilarity between the ground truth (reference) transcript and an ASR model's output. WER is computed by matching the words in the reference transcript and ASR output. WER is computed with numbers of substitutions (S) or words with spelling errors in ASR output, deletions (D) or words missing in ASR output, and insertions

---

[4] https://www.audacityteam.org/.

(I) or new words inserted in ASR output and (N), the total number of words in the reference transcript. Following is the calculation of WER:

$$WER = \frac{I + D + S}{N} \times 100 \tag{1}$$

A total of 3.6 h of Namma Halli Radio corpus, which is split into 10-s segments, is used in the experiments. The training set contained 2.7 h of audio randomly sampled, and the remaining 0.9 h of audio was used as the validation set. Two popular multilingual ASR models used in this study are Whisper [15], and Massively Multilingual Speech (MMS) [14]. Two native Kannada speakers manually corrected the initial fine-tuning corpus generated from a commercial ASR model with low WER. Correction includes adding missing words, removing extra or hallucinated words, and verifying the final transcripts by listening to the audio side by side.

The Whisper model's small variant ($openai/whisper - small$) trained on the Namma Halli radio corpus training set for 70 epochs achieved a WER of 72.13% on the validation set. Even using different methods in fine-tuning, such as training corpus augmentation (adding random Gaussian noise, stretching time, applying gain, and shifting the pitch) and using audio resources from OpenSLR[5] reported WER of 68.02% and 81.22% respectively. MMS model ($facebook/mms - 1b - fl102$) is fine-tuned for 50 epochs using a training split of the Namma Halli radio corpus. The fine-tuned MMS model could achieve a WER of 62.06% on the validation split, the best score in this study, and 82% of these were substitutions or spelling errors.

Achieving optimum WER requires fine-tuning very large ASR models requiring high computational resources. The fine-tuning process also requires a large audio corpus. The challenge is to build the smallest ASR model with the least possible WER when constrained by the limited corpus. As the main aim of this study is to follow an economically optimal approach, we settle for a WER of 62.06% in fine-tuning the ASR model, and 82% of these errors are spelling errors, and follow approaches in building knowledge management components to minimize the effect of WER.

3.2   N-Gram Fuzzy Search

The best fine-tuned ASR model, the fine-tuned MMS model ($facebook/mms - 1b - fl102$) transcriptions have 82% of substitutions or spelling errors with 62% WER. The search text assumed to be with correct spelling can be searched in the corpus based on the edit distance like Levenshtein Distance [9], which would either find an exact or fuzzy match. With either of these matches and the metadata to seek the match's location in the audio file, the user can be presented with matched audio contents and location in the audio to listen. By edit-distance-based text search in transcripts, the search in audio is achieved even with word errors in the transcripts. We have enabled n-gram search by detecting

---

[5] https://openslr.org/.

Algorithm 1: Fuzzy N-gram Search with Levenshtein Distance[9]

Input: Dictionary of Transcript Name and Content $TCrps = \{\{TName_1 : TContent_1\}, \{TName_2 : TContent_2\}, \ldots, \{TName_n : TContent_n\}\}$

Input: N-gram search text $SrTxt$

Output: Set of $[TName, NgramTxt, fDist]$ sorted in ascending order of $fDist$

1 $srtxt\_ngram\_size \leftarrow$ **get_word_count**$(SrTxt)$

2 $corpus\_ngrams \leftarrow \emptyset$

3 **foreach** $TName_i \in TCrps$ **do**

4      $transcript\_ngrams_i \leftarrow$ **get_ngrams**$(TContent_i, srtxt\_ngram\_size)$

5   **foreach** $NgramTxt_j \in transcript\_ngrams_i$ **do**

6          $corpus\_ngrams.$**add**$([TName_i, NgramTxt_j])$

7 $fuzzy\_ngrm\_matches \leftarrow \emptyset$

8 **foreach** $NgramTxt_k \in corpus\_ngrams$ **do**

9      $fDist_k \leftarrow$ **lev_dist**$(NgramTxt_k, SrTxt)$

10     $fuzzy\_ngrm\_matches.$**add**$([TName_k, NgramTxt_k, fDist_k])$

11 $fuzzy\_ngrams\_matches.$**sort**$(by = fDist, ascending = True)$

12 **return** $fuzzy\_ngrm\_matches$

---

the word count in the input text and searching for corresponding n-grams in the transcripts. Algorithm 1 shows the pseudo-code of search.

Figure 3 shows sample results in the keyword search interface[6] using fuzzy matching. General instructions for usage and some example keywords are displayed. The interface allows a keyword typed in the Kannada script or in the English script which can be converted using the *Transliterate* button. For each audio file, all occurrences of the searched keyword in that audio are displayed (in blue) along with the seek position in the audio. We also display popular named entities appearing along with the searched text (in green). Just clicking on any of the matched results will seek the audio to the corresponding timestamp and the user can hear the audio around the keyword. The user can also see the entire transcript for an audio using the *View transcript* button.

3.3 Named Entity Recognition Using Active Learning

Named Entity Recognition (NER) task aims to automatically identify and classify named entities, which are proper nouns present in the given natural language input. Person (PER), Location (LOC), and Organization (ORG) are the most widely used named entity classes. Many NER studies are limited to English because of multiple helping factors like the capitalization feature, making the first letter of proper nouns capital letter, and another factor is the vast amount of datasets from several works that can be used by succeeding studies. Kannada, similar to many other Indian languages, has complex grammar rules and agglutinative morphology, due to which a word can be inflected with more than one

---

[6] Demo app: http://103.156.19.244:33035/,
username: guest, password: guest123.

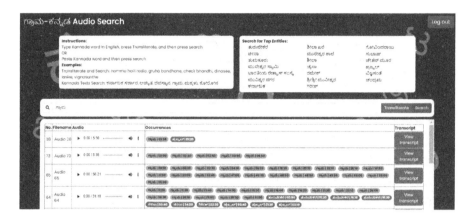

Fig. 3. Sample search result for the keyword *graama* (village). Matched text is shown in blue, most occurring entities are displayed in green for enriched search results (Color figure online)

suffix, and locating morpheme boundaries can be difficult as the root word and the suffixes form an entirely new word instead of just concatenating together. Also, very few studies have focused on the NER problem in Kannada. There also exist subtle differences between spoken Kannada and literary Kannada, which influences the prediction performance of a model trained only in literary Kannada.

For this study, we have trained the Kannada NER model with the colloquial Kannada transcripts corpus procured using the ASR task using the Active Learning (AL) [4] technique. An iteration in the AL cycle involves a human-in-the-loop style technique or an Oracle, correcting the predictions of a pre-trained Large Language Model (LLM). The corrected dataset will be the input for the next iteration of fine-tuning. The fine-tuning using the AL process outputs an iteratively built dataset and a model for Kannada NER. The proposed approach for fine-tuning a model using AL involves fine-tuning, predicting, and correcting.

Due to the scarcity of Kannada monolingual models, we use available multilingual models, multilingual-BERT or mBERT ($bert - base - multilingual - cased$) [5] and IndicBERT ($ai4bharat/indic - bert$) [8]. The AL technique was applied to the mBERT model to build the Kannada NER model of this study. WikiANN [13], a small NER dataset in Kannada, was used for the first iteration of fine-tuning and newspaper articles and transcripts corpus extracted using the ASR model as explained in Sect. 3.1 as unlabelled sentences for validation and with the five subsets of this dataset, five model building experiments were done and chose the best performing model. A human annotator validates the first fine-tuned model predictions on unlabelled sentences for the right predictions. The incorrect ones are corrected, and this new sample of correct predictions appended to the previous iteration dataset is the next iteration's fine-tuning dataset. F1-score, the harmonic mean of precision and recall, measures the model's perfor-

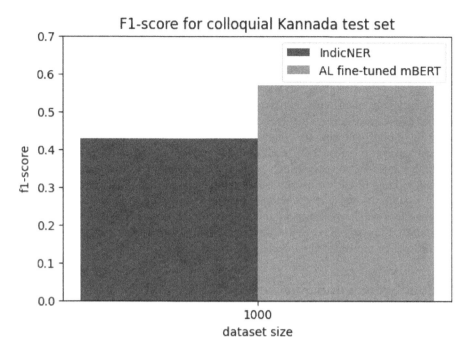

Fig. 4. Comparison of F1-scores of AL fine-tuned mBERT and vanilla IndicNER model from this study

mance. The saturation of the difference between observed F1-scores in consecutive iterations forms the stopping criteria. Figure 4 shows the F1-score of the best out of five AL fine-tuned mBERT models and the F1-score of the vanilla IndicNER model on a separate test dataset. The F1-scores of the AL fine-tuned mBERT model and the IndicNER model were 57.05% and 42.84% respectively.

The last iteration's fine-tuned model, or the Kannada NER model, will be the model for predicting named entities in colloquial corpus. The named entities extracted using the Kannada NER model aid the keyword search functionality as entity search recommendations for a user, as shown in Fig. 1. Predicted entity names are corrected for spelling since the corpus has misspelled words and are shown as search suggestions for the user. Figure 3 shows the top 20 entities in the corpus that are extracted using our Kannada NER model displayed as keyword suggestions to the user. The most frequently occurring entities in the transcripts corpus are of great significance to the community members and provide insights into the community knowledge, providing the entities as suggested searches act as a handy cue for a user unfamiliar with the community.

3.4 Knowledge Retrieval Using Question-Answering

Question-answering (QA) models effectively get human-like answers to queries made in natural language. QA models output relevant answers to any question after contextually understanding the question and searching for appropriate answers. Lewis et al. [10] demonstrated that Retrieval Augmented Generation (RAG) models can obtain competitive performance in open domain QA using a memory of a dense embedding vector index of Wikipedia. RAG models generate better answers than seq2seq models for language generation tasks.

As previously mentioned, construction of this component is under progress. We briefly discuss it here as it forms part of the future work. Using the question-answering model, we aim to benefit from the available transcripts corpus in accurate answer retrieval to a community-specific question the user poses. A community knowledge embeddings vector store created by extracting contextual embeddings of the transcripts corpus and used in the RAG technique will answer community-specific questions. The effect of expected spelling errors in the transcripts on the vector store must be tested. If it causes errors, we propose an automated process of correcting high-frequency words using a dictionary and edit distance to minimize the effect.

4   Conclusions and Future Work

This study proposes an architecture for AI-based assistance for managing oral community knowledge in low-resource and colloquial Kannada language. The goal is to preserve and access rural community knowledge that is vocal, uncodified, and unavailable in any global Big Data information systems. The need for more collective efforts for knowledge preservation in these communities is due to limited digital literacy, shortage of infrastructure, and vocal means of knowledge transfer. The proposed architecture uses speech modality to communicate with the user through an interface, and components use the textual transcripts in the background for easy processing. The speech interface enables even marginally literate community members to access internal community knowledge. As it is infeasible and impractical to record a massive amount of data in rural communities, we follow an economical and simple approach for extracting the transcripts of the limited available audio corpus and build a knowledge management framework using the transcripts corpus. We aim for this approach to apply to other low-resource scenarios for knowledge management in similar marginalized communities.

Future work involves implementing a Voice-based input/output interface for the search and knowledge retrieval using question-answering components, which is possible with current components in the architecture. The keyword search component currently processes ad-hoc input text and predicted entities from the NER model, and also input to the knowledge retrieval component is text. With the input to all three components being text and the Kannada ASR model fine-tuned on the colloquial corpus, in the architecture, the community members' speech queries converted to text by the Kannada ASR model will be input to the components. This enables search with speech input.

References

1. Aksënova, A., et al.: Accented speech recognition: benchmarking, pre-training, and diverse data (2022)
2. Baevski, A., Hsu, W.N., Conneau, A., Auli, M.: Unsupervised speech recognition. In: Ranzato, M., Beygelzimer, A., Dauphin, Y., Liang, P., Vaughan, J.W. (eds.) Advances in Neural Information Processing Systems, vol. 34, pp. 27826–27839. Curran Associates, Inc. (2021)
3. Baevski, A., Zhou, Y., Mohamed, A., Auli, M.: Wav2vec 2.0: a framework for self-supervised learning of speech representations. In: Larochelle, H., Ranzato, M., Hadsell, R., Balcan, M., Lin, H. (eds.) Advances in Neural Information Processing Systems, vol. 33, pp. 12449–12460. Curran Associates, Inc. (2020)
4. Cohn, D., Ghahramani, Z., Jordan, M.: Active learning with statistical models. In: Advances in Neural Information Processing Systems, vol. 7 (1994)
5. Devlin, J., Chang, M., Lee, K., Toutanova, K.: BERT: pre-training of deep bidirectional transformers for language understanding. CoRR abs/1810.04805 (2018). http://arxiv.org/abs/1810.04805
6. Duarte, F.: Amount of data created daily (2023). https://explodingtopics.com/blog/data-generated-per-day. Accessed 08 Oct 2023
7. Goodmann, E., Matienzo, M.A., VanCour, S., Dries, W.V.: Building the national radio recordings database: a big data approach to documenting audio heritage. In: 2019 IEEE International Conference on Big Data (Big Data), pp. 3080–3086 (2019). https://doi.org/10.1109/BigData47090.2019.9006520
8. Kakwani, D., et al.: IndicNLPSuite: monolingual corpora, evaluation benchmarks and pre-trained multilingual language models for indian languages. In: Findings of EMNLP (2020)
9. Levenshtein, V.I., et al.: Binary codes capable of correcting deletions, insertions, and reversals. In: Soviet Physics Doklady, vol. 10, pp. 707–710. Soviet Union (1966)
10. Lewis, P., et al.: Retrieval-augmented generation for knowledge-intensive NLP tasks (2021)
11. Mhaske, A., et al.: Naamapadam: a large-scale named entity annotated data for Indic languages. In: Proceedings of the 61st Annual Meeting of the Association for Computational Linguistics (Volume 1: Long Papers), pp. 10441–10456. Association for Computational Linguistics, Toronto (2023). https://doi.org/10.18653/v1/2023.acl-long.582, https://aclanthology.org/2023.acl-long.582
12. Najafabadi, M.M., Villanustre, F., Khoshgoftaar, T.M., Seliya, N., Wald, R., Muharemagic, E.: Deep learning applications and challenges in big data analytics. J. Big Data **2**(1), 1–21 (2015)
13. Pan, X., Zhang, B., May, J., Nothman, J., Knight, K., Ji, H.: Cross-lingual name tagging and linking for 282 languages. In: Annual Meeting of the Association for Computational Linguistics (2017)
14. Pratap, V., et al.: Scaling speech technology to 1,000+ languages. arXiv (2023)
15. Radford, A., Kim, J.W., Xu, T., Brockman, G., Mcleavey, C., Sutskever, I.: Robust speech recognition via large-scale weak supervision. In: Krause, A., Brunskill, E., Cho, K., Engelhardt, B., Sabato, S., Scarlett, J. (eds.) Proceedings of the 40th International Conference on Machine Learning. Proceedings of Machine Learning Research, vol. 202, pp. 28492–28518. PMLR (2023). https://proceedings.mlr.press/v202/radford23a.html
16. Verma, J.P., Agrawal, S., Patel, B., Patel, A.: Big data analytics: challenges and applications for text, audio, video, and social media data. Int. J. Soft Comput. Artif. Intell. Appl. (IJSCAI) **5**(1), 41–51 (2016)

17. Vryzas, N., Tsipas, N., Dimoulas, C.: Web radio automation for audio stream management in the era of big data. Information **11**(4) (2020). https://doi.org/10.3390/info11040205, https://www.mdpi.com/2078-2489/11/4/205
18. Wang, P., Wang, X., Liu, X.: Selection of audio learning resources based on big data. Int. J. Emerg. Technol. Learn. (Online) **17**(6), 23 (2022)
19. Zhang, J., et al.: Managing and analysing big audio data for environmental monitoring. In: 2013 IEEE 16th International Conference on Computational Science and Engineering, pp. 997–1004 (2013). https://doi.org/10.1109/CSE.2013.146
20. Zhang, Q., Yang, L.T., Chen, Z., Li, P.: A survey on deep learning for big data. Inf. Fusion **42**, 146–157 (2018). https://doi.org/10.1016/j.inffus.2017.10.006, https://www.sciencedirect.com/science/article/pii/S1566253517305328

Topic Modeling Applied to Reddit Posts

Maria Kędzierska[1], Mikołaj Spytek[1], Marcelina Kurek[1], Jan Sawicki[1], Maria Ganzha[1], and Marcin Paprzycki[2(✉)]

[1] Faculty of Mathematics and Information Science, Warsaw University of Technology, Koszykowa 75, 00-662 Warszawa, Mazowieckie, Poland
jan.sawicki2.dokt@pw.edu.pl
[2] Systems Research Institute, Polish Academy of Sciences, Newelska 6, 01-447 Warsaw, Mazowieckie, Poland
Marcin.Paprzycki@ibspan.waw.pl

Abstract. Text data is widely used for both commercial and research purposes. While extensive sources of text data are available within Internet forums, such as Reddit, their volume is vast and, typically, only a small subset of posts is studied. To overcame problem of data size, topic modeling can be applied, to extract the main ideas from the documents. However, as it will be shown, different modeling techniques may produce very different results. Specifically, in this contribution, an overview of the most popular topic models, used in natural language processing, and methods for their comparison, is provided. Moreover, a software solution for downloading, modeling, exploring, and comparing topics, contained in Reddit posts, is introduced. The proposed application is experimentally validated, by showing that the extracted topics reflect real-world events. Finally, obtained results are compared to these originating from a different tool, used for investigating topic popularity.

Keywords: NLP · text data processing · topic modeling · topic model evaluation · Reddit

1 Introduction

Nowadays, information is considered as one of the most valuable resources [1]. In this context, it is easy to notice that the largest repositories of text data are social media. Among them, Reddit is one of the most popular ones. It is also often used in current research on social networks [2,3]. However, as is the case with all social networks, its size makes it impossible to directly analyze/evaluate by humans, without limiting the study to a small number of posts. Hence, one

---

M. Kędzierska, M. Spytek, M. Kurek and J. Sawicki—These authors contributed equally to this work.

Supplementary Information The online version contains supplementary material available at https://doi.org/10.1007/978-3-031-58502-9_2.

of the ways to "deal with" large volumes of available data is by applying topic models [4–6], which are to extract "the most valuable parts" of text documents.

As there are multiple topic modeling techniques, developed for a different use cases, it may be of value to propose a comprehensive approach for their comparison. This should include metrics, which assign numerical values to selected aspects of obtained topics, as well as capability of human evaluation of the quality, understandability and interpretability of the resulting topics. Here, note that functionalized methods for comparison of results, delivered by different topic models, should be "easy to use", as they are to serve researchers from many disciplines, not always proficient in "computing".

In this context, the purpose of this work is to study the text data from Reddit, using topic modeling. Additionally, considered topic modeling methods are compared, using measures proposed in the literature. Furthermore, an application (outlined in Fig. 1), which enables users to explore Reddit has been developed. Hence, the main contributions of this work can be summarized as follows:

1. Popular topic modeling techniques are summarized. Moreover, it is experimentally shown that they achieve varying results, when extracting information from large collections of text data, especially in the context of topics changing over time. This is reflected in various performance measures, and easily noticeable in topic visualizations.
2. An open-source software solution, for the exploration of topics present in Reddit, using different modeling techniques, and comparing results within an interactive dashboard is proposed. The source code and use instructions are available at https://github.com/kaluskam/topic-models-comparison.
3. Using the developed tool it is shown that Internet forums, such as Reddit, do reflect events happening in the world. Moreover, topic modeling techniques can be useful for extracting such information, in a way that is understandable by humans.

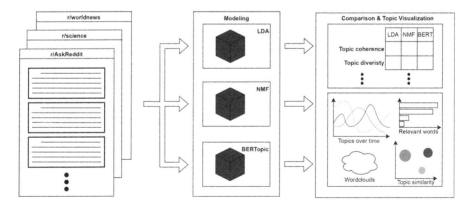

Fig. 1. A diagram illustrating the proposed solution.

2   Related Works

2.1   Reddit as a Data Source

Let us now outline the related state of the art, and start from the role of Reddit as the source of data. Reddit posts have been selected, since they are a popular in scientific research [2,3,7]. Analysis of literature shows that Reddit gained popularity in fields such as sociology, psychology, medicine, linguistics, and even environmental studies, by providing large and accessible (mostly textual) datasets. For example, researchers used Reddit posts to study social norms and decide, which factors cause people to judge the behavior of others in the way they do. Here, the anonymity of the forum allows for a comfortable expression of controversial thoughts and/or embarrassing stories [8]. Another study was focused on the relationship status of men [9]. Here, researchers proposed a theoretical framework, stating three main reasons why people stay single.

Reddit also helps to gather data for interdisciplinary research. For instance, a linguistic study was performed on patients with schizophrenia, based on posts from people who claim to have been diagnosed with this disease [10]. The researchers stated that gathering this amount of data without Reddit would be impossible, due to the relative rarity of this disorder.

While Reddit is used as a data source in multiple disciplines, there are drawbacks to using this data [11]. For instance, people posting on Reddit might not be "similar" to the general population. Moreover, since Reddit data is fundamentally different from data gathered from surveys, it might be of lesser quality.

Additionally, the downloading and processing of posts might pose technical challenges. Here, lack of tools for Reddit data processing and easy to use mechanisms for scrutinizing (e.g. visualizing) the Reddit data, is an important drawback. Hence, the recognized need for developing an automatic tool for Reddit data "inspection".

2.2   Topic Modeling

Let us now consider topic modeling, which is a process of extracting underlying semantic structure, from long texts, in the form of topics, represented by "a few words". While topic modeling gained popularity in the 1990s, new methods are constantly being developed [12]. Moreover, research has been conducted to find, which of methods are actually used and what drawbacks they have [13,14]. It was concluded that the Latent Dirichlet Allocation method [4] is the most popular approach to topic modeling, despite its limitations, e.g. poor handling of short documents, correlated topics, and complex relationships between topics.

However, other methods, such as Non-negative Matrix Factorization [6], Latent Semantic Analysis [15] and Probabilistic Latent Semantic Analysis [16] are also frequently used, as they are based on well-established mathematical concepts. Their popularity can be also attributed to the fact that they are present in well-known *Python* NLP packages, such as scikit-learn [17], gensim [18], text-summarizer[1] or sumy[2].

Easy availability of "building blocks" results in raising interest in methods based on machine learning. Here, examples are BERTopic [5] and W2V-LSA [19], which are both based on embeddings, acquired from large pre-trained language models.

The importance of topic models becomes apparent considering that scientists from different fields perform analyses of increasingly large text datasets. Topic modeling can make such studies achievable in bioinformatics [20] and social science [21]. However, trust and accessibility remain as important issues that need addressing.

Overall, the literature suggests a need for a tool that would support use and comparison of results delivered by multiple (different) topic modeling techniques. Such tool should be easy to use and accessible to people without advanced programming backgrounds.

2.3   Evaluation of Topic Models

The diversity of topic modeling approaches creates the need for developing methods for their evaluation. However, there are many aspects to the quality of captured topics, and it is difficult to capture them using a single metrics (i.e., an overall quality score). Therefore, the evaluation metrics usually deal with individual characteristics, and can be divided into different categories. Here, authors of [22], have grouped evaluation methods into: topic coherence, topic diversity, and topic significance.

Topic coherence metrics, proposed for example in [23,24], describe how the top words representing topics relate to one another. Such metrics are frequently used as a part of the evaluation process of obtained topics [25,26]. This is because they have a clear interpretations – they tell if found topics are human-interpretable, or if they are more likely just a "statistical noise".

Topic diversity metrics [27,28] measure how different are the obtained topics from one another. Better diversity values indicate better coverage of different aspects of the studied corpus. This group of metrics is sometimes used by researchers performing topic modeling studies [29], but they are applied less often than the coherence metrics.

Topic significance metrics, on the other hand, assess how well the topics reflect the corpus of documents. The most popular significance measures were introduced in [30,31], however, they are seldom used today.

An important aspect of evaluating topic models is availability of implemented metrics. While large number of topic models are available as *Python* libraries, topic evaluation metrics are not. The only topic coherence metrics are available in the Gensim [18] package. However, recently, an article [22] has been published, collecting multiple evaluation metrics, along with their implementation, as a *Python* package.

---

[1] https://github.com/ebenso/TextSummarizer.
[2] https://github.com/miso-belica/sumy.

3 Methods of Topic Modeling

Let us now present a more detailed description of the selected topics modeling approaches. Specifically, for each of them, a brief description of how it works, examples of usage in scientific studies, and list of drawbacks and limitations, are presented.

3.1 Latent Dirichlet Allocation

Perhaps the most popular topic model is Latent Dirichlet Allocation (LDA), first introduced in [4]. It assigns topics to documents, via an iterative process. With each pass of the algorithm, the topics should become more accurate. To ground the theory, let us define the following notation (inspired by the notation in [4]):

- A *word* is the smallest indivisible unit of text data. It is represented as a unit vector, with one element equal to 1. The set of words that can be used by an LDA model is finite, and its size is denoted by V. Hence, words are V-dimensional vectors.
- A *document* is a sequence of words $\mathbf{w} = (w_1, w_2, \ldots, w_n)$, where w_n represents the n-th word.
- A *corpus* is a set of documents $\mathbf{D} = \{\mathbf{w}_1, \mathbf{w}_2, \ldots, \mathbf{w}_M\}$, where M is its size.

With this notation, the idea behind the LDA model is as follows. It is assumed that each document is a probability mixture of many *latent* (hidden, unseen) topics and, in turn, each topic is a probability mixture of words from the vocabulary. The fitting of the model is a generative process, summarized as follows (see, [4] for more details):

1. Randomly choose $N \sim \text{Poisson}(\xi)$.
2. Randomly choose $\theta \sim \text{Dir}(\alpha)$.
3. For each of the N words w_i:
   (a) Randomly select a topic $z_i \sim \text{Multinomial}(\theta)$.
   (b) Select a word w_i from the probability distribution $p(w_i|z_i, \beta)$, a multinomial distribution conditioned on the topic z_i.

Here, $\text{Dir}(\alpha)$ represents a k-dimensional Dirichlet distribution, parameterized by a k-dimensional constant α, characterized by the probability density:

$$p(\theta, \alpha) = \frac{\Gamma(\sum_{i=1}^{k} \alpha_i)}{\prod_{i=1}^{k} \alpha_i} \theta_1^{\alpha_1 - 1} \ldots \theta_k^{\alpha_k - 1}, \tag{1}$$

where k is a hyperparameter of the model, representing the selected number of topics (assumed to be fixed). Another hyperparameter is the $k \times V$ matrix β, which is defined as follows: $\beta_{i,j} = p(w^j = 1|z^i = 1)$. In other words, the cell (i, j) of the matrix V contains the probability, with which word i belongs to the topic j. Here, it can be derived that the joint probability distribution of the topic mixture θ, topics $\mathbf{z}$ and words $\mathbf{w}$, given parameters α and β can be written as follows:

$$p(\theta, \mathbf{z}, \mathbf{w}|\alpha, \beta) = p(\theta|\alpha) \prod_{n=1}^{N} p(z_n|\theta)p(w_n|z_n, \beta). \tag{2}$$

This formula can be integrated, to get the marginal distribution of a single document:

$$p(\mathbf{w}|\alpha, \beta) = \int p(\theta|\alpha) \left(\prod_{n=1}^{N} \sum_{z_{dn}} p(z_{dn}|\theta)p(w_{dn}|z_{dn}, \beta) \right) d\theta, \tag{3}$$

and, by taking the product over all documents, the probability of the corpus becomes

$$p(D|\alpha, \beta) = \prod_{d=1}^{M} \int p(\theta_d|\alpha) \left(\prod_{n=1}^{N} \sum_{z_{dn}} p(z_{dn}|\theta)p(w_{dn}|z_{dn}, \beta) \right) d\theta_d. \tag{4}$$

Formulas 3 and 4 are the values, which specify which topics contribute to each document, and which topics contribute to the entire corpus.

3.1.1   Usage
Many studies have used the LDA to study topics in different document corpora. They include extracting topics from micro-blogs during the COVID-19 pandemic [32], finding in reviews complaints that people have about accommodations [33], or predicting crimes, based on topics extracted from user posts [34]. A survey, summarizing use of LDA in scientific articles was published in [35].

3.1.2   Drawbacks and Limitations
Despite its popularity, LDA has limitations. One of them is the fixed number of topics – the method does not allow for an adaptive selection of the best number of topics describing the documents. Another drawback is related to the fact that similar topics, with small differences are, most often, lumped into bigger topics, and this can lead to a loss of detail. The next problem is the fact that the generated topics are static. There is no possibility of adding a new topic to a fitted model, without recalculating the model from the scratch. Finally, LDA uses a bag-of-words representation of the corpus. This means that the sentence structure is not considered, when calculating the topic mixture of each document.

3.2   Non-negative Matrix Factorization

Whereas LDA is a probabilistic approach, the Non-negative Matrix Factorization (NMF) method has roots in multivariate analysis. It was first introduced in [6]. Interestingly, topic modeling is only one example of its use. Another example, for instance, is the extraction of features from the pictures of people's faces.

Regarding topic modeling, the assumption is that the corpus is represented as a $M \times V$ matrix X, where M depicts the number of topics, and V is the size of the vocabulary. Each cell at (i, j) a position of this matrix displays the number of occurrences of the j-th word in the document i. Given this assumption, it is postulated that there exist matrices W and H with non-negative values of shape $M \times k$ and $k \times V$, such that:

$$WH \approx X, \qquad (5)$$

where k is a chosen hyperparameter representing the number of topics. The matrices W and H are computed numerically, and many algorithms have been proposed for their quick calculation, depending on the desired application of the NMF method. This, and the fact that the process for their calculation is non-iterative, allows this method to be more time-efficient than the others. Obtained matrices contain all the relevant topic information. Each row of the matrix W represents how much each topic is connected with the document corresponding to the row, and each row of H states, which words contribute to the topic determined by the row of the matrix. A diagram describing the matrices of the NMF method and their shapes is presented in Fig. 2.

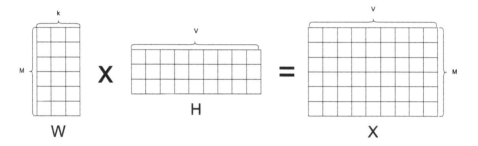

Fig. 2. Diagram of the NMF method.

3.2.1 Usage
While NMF is less popular than LDA, it was used, for example, for extracting topics from Twitter [36], or understanding clinical notes about patients diagnosed with COVID-19 [37]. NMF results are also compared to these from the LDA model, to ensure that the selected topics represent the documents well [38,39].

3.2.2 Drawbacks and Limitations
The NMF model shares many limitations with the LDA model. It is also static in nature, so it needs a preselected number of topics, which cannot be increased by enlarging the corpus with new documents. It cannot deal with correlated topics, and does not consider the order of the words in the sentences, despite using a different encoding of the corpus. A further drawback is that the attributions of words to the topics are not necessarily less or equal to 1. Although they can be used to assign relative importance, they cannot be treated as probabilities.

3.3 BERTopic

The BERTopic model is different from the previous two, as it uses a pre-trained language model, which inspects the semantic similarity between the words contained in the document. It was first proposed in [5]. Thanks to the well-documented open-source implementation, it has already gained popularity. Here, it is assumed that documents containing similar topics will be semantically similar (i.e. embeddings, attributed by the language model, will be similar among documents containing the same topics). The method of extracting topics from a corpus of documents proceeds in four steps.

1. The documents are converted to their embedding representations, using a pre-trained language model – BERT [40].
2. The embeddings are fed to a dimensionality reduction model – UMAP [41], for better clustering results.
3. The embeddings, with reduced dimensions, are clustered using HDBSCAN [42].
4. Human-readable descriptions are generated, using the TF-IDF technique, for each cluster separately, extracting the most meaningful words for the topics. Specifically, for each word in each document, a metric is calculated, and the words with the highest scores are chosen as topic descriptions. The metric is calculated as follows:

$$W_{t,d} = tf_{t,d} \log \frac{N}{df_t}, \tag{6}$$

where $tf_{t,d}$ represents the term frequency of term t in document d, df_t represents the number of documents that contain term t, and N is the number of documents in the corpus.

Notice that BERTopic assigns only one topic per document, whereas in the previous methods documents were seen as mixtures of different topics. This is because BERTopic uses clustering, which assigns each document to a single cluster.

3.3.1 Usage

Despite the fact that this method was introduced recently, it has already been applied, among others, in the analysis of public sentiment on the Internet, during the monkeypox outbreak [43], and topic extraction from financial policies [44].

3.3.2 Drawbacks and Limitations

Because of the specific internal structure of this model, some limitations arise. First, the BERTopic model does not allow for a selection of the desired number of topics. It generates as many topics, as there were clusters selected by the HDBSCAN method. Additionally, each document is only assigned one topic, instead of a mixture of topics, as in the two previous methods. The prolonged computation time is another disadvantage, as the use of a pre-trained language model for acquiring embeddings, for each document, is quite time-consuming.

3.4   Evaluation

Let us now consider the evaluation of trained topic models. As topic modeling is an unsupervised task, there is no single metric that describes the overall performance of the topic model (because there is no *ground truth* topic distribution). Therefore, researchers created different performance measures, focused on different aspects of the topics generated by the models. As noted above, they can be grouped into categories capturing (a) coherence, (b) similarity, and (c) diversity metrics. Each category can be based on a statistical approach or on text embeddings.

Statistical approaches use probabilities and distributions of topics to evaluate the fit of the evaluated method. Text embedding approaches are based on the embedding model [45]. An embedding model is a pre-trained model, which contains a multidimensional vector representation of words. These vectors reflect the semantic relationships between words – they can represent synonyms, antonyms, etc. Among many different static embedding models there is `word2vec-google-news-300` [46], containing 300-dimensional vectors, of 3 million words and phrases, which will further be used in the application of this paper.

3.4.1   Coherence Metric

Topic coherence metrics measure how the top-k words, from a given topic, relate to one another. These metrics are based on the Pointwise Mutual Information statistic, which is calculated as follows:

$$\text{PMI}(w_i, w_j) = \log \frac{\mathbb{P}(w_i, w_j)}{\mathbb{P}(w_i)\mathbb{P}(w_j)} \tag{7}$$

Here, for some metrics, the values of this statistic are normalized:

$$\text{NPMI}(w_i, w_j) = \frac{\text{PMI}(w_i, w_j)}{-\log \mathbb{P}(w_i, w_j)}. \tag{8}$$

The values $\mathbb{P}(w_i, w_j)$ are joint probabilities of both words w_i and w_j appearing in the same document, whereas $\mathbb{P}(w_i)$ indicates the probability of the occurrence of the word w_i in a document.

These values are further aggregated to measure the similarity of top words for each topic. For the reported analysis, c_V, c_{UMass}, c_{UCI} and c_{NPMI} coherence measures [23,24,47], have been used.

Two studies compared and contrasted different coherence measures [23,24] from the perspective of their relation to the way that humans rank of the topics. They indicate that the c_V coherence correlates the most with topics selected by humans.

Regarding coherence metrics, embedding models are used in the Pairwise Coherence and Centroid Coherence metrics. Pairwise Coherence is calculated as an average cosine similarity between each pair of words inside a topic. Cosine similarity is a similarity measure of two vectors irrespective of their size, the formula is calculated as follows:

$$Cos(x, y) = \frac{x \cdot y}{||x|| \cdot ||y||} \tag{9}$$

The Centroid similarity metric determines the center of a topic as an average of all word vectors included in a topic. Then, the cosine similarity calculation is performed between an average topic vector and each word vector inside a given topic.

Additionally, Pair Jaccard Similarity has been used in experiments. Pairwise Jaccard Similarity assesses the similarity between topics based on the Jaccard coefficient, which measures the size of the intersection relative to the size of the union of terms in two topics. Higher Jaccard similarity indicates greater overlap between topics [48].

3.4.2   Significance Metrics

Topic significance metrics [30,31] measure the distributions of topics in the documents, and specify if the found topics are "significant", i.e. if they reflect the documents, or if they are irrelevant. These metrics make use of the fact that significant topics would, most likely, only be comprised of a small part of the vocabulary, extracting only the relevant terms. That is, topics, which use many words for their representation, are probably insignificant.

These metrics calculate the Kullback-Leiber (KL) distance between topics, selected by the considered model, and some initial topic. The bigger this distance is, the more significant the topic should be.

Two significance metrics, first introduced in [30] are usually applied: *Uniform* and *Background*. The reference topic for the Uniform significance metric is a topic consisting of every word in the vocabulary, with equal probability. Clearly, such a topic does not summarize the documents well, so high values of the KL distance are desired.

The Background significance metric uses an initial topic that is equally likely to appear in all documents. Note that this is not a useful summary, as it does not separate the documents into different groups. Hence, big KL distances, between the selected topics and the reference topic, indicate "good performance" of the model.

3.4.3   Diversity Metrics

Topic diversity metrics help to understand how different are the topics, selected by the model, from one another. This metric helps reduce redundant topics and is, sometimes, used for the selection of the number of topics in the text.

The simplest diversity metric [28] measures the percentage of unique words in the top 25 words from each topic generated by the model. High values of this metric indicate that the selected topics are diverse, whereas values close to 0 suggest that there are many redundant topics.

Another diversity metric is the inverted rank-biased overlap metric (RBO) [49]. It is used to compare the similarity of two ranked lists. In the case of topic modeling evaluation, the top-k words in each topic are considered. This method is similar to the average overlap, but contains an additional weight for each rank, as the top positions are more significant than the bottom ones. Let us now dive deeper into the algorithm of the method.

Let S and T be two rankings, and S_i be the element in rank S at position i. Then, the set of the elements, starting from position c and ending on position d, in list S, is denoted as $S_{c:d}$. At each depth d, the size of the list intersection is named *overlap* of lists S and T to the depth d:

$$X_{S,T,d} = |S_{:d} \cap T_{:d}|. \tag{10}$$

Then, the agreement of lists S and T is defined as:

$$A_{S,T,d} = \frac{X_{S,T,d}}{d}. \tag{11}$$

Finally, the RBO metric is calculated as follows:

$$RBO(S,T,p) = (1-p) \sum_{d=1}^{\infty} p^{d-1} A_d, \tag{12}$$

where the term on a dth position has the value p^{d-1}, for $0 < p < 1$.

The resulting rank-biased overlap score is between 0 and 1, where 1 means identical lists. The final score of a diversity metric is obtained as $1 - RBO(S,T,p)$.

Another topic diversity metric is Log Odds Ratio [50]. The purpose of this metric is to compare the use of the word w across different documents. Unlike the previous metrics, it is calculated on word probabilities for each topic. Log Odds of a word w in document i is calculated as:

$$\log O_w^i = \log \frac{f_w^i}{1 - f_w^i}, \tag{13}$$

where f_w^i indicates the frequency of word w in document i.

The formula for the Log odds ratio is:

$$\log \frac{O_w^i}{O_w^j} = \log \frac{f_w^i}{1 - f_w^i} - \log \frac{f_w^j}{1 - f_w^j}. \tag{14}$$

Embedding models are also used in diversity metrics calculation. In the case of diversity metrics, the vector representation of words, derived from an embedding model, is combined with the inverted rank-biased overlap calculation method. The difference in calculating the inverted rank-biased overlap with an embedding model is that the ranked lists consist of multidimensional vectors representing each word, instead of a word itself. This approach leads to representing the similarity of not only words but also the relationships between them.

4   Data Acquisition and Preparation

The data used in this work was collected from Reddit, using the open REST Pushshift API. The API is made available by the moderators of the *r/Datasets* subreddit moderators. The posts are available for anybody for free, however, the access is rate limited, so the process of downloading data is quite time-consuming. Moreover, within last few months (mid 2023) Reddit started to reduce access to its data (among others, as a response to large language model training data scraping)[3,4]. As a result, an alternative approach to "live" access to Reddit may need to be developed. However, the remaining parts of the tool would remain unchanged. Moreover, this tool can be used to interact with "Reddit data collections" (which systematically materialize across dataset repositories). We use the *psaw Python* package, which simplifies the procedure of creating requests for the API, by wrapping the most popular use cases into convenient functions, e.g. downloading posts, metadata filtering, date-filtering etc.

4.1   Data Preprocessing

Before feeding the data into the model it needs to be preprocessed. For the processing, common and well-researched text preparation techniques are used [51,52]. They can be found in Python [53] libraries NLTK [54], spaCy [55], scikit-learn [56]. The processing pipeline consists of the steps.

(1) The punctuation and digits are removed, as are stopwords [57]. Apart from the standard stop words such as *the, in, at,* etc.), other subreddit-specific words are also removed, e.g. e.g., *advice* on subreddits related to giving users advice. (2) Text data often contain phrases in which some words have different meanings together than separately (e.g., *Chinese food* means something different from food coming from China). To ensure this altered meaning is preserved, tokens comprised of two words are generated and added to the corpus for further analysis. A possibility of adding *n-grams* of higher order exists but this slows computational time significantly and has diminishing returns for model performance, so it has not been implemented in the system. (3) The words are further lemmatized to acquire morphological roots. Text data prepared in this way is then converted to a desired output format – a list of documents, where each document is stored as a list of strings, each of those being a single token.

5   Developed Solution

The main goal of reported work was to provide a software open-source application, for the exploration and comparison of topics from Reddit posts. Moreover, proposed topics were to be proposed by different topic modeling methods.

---

[3] https://www.reddit.com/r/reddit/comments/12qwagm/an_update_regarding_re ddits_api/.

[4] https://www.reddit.com/r/modnews/comments/13wshdp/api_update_continued _access_to_our_api_for/.

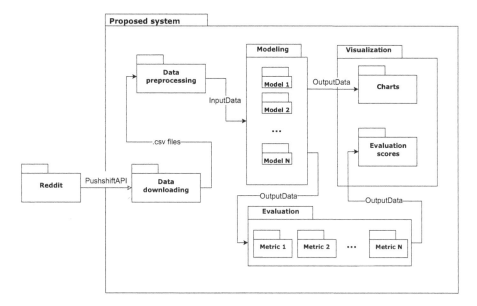

Fig. 3. Diagram of modules in the proposed solution.

The application is written in *Python* and consists of 5 modules, described in the appendix. Developed code uses multiple *Python* packages [17,18,22,42]. The user interface is an interactive dashboard, which allows the user to select various criteria for modeling (e.g. source subreddits of the posts to be modeled, the considered time period, topic modeling technique, number of topics, etc.). For easy access, for future researchers and developers, the code is documented using *Python docstrings*. The application modules and connections between them are visualized in Fig. 3. Let us now describe each module in more detail.

- *Data extraction module* communicated with Reddit servers using the REST Pushshift API, which was made available by the moderators of the *r/Datasets* subreddit using a *Python* package – *psaw*, as a wrapper API. It supports downloading posts from a selected time range and/or a specific subreddit. It also allows including only the necessary columns as the Reddit API provides additional metadata (number of votes for each post, author, number of comments, etc.) The object returned by calling this function is a dataframe, containing the posts satisfying the provided conditions. Each posts contains also selected additional metadata (such as title, source subreddit name, and date and time of the submission). In this form, it can be further processed (e.g. by the preprocessing module).
- *Processing module* applies necessary text processing described in Sect. 4.1. The resulting data is converted to standard data frames [58].
- *Modelling module* consists of models, which can be used to extract topics from the documents. Provided functions allow, among others, model training, predicting the topic distribution in the documents, assigning the most probable topic to each document, etc. The application comes with three integrated

topic modeling techniques: Latent Dirichlet Allocation, Non-negative Matrix Factorization, and BERTopic (described in detail in Sect. 3). Due to the modular design, adding new topic modeling algorithms should be "easy".

- *Evaluation module* supports comparison of topics returned by the models from the *Modelling module* using given metric: coherence metrics, diversity metrics, and topic significance metrics (see Sect. 3.4). Besides the function to calculate the metric value, each metric contains metadata about the metric: how to interpret this score, which category of metrics it belongs to, if higher or lower values are better, and the range of possible values.
- *Visualization module* creates interactive visualization of topics. It allows easy investigation and exploration of topics, given different criteria – subreddit subset, narrow or wide time period, etc. The available visualizations include: word distribution in the selected topic, a wordcloud, topic popularity distribution over time, chart showing the relative distances and popularity of topics using dimensionality reduction techniques.

The full technical overview of the implementation, as well as instructions on how to use the application, are provided in the supplementary materials available online.

6   Experiments with Reddit Data

Using the described methods, within the implemented application, several experiments have been performed. They were aimed at verifying theoretical set up, while showcasing practical applications of the explored methods, using real-life data. Let us now describe, in detail, the performed experiments.

6.1   Experiment 1: Connections Between Extracted Topics and Real-Life Events

In order to test the quality of topic selection, performed by the models, the selected topics have been "confronted" with real-world events. For this purpose, the *r/netflix* subreddit was selected. There, users post discussions about TV series, which they watch on *Netflix*. Obviously, this subreddit contains mainly discussions about "current events" relevant to the users, but the posts are still thematically and structurally diverse. The structural difference originates from the fact that posts on *r/netflix* significantly vary in length, from just one or two sentences, to a few paragraphs. Thematically, the selected subreddit is also very diverse; i.e. it contains various types of messages, e.g. TV series summaries, recommendation posts, reviews, or speculations about future seasons of a given series.

Next, all three topic models: NMF, LDA, and BERTopic were applied to posts sourced from these subreddits from October 1st, 2019 to September 30th, 2022. The number of topics to be found, was set to 20 for each model. Later, for each of the two subreddits, topics were selected, which appeared in the output of at least two out of the three models. The topics-over-time visualizations, for

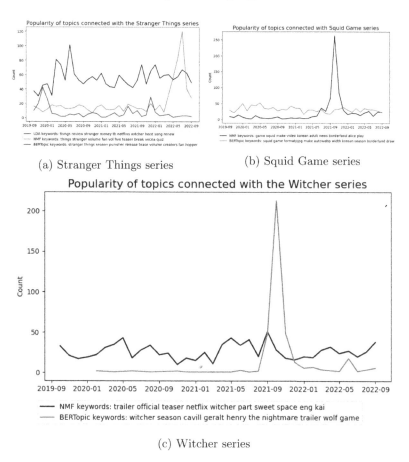

(a) Stranger Things series

(b) Squid Game series

(c) Witcher series

Fig. 4. Comparison of topic popularity using different methods on *r/netflix* subreddit.

all three models and the chosen subset of topics, are depicted within Fig. 4, with the events corresponding to the topics added to the plots. Additionally, the performance metrics are combined in Table 1, with the best values marked in bold.

This experiment tested:

- if the topics across the various models are interpretable (is the referred event understandable),
- if the topic representations are understandable – the topic concerning the same event is usually represented using a different set of words in the outputs of different models,
- if the best fitted model has a reflection in the calculated performance metrics; here, "best fitted" means the one, for which the distribution of the topic over time makes the most sense,
- the shape of the topic distributions, which describes whether a given topic model is capable of finding dynamically changing topics, or if such distribution of topics causes issues with a given method.

6.1.1 Results of Experiment 1

Two out of the three models: NMF, and BERTopic, extracted topics connected with the Stranger Things, the Squid Game, and the Witcher series. Interestingly, among the topics found using LDA, only a topic concerning the Stranger Things series could be identified. Figure 4 presents the topics-over-time visualizations of the topics selected using different methods. In Fig. 4a it can be seen that BERTopic found a larger number of posts in late 2019, just a few months after the release of the show's third season, whereas the topic found by the NMF shows a spike in May and June 2022 when the fourth season was being released. The number of posts assigned to this topic, by LDA, is quite stable and does not seem to correlate with any event connected with the Stranger Things series. In Fig. 4b topics related to the Squid Game series are shown. A peak in the number of posts, attributed to this topic by the NMF method, can be seen in October 2021, corresponding to the release of the show. The number of posts assigned to this topic by BERTopic is stable. However, when it comes to the Witcher series (Fig. 4c) the opposite is true. The topic found by BERTopic shows a spike around November 2021, which corresponds to the release of the show's second season, whereas the number of posts related to the topic found by the NMF model remains constant.

Table 1. Comparison of the evaluation metrics for different models fitted on posts from the *r/netflix* subreddit. Best values are bolded.

	NMF	LDA	BERTopic
KL Uniform	0.688	**0.171**	0.466
KL Background	**0.680**	0.682	0.691
RBO	0.018	0.001	**0.033**
Word Embedding Pairwise Similarity	**0.110**	0.093	0.101
Word Embedding Centroid Similarity	**0.449**	0.405	0.432
Pairwise Jaccard Similarity	0.016	0.001	**0.025**
UMass Coherence	-3.560	-4.135	**-5.088**
CV Coherence	**0.498**	0.469	0.481
CUCI Coherence	**-0.221**	-1.591	-0.621
CNPMI Coherence	0.058	-0.009	**0.088**
Word Embedding Pairwise Coherence	0.022	0.037	**0.010**
Word Embedding Centroid Coherence	0.802	0.784	**0.743**
Topic Diversity	**0.790**	0.990	0.830
Log Odds Ratio	0.891	**0.440**	0.917

The NMF and BERTopic both got the best results out of the three methods in 6 out of 14 considered metrics, whereas LDA was best in 2 out of 14 metrics. While this is not a clear indications that NMF and BERTopic are better, it is consistent with the fact that topics found by the NMF and the BERTopic methods have been better connected with the studied series.

The poor performance of the LDA method, despite its popularity in the research community, might be related to the fact that, in the literature it is reported very often that LDA is extensively manually tuned for a particular dataset. On the other hand, such hyperparameter tuning is extremely difficult to instantiate in a general application that is to work for extremely heterogeneus data that differs in number of posts, post lenghts, text complexity, domain-specific language etc. Here, note also that, in the considered scenario, it is not known in advance what data will the "user" ask to retrieve from Reddit. At the same time, the LDA supported research, usually, started to form a specific dataset, for which hyperparameters could have been tuned.

6.2   Experiment 2: Comparison of the Selected Topics with Google Trends

Another tool, often used to gauge the popularity of different topics on the Internet, is Google Trends API. It can be used to obtain information about how often different searches were submitted to the Google search engine, during different time periods. Hence, the decision to compare the popularity of the topics found by the models within the Reddit posts, to the popularity of worldwide Google searches concerning the same topics (in the same time frame). This is motivated by a previous study, which found a large overlap between Google Trends and Reddit topic space [59].

For this purpose, the three topic models: LDA, NMF and BERTopic have been applied to data from the *r/worldnews* subreddit, from October 1st, 2019 to September 30th, 2022. It was "requested" that 20 topics are to be found by each model. Then for each model, selected topics have been turned into potential Google searches; i.e. searches that would best describe the selected topics, while being "likely looked up" by people. Finally, the "shapes" of the topic-over-time distribution graphs (in Reddit) have been compared with the search popularity graphs, obtained from Google Trends. Due to the decision to set the smallest unit of time to a *month*, the Google Trends score presented on plots is the sum of Google Trends scores that appeared for each week in the month (the Google Trends units are arbitrary – relative to the most popular score of the topic). The same procedure has then been repeated for the data from *r/netflix*.

6.2.1   Results from the *r/worldnews* Subreddit

The topics selected for analysis extracted from the *r/worldnews* subreddit are presented in Table 2, along with the corresponding Google search. In some cases, the topics covered two different events. Hence, two Google searches have been formulated.

In Fig. 5, topics extracted by the NMF method are compared with the corresponding Google Trends results. It can be seen that, especially for the topic concerning the Russian-Ukrainan war and the COVID-19 outbreak, the shapes are very similar. In the case of the topic concerning the COVID-19 Vaccine, the discussion on Reddit began much earlier than the corresponding Google searches. This might be caused by the news reports concerning the development of the vaccine, months before it became available to the wider public. The smallest correlation can be seen in the topic concerning the Impeachment of Donald Trump.

There are two distinct spikes, corresponding to the Impeachment hearings and the inauguration of the new president of the US.

Topics found by the LDA method (Fig. 6) describe events contained in the posts. However, there is no significant correlation between their distribution and results from Google Trends. This may suggest an inconsistency between the events discussed on Reddit and events appearing in the Google Trends, which represent Google searches.

In the case of topics acquired by the BERTopic model (Fig. 7) the highest correlation between the number of posts and the Google Trends results is visible in the topic concerning the Hong Kong protests. The shapes of the lines are almost identical, they both have a secondary peak around May 2020. In the case of the NASA and SpaceX topic, the Google Trends result peaks about 6 months before the Reddit posts. This might be caused by the fact that the Google searches are related to a different event than the one discussed on Reddit. When one considers the topic concerning Boris Johnson, it can be seen that it is most popular within Google searches around the beginning and the end of his role as the Prime Minister of the UK, whereas the number of posts on Reddit is quite high (and similar) throughout his term. It should also be noted that despite the topic containing the Brexit keyword, Google searches about this event do not seem to correlate with the Reddit topic. This, again, shows an inconsistency between the behaviour of Reddit topics (representing "interests" of Reddit users) and Google searches (powered by Google users).

Table 2. Words representing extracted topics from the *r/worldnews* subreddit and corresponding Google Trends searches.

NMF	
Words comprising topic	Google Trends search
coronavirus, case, confirm, test, first, outbreak, deaths, death, toll, health	Coronavirus disease 2019
covid, vaccine, case, test, uk, positive, vaccines, get, deaths, variant	COVID-19 Vaccine
ukraine, russia, war, putin, warn, invasion, nato, weapons, biden, invade	War Russia-Ukraine 2022
trump, president, donald, biden, call, house, impeachment, administration, white, twitter	Impeachment of Donald Trump
LDA	
Words comprising topic	Google Trends search
ukraine, russia, say, russian, us, yous, ukrainian, military, force, call	Ukraine Russia
putin, live, free, stream, nord, open, part, least, major, update	Nord Stream/Vladimir Putin
BERTopic	
Words comprising topic	Google Trends search
hong, kong, protest, protesters, china, police, law, chinese, tiananmen, prodemocracy	Hong Kong protests
nasa, space, spacex, earth, telescope, moon, mar, webb, scientists, rover	NASA and SpaceX
boris, johnson, brexit, uk, eu, minister, tory, say, election, party	Boris Johnson/Brexit

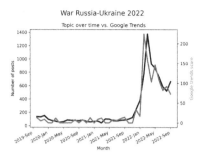

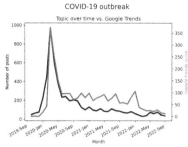

(a) **Topic keywords:** ukraine, russia, war, putin, warn, invasion, nato, weapons, biden, invade

(b) **Topic keywords:** coronavirus, case, confirm, test, first, outbreak, deaths, death, toll, health

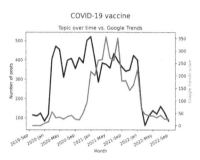

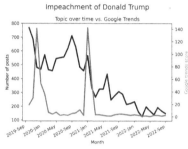

(c) **Topic keywords:** covid, vaccine, case, test, uk, positive, vaccines, get, deaths, variant

(d) **Topic keywords:** trump, president, donald, biden, call, house, impeachment, administration, white, twitter

Fig. 5. Comparison of topics found by NMF model on the *r/worldnews* subreddit with Google Trends search.

6.2.2 Results from the *r/netflix* Subreddit

A similar analysis was performed for the *r/netflix* subreddit. The studied topics are presented in Table 3, along with their corresponding Google Trends searches. For topics covering two separate issues, two searches were proposed and analyzed.

In Fig. 8 it can be seen, that the NMF method found topics that correlate extremely well with the equivalent Google searches. The shapes of the lines are practically identical for the topics concerning Squid Game, Stranger Things, and La Casa de Papel. For the Witcher series, the correlation is less pronounced but still noticeable, despite the chaotic nature of the number of posts.

In contrast, again, the topic found by the LDA method (Fig. 9) does not seem to correlate well with the Google searches. It contains keywords for both the Stranger Things and the Witcher, along with some other ones that seem quite random. However, the Google Trends results for both of these shows are

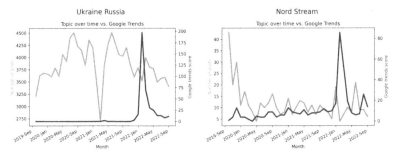

(a) **Topic keywords:** ukraine, rus- (b) **Topic keywords:** putin, live,
sia, say, russian, us, yous, ukrainian, free, stream, nord, open, part, least,
military, force, call   major, update

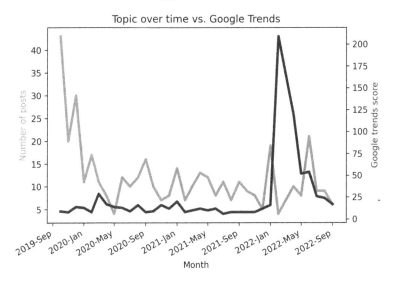

(c) **Topic keywords:** putin, live, free, stream, nord, open, part, least,
major, update

Fig. 6. Comparison of topics found by LDA model on the *r/worldnews* subreddit with
Google Trends search.

not similar at all. This, again, could have been caused by the topic complexity, domain-specific language and the inner proprietary mechanisms of Google
Trends.

The topics selected by the BERTopic model (Fig. 10) correspond quite well
with the Google Trends results. In the case of the Queen's Gambit series the peak
of posts attributed to this topic comes a few months before the relevant peak in
Google searches, whereas when it comes to the Lucifer series, the situation is the

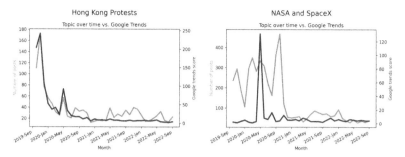

(a) **Topic keywords:** hong, kong, protest, protesters, china, police, law, chinese, tiananmen, prodemocracy

(b) **Topic keywords:** nasa, space, spacex, earth, telescope, moon, mar, webb, scientists, rover

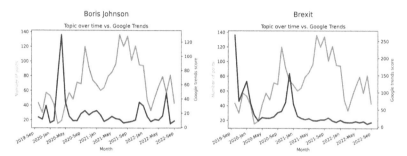

(c) **Topic keywords:** boris, john-son, brexit, uk, eu, minister, tory, say, election, party

(d) **Topic keywords:** boris, john-son, brexit, uk, eu, minister, tory, say, election, party

Fig. 7. Comparison of topics found by BERTopic model on the *r/worldnews* subreddit with Google Trends search.

opposite. This seems very interesting, but we cannot explain this relationship. Perhaps it is worth investigating by performing an in-depth study, which topics first emerge in Google searches, and which are first discussed on Reddit, and why. However, such study was out of scope of this contribution. In the case of topics relating to the Squid Game and the Breaking Bad, there is no correlation with the equivalent Google searches.

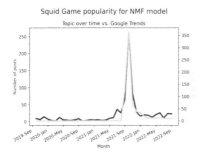
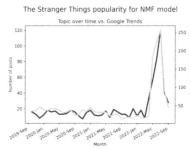

(a) **Topic keywords:** game, squid, make, video, korean, adult, borderland, alice, play

(b) **Topic keywords:** things, stranger, volume, fan, vol, five, teaser, break, vecna, quiz

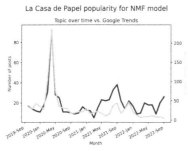
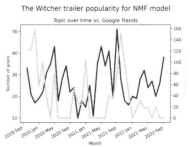

(c) **Topic keywords:** money, heist, part, de, casa, papel, la, top, break, korea

(d) **Topic keywords:** trailer, official, teaser, netflix, witcher, part, sweet, space, eng, kai

Fig. 8. Comparison of topics found by NMF model on the *r/netflix* subreddit with Google Trends search.

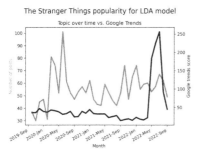
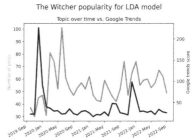

(a) **Topic keywords:** things, review, stranger, money, th, netflixs, witcher, heist, song, renew

(b) **Topic keywords:** things, review, stranger, money, th, netflixs, witcher, heist, song, renew

Fig. 9. Comparison of topics found by LDA model on the *r/netflix* subreddit with Google Trends search.

Table 3. Words representing extracted topics from the *r/netflix* subreddit and corresponding Google Trends searches.

NMF	
Words comprising topic	Google Trends search
game, squid, make, video, korean, adult, news, borderland, alice, play	Squid Game
things, stranger, volume, fan, vol, five, teaser, break, vecna, quiz	Stranger Things
money, heist, part, de, casa papel, la, top, break, korea	Casa del Papel
trailer, official, teaser, netflix, witcher, part, sweet, space, eng, kai	Witcher trailer/Witcher
LDA	
Words comprising topic	Google Trends search
gambit, queen, chess, vfx, the, beth, ceiling, harmon, piano, gaprindashvili	Gambit Queen
BERTopic	
Words comprising topic	Google Trends search
things, review, stranger, money, th, netflixs, witcher, heist, song, renew	Witcher/Stranger Things
lucifer, season, five, show, go, devil, things, chloe, release, angel	Lucifer
saul, call, better, season, break, bad, watch, available, episode, air	Breaking Bad
squid, game, formatpjpg, make, autowebp, width, korean, season, borderland, draw	Squid Game

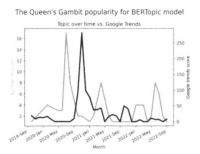

(a) **Topic keywords:** gambit, queen, chess, vfx, the, beth, ceiling, harmon, piano, gaprindashvili

(b) **Topic keywords:** lucifer, season, five, show, go, devil, things, chloe, release, angel

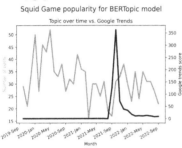

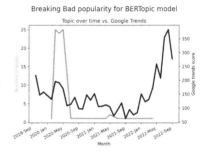

(c) **Topic keywords:** squid, game, formatpjpg, make, autowebp, width, korean, season, borderland, draw

(d) **Topic keywords:** saul, call, better, season, break, bad, watch, available, episode, air

Fig. 10. Comparison of topics found by BERTopic model on the *r/netflix* subreddit with Google Trends search.

7   Concluding Remarks

In this work, an open-source software solution, for the exploration of topics contained in posts from Reddit, using different natural language processing techniques was introduced. Moreover, this tool facilitates comparison of different topic modeling techniques. Developed comparisons (1) use multiple evaluation metrics, and (2) can be based on "manual" evaluation of the produced topics, using the provided visualizations.

The developed tool has been experimentally validated. The results show that use of topics modeling can turn Reddit into a valuable source of information. Obtained topics illustrate what Reddit users are interested in, and when such interest materializes. However, the correlation between topics extracted from subreddits and information searched in Google is not a simple one. The NMF approach seems to generate most convincing topics and matches best with what can be observed in Google Trends. The BERTopic model delivers results that are quite similar to these originating from the NMF approach. Interestingly, results obtained by using LDA are "strange" and least comprehensible. They have the lowest correlation with Google Trends. The reason for this may be worthy to be further explored in future works.

The proposed application can be further extended. First, other existing (implemented) topic modelling approaches can be added, just by standardizing their inputs and outputs. The same can be said about metrics and the evaluation module. However, here, not many ready implementations exist, as most metrics have been proposed and used (without available code) in a given article. It is also possible to add more topic visualizers, if needed for a specific ongoing research.

Second, there are possible improvements to the application. One of issues, is the long wait time of modeling and evaluation steps. To confront this issue, models used in reported experiments were precalculated and cached. However, there is room for improvement in this domain. Unfortunately, an issue of "online" open access to Reddit data may needs to be investigated (and successfully addressed) first.

Third, in the preliminary results of experiments presented in this contribution, it was shown that some topics are present in the Reddit threads earlier than in the Google searches, and for some topics the situation is the opposite. Further analysis of this phenomenon may bring about interesting results.

Finally, note that Reddit is not the only big online text data source. Other services, like X (Twitter), various news sites, or forums such as Quora and Stack Exchange, may be considered for topic analysis. In these cases, methods similar to the ones described above may be of value and immediate application.

References

1. Piwowar, H.A., Vision, T.J., Whitlock, M.C.: Data archiving is a good investment. Nature **473**(7347), 285 (2011)
2. Sawicki, J., Ganzha, M., Paprzycki, M., Badica, A.: Exploring usability of reddit in data science and knowledge processing. Scalable Comput.: Pract. Exp. **23**(1), 9–22 (2022)
3. Proferes, N., Jones, N., Gilbert, S., Fiesler, C., Zimmer, M.: Studying reddit: a systematic overview of disciplines, approaches, methods, and ethics. Soc. Media + Soc. **7**(2) (2021)
4. Blei, D.M., Ng, A.Y., Jordan, M.I.: Latent Dirichlet allocation. J. Mach. Learn. Res. **3**, 993–1022 (2003)
5. Grootendorst, M.: BERTopic: neural topic modeling with a class-based TF-IDF procedure. arXiv preprint arXiv:2203.05794 (2022)
6. Lee, D.D., Seung, H.S.: Learning the parts of objects by non-negative matrix factorization. Nature **401**(6755), 788–791 (1999)
7. Jamnik, M.R., Lane, D.J.: The use of reddit as an inexpensive source for highquality data. Pract. Assess. Res. Eval. **22**(1), 5 (2017)
8. De Candia, S., De Francisci Morales, G., Monti, C., Bonchi, F.: Social norms on reddit: a demographic analysis. In: 14th ACM Web Science Conference 2022, pp. 139–147 (2022)
9. Apostolou, M.: Why men stay single? Evidence from reddit. Evol. Psychol. Sci. **5**(1), 87–97 (2019)

10. Zomick, J., Levitan, S.I., Serper, M.: Linguistic analysis of schizophrenia in reddit posts. In: Proceedings of the Sixth Workshop on Computational Linguistics and Clinical Psychology, pp. 74–83 (2019)
11. Amaya, A., Bach, R., Keusch, F., Kreuter, F.: New data sources in social science research: things to know before working with reddit data. Soc. Sci. Comput. Rev. **39**(5), 943–960 (2021)
12. Churchill, R., Singh, L.: The evolution of topic modeling. ACM Comput. Surv. **54**(10s), 1–35 (2022)
13. Kherwa, P., Bansal, P.: Topic modeling: a comprehensive review. EAI Endors. Trans. Scalable Inf. Syst. **7**(24) (2019)
14. Vayansky, I., Kumar, S.A.: A review of topic modeling methods. Inf. Syst. **94**, 101582 (2020)
15. Landauer, T.K., Foltz, P.W., Laham, D.: An introduction to latent semantic analysis. Discourse Process. **25**(2–3), 259–284 (1998)
16. Hofmann, T.: Probabilistic latent semantic analysis. In: Uncertainty in Artificial Intelligence (UAI 99), Stockholm, Sweden (1999)
17. Pedregosa, F., et al.: Scikit-learn: machine learning in Python. J. Mach. Learn. Res. **12**, 2825–2830 (2011)
18. Rehurek, R., Sojka, P.: Gensim - python framework for vector space modelling. NLP Cent. Fac. Inform. Masaryk Univ. Brno Czech Republic **3**(2), 2 (2011)
19. Kim, S., Park, H., Lee, J.: Word2vec-based latent semantic analysis (W2V-LSA) for topic modeling: a study on blockchain technology trend analysis. Expert Syst. Appl. **152**, 113401 (2020)
20. Liu, L., Tang, L., Dong, W., Yao, S., Zhou, W.: An overview of topic modeling and its current applications in bioinformatics. Springerplus **5**(1), 1–22 (2016)
21. Ramage, D., Rosen, E., Chuang, J., Manning, C.D., McFarland, D.A.: Topic modeling for the social sciences. In: NIPS 2009 Workshop on Applications for Topic Models: Text and Beyond, vol. 5, pp. 1–4 (2009)
22. Terragni, S., Fersini, E., Galuzzi, B.G., Tropeano, P., Candelieri, A.: OCTIS: comparing and optimizing topic models is simple! In: Proceedings of the 16th Conference of the European Chapter of the Association for Computational Linguistics: System Demonstrations, pp. 263–270 (2021)
23. Lau, J.H., Newman, D., Baldwin, T.: Machine reading tea leaves: automatically evaluating topic coherence and topic model quality. In: Proceedings of the 14th Conference of the European Chapter of the Association for Computational Linguistics, pp. 530–539 (2014)
24. Röder, M., Both, A., Hinneburg, A.: Exploring the space of topic coherence measures. In: Proceedings of the Eighth ACM International Conference on Web Search and Data Mining, pp. 399–408 (2015)
25. Latif, S., Shafait, F., Latif, R., et al.: Analyzing LDA and NMF topic models for Urdu tweets via automatic labeling. IEEE Access **9**, 127531–127547 (2021)
26. Liu, S., Zhang, R.-Y., Kishimoto, T.: Analysis and prospect of clinical psychology based on topic models: hot research topics and scientific trends in the latest decades. Psychol. Health Med. **26**(4), 395–407 (2021)
27. Bianchi, F., Terragni, S., Hovy, D.: Pre-training is a hot topic: contextualized document embeddings improve topic coherence. In: Proceedings of the 59th Annual Meeting of the Association for Computational Linguistics and the 11th International Joint Conference on Natural Language Processing (Volume 2: Short Papers), pp. 759–766. Association for Computational Linguistics (2020)
28. Dieng, A.B., Ruiz, F.J., Blei, D.M.: Topic modeling in embedding spaces. Trans. Assoc. Comput. Linguist. **8**, 439–453 (2020)

29. Keane, N., Yee, C., Zhou, L.: Using topic modeling and similarity thresholds to detect events. In: Proceedings of the The 3rd Workshop on EVENTS: Definition, Detection, Coreference, and Representation, pp. 34–42 (2015)
30. AlSumait, L., Barbará, D., Gentle, J., Domeniconi, C.: Topic significance ranking of LDA generative models. In: Buntine, W., Grobelnik, M., Mladenić, D., Shawe-Taylor, J. (eds.) ECML PKDD 2009. LNCS (LNAI), vol. 5781, pp. 67–82. Springer, Heidelberg (2009). https://doi.org/10.1007/978-3-642-04180-8_22
31. Terragni, S., Nozza, D., Fersini, E., Enza, M.: Which matters most? Comparing the impact of concept and document relationships in topic models. In: Proceedings of the First Workshop on Insights from Negative Results in NLP, pp. 32–40 (2020)
32. Xue, J., et al.: Twitter discussions and emotions about the COVID-19 pandemic: machine Learning approach. J. Med. Internet Res. **22**(11), 20550 (2020)
33. Guo, Y., Barnes, S.J., Jia, Q.: Mining meaning from online ratings and reviews: tourist satisfaction analysis using latent Dirichlet allocation. Tour. Manage. **59**, 467–483 (2017)
34. Wang, X., Gerber, M.S., Brown, D.E.: Automatic crime prediction using events extracted from twitter posts. In: Yang, S.J., Greenberg, A.M., Endsley, M. (eds.) SBP 2012. LNCS, vol. 7227, pp. 231–238. Springer, Heidelberg (2012). https://doi.org/10.1007/978-3-642-29047-3_28
35. Jelodar, H., et al.: Latent Dirichlet allocation (LDA) and topic modeling: models, applications, a survey. Multimed. Tools Appl. **78**(11), 15169–15211 (2019)
36. Athukorala, S., Mohotti, W.: An effective short-text topic modelling with neighbourhood assistance-driven NMF in twitter. Soc. Netw. Anal. Min. **12**(1), 1–15 (2022)
37. Meaney, C., et al.: Non-negative matrix factorization temporal topic models and clinical text data identify COVID-19 pandemic effects on primary healthcare and community health in Toronto. Canada. J. Biomed. Inform. **128**, 104034 (2022)
38. Chen, Y., Zhang, H., Liu, R., Ye, Z., Lin, J.: Experimental explorations on short text topic mining between LDA and NMF based schemes. Knowl.-Based Syst. **163**, 1–13 (2019)
39. Suri, P., Roy, N.R.: Comparison between LDA & NMF for event-detection from large text stream data. In: 2017 3rd International Conference on Computational Intelligence & Communication Technology (CICT), pp. 1–5. IEEE (2017)
40. Devlin, J., Chang, M.-W., Lee, K., Toutanova, K.: BERT: pre-training of deep bidirectional transformers for language understanding. In: Proceedings of the 2019 Conference of the North American Chapter of the Association for Computational Linguistics: Human Language Technologies, Volume 1 (Long and Short Papers), pp. 4171–4186. Association for Computational Linguistics, Minneapolis (2019)
41. McInnes, L., Healy, J., Saul, N., Großberger, L.: UMAP: uniform manifold approximation and projection. J. Open Sour. Softw. **3**(29), 861 (2018)
42. McInnes, L., Healy, J., Astels, S.: HDBSCAN: hierarchical density based clustering. J. Open Sour. Softw. **2**(11), 205 (2017)
43. Ng, Q., Yau, C., Lim, Y., Wong, L., Liew, T.: Public sentiment on the global outbreak of monkeypox: an unsupervised machine learning analysis of 352,182 twitter posts. Public Health **213**, 1–4 (2022)
44. Clapham, B., Bender, M., Lausen, J., Gomber, P.: Policy making in the financial industry: a framework for regulatory impact analysis using textual analysis. J. Bus. Econ. 1–52 (2022)
45. Belford, M., Greene, D.: Comparison of embedding techniques for topic modeling coherence measures. In: Proceedings of the Poster Session of the 2nd Conference (2019)

46. Mikolov, T., Yih, W.-T., Zweig, G.: Linguistic regularities in continuous space word representations. In: Proceedings of the 2013 Conference of the North American Chapter of the Association for Computational Linguistics: Human Language Technologies, pp. 746–751 (2013)
47. Rosner, F., Hinneburg, A., Röder, M., Nettling, M., Both, A.: Evaluating topic coherence measures. arXiv preprint arXiv:1403.6397 (2014)
48. O'callaghan, D., Greene, D., Carthy, J., Cunningham, P.: An analysis of the coherence of descriptors in topic modeling. Expert Syst. Appl. **42**(13), 5645–5657 (2015)
49. Webber, W., Moffat, A., Zobel, J.: A similarity measure for indefinite rankings. ACM Trans. Inf. Syst. (TOIS) **28**(4), 1–38 (2010)
50. Monroe, B.L., Colaresi, M.P., Quinn, K.M.: Fightin' words: lexical feature selection and evaluation for identifying the content of political conflict. Polit. Anal. **16**(4), 372–403 (2017)
51. Kannan, S., et al.: Preprocessing techniques for text mining. Int. J. Comput. Sci. Commun. Netw. **5**(1), 7–16 (2014)
52. Sun, X., Liu, X., Hu, J., Zhu, J.: Empirical studies on the NLP techniques for source code data preprocessing. In: Proceedings of the 2014 3rd International Workshop on Evidential Assessment of Software Technologies, pp. 32–39 (2014)
53. Python, W.: Python. Python Releases for Windows 24 (2021)
54. Hardeniya, N., Perkins, J., Chopra, D., Joshi, N., Mathur, I.: Natural Language Processing: Python and NLTK. Packt Publishing Ltd. (2016)
55. Vasiliev, Y.: Natural Language Processing with Python and spaCy: A Practical Introduction. No Starch Press (2020)
56. Pedregosa, F., et al.: Scikit-learn: machine learning in python. J. Mach. Learn. Res. **12**, 2825–2830 (2011)
57. Kaur, J., Buttar, P.K.: Stopwords removal and its algorithms based on different methods. Int. J. Adv. Res. Comput. Sci. **9**(5), 81–88 (2018)
58. Nicoletti, P.: IEEE 802.11 frame format. XP055083596 (2005)
59. Sawicki, J., Ganzha, M., Paprzycki, M., Bădică, A.: Exploring usability of reddit in data science and knowledge processing. arXiv preprint arXiv:2110.02158 (2021)

Twitter Sentiment Analysis in Resource Limited Language

Riya Gupta, Sandli Agarwal, Shreya Garg, and Rishabh Kaushal$^{(\boxtimes)}$ ⓘ

Indira Gandhi Delhi Technical University for Women, Kashmere Gate,
Delhi 110006, India
`rishabhkaushal@igdtuw.ac.in`

Abstract. Sentiment analysis is essential for understanding public opinion and user feedback in various languages. However, a language barrier
often limits the use of existing models which are primarily pre-trained
on English. Therefore, previous approaches have focused on building
language-specific models for non-English languages. In this work, we
investigate the efficacy of low resource language specific models (like
GreekBERT) and compare their performance with RoBERTa model for
predicting sentiments in Greek and English language tweets. More specifically, we explore whether Greek tweets translated to English and fed
to RoBERTa model performs better than Greek tweets directly fed to
GreekBERT model. We find the RoBERTa model performs well not only
for the English tweets but also for the non-English tweets (Greek) translated to English. We present a detailed summary of model performance
for sentiment classsification of non-English (Greek) tweets.

Keywords: Sentiment Analysis · Text Classification · Resource
Limited Language Model

1 Introduction

Today, social media platforms, particularly Twitter (now X), have become a
global stage for expressing opinions, emotions, and sentiments on various topics.
Understanding the sentiments of social media users is a critical task for businesses, governments, and researchers alike. It provides invaluable insights into
public opinion, customer feedback, and emerging trends. However, when analytical lenses are extended beyond English-speaking Twitter users, it is challenging to find sentiments due to limited non-English language resources. Previous
approaches primarily focus on language-specific models, constraining their usage
to a single language. Consequently, there are different bidirectional encoder representations from Transformers (BERT) based on language-specific models like
RoBERTa for English, the GreekBERT model for Greek, the BETO model for
Spanish, etc. However, building a language-specific model requires a sizeable
language-specific corpus. In this work, we adopt a two-step approach in which
we first translate the non-English text into English and then apply a single

BERT model trained in English to find sentiment expressed in different languages. RoBERTa (pre-trained on English corpus of data) works well on both English and translated English language tweets. Translation is a good process, enabling us to use a single BERT model for various languages. The main contributions of our work are

- RoBERTa model, trained on resource-rich language (English), performs well on resource-limited language (Greek) for the text classification task of sentiment prediction.
- We compare and perform detailed experiments with different vectorization and machine learning models for predicting sentiments for Greek tweets.

The rest of the paper is organized as follows. Section 1, which is this section, briefly introduces the research problem, highlighting the significance of multilingual sentiment analysis in today's globalized and interconnected world. Section 2 delves into the background and the existing landscape of sentiment analysis, emphasizing the limitations encountered when extending sentiment analysis to multiple languages. In Sect. 3, we explain the dataset and related preprocessing. Further, we explain our sentiment analysis approach to multilingual Twitter data. The comparative study involves RoBERTa and the GreekBERT model. Section 4 focuses on the analysis results, demonstrating the advantages of leveraging the RoBERTa model. Finally, Sect. 5 offers a conclusion, summarizing the key contributions of the work and the potential for extending the work in the future.

2   Related Work

This work is inspired by the work of Antypas et al. [1], who investigated sentiment analysis to understand the impact of sentiment on the virality of tweets. They worked on English, Spanish, and Greek sentences and used different models, namely, SVM, LSTM, BERT-based models, and XLM-T, to find the best sentiment classifier for the prediction of sentiments in tweets. Besides the above, we also referred to other works (Table 1) on sentiment classification that use the same dataset as proposed by Antypas et al. [1]. M Pota et al. [13] investigated sentiment analysis of multilingual tweets by transforming tweets, which are made up of random words and unique symbols, to make them easier to analyze using a BERT model that's been trained on well-structured text and refined on tweets that have been transformed for sentiment analysis. They used English and Italian datasets, Pre-processed, and then used the BERT BASE model, which employs $L = 12$, $A = 12$, and $H = 768$. BERT inputs a sequence of 512 tokens and returns a representation of every token in the sequence, and they use the same dataset as ours for the English language. Barriere et al. [2] also investigated sentiment analysis on five different languages (English et al.) and used RoBERTa and XLM-RoBERTa(multilingual) for classification and also compared monolingual and multilingual models, and they used the same dataset as ours for English and Spanish languages.

Table 1. Comparative analysis between prior research works who have used **same dataset** as we have used in this paper.

Author(s)	Brief Description	Results
Antypas et al. [1][a]	They investigated sentiment analysis to understand sentiment's impact on tweets' virality. They worked on English, Spanish, and Greek datasets and used different models like SVM, LSTM, BERT-based models, XLM-T, etc., to find the best sentiment classifier among all of them and also applied statistics to understand the difference in sentiments of tweets posted by government and opposition	they got F1 avg score as 80 for English dataset using RoBERTa-base and 49 for Greek dataset using palobert-base-greek-uncased-v1
M Pota et al. [13][b]	BERT-based sentiment analysis on multilingual tweets, used English and Italian datasets, pressed them, and then used the BERT BASE model using A = 12, L = 12, and H = 768. BERT inputs a sequence of 512 tokens and returns a representation of each token in a sequence that is pre-trained on plaintext and fined-tuned on pre-processed tweets	results of this paper include 0.688 as Ravg,0.681 as F score, and 0.677 as accuracy
Barriere et al. [2][c]	they worked on sentiment analysis on five different languages (English et al., Italian, and French) and used RoBERTa and XLM-RoBERTa(multilingual) for classification and also compared monolingual and multilingual models	results of this paper include 72.8 Rec, 71.7 as F1mac and 72.3 as F1pn using RoBERTa on English tweets and got 69.8 Rec,69.6 as F1mac and 78.2 as F1pn using multilingual model on Spanish tweets

[a] https://www.sciencedirect.com/science/article/pii/S2468696423000010.
[b] https://www.sciencedirect.com/science/article/pii/S0957417421005601.
[c] https://arxiv.org/abs/2010.03486.

Next, we also briefly explain prior works that have worked on sentiment classification but used different datasets. Manias et al. [9] worked on six different languages (English et al., and Chinese) and applied multilingual BERT for sentiment analysis. Mujahid et al. [11] worked on a dataset in the Arabic language and then applied BERT and Roberta for sentiment analysis. They used a bag of words and term frequency-inverse document frequency for extracting key features, and different machine learning models were also used. Umair et al. [14] proposed a BERT+NBSVM model for sentiment analysis of Covid-19 vaccine tweets. Mabokela et al. [8] worked on sentiment analysis by using various models like BERT, mBERT, NB, SVM, CNN, and LSTM on different languages like English, Spanish, Greek, Tamil, Persian and compared all these models. Khan et al. [6] worked on sentiment analysis in the Urdu language and used fine-tuned multilingual BERT model for sentiment classification, and some ML and deep learning models were also used. Islam et al. [5] worked on sentiment analysis in the Bengali language and used multilingual BERT, which was trained via transfer learning, and also compared this model with other models trained with different word embedding techniques. Kumar et al. [7] worked on sentiment analysis on English language tweets and did a comparative study of different ML models and BERT. Muhammad et al. [10] worked on sentiment analysis on Nigerian language tweets and used different models like mBERT, XLM-R, and RemBERT for classification. Ohman et al. [12] worked on sentiment analysis on English and Finnish language tweets and used BERT and SVM on English tweets and FinBERT on Finnish tweets. Bello et al. [3] worked on sentiment analysis on English language tweets by combining the knowledge built into the pre-trained BERT with the knowledge of the deep learning classifier for sentiment detection by first tokenizing text using BERT then using classifiers such as CNN, RNN, or BiLSTM. Guven et al. [4] worked on sentiment analysis on Turkish language tweets using Turkish BERT and multilingual Bert and also different ML models like Logistics Regression, Random Forest, and Naive Bayes and compared accuracies off all, and BERT outperformed all ML models by a significant margin.

3   Proposed Methodology

3.1   Dataset and Preprocessing

The dataset is taken from the work of Antypas et al. [1], who studied the impact of sentiment on the virality of tweets. They worked on tweets in three languages, namely, English, Spanish and Greek. The dataset is available in public[1] domain. In our work, we have taken 900 tweets from English and Greek languages only. We applied standard data preprocessing techniques. We removed null and duplicate values in the dataset to prevent redundancy. Since we wanted only three types of labels [−1, 0, 1], so we removed tweets containing the label 'x'.

3.2   Recap of BERT Model

Since we use BERT-based models for sentiment analysis, we briefly describe these models in this section. RoBERTa is an English pre-trained transformers model, whereas GreekBERT is a similar model but pre-trained in the Greek language. In this section, we further describe the working of RoBERTa model, which was trained without human labelling using self-supervised learning. The

[1] https://github.com/cardiffnlp/politics-and-virality-twitter/tree/main/data/annotation.

model is based on the Masked Language Modelling (MLM) technique in which some of the words in a given sentence are masked; the model is trained to predict these masked words. In contrast to conventional RNNs or auto-regressive models, RoBERTa acquires a bidirectional representation, which helps in linguistic comprehension. Key components in the RoBERTa model are explained below.

– Input Embedding Layer: The input sequence of tokens is represented as a matrix

$$X \in R \wedge (L * d), \tag{1}$$

where L is the sequence length, and d is the dimension of token embeddings.

– Transformer Encoder Layers: The base architecture of the model consists of a stack of N transformer encoder layers (N = 12 for the base model).

– Multi-Head Self-Attention Mechanism: The self-attention mechanism calculates attention scores for each token in the input sequence, allowing the model to focus on different parts of the input. Self-Attention Score is represented as below.

$$A(Q, K, V) = softmax(\frac{Q * K \wedge T}{\sqrt{d}}) * V \tag{2}$$

where Q, K, and V are query, key, and value matrices derived from the input embedding layer, X. $\sqrt{d}$ is the scaling factor. The softmax function normalizes the scores. The attention mechanism can be performed in multiple heads to capture different relationships within the input.

– Feed-Forward Neural Network Layer: After self-attention, the output is passed through a feed-forward neural network, which consists of two fully connected layers with a ReLU activation function:

$$FFN(X) = max(0, X * W_1 + b_1) * W_2 + b_2 \tag{3}$$

where X is the input from self-attention. W_1, b_1, W_2, and b_2 are learnable weight matrices and bias terms.

– Layer Normalization and Residual Connections: After each sub-layer (self-attention and feed-forward layers), layer normalization is applied, and the results are added to the original input in a residual connection. Layer Normalization and Residual are expressed below.

$$LayerNorm(X + SubLayer(X)) \tag{4}$$

– Positional Encodings: To account for the position of tokens in the sequence, RoBERTa uses learned positional encodings that are added to the token embeddings. The position encodings depend on the position of each token in the sequence.

– Classification Head: RoBERTa adds a classification head on top of the encoder layers for downstream tasks. This head includes fully connected layers and task output, which is expressed below.

$$Y = \sigma(X * W_3 + b_3) \tag{5}$$

where Y is the output for the specific task, and X is the output of the encoder layers. W_3 and b_3 are task-specific weight matrices and bias terms. σ symbol represents the activation function suitable for the task (e.g., softmax for classification).

– Pretraining and Fine-Tuning: During pretraining, the model is pre-trained on a large corpus of text. After pre-training, it can be fine-tuned on specific NLP tasks using task-specific labeled data. Fine-tuning typically involves training additional task-specific layers while keeping the pre-trained RoBERTa base fixed.

3.3   Experiment Design

We performed the following experiments for English and Greek text, as listed below.

– English tweets:
  • Eng-RoBERTa Model: Tweets in English were directly fed into RoBERTa model.
  • Eng-Gr-GreekBERT Model: Alternatively, tweets in English were first translated to Greek, and then GreekBERT was used.
– Greek tweets:
  • Gr-GreekBERT Model: Tweets in Greek were directly fed into Greek-BERT model.
  • Gr-Eng-RoBERTa Model: Alternatively, tweets in Greek were first translated to English, and then RoBERTa was applied.

For language translations, we use the latest version of Google Translate[2] and installed related packages, namely, *langdetect* and *translate*. Next, we explain our experimental setups for both RoBERTa and GreekBERT models.

– RoBERTa: RoBERTa is a powerful pre-trained language model optimized for a wide range of NLP tasks and has demonstrated exceptional performance in tasks like sentiment analysis, text classification, machine translation, and more.
  • First, we initialized a fast tokenizer specifically designed for the RoBERTa model. It uses the "roberta-base" pre-trained model. This tokenizer can efficiently process large amounts of text data and convert them into numerical tokens.

---

[2] https://translate.google.com/.

- Then, we computed *max_length* as the longest token sequence found in the training data when using the RoBERTa tokenizer, with a constraint of 512 tokens per sequence. This value is important for managing input text lengths and ensuring they do not surpass the model's token processing capacity.
- Then we used *tokenize_roberta* function, which tokenizes a list of text data using the RoBERTa tokenizer, returning input IDs and attention masks. It ensures that the tokenized sequences are padded to the specified *max_len* (defaulting to MAX_LEN) and includes special tokens for RoBERTa's input format.
- Then, the pre-defined *tokenize_roberta* function is used to tokenize the text data for the training (X_train), validation ($X\_validate$), and test (X_test) sets. The resulting tokenized sequences are prepared for each dataset, including input IDs and attention masks. This tokenization process ensures that the text data adheres to a maximum token length of MAX_LEN, typically 100 tokens.
- Next, we create and train the model using the *create_model* function and fitting it.

– GreekBERT: The Greek version of BERT is used as below.

- We used a *bert_tokenizer* to tokenize text data in the data. The function calculates the maximum token length for these tokenized sequences with a limit of 512 tokens. The result, stored in *max_len*, represents the longest token sequence length found in the data, helping to set constraints for text input lengths when working with the BERT model.
- Token lengths for the data in the test set are calculated using the BERT tokenizer with a maximum limit of 512 tokens. If a tokenized sequence exceeds 80 tokens, the function prints the index and the corresponding text, allowing us to identify and inspect text samples in the test set that are longer than the defined threshold for potential further analysis or handling.
- Then, we initialized the BERT-based model and its corresponding tokenizer for Greek text. Specifically, it loads the $bert - base - greek - uncased - v1$ model and tokenizer for a sequence classification task with three output labels.
- Then, we did train-test data splitting and applied two functions for preparing text data for training a machine learning model:
  * *convert_example*: Converts raw text data and labels them into input examples, a format suitable for model training. It processes both training and testing data, applying a BERT-like tokenizer.
  * *convert_tfdataset*: Takes the $InputExamples$, tokenizes them using the provided tokenizer, and organizes them into a TensorFlow dataset. This function prepares the data for training deep learning models, such as BERT-based models, by ensuring consistent input format and tokenization for input features and labels.
- Now, training data is converted into suitable $InputExamples$, a data structure used in NLP models, and then into a TensorFlow dataset using

the pre-defined tokenizer. The data is shuffled, batched, and repeated to prepare it for model training. A learning rate schedule with exponential decay is defined for the optimizer for early stopping to avoid overfitting. The model is compiled with a suitable optimizer and a suitable loss function. Model training is executed on the prepared training data for four epochs, aiming to update the model's parameters and improve its performance over the training data.

- Next, we configured a deep learning model for training, which uses the Adam optimizer with a learning rate schedule and other settings. The loss function is set for sparse categorical cross-entropy, and accuracy is included as a metric to monitor during model training.

4   Results and Observations

Recall that in this work, we look for answers to the following research questions.

- RQ1: Which approaches better detect sentiment for Greek (resource-limited) tweets? (1) Applying GreekBERT directly on Greek tweets, or (2) Translating Greek tweets to English (resource rich) and then applying RoBERTa model.
- RQ2: What is the model performance for the best approach from the above two options?
- RQ3: Which machine learning model performs best for sentiment detection of Greek (resource-limited) tweets?

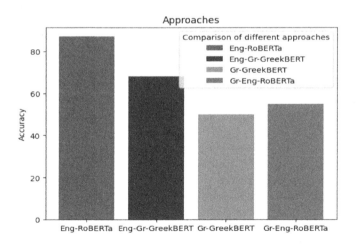

Fig. 1. Comparison of different approaches

4.1   RQ1: Best Approach

In Fig. 1, we compare the accuracy of two approaches, namely, (1) applying GreekBERT directly on Greek tweets or (2) translating Greek tweets to English (resource rich) and then applying the Roberta model. For the resource-rich language (English) tweets, we find that the BERT model (RoBERTa) trained on rich language (English) gives the best result. We observe that $Eng - RoBERTa$ model performs better than $Eng - Gr - GreekBERT$ model. The Eng-RoBERTa model's sentiment classification accuracy for English tweets turned out to be more than 80% Likewise, for the resource-limited language (Greek) tweets, we find that the same BERT model (RoBERTa) trained on rich language (English) gives the best result even on English text, which is obtained by translating Greek tweets to English. We find that Greek tweets, when translated to English and passed to the RoBERTa model, give an accuracy of more than 50% as compared to using the GreekBERT model on Greek tweets. Consequently, the BERT model trained on resource-rich language (English) works well for both English and non-English languages. In the Future, it would be worth experimenting with other non-English languages to find whether the RoBERTa model or language-specific model works better.

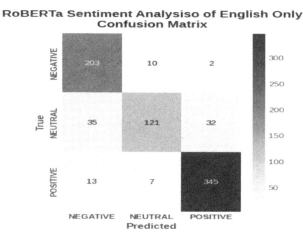

Fig. 2. Confusion Matrix of Eng-RoBERTa model on English tweets.

4.2   RQ2: Best Model Performance

Given that we show that RoBERTa model performs well on both English tweets and Greek tweets translated to English, in this subsection, we show the results of RoBERTa model performance in detail. Figures 2 and 3 show the confusion matrix and classification report of the Eng-RoBERTa model, respectively, on English tweets. Figure 2 depicts that 203, 121, and 345 predictions are correct for all three sentiment classes, namely, negative, neutral, and positive, respectively. Mis-classified negative tweets are mostly wrongly classified as neutral, ten as compared to 2. However, misclassified positive tweets are wrongly classified more as negative (13 instances) than neutral (7 instances). Wrongly classified neutral tweets are equally misclassified as positive (32 instances) and negative (35 instances). Figure 3 shows the classification report for the Eng-RoBERTa model. Performance for positive class English tweets is the best with precision, recall, and F1-score of 0.91, 0.95, and 0.93, respectively. Neutral tweets have a better precision of 0.88 than the recall of 0.64, with 0.74 as the F1-score. Negative tweets have a better recall of 0.94 than a precision of 0.81, with 0.87 as the F1 score.

Classification Report for RoBERTa:

	precision	recall	f1-score	support
Negative	0.81	0.94	0.87	215
Neutral	0.88	0.64	0.74	188
Positive	0.91	0.95	0.93	365
micro avg	0.87	0.87	0.87	768
macro avg	0.87	0.84	0.85	768
weighted avg	0.87	0.87	0.87	768
samples avg	0.87	0.87	0.87	768

Fig. 3. Classification Report of Eng-RoBERTa model.

Figures 4 and 5 show the confusion matrix and classification report of the Gr-Eng-RoBERTa model, respectively, for Greek tweets, which were translated into English. As shown in Fig. 4, we observe that test data comprised 20 positive, 17 neutral, and 10 negative sentiment Greek tweets. Out of 10 negative Greek tweets, six are correctly predicted. Out of 20 positive Greek tweets, all of them are predicted correctly. Finally, we observe that all 17 neutral Greek tweets are misclassified as positive. In Fig. 5, we depict the classification report for the Gr-Eng-RoBERTa model for the Greek tweets translated into English. We observe that negative Greek tweets have the best precision of 1.0 than recall of 0.6, with 0.75 as the F1-score. Positive Greek tweets have the best recall of 1.0 with precision of 0.49 and 0.66 as the F1-score. The model performs poorly for the neutral tweets.

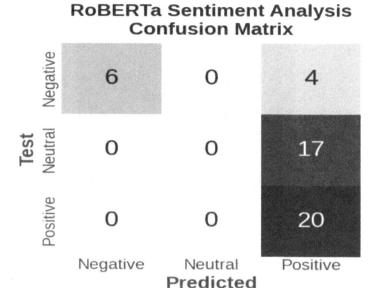

Fig. 4. Confusion matrix of Gr-Eng-RoBERTa model.

```
Classification Report for RoBERTa:

                precision    recall  f1-score   support

    Negative       1.00      0.60      0.75        10
     Neutral       0.00      0.00      0.00        17
    Positive       0.49      1.00      0.66        20

   micro avg       0.55      0.55      0.55        47
   macro avg       0.50      0.53      0.47        47
weighted avg       0.42      0.55      0.44        47
 samples avg       0.55      0.55      0.55        47
```

Fig. 5. Classification report of Gr-Eng-RoBERTa model.

4.3   RQ3: Best Classifier

In this sub-section, we aim to find the best machine-learning classifier for detecting the sentiment of Greek tweets. We translate Greek tweets to English and

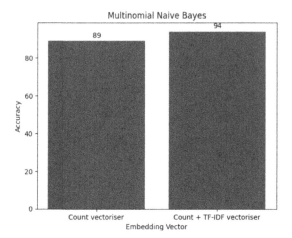

Fig. 6. Performance comparison of embedding techniques for Multinomial Naive Bayes model.

then apply different ML models with different embedding techniques. In Fig. 6, we compare the performance of embedding techniques for the Multinomial Naive Bayes model. We find that the TF-IDF vectorization approach performs better than the count vectorizer (Bag of Word, BoW) approach with accuracies of 94% and 89%, respectively. Next, in Fig. 6, we compare the performance of embedding techniques for the Logistic Regression model. We find that the count vectorizer (Bag of Word, BoW) performs better than the TF-IDF approach with accuracies of 97.87% and 95.74%, respectively (Fig. 7).

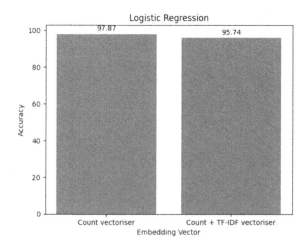

Fig. 7. Performance comparison of embedding techniques for Logistic Regression model.

5   Future Work and Conclusion

In this work, we focus on an approach for sentiment analysis of tweets from resource-limited languages (e.g. Greek) and compare it with sentiment analysis for English tweets. We found that RoBERTa base BERT model performs well on both English and tweets translated from Greek. RoBERTa model outperforms the Greek BERT model, which is only pre-trained on the Greek corpus of data, which is a low-resource language. However, RoBERTa is pre-trained in the English Language, which is trained on resource-rich language (English) and gives better results. So, translating low-resource language (Greek) tweets to English and then applying Roberta BERT gives excellent results. This work can benefit those researchers who want to study the impact of BERT-based models on language and translated language and whether BERT performs better in the original language or in the translated language.

In the Future, this work can be extended in many ways. First, we can experiment with more resource-limited languages rather than restricting ourselves to only Greek. Second, more advanced state-of-the-art language models can be explored in predicting the sentiment of tweets. Third, the efficacy of the proposed approach for text classification can be tried with problems other than sentiment.

References

1. Antypas, D., Preece, A., Camacho-Collados, J.: Negativity spreads faster: a large-scale multilingual twitter analysis on the role of sentiment in political communication. Online Soc. Netw. Media **33**, 100242 (2023)
2. Barriere, V., Balahur, A.: Improving sentiment analysis over non-English tweets using multilingual transformers and automatic translation for data-augmentation. arXiv preprint arXiv:2010.03486 (2020)
3. Bello, A., Ng, S.-C., Leung, M.-F.: A BERT framework to sentiment analysis of tweets. Sensors **23**(1), 506 (2023)
4. Guven, Z.A.: Comparison of BERT models and machine learning methods for sentiment analysis on Turkish tweets. In: 2021 6th International Conference on Computer Science and Engineering (UBMK), pp. 98–101. IEEE (2021)
5. Islam, K.I., Islam, M.S., Amin, M.R.: Sentiment analysis in Bengali via transfer learning using multi-lingual BERT. In: 2020 23rd International Conference on Computer and Information Technology (ICCIT), pp. 1–5. IEEE (2020)
6. Khan, L., Amjad, A., Ashraf, N., Chang, H.-T.: Multi-class sentiment analysis of Urdu text using multilingual BERT. Sci. Rep. **12**(1), 5436 (2022)
7. Sai Kumar, T.S., Arunaggiri Pandian, K., Thabasum Aara, S., Nagendra Pandian, K.: A reliable technique for sentiment analysis on tweets via machine learning and BERT. In: 2021 Asian Conference on Innovation in Technology (ASIANCON), pp. 1–5. IEEE (2021)
8. Mabokela, K.R., Celik, T., Raborife, M.: Multilingual sentiment analysis for under-resourced languages: a systematic review of the landscape. IEEE Access (2022)
9. Manias, G., Mavrogiorgou, A., Kiourtis, A., Symvoulidis, C., Kyriazis, D.: Multilingual text categorization and sentiment analysis: a comparative analysis of the utilization of multilingual approaches for classifying twitter data. Neural Computing and Applications, pp. 1–17 (2023)

10. Muhammad, S.H., et al.: NaijaSenti: a Nigerian twitter sentiment corpus for multilingual sentiment analysis. arXiv preprint arXiv:2201.08277 (2022)
11. Mujahid, M., Kanwal, K., Rustam, F., Aljadani, W., Ashraf, I.: Arabic ChatGPT tweets classification using RoBERTa and BERT ensemble model. ACM Trans. Asian Low-Resour. Lang. Inf. Process. **22**(8), 1–23 (2023)
12. Öhman, E., Pàmies, M., Kajava, K., Tiedemann, J.: XED: a multilingual dataset for sentiment analysis and emotion detection. arXiv preprint arXiv:2011.01612 (2020)
13. Pota, M., Ventura, M., Fujita, H., Esposito, M.: Multilingual evaluation of preprocessing for BERT-based sentiment analysis of tweets. Expert Syst. Appl. **181**, 115119 (2021)
14. Umair, A., Masciari, E., Madeo, G., Ullah, M.H.: Sentimental analysis of COVID-19 vaccine tweets using BERT+NBSVM. In: Koprinska, I., et al. (eds.) ECML PKDD 2022. CCIS, vol. 1752, pp. 238–247. Springer, Cham (2023). https://doi.org/10.1007/978-3-031-23618-1_16

Querying Healthcare Data in Knowledge-Based Systems

Kanika Soni, Shelly Sachdeva(✉), and Anupama Minj

National Institute of Technology Delhi, Delhi, India
`shellysachdeva@nitdelhi.ac.in`

Abstract. In the ever-evolving healthcare landscape, integrating knowledge-based systems into data querying processes is becoming imperative. The existing challenges in querying healthcare data lie in the complexity of extracting meaningful insights from vast and heterogeneous datasets. EHRs store different forms of data, and query systems' scalability and performance, especially considering the increasing volume of EHR data, are the main challenges faced. To overcome these challenges, the paper proposes a system with a user-friendly graphical interface for creating Archetype Query Language (AQL) queries in openEHR systems. It consists of three components: User Interface, which allows the user to specify query parameters, modify EHRs paths, filter data, and customize query results; Query builder, which creates the AQL query based on input from the User Interface and Repository of Documents where the compositions are stored and the query result obtained from this component is sent back to User Interface. It stands out with its innovative approach, systematically extracting openEHR schemas and simplifying the creation of complex AQL queries. The system's effectiveness and user satisfaction make learning, using, and developing queries for graph-driven healthcare data knowledge easy. The system enhances the overall functionality and usability of the query builder within the system. It offers a pathway to improved clinical decision-making and patient care outcomes.

Keywords: Knowledge-Based System · OpenEHR · Knowledge Graph · Querying · Healthcare

1 Introduction

Knowledge-based systems (KBS) have played a pivotal role in various domains, offering intelligent decision support and problem-solving capabilities. It represents an artificial intelligence (AI) branch that leverages human knowledge to solve complex problems and make informed decisions. These systems are designed to store, manipulate, and apply knowledge to solve complex problems, make decisions, or provide recommendations. KBS utilizes a knowledge base, an inference engine, and a user interface as its core components. Knowledge has been considered one of the most essential resources in an organization because it can make organizational and individual actions more intelligent, efficient, and effective. It stimulates the elaboration of innovative and continuously excellent products and services in complexity, flexibility, and creativity [1].

The healthcare environment has significantly transformed with the introduction of Electronic Health Records (EHRs), which provide effective data management solutions. An EHRs is a systematic electronic collection of health information about patients, such as medical history, medication orders, vital signs, laboratory results, radiology reports, and physician and nurse notes [2]. Yet, the smooth transmission of critical patient data is still a difficult objective in the complex network of healthcare systems, where innumerable clinics and hospitals use different information systems. Standardization and interoperability have become essential in EHRs to address this challenge, driving the need for knowledge-based systems beyond mere data storage. Several standards, including the Health Level 7 (HL7) Clinical Document Architecture (CDA) [3], CEN EN 13606 EHRcom [4], and openEHR [5], are actively developed to address the EHRs interoperability issue [6]. This paper focuses on how OpenEHR can be viewed as a knowledge-based system, archetype as a knowledge graph structure, and querying in Knowledge-based systems.

1.1 OpenEHR as a Knowledge-Based System

OpenEHR can be viewed as a Knowledge-based System due to its distinctive design and method of maintaining electronic health records (EHRs). It is built on the principle of semantic interoperability. It means that it doesn't just store data; it understands the meaning and context of that data. It achieves this by employing standardized clinical ontologies and terminologies. These ontologies provide a common language for describing medical concepts, ensuring that healthcare professionals, systems, and organizations can share and interpret data consistently. This level of semantic understanding is a trademark of knowledge-based systems. OpenEHR uses a dual-level modeling approach consisting of the Reference Model (RM) [7] and the Archetype Model (AM) [7]. The Reference Model provides a foundational framework for data storage and processing. It includes generic data structures representing a wide range of clinical information. The Archetype Model, on the other hand, adds a semantic layer to this data. It defines domain-specific structures and constraints using archetypes [8] and templates. These archetypes describe clinical concepts, events, and entities, effectively encoding domain knowledge into the system, as shown in Fig. 1 [9]. This dual-level modeling ensures that EHRs don't just contain data points but encapsulate knowledge about patient conditions, treatments, and more. OpenEHR is designed to accommodate evolving medical knowledge. When medical practices or guidelines change, the archetypes and templates can be updated to reflect the latest standards. This adaptability ensures that EHRs remain aligned with current medical knowledge and practices, further solidifying OpenEHR's status as a knowledge-based system.

1.2 Archetype as a Knowledge Graph Structure

A knowledge graph is a structured knowledge in a graphical representation [12]. [10] defined a knowledge graph as a "graph of data intended to accumulate and convey knowledge of the real world, whose nodes represent entities of interest and whose edges represent potentially different relations between these entities". Knowledge graphs have been used in many domains like healthcare, education, information and communication technology, science and engineering, finance, society and politics, and travel [11].

Archetype Definition Language (ADL) [13], Extensible Markup Language (XML) [14], Web Ontology Language (OWL) [15], Object Constraint Language (OCL) [16], and Knowledge Interchange Format (KIF) [17] are knowledge technologies for the representation of archetypes.

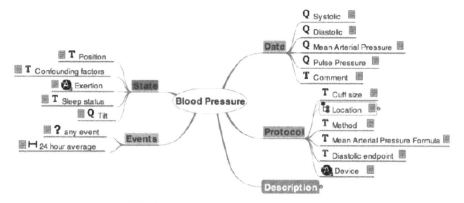

Fig. 1. Blood pressure Archetype structure

ADL is a language designed for modeling archetypes and structured representations of clinical concepts in healthcare systems. To specify constraints, ADL uses an object-oriented reference model, expressed using Unified Modeling Language (UML). ADL allows for the expression of archetype constraints in a structured and nested manner, making it suitable for complex healthcare models. While XML is widely used for web document models, it doesn't inherently support object-oriented semantics or archetype constraints. XML Schema can define data structures but is not well-suited for representing archetype constraints in a structured way. OWL is used for building ontologies on the Semantic Web. While powerful for representing knowledge and relationships, it may not directly express archetype constraints without explicitly defining a reference model. It operates on first-order predicate logic (FOPL) statements, making it less suitable for framing archetypes structurally. OCL is a language for specifying constraints in object-oriented models. It supports various constraint types, including pre- and post-conditions and class variants. While OCL is expressive for modeling constraints, it lacks a built-in mechanism for path traversal within complex structures. KIF is a language for expressing knowledge through first-order predicate logic statements. When describing archetypes, existing information models and terminologies must be converted into KIF statements. It offers expressiveness in logic but does not inherently support structural representation.

Regarding path traceability, ADL uses a path syntax similar to XPath for navigating nested structures, making it convenient for dealing with complex hierarchies. XML includes an XPath mechanism for path traversal. OWL and OCL have similar path syntax, but neither has a dedicated built-in path mechanism. Regarding ontology sections, ADL provides separate ontologies per archetype, facilitating independence from natural language and terminology issues. The other languages mentioned lack built-in syntax for handling this aspect, requiring additional efforts to represent semantics and translations.

1.3 Archetype Definition Language

Archetype Definition Language (ADL) is a formal language used in clinical informatics and healthcare to define and represent clinical archetypes. ADL is a way to structure and standardize medical data, similar to how forms are used daily. Each archetype in ADL is created to a reference model, which means it's designed to conform to specific healthcare standards. These archetypes can be used as templates to structure and validate medical data locally. ADL is based on frame logic queries, knowledge representation, and ontology language. Frame logic queries help define and describe various aspects of data and knowledge. An ADL archetype is designed to capture any archetype's whole meaning and semantics. It's intended to be a precise and complete representation of the archetype's characteristics. The ADL language is structured to closely resemble the Archetype Object Model (AOM) [18]. AOM is a definitive model that describes how archetypes should be structured and what relationships should exist within them. It's like a set of rules for creating an archetype. ADL serves as a textual representation of these characteristics, allowing for a formal and structured way of specifying constraints on data instances adhering to a Reference Model (RM).

An archetype expressed in ADL consists of four main parts. These are Header, Definition, Ontology, and Revision History as shown in Fig. 2.

The header section contains metadata about the archetype, such as its name, author, creation date, and other relevant information. The Definition section describes the modeled clinical concept in terms of a specific Reference Model (RM) class. Constraints are applied to properties of classes and attributes. For instance, constraints might specify the allowed number of occurrences or the permissible values for specific attributes. In the ontology section, the entities defined in the definition section are further described and connected to standardized terminologies. It helps establish a common understanding of the clinical terms and concepts used in the archetype. The revision history section keeps track of any changes made to the archetype over time. It serves as an audit trail, documenting the evolution of the archetype.

ADL can be used to describe constraints on data instances based on formal object models. It also introduces three specific syntaxes within ADL: Constraint ADL (cADL), Data Definition ADL (dADL), First-Order Predicate Logic (FOPL).

cADL: cADL is a syntax within ADL used to express constraints on data instances. These constraints help define how data adhering to a specific object model should behave or be structured. It allows you to specify rules and limitations on data formally. dADL: dADL is another syntax within ADL, and it's used to define the data itself. It describes the data's structure and attributes, which can appear in various sections of an ADL archetype, including Language, description, ontology, and revision history. Essentially, dADL helps specify the content of the archetype. First-Order Predicate Logic (FOPL): ADL also includes a version of first-order predicate logic, a formal logic system used to express statements and constraints. This logic is particularly useful for describing relationships and conditions in archetypes, mainly when the archetypes are based on information models like those expressed in UML (Unified Modeling Language). With

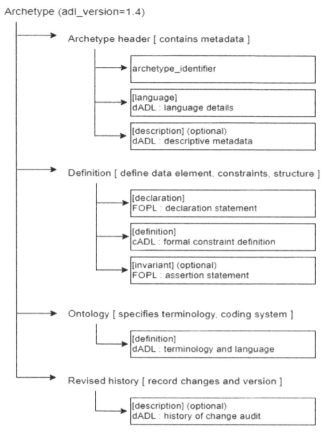

Fig. 2. Archetype Definition Language Structure

these syntaxes, ADL can be used to create archetypes for various domains with formal object models describing data instances. It allows you to define constraints and rules for data within these models. When these archetypes are used in specific contexts, they can be combined into larger structures using templates. Templates are a way to assemble archetypes with additional local or specialized constraints. In the past, healthcare data, including archetypes, was sometimes expressed in XML format. Archetypes are designed to connect medical information to standardized terminologies. They can be addressed or located using path expressions, similar to how XML data can be navigated using XPath expressions. Special tools are available to convert ADL into various XML formats. It means that the healthcare data structured using ADL can be transformed into XML, which computer systems can efficiently process.

1.4 Query Language

A query language is crucial for data retrieval and analysis in database management. It allows users to extract and manipulate database data according to their needs. EHRs systems often use clinical terminologies and coding systems to represent patient data. There are many query languages used. Some of them are Structured Query Language (SQL) [19], XQuery [20], Clinical Quality Language (CQL) [21], Cerner Command Language (CCL) [22], EHR Query Language (EQL) [23], and Archetype Query Language (AQL) [24].

Archetype Query Language. AQL is a declarative query language explicitly developed for expressing queries in searching data within EHRs. It is designed to be neutral, meaning it can work with various EHRs systems, programming languages, and system environments. AQL is closely tied to the openEHR archetype model and semantics, which provide a standardized way to structure healthcare data. The specifications for AQL and EHRs are based on an object-oriented framework. This framework allows for the organization of healthcare data in a structured and hierarchical manner, making it suitable for querying complex medical records. AQL builds upon its predecessor, EQL (EHR Query Language), with two notable innovations: It uses the openEHR path mechanism to represent query criteria and results. It introduces a 'containment' mechanism to indicate data hierarchy and constrain the source data for the query.

The OpenEHR Path Mechanism allows the specification of any node within a top-level structure using a path compatible with semantic levels and X-path. It simplifies the process of navigating and querying complex hierarchical healthcare data. AQL queries are structured using SELECT, FROM, and WHERE clauses, similar to common database query languages. However, AQL considers the hierarchical structure of EHRs data and introduces a containment constraint to specify relationships between parent and child archetypes. A key part of the AQL syntax is the class expression, which consists of the openEHR RM class name (mandatory), A variable name (optional), and An archetype predicate (optional).

Figure 3 displays the AQL structure; the query selects the 'systolic blood pressure' from observation with ehr_id. AQL has certain advantages over other query languages. Users must know the persistence data structure of an EHRs to query by other query languages. Queries of other languages cannot be used on systems with different data stores. AQL uses the OpenEHR Reference model for querying. AQL provides overlapping semantics/use of the FROM block. OpenEHR stores data in (JSON + XML + Relational) format.

```
Select  c/content[OBSERVATION.blood_pressure.v2]/data[at0001]/events[at0006]/data[at0003]/items[at0004]/value
AS systolic_b
FROM EHR e CONTAINS COMPOSITION c WHERE e/ehr_id/value='550e8400-e29b-41d4-a716-446655440000'"
```

Fig. 3. AQL structure

1.5 Query Builder

A query builder is a tool or software application that allows users to create and customize queries to access and retrieve data from healthcare databases or information systems.

These databases often store vast amounts of patient-related information, medical records, and other healthcare data. The query builder simplifies extracting specific information by providing a user-friendly interface where users can define their search criteria without manually writing complex database queries. It can be beneficial for healthcare professionals, administrators, or researchers who may not have extensive programming or database query language skills.

The introduction of EHRs has brought a transformative impact on healthcare by improving the quality of patient data. Within this evolving digital healthcare ecosystem, pursuing semantic interoperability has become a main objective, aiming not just for data exchange but also to share understandable healthcare information across diverse platforms and systems. OpenEHR and FHIR have emerged as vital contributors to the quest for semantic interoperability. These standards are pivotal in realizing seamless data communication between different healthcare systems. EHRs aim to capture a large amount of data, resulting in large datasets containing structured and unstructured data. So, several factors contribute to the complexity of EHRs data, making querying a vital tool for managing and extracting useful information. AQL is a powerful language for querying clinical information structured according to openEHR standardized data models. It enables the user to navigate complex and hierarchical clinical data with precision, ensuring the extraction of the correct information. However, the AQL syntax is difficult and requires a user interface. Creating a user interface for the AQL poses challenges due to the intricate nature of healthcare data and the lack of an intuitive, standardized querying system. Users often face complexities in formulating AQL queries and interpreting results, hindering widespread adoption. The key contributions of this paper are:-

1. The paper proposes an Interactive Graphical User Interface featuring a query builder to facilitate seamless query creation for querying healthcare data within a knowledge-based system.
2. The proposed system comprises a User Interface, Query Builder, and Repository of Documents. All the components enhance the overall user experience, streamline query creation, and establish a robust document management system within the knowledge-based system.
3. We evaluated the features of the proposed approach against different visualization tools using parameters such as language used, technique used, etc.
4. It focuses on improving the overall querying experience for healthcare professionals by proposing user-friendly query interfaces, acknowledging the role of a positive user experience in the effectiveness of EHRs systems.

Further, this paper explores the existing query language, EHRs-based query interface, and knowledge graph in EHRs in Sect. 2. The proposed approach is discussed in Sect. 3. The implementation details and results are given in Sect. 4 and Sect. 5, respectively. Finally, Sect. 6 gives the conclusions.

2 Related Work

This section presents existing query languages for EHRs, existing query interfaces, and the related knowledge graph work in healthcare. The open standard and architecture known as OpenEHR, which stands for "Open Electronic Health Record," aims to completely alter how EHRs are created, maintained, and distributed in healthcare systems. OpenEHR's approach involves clinicians defining EHRs data structure and contents, promoting interoperability among organizations [25]. It provides a thorough and adaptable method for managing medical data while assuring semantic interoperability, scalability, and clinical data quality. It strongly emphasizes semantic interoperability, ensuring that health data is exchanged and retains its clinical meaning. It adopts a dual-model architecture consisting of the Reference and Archetype Models. This architecture distinguishes between the structure of health records and the clinical content, allowing for flexibility in data representation and knowledge capture. [25] discuss the semantic compatibility of dual model architecture-based EHRs standards, including OpenEHR and ISO EN 13606. [26] discuss on archetypes and templates highlights the innovative approach of openEHR, which facilitates consistent data representation and semantic interoperability across diverse healthcare systems. EHRs have revolutionized healthcare data management, but their effectiveness is heavily dependent on the ease of querying and retrieving relevant patient data.

2.1 Query Languages for EHRs

An effective query language in EHRs is paramount for extracting valuable insights from vast healthcare datasets. A well-designed query language facilitates patient information's seamless retrieval and analysis, improving healthcare decision-making. Query Languages for EHRs include SQL, XQuery, CQL, CCL, EQL, and AQL. Each query language is associated with particular standards, ranging from OpenEHR and HL7 FHIR to generic XML data standards and widely used SQL databases. The choice of the best query language hinges on the specific requirements and goals of the healthcare system. For instance, AQL excels in complex EHRs queries, research, and quality improvement, making it ideal for systems prioritizing interoperability and intricate data retrieval. In contrast, the EQL is well-suited for organizations aiming to facilitate EHRs data exchange, mobile health applications, and patient portals while emphasizing simplicity. XQuery is a versatile tool for generic XML document querying but may not best fit for healthcare-specific applications. SQL is a robust and widely applicable option for general database querying and healthcare analytics. The CQL is valuable for clinical decision support, healthcare analytics, and quality improvement initiatives. Meanwhile, CCL explicitly targets organizations that use Cerner's EHRs system, offering capabilities for querying and reporting on Cerner EHRs data and healthcare analytics. Ultimately, the decision should align with the unique data management requirements, existing infrastructure, and expertise available within the organization, ensuring that the chosen query language effectively serves the organization's goals and resources.

2.2   Existing Query Interfaces

Visual query interfaces in EHRs are crucial in simplifying data access and analysis. It has gained prominence due to its ability to enhance data accessibility, clinical decision-making, and patient care. Research shows that these interfaces provide a user-friendly means for healthcare professionals to extract and understand patient data quickly, improving overall efficiency and quality of care. [27] discusses the challenges of using AQL (Archetype Query Language) for querying EHRs databases, especially for semi-skilled users. It proposes an alternative approach using XQBE (XQuery By Example) as a high-level interface for querying EHRs databases. To enable XQBE at the user level, the proposal suggests converting ADL into an equivalent XML instance. Patient data description is converted to XML format and reformed to suit the adoption of the XQBE interface. It allows users to use the XQBE query interface directly to access patient data, eliminating the need to learn and use AQL. [28] presents the development of an Interactive User Interface (ETable) for querying and navigating databases. The ETable allows users to incrementally construct complex queries and perform Create, Read, Update, and Delete operations on SQL databases. [29] presents a promising solution for simplifying the interaction with EHRs, with potential areas for improvement and expansion in functionality to meet the evolving needs of healthcare professionals and patients. It involves bypassing the need for users to learn Archetype Query Language (AQL) directly and leveraging document embedding to handle complex queries from multiple documents. [30] presents a method for automatically generating user interfaces (UIs) for displaying structured hierarchical data. The proposed method uses a horizontally unconstrained table layout, which allows for an unlimited level of hierarchy and increases the compactness and readability of the UI. The proposed algorithm generates the UI by first sorting the data based on its hierarchical structure and then applying a series of rules to determine the placement of each element within the table. SIEUFERD [31], a visual query system presented in this paper, allows users to interact with relational databases by directly manipulating results, providing SQLlike expressiveness from a pure direct manipulation interface. [32] offers a survey of techniques that make data visualization more efficient and effective. It discusses three main areas: visualization specifications, efficient approaches for data visualization, and data visualization recommendations. The paper concludes that data visualization is crucial in today's data-driven business world and suggests a need for further research in this field. The choice of tool would depend on the specific requirements of the research or data retrieval task, considering factors such as query complexity, data domain, and user expertise.

2.3   Knowledge Graph in EHRs

The openEHR approach has been used to address many challenges, such as improving the semantic interoperability of clinical data registries [26]. Using the openEHR modeling approach, [33] research created the COVID-19 openEHR template based on the most recent Chinese guideline. It demonstrated the Methodology's capacity to model and share information quickly by reusing the preexisting archetypes, which is especially helpful in a new and constantly evolving field like COVID-19. Semantic health knowledge graphs have gained prominence in healthcare data management and querying.

Table 1. Knowledge graph application in EHRs

Paper	About
Adverse Drug Reaction Discovery Using a Tumor-Biomarker Knowledge Graph [34]	Adverse drug reactions (ADRs) are a significant concern for public health and highlight the need for early detection to ensure drug development and patient safety
Knowledge guided graph attention network for detecting healthcare misinformation [35]	Addresses the issue of healthcare misinformation in online platforms, which can negatively impact public health due to the spread of inaccurate or incomplete medical information
COVID-19 literature knowledge graph construction and drug repurposing report generation [36]	Created a powerful tool called COVID-KG to help scientists and doctors understand COVID-19 better
Gamenet: Graph augmented memory networks for recommending medication combination [37]	Knowledge about Drug-drug interactions
Learning an expandable EMR-based medical knowledge network to enhance clinical diagnosis [38]	Develop an expandable MKN based on Chinese Electronic Medical Records (CEMRs) to improve initial clinical diagnosis. It means creating a system that can continuously grow and strengthen its knowledge base
Robustly extracting medical knowledge from EHRs: a case study of learning a health knowledge graph [39]	Used EHRs data to build a knowledge graph that can help in diagnosing diseases based on symptoms

Knowledge graphs have been studied in various healthcare fields, as shown in Table 1. One of them is Adverse drug reactions (ADRs) [34]. It is a significant concern for public health. It highlights the need for early detection to ensure drug development and patient safety. [34] used machine learning methods to create a Tumor-Biomarker Knowledge Graph (TBKG) that includes four types of nodes: Tumor, Biomarker, Drug, and ADR. Their approach helps identify potential ADRs related to anti-tumor drugs and explains these predictions. [35] addresses the issue of healthcare misinformation in online platforms, which can negatively impact public health due to the spread of inaccurate or incomplete medical information. [36] created a powerful tool called COVID-19 to help scientists and doctors understand COVID-19 better. They read many scientific papers and turned the information into innovative maps called knowledge graphs (KGs). Predicting drug-drug interactions (DDIs) is essential for patient safety during clinical trials. Knowledge graphs are also used to identify biomolecular features that can help classify drugs as causative or not for specific types of adverse drug reactions (ADRs), such as drug-induced liver injuries (DILI) and severe cutaneous adverse reactions (SCAR). One particular application in healthcare is providing recommendations for medications. It can be challenging, especially for patients with complex health conditions who may require multiple medications. Recommending the right combination of medications is crucial to ensure patient safety and effectiveness of treatment. Existing approaches to medication recommendations might not take into account a patient's unique health history, and they might overlook potential interactions between different drugs. GAMENet [37] was introduced as a deep learning model integrating longitudinal patient EHR data (historical health data over time) and drug knowledge about DDIs. Current medical knowledge graph construction studies focus less on utilizing real-world data sources and more on general methodologies and opportunities. A knowledge graph constructed from EHRs data obtains real-world data from healthcare records [38]. EHRs are a valuable source of information for learning medical knowledge. Researchers aim to use this data to build a knowledge graph that can help diagnose diseases based on symptoms [39], acknowledging that clinicians tend to focus on clinical information relevant to their specialties when using EHRs. This specialization can lead to a lack of attention to information outside their expertise, potentially resulting in delayed diagnoses or improper management of diseases.

3   Querying Knowledge-Based System

Querying Healthcare Data in a Knowledge-Based System involves data extraction, implementing an Archetype Query Language (AQL)-based query builder, and querying. The system has three components. These are user interface query builders and a repository of documents, as shown in Fig. 4.

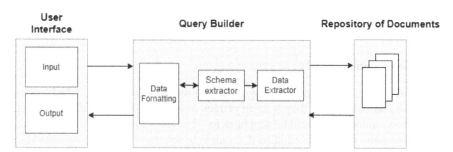

Fig. 4. Architecture Diagram

User Interface (UI): The UI is the component with which the end user directly interacts. It provides a graphical interface for users to input their requirements. The interface is designed to be intuitive, user-friendly, and easy to navigate, enabling users to select patients and compositions, define the WHERE clause, set postprocessing functions like limit, offset, and order by, and finally generate the AQL query. To enhance the user experience, it may also include additional features like tooltips, autocomplete functions, and visual cues to guide users through the query-building process.

Query Builder: Based on the user's input from the UI, the Query Builder constructs the AQL query. It involves complex algorithms and data processing techniques to ensure the generated queries are accurate, efficient, and optimized for the best performance.

Query Builder has Schema Extractor as subcomponents. The Schema Extractor interacts with the EHR's underlying data structure. It pulls out the necessary data from the composition schema, such as the elements and their paths within the EHRs, enabling the Query builder to construct accurate and effective queries. Data Extractor communicates with the FHIR and openEHR endpoints, essentially the servers where the EHR data is stored. It sends the generated AQL queries to the EHRBase to retrieve the data. EHRBase [40] is an open-source platform for managing EHRs. It is designed to provide a flexible and scalable solution for storing, retrieving, and managing health-related data in a standardized and interoperable manner. This component must handle network communication, server responses, and possible errors or timeouts during the data fetching. Data Formatting job is to present the data in the UI. It might involve filtering, sorting, or other forms of data manipulation to make the data more accessible for the end user to understand. This component is crucial in ensuring the raw data is transformed into a valid, meaningful, and easy-to-understand format.

Repository of Documents: It stores the Compositions [21] within the EHRs system and is the backbone for organizing and managing healthcare data. Compositions represent a structured collection of patient information offering a comprehensive view of a patient's health history. It stores the compositions in JSON format.

4   Implementation

This section explains the detailed implementation, how the user requests the query and gets the response back, and what software and hardware requirements are needed to set up this system. Finally, the results and comparison between existing and proposed approaches will be presented.

4.1   Implementation Details

The user will directly contact the UI by providing the information, i.e., which patient information and observation they want to extract, and the output query extracted from the repository of documents will be sent back to UI as shown in Fig. 5.

Figure 6 shows the implementation diagram in which the Clinical Knowledge Manager (CKM) [41] and openEHR Archetype Designer [42] are used in the template generation layer to create a standardized template for collecting and storing EHRs data. The CKM provides a comprehensive library of clinical concepts and terminologies to create the template based on the healthcare organization's specific needs. The openEHR Archetype Designer, on the other hand, is a tool that allows healthcare professionals to design and manage templates according to openEHR specifications. Ultimately, the generated template is exported into ODT or JSON format.

Once the template is generated, the form generation phase begins, where Medblocks UI [43] and Svelte [44] are used to create the UI for the EHRs-based application. Medblocks UI provides a set of HTML snippets that can be easily integrated into the application to create a visually appealing and user-friendly interface. On the other hand, Svelte is a front-end JavaScript framework that allows developers to create dynamic and interactive forms for data entry and retrieval.

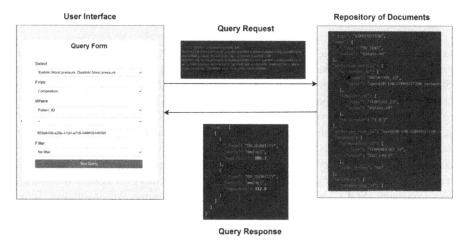

Fig. 5. Query Processing Diagram

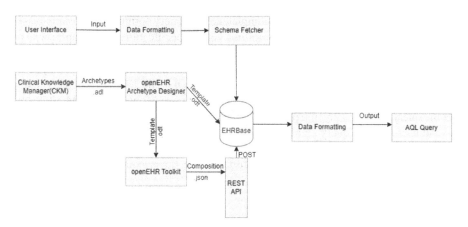

Fig. 6. Implementation Diagram

Finally, the backend EHRbase REST API setup using Docker [45] provides the necessary infrastructure for storing and accessing the EHRs data. The API setup uses Docker containers to deploy the EHRbase server, which provides FHIR and openEHR endpoints for accessing patient demographic data and EHRs entries. The API also supports various authentication and authorization mechanisms to ensure the security and privacy of the EHRs data.

4.2 Software and Hardware Configurations

OS: Linux/Mac/Windows; RAM: 4GB/8GB; Processor: 11th Gen Intel Core i5; Google Chrome, Microsoft Edge or other; Docker Desktop: 4.25.2; Java: 21.0.1; Internet.

5 Results

A user interface is depicted in Fig. 7, wherein the user chooses the "systolic blood pressure" and "diastolic blood pressure" from observation, with the Patient_ID being "550e8400-e29b-41d4-a716-446655440000" and the filter being "No filter". The query builder generates the AQL query based on user input provided through the user interface, and the query result of the generated AQL query is returned to the user interface. The query result is shown in Fig. 8. In query visualization tools, as shown in Table 2, various approaches have been explored to enhance the interpretation and formulation of queries. In query visualization tools, multiple approaches have been studied to enhance the interpretation and formulation of queries. QueryVis utilizes Structured Query Language (SQL) and employs diagrammatic reasoning with inspiration from Unified Modeling Language (UML), resulting in faster interpretation with fewer errors, as evidenced by user studies. Relational Diagrams, also employing SQL, utilize nested negated bounding boxes inspired by Peirce's beta graph, ensuring unambiguous interpretation for any nesting depth, even in the case of disconnected components. Visual SQL, grounded in SQL, adopts an entity-relationship representation paradigm, leading to higher conceptual correctness and completeness in query formulation. Polaris takes a different route by automatically compiling visual specifications into graphical displays, combining statistical analysis and visualization with SQL for generating rich and expressive visualizations in multidimensional database exploration. AQL-MongoDB interpreter integrates Archetype Query Language (AQL) and MongoDB Query Language, showing nuanced performance differences between MongoDB and MySQL for specific query types. Lastly, the proposed approach employs AQL, focusing on interactive and user-friendly query creation by extracting specific data elements via recursive parsing, promising precision in AQL queries. This approach stands out for its ability to provide an interactive and user-friendly Interface and a query builder.

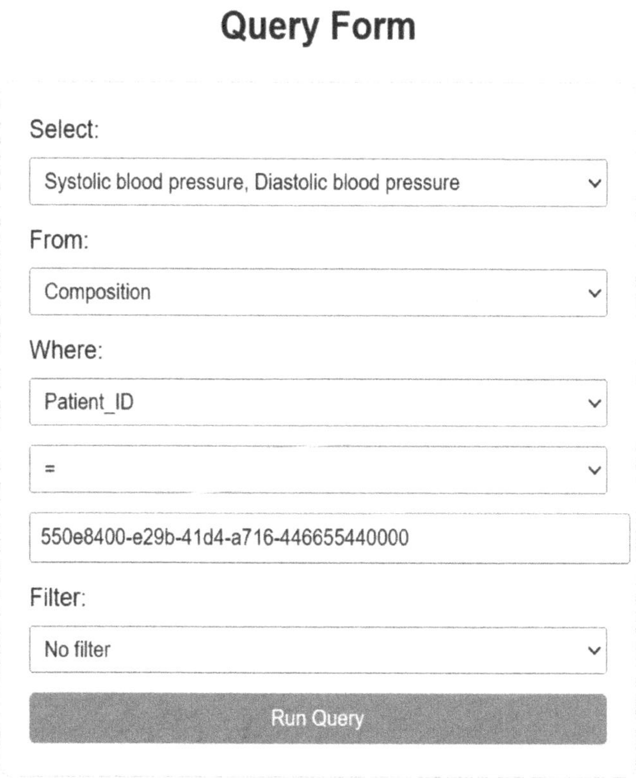
Query Form
Select:
Systolic blood pressure, Diastolic blood pressure
From:
Composition
Where:
Patient_ID
=
550e8400-e29b-41d4-a716-446655440000
Filter:
No filter
Run Query

Fig. 7. User Interface

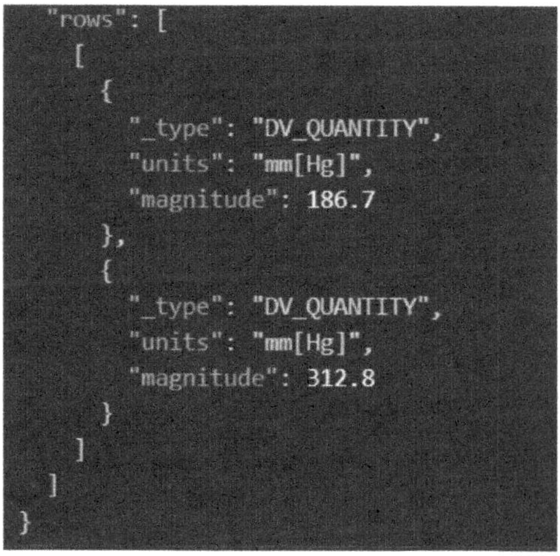
"rows": [
[
{
"_type": "DV_QUANTITY",
"units": "mm[Hg]",
"magnitude": 186.7
},
{
"_type": "DV_QUANTITY",
"units": "mm[Hg]",
"magnitude": 312.8
}
]
]
}

Fig. 8. Query Result

Table 2. Comparison between different query visualization tools and the proposed approach

Query Visualization Tools	Language Used	Technique Used	Results
QueryVis [46]	Structured Query Language	Diagrammatic reasoning, UML-inspired	Faster interpretation with fewer based on user study
AQL-MongoDB interpreter [47]	Archetype Query Language, MongoDB Query Language	AQL into MongoDB interpreter, Integration of AQL's semantic querying capabilities with MongoDB's document-based NoSQL storage	Exaggerated single-patient queries behave better in MongoDB, but exaggerated all-patient queries typically behave better in MySQL, and the projection query also behaves considerably better in MongoDB than MySQL
Visual SQL [48]	Structured Query Language	Based on the paradigm of entity-relationship representation	Higher conceptual correctness and conceptual completeness in query formulation
Polaris [49]	Structured Query Language	Automatic compilation of visual specifications into graphical displays, combining statistical analysis and visualization	Generation of rich, expressive visualizations for multidimensional database exploration
Proposed Approach	Archetype Query Language	Extraction of specific data elements through recursive parsing	Interactive and user-friendly, create AQL queries precisely

6 Conclusions

The incorporation of the proposed approach to openEHR and EHRBase platforms will help make it possible for medical practitioners to examine and access EHR data without needing to be proficient in AQL or schema expertise. The user-friendly visual query interface will make data retrieval quick and easy, and its export features will help with data integration and sharing even more. The proposed approach will make the querying system a vital tool for streamlining data management in the healthcare industry.

References

1. Rocha, E.S.B., et al.: Knowledge management in health: a systematic literature review. Rev. latino-americana enfermagem **20**, 392–400 (2012)
2. Campanella, P., et al.: The impact of electronic health records on healthcare quality: a systematic review and meta-analysis. Eur. J. Public Health **26**(1), 60–64 (2016)
3. Dolin, R.H., et al.: The HL7 clinical document architecture. J. Am. Med. Inform. Assoc. **8**(6), 552–569 (2001)
4. CEN EN 13606-1. Health informatics–Electronic health record communication–Part 1: Reference model. Draft European Standard for CEN Enquiry prEN 13606-1. European Committee for Standardization, Brussels, Belgium (2004)
5. Kalra, D., Beale, T., Heard, S.: The openEHR foundation. Stud. Health Technol. Inform. **115**, 153–173 (2005)
6. Eichelberg, M., et al.: A survey and analysis of electronic healthcare record standards. ACM Comput. Surv. (CSUR) **37**(4), 277–315 (2005)
7. Beale, T., Heard, S.: openEHR architecture: architecture overview in the openEHR release 1.0.2. In: Beale T and Heard S, eds. openEHR Foundation (2008)
8. Blobel, B., Pharow, P. (eds.): Advanced Health Telematics and Telemedicine: The Magdeburg Expert Summit Textbook, vol. 96. IOS Press (2003)
9. Towards the interoperability of computerised guidelines and electronic health records: an experiment with openEHR archetypes and a chronic heart failure guideline – Scientific Figure on ResearchGate. https://www.researchgate.net/figure/openEHR-archetype-for-the-blood-pressure-concept-diagram-taken-from-the-openEHR_fig1_220836902
10. Hogan, A., et al.: Knowledge graphs. ACM Comput. Surv. (CSUR) **54**(4), 1–37 (2021)
11. Abu-Salih, B.: Domain-specific knowledge graphs: a survey. J. Netw. Comput. Appl. **185**, 103076 (2021)
12. Sheth, A., Padhee, S., Gyrard, A.: Knowledge graphs and knowledge networks: the story in brief. IEEE Internet Comput. **23**(4), 67–75 (2019)
13. Archetype Definition Language 1.4 (ADL1.4). Archetype Definition Language 1.4 (ADL1.4). https://specifications.openehr.org/releases/AM/latest/ADL1.4.html
14. Extensible Markup Language (XML). https://www.w3.org/XML/
15. Web Ontology Language (OWL). https://www.w3.org/OWL/
16. Object Constraint Language (OCL). https://www.omg.org/spec/OCL/2.4/About-OCL/
17. Knowledge Interchange Format. http://www-ksl.stanford.edu/knowledge-sharing/kif/
18. Beale, T., Heard, S.: openEHR specification project release 101. 1.4. 0. The openEHR Foundation, London (2007)
19. Foster, E.C., Godbole, S.V., Foster, E.C., Godbole, S.V.: Overview of SQL. Database Syst.: Pragmatic Approach 171–175 (2014)
20. Boag, S., et al.: XQuery 1.0: an XML query language (2002)
21. Clinical Quality Language. https://cql.hl7.org/
22. Cerner interoperability solution. https://www.cerner.com/solutions/interoperability
23. Ma, C., et al.: EHR query language (EQL)-a query language for archetype-based health records. Medinfo **129**, 397–401 (2007)
24. Archetype Query Language. https://specifications.openehr.org/releases/QUERYLANGUAGE/latest/AQL.html
25. Martínez-Costa, C., Menárguez-Tortosa, M., Fernández-Breis, J.T.: An approach for the semantic interoperability of ISO EN 13606 and OpenEHR archetypes. J. Biomed. Inform. **43**(5), 736–746 (2010)
26. Min, L., et al.: An openEHR based approach to improve the semantic interoperability of clinical data registry. BMC Med. Inform. Decis. Making **18**(1), 49–56 (2018)

27. Sachdeva, S., Bhalla, S.: Implementing high-level query language interfaces for archetype-based electronic health records database. In: International Conference on Management of Data (COMAD) (2009)
28. Kahng, M., et al.: Interactive browsing and navigation in relational databases. arXiv preprint arXiv:1603.02371 (2016)
29. Soni, K., Sachdeva, S., Goyal, A., Gupta, A., Bose, D., Bhalla, S.: Saral Anuyojan: an interactive querying interface for EHR. In: Sachdeva, S., Watanobe, Y., Bhalla, S. (eds.) BDA 2022. LNCS, vol. 13830, pp. 163–176. Springer, Cham (2023). https://doi.org/10.1007/978-3-031-28350-5_13
30. Bakke, E., Karger, D.R., Miller, R.C.: Automatic layout of structured hierarchical reports. IEEE Trans. Visual Comput. Graphics 19(12), 2586–2595 (2013)
31. Bakke, E., Karger, D.R.: Expressive query construction through direct manipulation of nested relational results. In: Proceedings of the 2016 International Conference on Management of Data (2016)
32. Qin, X., et al.: Making data visualization more efficient and effective: a survey. VLDB J. 29, 93–117 (2020)
33. Li, M., et al.: Development of an openEHR template for COVID-19 based on clinical guidelines. J. Med. Internet Res. 22(6), e20239 (2020)
34. Wang, M., et al.: Adverse drug reaction discovery using a tumor-biomarker knowledge graph. Front. Genet. 11, 625659 (2021)
35. Cui, L., et al.: Deterrent: Knowledge guided graph attention network for detecting healthcare misinformation. In: Proceedings of the 26th ACM SIGKDD International Conference on Knowledge Discovery & Data Mining (2020)
36. Wang, Q., et al.: COVID-19 literature knowledge graph construction and drug repurposing report generation. arXiv preprint arXiv:2007.00576 (2020)
37. Shang, J., et al.: GameNet: graph augmented memory networks for recommending medication combination. In: Proceedings of the AAAI Conference on Artificial Intelligence, vol. 33, no. 01 (2019)
38. Xie, J., et al.: Learning an expandable EMR-based medical knowledge network to enhance clinical diagnosis. Artif. Intell. Med. 107, 101927 (2020)
39. Chen, I.Y., et al.: Robustly extracting medical knowledge from EHRs: a case study of learning a health knowledge graph. In: Pacific Symposium on Biocomputing 2020 (2019)
40. EHRBase. https://ehrbase.org/
41. Ocean Health Systems, Sebastian Garde. Clinical Knowledge Manager. Clinical Knowledge Manager. https://ckm.openehr.org/ckm/
42. Archetype Designer. https://tools.openehr.org/designer/
43. Ramesh, S.: Introducing medblocks ui. https://blog.medblocks.org/2021-01-26-introducing-medblocks-ui/
44. Svelte. https://svelte.dev/
45. REST API J. Ratliff, Docker: Accelerated, containerized application development (2022). https://www.docker.com
46. Leventidis, A., et al.: QueryVis: logic-based diagrams help users understand complicated SQL queries faster. In: Proceedings of the 2020 ACM SIGMOD International Conference on Management of Data (2020)
47. Ramos, M., et al.: An archetype query language interpreter into MongoDB: managing NoSQL standardized electronic health record extracts systems. J. Biomed. Inf. 101, 103339 (2020)

48. Jaakkola, H., Thalheim, B.: Visual SQL – high-quality ER-based query treatment. In: Jeusfeld, M.A., Pastor, Ó. (eds.) ER 2003. LNCS, vol. 2814, pp. 129–139. Springer, Heidelberg (2003). https://doi.org/10.1007/978-3-540-39597-3_13

49. Stolte, C., Tang, D., Hanrahan, P.: Polaris: A system for query, analysis, and visualization of multidimensional relational databases. IEEE Trans. Visual Comput. Graphics **8**(1), 52–65 (2002)

IGUANER - DIfferential Gene Expression and fUnctionAl aNalyzER

Valentina Pinna[1], Jessica Di Martino[2], Franco Liberati[1,2],
Paolo Bottoni[1(✉)], and Tiziana Castrignanò[2]

[1] Sapienza University of Rome, Rome, Italy
pinna.1837949@studenti.uniroma1.it, {liberati,bottoni}@di.uniroma1.it
[2] University of Tuscia, Viterbo, Italy
{jessica.dimartino,franco.liberati,t.castrignano}@unitus.it

Abstract. In the past fifteen years, the advent of Next-Generation Sequencing technologies, characterized by high efficiency and reduced costs, has marked a pivotal turn for research across various fields including molecular biology, genetics, and molecular medicine. Projects that would have previously required extensive timeframes and significant investments can now be completed swiftly at a fraction of the cost. A direct consequence of the proliferation of these systems is the exponential increase in data generated by RNA-Seq experiments. Much of this data originates from biological samples (cells, tissues, mucus, etc.) of organisms with either absent or incomplete genomic annotations. Compounding this issue is the fact that the surge in data has not been matched by the development of adequate software tools capable of analyzing RNA-Seq data for such organisms. Currently available tools have several limitations: a) they operate in silos, so they only support certain types of analyses, thus complicating the biological interpretation of results; b) they are often executable only via Web interfaces, overlooking the parallelism and efficiency offered by modern supercomputers; c) functional analysis tools rely on outdated functional annotations or support only a limited set of organisms with genomic annotation; d) only one comparison (between two different experimental conditions) can be tested at each run. In order to overcome these limitations, we present IGUANER - (DIfferential Gene expression and fUnctionAl aNalyzER), a software aimed at ensuring the capability for integrated and up-to-date analysis of RNA-Seq data from any organism, regardless of the level of genomic annotation.

Keywords: 'omics' databases · Format independence · Interactive queries

1 Introduction

Biological research has recently seen a massive increase in genomic information, primarily due to *Next-Generation Sequencing* (NGS) technologies, leading to a significant growth in both the amount and variety of raw sequencing data. As a

S. Sachdeva and Y. Watanobe (Eds.): BDA 2023, LNCS 14516, pp. 78–93, 2024.
https://doi.org/10.1007/978-3-031-58502-9_5

result, bioinformatics has become a major player in the 'big data' field, opening up new opportunities for discovery [5,7,15,41]. At the same time, there has been a substantial increase in the amount of biological data stored in genomic databases [6,14,31], collected from extensive NGS experiments [10,43].

The rapidly growing collection of genetic data provides exceptional opportunities for research. However, it also requires the creation of more advanced methods for effective data mining and analysis [3,8]. Although modern sequencing platforms like PacBio and MinIon have been developed for generating long reads, fully determining an organism's genome is still a complex and costly process, requiring considerable time and financial resources [46].

The need for a deeper understanding of cell functions, not achievable through genome analysis alone, has led to the widespread adoption of the RNA-Seq technique, which uses Next-Generation Sequencing (NGS) technologies to identify and quantify RNA molecules in a biological sample [33]. RNA-Seq provides a comprehensive view of the transcriptome, which is the complete set of RNA transcripts. It reflects the dynamic presence and abundance of RNA in cells at the time of sampling. After RNA-seq sequencing, the reads are either aligned to a reference genome or transcripts, or assembled *de novo* without genomic sequence [9,28,29,37,38]. This process creates a transcription map at the genomic scale, detailing the structure and/or expression level of each gene [47].

Among the various pieces of software that aim at evaluating gene expression levels (i.e. *counts*) in different experimental conditions, StringTie [40] is the most widely used one in presence of a reference genome, whilst Salmon [39] is exploited when only the trascriptome is available. These tools allow quantification of RNA and must be used alternatively. The quantification step is mandatory in RNA-Seq Analysis; indeed the quantification output files containing the *counts* are needed to accomplish the other core step of differential gene expression analysis.

The latter is a method to compare the levels of gene expression between two or more groups under varying conditions, such as different time points, environmental stresses, or between healthy and diseased tissues. The objective is to identify genes that show statistically significant differences in expression levels (named *differentially expressed genes - degs*), indicating that they may be involved in the processes or conditions being studied [13].

By analyzing patterns of up- or down-regulation of genes, researchers can infer their roles in cellular functions, understand the molecular mechanisms underlying certain conditions, and potentially identify targets for therapeutic intervention. This analysis is crucial for understanding complex biological responses and is a foundational tool in functional genomics [18].

To support researchers, we introduce IGUANER, an automated bioinformatics pipeline for analysis of *degs* in organisms at any level of genomic annotation. Even in the absence of a reference genome, IGUANER can perform differential gene expression analysis along with the corresponding functional analysis. IGUANER process is fully automated, starting from just a few input data (the quantification files containing the *counts*, the transcriptome -in some cases- and the phenotypic data file). The pipeline is thus capable of providing results, regardless of the number of comparisons to be made between the phenotypic conditions.

Full automation makes IGUANER a strong candidate for big data analysis of massive datasets, and deployment on high-performance computing platforms.

For better understanding, we underline the difference between model and non-model organisms. These terms receive various definitions, in particular from the purely biological field or the bioinformatics one. In this paper we use the model adjective when referring to organisms for which a well-annotated reference genome exists, and the non-model adjective to denote the remaining ones.

In the rest of the paper, after reviewing related work in Sect. 2, we provide an overview on the software that IGUANER leverages, in Sect. 3, while Sect. 4 presents the typical processes performed with IGUANER. Results are discussed in Sect. 5 and Sect. 6 draws conclusions and points to future work.

2   Related Work

In Tables 1 (all tools, most of which supporting differential gene expression analysis) and 2 (those also implementing functional analysis) we compare specifications of currently available and automated tools for RNA-Seq analysis.

Table 1. Automated tools for differential gene expression analysis.

Tool	UI	Hosting	*Counts* source	Phenotypic data source	Only genome reference-based	Reference
IDEAMEX	Web GUI	Remote	Matrix	Online form	No	[20]
RobiNA	Web GUI	Remote	Matrix /FASTQ /SAM /BAM	Online form	No	[30]
iDEP	Web GUI	Remote	Matrix	File	No	[16]
IRIS-EDA	Web GUI	Remote	Matrix	File	No	[36]
aTAP	Web GUI	Remote	FASTQ	Online form	No	[45]
UTAP	Web GUI	Remote	FASTQ /BCL	Online form	Yes	[26]
MAP-RSeq	CLI	Local	FASTQ	File	No	[21]
aRNApipe	CLI	Local	FASTQ	File	Yes	[1]
TCC-GUI	Web GUI	Remote	Matrix	Online form	No	[44]
GENAVi	Web GUI	Remote	Matrix	File	Yes	[42]

These tools show some limitations: (1) Almost all of them can only be run via a Web interface and remotely. (2) No tool directly accepts files already produced by Salmon as input. (3) Only matrices or files that can be processed by quantification tools are accepted. (4) Finally, half of them allow phenotypic data to be provided only by filling a form field, but this is an error-prone strategy.

For the subset of software able to perform functional analysis we observe the following: (1) Few species are properly supported (i.e. the experimental validated annotations are not always used when they exist and/or prediction is not performed when necessary). (2) The genome/transcriptome full annotation phase must be carried out whenever the analysis is launched (retrieved annotations cannot be reused subsequently, due to their temporariness). (3) KEGG analysis is not always possibile. (4) Finally, continuos update is not guaranteed.

Table 2. Automated tools for both differential gene expression and functional analysis.

Tool	Only genome reference-based	Properly supported species	Level	Reusable	GO	KEGG	Continuous update	Reference
iDEP	No	Subset; input-dependent for others	Experiment-based only for supported species; input-dependent for others	No	Yes	Yes	No	[16]
aTAP	No	All	Prediction-based only	No	Yes	No	No	[45]
GENAVi	Yes	Mouse, human	Experiment-based only	No	Yes	Yes	No	[42]

3   Components of the Iguaner Platform

IGUANER is a gene expression analysis software relying on the integration of various key technologies. The primary development platform is Python, a programming language known for its simplicity, readability, and flexibility, making it ideal for scientific projects, particularly in the analysis of biological data.

Part of the IGUANER code is in the R language, renowned for its advanced capabilities in statistical analysis of biological data [48]. To efficiently manage the storage and access of GO/KEGG data, IGUANER has incorporated the MongoDB[1] database management system, providing a solid framework to handle substantial volumes of biological data. Indeed, MongoDB significantly contributes to the completeness and reliability of the platform.

---

[1] https://www.mongodb.com/.

In summary, IGUANER is a software primarily developed in Python, with crucial components implemented in R, and using the MongoDB database to ensure a comprehensive and efficient platform for functional analysis. IGUANER extensively leverages third-party software to optimize its capabilities.

The core component of IGUANER, in Python, benefits from various libraries and packages devoted to analysis of biological data, such as: `Matplotlib` [19], and `Pandas` [34]. These packages offer advanced functionalities for data analysis, including data manipulation, visualization, and statistical analysis. Concerning the component developed with R, the major packages are `dplyr` [51], `tidyr` [50], `DESeq2` [32], `ggplot2` [49], `clusterProfiler` [52,53]. The first two packages deal with data manipulation, the third one aims at identifying differentially expressed genes, and the last two ones are concerned with data visualization and in statistical analysis. These components have been seamlessly integrated into IGUANER to ensure precise and reliable gene expression analysis.

IGUANER includes seven distinct modules (see Fig. 1), among which the differential gene expression analysis module and the functional analysis module represent the core components. These central modules (highlighted in blue in Fig. 1) are crucial in achieving the main goals of the analysis.

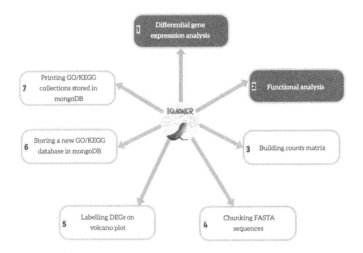

Fig. 1. The seven IGUANER software modules. (Color figure online)

Herein, we provide a concise description of each module:

1. **Differential gene expression analysis - *degs* analysis:** This module identifies variations in gene expression levels between different sample groups in genomic studies. This analysis hinges on comparing the RNA expression levels of genes across different conditions, such as diseased vs. healthy tissues, treated vs. untreated cells, or various developmental stages.

2. **Functional analysis:** This module assigns biological meaning to the variations observed in the identification of differentially expressed genes. Through the use of databases such as Gene Ontology [2,12] and KEGG Pathway [22,24,25], it analyzes the biological functions, cellular processes and metabolic pathways involved in the gene identifications, providing a comprehensive overview of the biological implications.

3. **Building the *counts* matrix:** This module builds a CSV counting matrix, an essential step for quantitatively representing gene expression transcripts. It transforms the raw data generated by StringTie into a tabular structure, facilitating further statistical analysis and data visualization.

4. **Chunking the FASTA sequence file:** When the sequences contained in the FASTA file are too large to be processed in a single step by common functional annotation tools, e.g., eggNOG-mapper and BlastKOALA, this module splits the file, optimizing the annotation process and ensuring the efficient management of large transcriptomic datasets.

5. **Labelling annoted DEGs on volcano plot:** Data visualization is enriched by identifying and labeling genes of interest on a scatterplot (volcano plot). It facilitates rapid visual interpretation of significant gene expression differences, highlighting salient points in the context of the analysis.

6. **Storing new GO/KEGG database in MongoDB:** This module enables the integration of new GO and KEGG databases, so that users can customize and update functional annotation resources for future analyses.

7. **Printing GO/KEGG database stored in MongoDB:** It provides clear functionality for data visualization, allowing users to print and access collections of GO/KEGG data stored in MongoDB, promoting transparency and facilitating user inspection of available functional annotation resources.

4   The IGUANER Workflow

The strength of IGUANER lies in its ability to analyze data derived from RNA-Seq experiments of both model and non-model organisms.

In order to analyze each scenario, IGUANER processes the data by applying two main workflows, for analysing differential gene expression and functionalities.

4.1   The Differential Gene Expression Analysis

We first illustrate the workflow of the activities for analysing differential gene expressions, shown in Fig. 2 for the case of model organisms.

1. **StringTie output preprocessing:** This initial phase is performed *iff* the quantification results come from StringTie (i.e. in the case of model organisms, when a genome annotation exists). It returns the gene *counts* matrix.

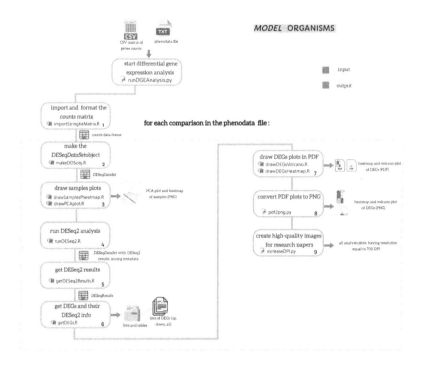

Fig. 2. Workflow for differential gene expression analysis on model organisms.

2. ***Counts* files import:** The provided matrix (in step 1 - model organisms) or quantification files returned by Salmon (non model organisms) are imported.

3. **Building of the *DESeqDataSet* object:** The *counts* matrix or files are used along with the phenotypic data file to make the *DESeqDataSet*, which is needed in order to run DESeq2 analysis for each phenotypic comparison.

4. **Samples plotting:** Samples are represented in PCA and heatmap plots in order to explore similarity of samples and therefore to evaluate their quality.

5. **Running the DESeq2 analysis:** The DESeq2 analysis is performed by calling the *DESeq()* function provided by the DESeq2 package.

6. **Results extraction:** The DESeq2 analysis results are extracted by calling the *results()* function (provided by the DESeq2 package) which returns a *DESeqResults* object.

7. ***DEGs* mining:** The *degs* along with their characterizing parameters (*log2-FoldChange*, *adjusted p-value*, etc.) are extracted by calling the *results()* function of DESeq2, which returns a *DESeqResults* object.

8. ***DEGs* sequences extraction:** This phase is exploited if and only if *counts* come from Salmon (i.e. the organism of interest is non-model, therefore trascriptome is used). *Degs* are transcripts and their sequences are saved into FASTA files. A new FASTA file is created for each *degs* list file.

9. **DEGs plotting:** *Degs* are graphically represented in heatmap and volcano plots. All figures are saved in PDF format because of some graphical packages issues in saving in common images format (PNG, JPEG, etc.).

10. **Converting PDF plots:** Aimed at creating high quality images.

4.2   Functional Analysis

The workflow of the activities related to functional analysis is shown in Fig. 3, again for the case of model organisms.

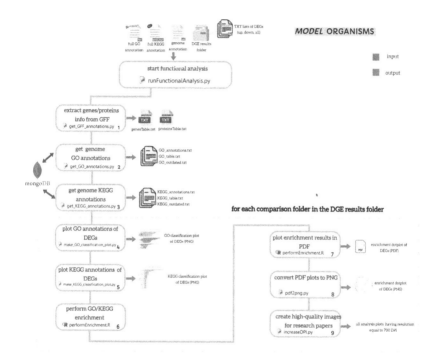

Fig. 3. Workflow for functional analysis on model organisms.

1. **Genes and proteins collecting:** This phase is performed *if* and only if the organism of interest is model. All the genes and proteins revealed by the reference genome and properly stored in specific annotation files, typically in GFF format, are collected and stored in two structured files (in TSV format) required to perform the functional annotation step.

2. **GO functional annotation processing:** All GO annotations (i.e. mappings between genes/transcripts and GO terms -biological processes, molecular functions, cellular components-) which have been retrieved/predicted by the chosen GO functional annotation tool, are processed in order to store a comprehensive, well-structured and updated functional annotation.

This step is performed by interacting with MongoDB. Indeed output files from functional annotation tools contain only terms IDs, without providing any description of them. The interaction with MongoDB enriches functional annotation results, by adding biological meanings to raw IDs.

3. **KEGG functional annotation processing:** This step is carried out as the previous one, but differs in the type of functional data to process: in this case we deal with KEGG pathways instead of GO terms.

4. **Plotting of GO annotations of *degs*:** A plot is drawn for each *degs* list and for each comparison folder (referred to the corresponding comparison in the phenotypic data file), where all associated GO annotations are graphically represented in horizontal bar diagram.

5. **Plotting of KEGG annotations of *degs*:** This step is similar to the previous one, but plotting KEGG annotations instead of the GO ones.

6. **GO enrichment analysis of *degs*:** This phase is performed for each *degs* list and for each comparison. It aims at identifying the statistically enriched functional categories (GO terms in this case) with respect to what is expected by chance. It is accomplished by calling the function *enricher()* from the `clusterProfiler` package, that performs some statistical tests. All results are stored in a *data.frame* object.

7. **Plotting of GO enrichment results:** Results obtained in the previous step are plotted on a dotplot and stored in PDF format.

8. **KEGG enrichment analysis of *degs*:** This step is analogous to step 3, but enrichment regards KEGG pathways in this case.

9. **Plotting of KEGG enrichment results:** This step is analogous to step 4, but starting from KEGG enrichment results.

10. **Converting PDF plot:** Aimed at creating high quality images.

Initially, before running the functional analysis, functional annotation of *degs* is carried out. It consists of the assignment of biological functions through access to database such as the Gene Ontology and KEGG Pathway database and it is fulfilled by the means of specific tools. The choice of which tools to use varies according to the functional annotation level of a given organism. In general, one of the following three cases can happen:

a. The organism is model and the experimentally validated (hence available) functional annotation is complete. GO functional annotation must be performed via the UniProt resource [11]. KEGG functional annotation has to be performed by accessing annotations stored by KEGG Pathway database.

b. The organism is model, the experimentally validated functional annotation is partial, but the incompleteness only refers to KEGG annotations. GO functional annotation is accomplished as in case a. The lack of experimentally validated KEGG annotations in KEGG Pathway database forces the use of a KEGG annotation predicting tool, BlastKOALA [23] in our case.

c. The organism is non-model. As there is no experimentally validated annotation, GO and KEGG annotations must be predicted, which we perform by means of eggNOG-mapper [4] an annotation tool for both GO and KEGG.

In summary, IGUANER's approach offers a high degree of precision in addressing both model and non-model organisms, as a result of its ability to integrate critical steps for comprehensive RNA-Seq analysis.

5   Results

Running IGUANER on processed RNA-seq data, specifically the differential gene expression and functional analysis ones generated by its two main modules, results into the production of various data sets and plots. Particularly for the module of differential gene expression analysis, the outputs include: 1) PCA plots and heatmaps of the samples representing the raw values extracted from the count matrices; 2) the lists of differentially expressed genes (*degs*) in various pairwise comparisons of phenotypic conditions; 3) generation of heatmaps and volcano plots for the different *degs* lists obtained. In the functional analysis of the DEG lists derived in the previous step, the outputs comprise: 1) GO annotation data and KEGG annotation; 2) GO and KEGG classification plots for each produced *degs* list; 3) gene set enrichment plots for each *degs* list generated.

In detail, Fig. 4 represents the outcome of Principal Component Analysis (PCA) applied to the transcriptomic data of a non-model organism. PCA is a dimensionality reduction technique that visualizes the overall variation in data, allowing a rapid assessment of relationships and differences between samples. Each point on the plot corresponds to a sample, and the distance between points reflects differences in gene composition. This type of visualization provides an intuitive overview of the similarity or diversity among samples, enabling users to assess the biological coherence of the data and identify any distinctive patterns in the analyzed experimental groups.

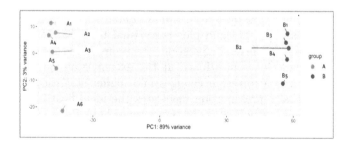

Fig. 4. PCA plot of samples: transcriptomic data from a non model organism.

Figure 5 depicts the heatmap of differentially expressed genes (degs) obtained after the analysis of transcriptomic data from a non-model organism. The heatmap illustrates the variation in gene expression across samples, highlighting the relative expression levels for each gene. Colors on the map reflect expression values, enabling a quick identification of distinctive gene expression patterns or clusters with similar behaviors. This graphical representation is valuable for understanding the dynamics of gene expression across different experimental conditions and identifying groups of genes that exhibit coordinated regulations.

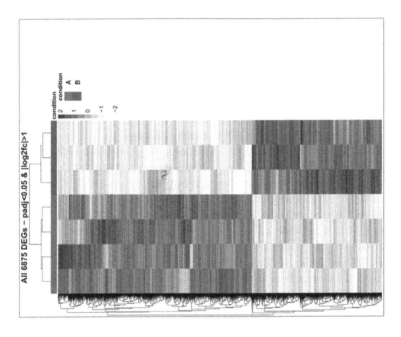

Fig. 5. Heatmap of *degs*: transcriptomic data from a non model organism.

Figure 6 shows the volcano plot of differentially expressed genes (*degs*), obtained from the analysis of data from *Homo sapiens* to study changes induced by melanoma disease. The volcano plot is a visual tool that intuitively highlights genes showing significant expression variations in terms of fold-change and adjusted p-value. Genes positioned at the extremes of the plot represent those with the greatest expression changes and higher statistical significance. This type of graphical representation facilitates the identification of key genes involved in melanoma pathology, providing a snapshot of the gene expression changes associated with the disease.

Figure 7 depicts the enrichment dot plot of differentially expressed genes (degs), obtained when analyzing transcriptomic data from a non-model organism. The dot plot visually represents the enriched gene sets derived from functional annotation analyses. Each dot corresponds to a gene set, and its position reflects the enrichment significance and the number of genes associated with that set. This graphical representation enables a quick assessment of the functional pathways and biological processes that are significantly enriched among the differentially expressed genes. It provides valuable insights into the underlying functional themes associated with the experimental conditions studied.

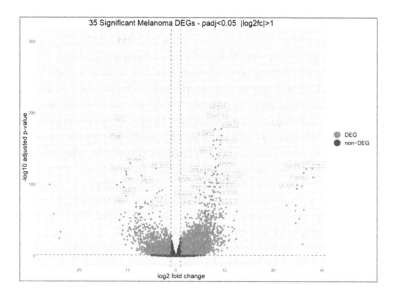

Fig. 6. Volcano plot of *degs*: data from *Homo sapiens*, melanoma pathology.

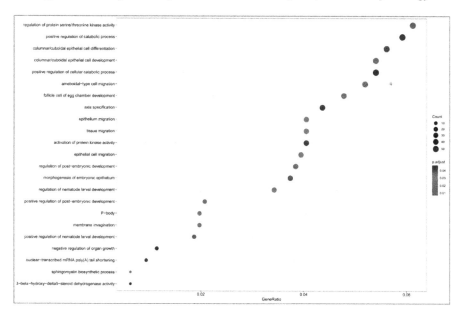

Fig. 7. Enrichment dotplot of *degs* of a non model organism.

6   Conclusions

Currently, IGUANER is in an advanced testing phase, demonstrating success in the analysis of RNA-Seq data from various model and non model species, including *Bombina pachypus, Salamandra salamandra, Mus musculus, Homo sapiens Anisakis pegreffii, Contracaecum osculatum,* and *Culex pipiens.* It is noteworthy that only about one third of the aforementioned list encompasses model organisms for which various analytical software tools are already available. IGUANER emerges as a strategically significant software for conducting both differential and functional gene expression analysis, particularly in non-model organisms that are of ecological significance for biodiversity conservation. Within this framework, the transcriptomic analysis of non-model organisms addresses a gap in the availability of software tools. Regarding the added value of IGUANER for model organisms, to our knowledge, there currently exists no software able to execute an arbitrary number of phenotypic comparisons in a single run. This level of automation significantly enhances the speed of transcriptomic analysis production, even in model organisms. All tests were conducted on a common platform, a PC running the Windows operating system.

The approach behind IGUANER, integrating two types of analyses with differentiated input based on the level of genomic annotation and facilitating a unified update of functional annotation files, positions the software as a highly versatile tool for the scientific community, including the medical field.

The runtime for gene expression analysis on Windows varies between 10 and 30 min, depending on the number of quantified genes/transcripts. For functional analysis, the time ranges from 15 to 35 min, based on the number of existing or predicted functional annotations. It is emphasized that the runtime of the latter analysis is directly proportional to the time required to generate functional annotation files. If these functional files are already available, a significant reduction in time is observed, as classification diagrams are generated directly, and only enrichment is performed.

Among potential future developments, we consider the design of a Web interface to simplify software accessibility and usability. Additionally, we plan to explore the possibility of integration with other analysis software, sometimes non-automated like WCGNA [27], and the inclusion of additional functional annotation databases such as Pfam [35], Reactome [17], and others.

Acknowledgments. Part of this research is based on the Cooperative Research Project at the Research Center for Biomedical Engineering CRP-BE-2057.

References

1. Alonso, A., et al.: aRNApipe: a balanced, efficient and distributed pipeline for processing RNA-Seq data in high-performance computing environments. Bioinformatics **33**(11), 1727–1729 (2017). https://doi.org/10.1093/bioinformatics/btx023
2. Ashburner, M., et al.: Gene ontology: tool for the unification of biology. Nat. Genet. **25**(1), 25–29 (2000). https://doi.org/10.1038/75556
3. Bolis, M., et al.: Network-guided modeling allows tumor-type independent prediction of sensitivity to all-trans-retinoic acid. Ann. Oncol. **28**(3), 611–621 (2017). https://doi.org/10.1093/annonc/mdw660

4. Cantalapiedra, C.P., et al.: eggnog-mapper v2: functional annotation, orthology assignments, and domain prediction at the metagenomic scale. Mol. Biol. Evol. **38**(12), 5825–5829 (2021). https://doi.org/10.1093/molbev/msab293

5. Castrignanò, T., et al.: ASPIC: a web resource for alternative splicing prediction and transcript isoforms characterization. Nucleic Acids Res. **34**(WEB. SERV. ISS.), W440–W443 (2006). https://doi.org/10.1093/nar/gkl324

6. Castrignanò, T., et al.: ASPicDB: a database resource for alternative splicing analysis. Bioinformatics **24**(10), 1300–1304 (2008). https://doi.org/10.1093/bioinformatics/btn113

7. Castrignanò, T., et al.: ELIXIR-IT HPC@CINECA: high performance computing resources for the bioinformatics community. BMC Bioinform. **21** (2020). https://doi.org/10.1186/s12859-020-03565-8

8. Chiara, M., et al.: CoVaCS: a consensus variant calling system. BMC Genom. **19**(1) (2018). https://doi.org/10.1186/s12864-018-4508-1

9. Chiocchio, A., et al.: Brain *de novo* transcriptome assembly of a toad species showing polymorphic anti-predatory behavior. Sci. Data **9**(1) (2022). https://doi.org/10.1038/s41597-022-01724-5

10. Cirilli, M., et al.: PeachVar-DB: a curated collection of genetic variations for the interactive analysis of peach genome data. Plant Cell Physiol. **59**(1) (2018). https://doi.org/10.1093/pcp/pcx183

11. Consortium, T.U.: UniProt: the universal protein knowledgebase in 2023. Nucleic Acids Res. **51**(D1), D523–D531 (2022). https://doi.org/10.1093/nar/gkac1052

12. Consortium The Gene Ontology: The gene ontology knowledgebase in 2023. Genetics **224**(1), iyad031 (2023). https://doi.org/10.1093/genetics/iyad031

13. Costa-Silva, J., Domingues, D., Lopes, F.M.: RNA-Seq differential expression analysis: an extended review and a software tool. PLoS ONE **12**(12), e0190152 (2017). https://doi.org/10.1371/journal.pone.0190152

14. Flati, T., et al.: A gene expression atlas for different kinds of stress in the mouse brain. Sci. Data **7**(1) (2020). https://doi.org/10.1038/s41597-020-00772-z

15. Flati, T., et al.: HPC-REDItools: a novel HPC-aware tool for improved large scale RNA-editing analysis. BMC Bioinform. **21** (2020). https://doi.org/10.1186/s12859-020-03562-x

16. Ge, S.X., Son, E.W., Yao, R.: iDEP: an integrated web application for differential expression and pathway analysis of RNA-Seq data. BMC Bioinform. **19**(1) (2018). https://doi.org/10.1186/s12859-018-2486-6

17. Gillespie, M., et al.: The reactome pathway knowledgebase 2022. Nucleic Acids Res. **50**(D1), D687–D692 (2022). https://doi.org/10.1093/nar/gkab1028

18. Huang, Q., et al.: RNA-Seq analyses generate comprehensive transcriptomic landscape and reveal complex transcript patterns in hepatocellular carcinoma. PLoS ONE **6**(10), e26168 (2011). https://doi.org/10.1371/journal.pone.0026168

19. Hunter, J.D.: Matplotlib: a 2D graphics environment. Comput. Sci. Eng. **9**(3), 90–95 (2007). https://doi.org/10.1109/MCSE.2007.55

20. Jimenez-Jacinto, V., Sanchez-Flores, A., Vega-Alvarado, L.: Integrative differential expression analysis for multiple experiments (IDEAMEX): a web server tool for integrated RNA-Seq data analysis. Front. Genet. **10**(MAR) (2019). https://doi.org/10.3389/fgene.2019.00279

21. Kalari, K.R., et al.: MAP-RSeq: mayo analysis pipeline for RNA sequencing. BMC Bioinform. **15**(1) (2014). https://doi.org/10.1186/1471-2105-15-224

22. Kanehisa, M., Goto, S.: KEGG: Kyoto encyclopedia of genes and genomes. Nucleic Acids Res. **28**(1), 27–30 (2000). https://doi.org/10.1093/nar/28.1.27

23. Kanehisa, M., Sato, Y., Morishima, K.: BlastKOALA and ghostKOALA: KEGG tools for functional characterization of genome and metagenome sequences. J. Mol. Biol. **428**(4), 726–731 (2016). https://doi.org/10.1016/j.jmb.2015.11.006

24. Kanehisa, M., et al.: KEGG: new perspectives on genomes, pathways, diseases and drugs. Nucleic Acids Res. **45**(D1), D353–D361 (2017). https://doi.org/10.1093/nar/gkw1092

25. Kanehisa, M., et al.: KEGG for taxonomy-based analysis of pathways and genomes. Nucleic Acids Res. **51**(D1), D587–D592 (2023). https://doi.org/10.1093/nar/gkac963

26. Kohen, R., et al.: UTAP: user-friendly transcriptome analysis pipeline. BMC Bioinform. **20**(1) (2019). https://doi.org/10.1186/s12859-019-2728-2

27. Langfelder, P., Horvath, S.: WGCNA: an R package for weighted correlation network analysis. BMC Bioinform. **9**(1), 559 (2008). https://doi.org/10.1186/1471-2105-9-559

28. Libro, P., et al.: First brain *de novo* transcriptome of the Tyrrhenian tree frog, Hyla sarda, for the study of dispersal behavior. Front. Ecol. Evol. **10** (2022). https://doi.org/10.3389/fevo.2022.947186

29. Libro, P., et al.: *De novo* transcriptome assembly and annotation for gene discovery in salamandra salamandra at the larval stage. Sci. Data **10**(1) (2023). https://doi.org/10.1038/s41597-023-02217-9

30. Lohse, M., et al.: RobiNA: a user-friendly, integrated software solution for RNA-Seq-based transcriptomics. Nucleic Acids Res. **40**(W1), W622–W627 (2012). https://doi.org/10.1093/nar/gks540

31. Lombardozzi, V., et al.: An interactive database for an ecological analysis of stone biopitting. Int. Biodeterior. Biodegrad. **73**, 8–15 (2012). https://doi.org/10.1016/j.ibiod.2012.04.016

32. Love, M.I., Huber, W., Anders, S.: Moderated estimation of fold change and dispersion for RNA-Seq data with DESeq2. Genome Biol. **15**(12), 550 (2014). https://doi.org/10.1186/s13059-014-0550-8

33. Marguerat, S., Bähler, J.: RNA-Seq: from technology to biology. Cell. Mol. Life Sci. **67**(4), 569–579 (2010). https://doi.org/10.1007/s00018-009-0180-6

34. McKinney, W.: Data structures for statistical computing in python. In: van der Walt, S., Millman, J. (eds.) Proceedings of the 9th Python in Science Conference, pp. 56–61 (2010). https://doi.org/10.25080/Majora-92bf1922-00a

35. Mistry, J., et al.: Pfam: the protein families database in 2021. Nucleic Acids Res. **49**(D1), D412–D419 (2021). https://doi.org/10.1093/nar/gkaa913

36. Monier, B., et al.: IRIS-EDA: an integrated RNA-Seq interpretation system for gene expression data analysis. PLoS Comput. Biol. **15**(2) (2019). https://doi.org/10.1371/journal.pcbi.1006792

37. Palomba, M., et al.: *De novo* transcriptome assembly and annotation of the third stage larvae of the zoonotic parasite Anisakis pegreffii. BMC Res. Notes **15**(1) (2022). https://doi.org/10.1186/s13104-022-06099-9

38. Palomba, M., et al.: *De novo* transcriptome assembly of an Antarctic nematode for the study of thermal adaptation in marine parasites. Sci. Data **10**(1) (2023). https://doi.org/10.1038/s41597-023-02591-4

39. Patro, R., et al.: Salmon provides fast and bias-aware quantification of transcript expression. Nat. Methods **14**(4), 417–419 (2017). https://doi.org/10.1038/nmeth.4197

40. Pertea, M., et al.: StringTie enables improved reconstruction of a transcriptome from RNA-Seq reads. Nat. Biotechnol. **33**(3), 290–295 (2015). https://doi.org/10.1038/nbt.3122

41. Picardi, E., et al.: ExpEdit: a webserver to explore human RNA editing in RNA-Seq experiments. Bioinformatics **27**(9), 1311–1312 (2011). https://doi.org/10.1093/bioinformatics/btr117

42. Reyes, A., et al.: GENAVi: a shiny web application for gene expression normalization, analysis and visualization. BMC Genom. **20**(1) (2019). https://doi.org/10.1186/s12864-019-6073-7

43. Schmidt, B., Hildebrandt, A.: Next-generation sequencing: big data meets high performance computing. Drug Discov. Today **22**(4), 712–717 (2017). https://doi.org/10.1016/j.drudis.2017.01.014

44. Su, W., Sun, J., Shimizu, K., Kadota, K.: TCC-GUI: a shiny-based application for differential expression analysis of RNA-Seq count data. BMC Res. Notes **12**(1) (2019). https://doi.org/10.1186/s13104-019-4179-2

45. Surachat, K., et al.: aTAP: automated transcriptome analysis platform for processing RNA-Seq data by de novo assembly. Heliyon **8**(8) (2022). https://doi.org/10.1016/j.heliyon.2022.e10255

46. Tripathi, R., et al.: Next-generation sequencing revolution through big data analytics. Front. Life Sci. **9**(2), 119–149 (2016). https://doi.org/10.1080/21553769.2016.1178180

47. Wang, Z., Gerstein, M., Snyder, M.: RNA-Seq: a revolutionary tool for transcriptomics. Nat. Rev. Genet. **10**(1), 57–63 (2009). https://doi.org/10.1038/nrg2484

48. Weaver, K., et al.: An Introduction to Statistical Analysis in Research: With Applications in the Biological and Life Sciences. Wiley, Hoboken (2017). https://doi.org/10.1002/9781119454205

49. Wickham, H.: ggplot2: Elegant Graphics for Data Analysis. Springer, New York (2016), https://ggplot2.tidyverse.org

50. Wickham, H., Vaughan, D., Girlich, M.: tidyr: tidy messy data (2023). https://tidyr.tidyverse.org

51. Wickham H., et al.: dplyr: a grammar of data manipulation (2023). https://dplyr.tidyverse.org

52. Wu, T., et al.: clusterprofiler 4.0: a universal enrichment tool for interpreting omics data. Innov. (Camb.) **2**(3), 100141 (2021). https://linkinghub.elsevier.com/retrieve/pii/S2666675821000667

53. Yu, G., et al.: clusterProfiler: an R package for comparing biological themes among gene clusters. OMICS: J. Integr. Biol. **16**(5), 284–287 (2012). https://doi.org/10.1089/omi.2011.0118

Data Science: Architectures and Systems

Boosting Diagnostic Accuracy of Osteoporosis in Knee Radiograph Through Fine-Tuning CNN

Saumya Kumar, Puneet Goswami$^{(\boxtimes)}$, and Shivani Batra$^{(\boxtimes)}$

Department of Computer Science and Engineering, SRM University, Delhi NCR,
Sonepat 131029, India
goswamipuneet@gmail.com, ms.shivani.batra@gmail.com

Abstract. Osteoporosis is a serious worldwide medical problem that might be challenging to identify promptly owing to the absence of indicators. At the moment, DEXA scans, CT scans, and other techniques with expensive devices and payroll expenses are the mainstays of osteoporosis evaluation. Consequently, an improved, accurate and affordable approach is essential for osteoporosis diagnosis. With the advancement of deep learning, systems for the automated identification of illnesses are regularly presented. Leveraging datasets from chest X-rays accessible for free, the present research assesses the efficacy of several convolutional neural network (CNN) models with the best extreme parameters for osteoporosis detection. Both custom CNN designs and already trained CNN structures for VGG-16 have been incorporated into the assessed system. According to the research results, the VGG-16 with fine-tuning outperformed the one without fine-tuning with an 86.36% accuracy, 86.67% precision, 86.36% recall and 86.34% f1-score, which makes it a potential and reliable model for osteoporosis prediction. The automated diagnosis approach built on CNN can help practitioners promptly, correctly, and reliably identify osteoporosis. This development results from enhanced patient outcomes and increased system productivity.

Keywords: Convolutional Neural Network · Fine-tuning · Knee · Osteoporosis · VGG-16 · X-Rays

1 Introduction

Osteoporosis has grown to be a global health issue of great significance due to the ageing population in our culture. The WHO defines osteoporosis as a chronic orthopedic illness marked by reduced density of bones, compromised cartilage microarchitecture, and elevated vulnerability and breakage propensity. Europe had thirty-two million occurrences in 2019 (5.6% of the continent's inhabitants were fifty years old or older) [1]. Lifestyle factors, particularly nutrition and exercise, impact the progression of this condition. As a result, it is reasonable to assume that a global epidemic will make things terrible and have a big impact on how quickly people's diseases develop. The rate of occurrence is expected to rise sharply in the coming years, according to predictions [1]. In previous years, individuals were sent for subsequent exams specifically for osteoporosis more seldom [2], so many remain ignorant concerning their illness. Osteoporosis is typically discovered when it has progressed, and osteoporotic fractures have already occurred. The vertebral column is particularly at risk from osteoporosis. As a result, ongoing study is required to provide the finest screening technique that could facilitate the early identification of osteoporosis [3]. Most studies in this field indicate that examining cartilage structure yields superior outcomes [4–7].

Techniques for machine learning (ML), particularly deep learning (DL) techniques, have developed quickly in the past few decades. Artificial neural networks (ANN) are the foundation of the ML paradigm known as DL [8]. They typically employ several levels of linked neural networks. ML performs image recognition quite effectively, particularly for biomedical photos. ANN has been used in recent research to diagnose intramucosal stomach cancer [9], persistent renal failure [10], major melancholy and bipolar disorders [11], and even COVID-19 [12,13]. Deep learning-based innovative techniques for detecting osteoporosis have also been published [14,15].

Researchers' interest has been drawn to image processing due to recent substantial developments, which have created accurate yet affordable architectures. Deep convolutional neural network (DCNN) architectures are currently gaining prominence as potent tools, and various techniques and architectures have been developed [16–18]. Convolutional neural network (CNN) models make it easier to analyze vast volumes of data and use cutting-edge techniques, providing answers to challenging clinical issues. CNNs' impressive performance in disease diagnosis lays a strong platform for their use in detecting dangerous osteoporosis. With the help of this innovation, individuals have a rare chance to get a quick, secure, and affordable diagnostic.

Much curiosity has been generated by the widespread adoption of DCNNs and associated encouraging outcomes in the identification of osteoporosis. However, several issues must be resolved for individuals to attain all of their abilities. The investigators of the research [19] outlined a few of the difficulties in using DCNNs. Some of these obstacles are the lack of vast, heterogeneous records, the requirement for particular expertise in creating and improving system designs, and the comprehensibility of a system's conclusion. DCNN effectiveness is also impacted by the standard of the source pictures and the presence of distracting variables. Using CNNs for osteoporosis presents additional difficulties, as described in the study [20], particularly the problem of unbalanced data.

The unbalanced datasets caused by the scarcity of favourable instances relative to the richness of unfavourable instances bring bias into the learning procedure and reduce the CNNs' precision. The researchers explore many approaches to the unbalanced data challenge, including over-sampling, under-sampling, and cost-sensitive training. The potential of overfitting while employing DCNNs is a further problem raised by the researchers in a particular study [21] that relates to the sparse osteoporosis samples. The researchers suggest using data augmentation approaches to address this problem. Choosing the best strategy among the vast array of alternatives offered in the ML and DL fields is hard and takes a while. Additionally, there remains room for enhancement even if many conventional techniques used in these disciplines have been the subject of substantial investigation. However, improving these techniques might be very difficult technically [22].

The proposed investigation intends to evaluate CNN's performance in identifying osteoporosis from chest X-rays. The study aims to compare the efficacy of VGG-16 with fine-tuning and pre-trained VGG-16 models using TL. These methods divide chest X-ray (CXR) pictures into the osteoporosis and normal categories. Simulations are assessed using a variety of effectiveness indicators, including accuracy, F1 score, precision, recall, and area under the curve (AUC). To assess their respective efficacy, the outcomes from each strategy are juxtaposed. Significant achievements are made through the proposed work:

- Creation of a reliable DL model for X-ray-based osteoporosis diagnosis that provide more accurate results.
- For identifying the best resultant CNN model for diagnosing osteoporosis, the different pre-trained model is compared to CNN simulations created from the beginning.
- System hyper-parameter tuning to offer clever methods for precise osteoporosis diagnosis.

2 Literature Survey

CNNs are widely employed for locating problems as DL technology advances. Still, most of this research refers to detecting centroid points as spinal identification. Chen et al. applied sophisticated CNN characteristics to depict bones using a 3D CT consumption, which prevented the identification of misaligned centroids using a random forest model [23]. By employing a message-passing arrangement to retrain the CNN's centroid likelihood connect and sparse normalization to enhance the positioning outcomes, Dong et al. determined the likelihood of each vertebral central point at every pixel [24]. Instead of using a likelihood distribution of the centroid point, it could be simpler when recognizing the markings and box borders of the bone segments. To improve the categorization of vertebral divisions and the consciousness of inaccurate identification, Zhao et al. presented a category-consistent self-calibration system that can be used to reliably forecast the boundaries of every bone [25]. All these techniques help us locate vertebral bones from the perspective of the cortex. Still, we need a condensed picture of the intervertebral from the lateral perspective.

Yoo et al. [26] developed a support vector machine (SVM) approach to identifying osteoporosis in postmenopausal women employing age, stature, body mass index, high blood pressure, high cholesterol levels, and other parameters in developing the osteoporosis forecast. They discovered that the SVM simulation is superior to conventional osteoporosis self-evaluation instruments [26].

A J48 decision frequency system was developed by Pedrassani de Lira et al. to diagnose osteoporosis using a variety of markers, including age, a history of broken bones, the overall amount of prior broken bones, and prior vertebral fractures [27] To diagnose osteoporosis, Tafraouti et al. collected characteristics from X-ray pictures and used an SVM framework [28], which can separate those with the condition from healthy individuals. In this study, Kilic and Hosgormez used an arbitrary subspace approach and a random forest ensemble framework to identify osteoporosis. Osteoporosis was identified by Jang et al. using a DL technique [29]. The findings from the study demonstrate the potential for spontaneous automated osteoporosis detection in a medical setting [30] using X-ray based on DL algorithms.

According to the mineral content of bone, the L1-L4 spinal column was marked in the most recent study by Xue et al. and separated into three distinct groups: osteoporosis, osteopenia, and normal. The research was highly accurate [31]. A unique technique for detecting osteoporosis has been established by Dzierzak and Omiotek using DCNN and CT scans of the backbone. They used an extensive data set to prepare the system to overcome the problem of tiny sample sizes, which led to the effective categorization of osteoporosis and normal instances. This strategy demonstrated encouraging outcomes for accurately identifying osteoporosis by CT scans [32]. In these techniques, the picture comprising only the relevant area is the information resource for both the conventional ML procedure and the currently prevalent DL technique. Pre-processing in this manner is difficult, costly, and ineffective.

3   Materials and Methods

Leveraging X-rays, the purpose is to develop a binary classification framework backed by DL to identify osteoporosis. The purpose is to create a powerful DL framework with precise projections and a lightweight design.

3.1   Investigation Design and Dataset

The current investigation aims to diagnose osteoporosis in X-rays of the knee. We used a segmented collection to recreate the osteoporosis diagnosis spectrum in the DXA technique. For data standardization and enhancement, the Keras DL modules have been used. The VGG-16 TL deep neural network has been employed to diagnose osteoporosis through knee scans. The VGG-16 framework has been chosen because it was extensively used and acknowledged as the best choice for commercial and clinical image classification projects. However, it has yet to be straightforward to apply to the diagnosis of osteoporosis from individual knee X-rays. To enable the use of a TL strategy for massive picture identification, VGG-16 has also been educated on massive datasets. Parameter fine-tuning is justified since studies demonstrate it improves a DL algorithm's efficiency over randomization of parameters [33]. The knee X-ray collection was chosen since there has been a dearth of DL studies regarding knee X-ray categorization of

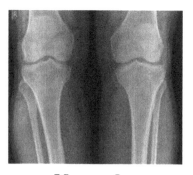 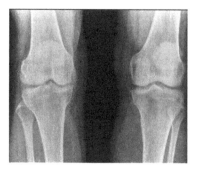

Normal   **Osteoporosis**

Fig. 1. Sample Knee Scans

osteoporosis. A sample knee scan is presented in Fig. 1. Leveraging innovative evaluation techniques, we evaluated the correctness of the TL model's osteoporosis predictive diagnosis alongside and without parameters fine-tuning. The observations were gathered through data that [34] published in Mendeley. Data enhancement in Python was used to enhance the dataset pictures quantitatively. The collection included 372 pictures, of which 186 were classified as normal and the remaining as osteoporosis.

3.2   Data Pre-processing

Grayscale Conversion. Red Green Blue (RGB)-formatted photos constitute the collection of X-rays. For every one of the pixels in an RGB picture, a 3D byte array contains colour information. Modelling and learning become more difficult while using the RGB colour scheme. Black and white and monochrome photos are favoured because they reduce computing overhead. Since the technique of our investigation relies on information from knee X-rays, colour in a X-ray is not significant to assessment. The X-rays were changed from RGB to grayscale for the reason above, considering that grayscale pictures are simpler for building a model.

Data Normalization. Data normalization transforms visual data pixels into a specified spectrum: $(0, 1)$ or $(-1, 1)$. Usually, pictures have pixel values between 0 and 255. Massive numbers can impede or hinder the development procedure for deep neural networks. Consequently, image standardization is advised as a best practice: the values of pixels vary from 0 to 1.

Data Augmentation. It is crucial to be certain that DL models receive adequate training information while interacting with it. Data augmentation is applying multiple adjustments to the initial pictures to produce multiple changed versions of a single picture. However, the augmentation techniques employed cause certain replicas to vary from one another. For this investigation, augmentation was carried out employing the Python-based Keras ImageDataGenerator.

3.3 Transfer Learning with Fine Tuning

VGG16 and the parameter fine-tuning version of VGG16 comprised the two CNN cohorts employed in the present investigation. The second deployment, which differs from the first, employed parameter fine-tuning, whereas the first did not. The classification layer of the VGG-16 network was altered, the quantity of trainable levels was changed, and fresh levels were added to increase the system's efficacy. With this strategy, we hoped to help the system pick up more precise elements important for our categorization task. The altered VGG-16 design (presented in Fig. 2) exemplifies the alteration of the categorization layers, the addition of two more levels, and the maintenance of the previous layers by maintaining their frozen state.

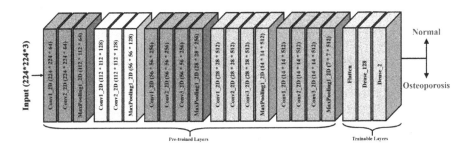

Fig. 2. Fine-tuned VGG-16 employed in current research

4 Results

4.1 Experimental Setup

The preliminary collection of the sampled photos was divided into five folds arbitrarily. As a result, overfitting was avoided when a 5-fold cross-validation was done on the system's learning. During every fold, data collection had been separated into distinct training and validation sets employing an eighty to twenty division. It was determined to evaluate the learning state during training using a validation set entirely distinct from the other training sets. Following the conclusion of the first model learning stage, the additional isolated fold was used as a validation set, and the prior validation set was reused as a component of the training set to assess the system training. For both models in this investigation, this cross-validation procedure was conducted. These models were trained and tested on the graphics processing unit of Google Collabs. The DL structures have been built using the Keras toolkit and TensorFlow. Precision, recall and F1-score indicators have been chosen to properly evaluate the system's achievement accuracy.

4.2   Prediction Performance

The CNN simulations used in this study have been evaluated on a collection of knee X-ray from osteoporosis patients. For both TL simulations, the data collection has been split into test and training segments in an 80:20 ratio. There were 50 training epochs for every simulation. As the data collection objective contains two categories, binary_crossentropy was implemented as the loss measure for every simulation. The selected optimizer, RMSprop, has a learning rate of 0.001. The Keras assess operation was used on the constructed model using the test sample as an input to assess the simulation's correctness. A visual representation of the performance indicators variance between the two VGG-16 TL framework executions is shown in Fig. 3.

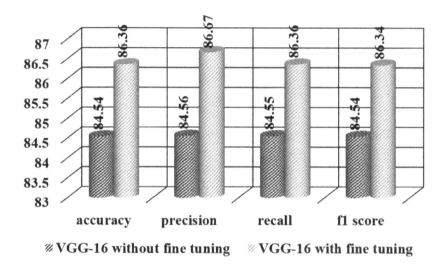

Fig. 3. Performance of models employed in current research

The VGG-16 with fine-tuning outperformed the one without fine-tuning with an 86.36% accuracy, 86.67% precision, 86.36% recall and 86.34% f1-score. The VGG-16 without fine-tune tuning achieved 84.54% accuracy, 84.56% precision, 84.55% recall and 84.54% f1-score. The accuracy and loss graph of the VGG-16 model without fine-tuning is presented in Fig. 4 and Fig. 5, respectively. Further, the accuracy and loss graph of the VGG-16 model with fine-tuning is illustrated in Fig. 6 and Fig. 7, respectively.

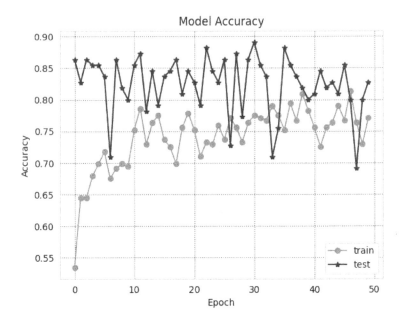

Fig. 4. Accuracy graph of VGG-16 model without fine-tuning

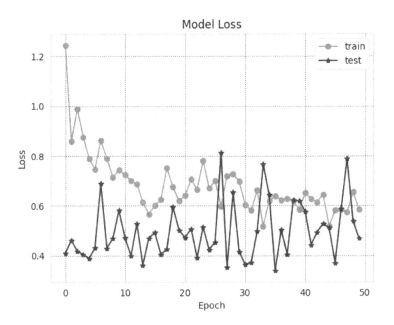

Fig. 5. Loss graph of VGG-16 model without fine-tuning

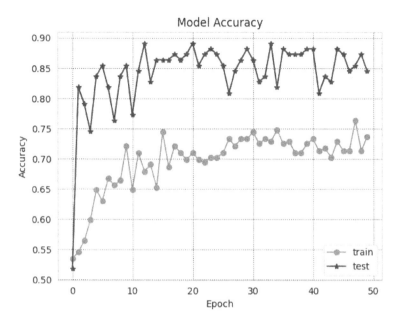

Fig. 6. Accuracy graph of VGG-16 model with fine-tuning

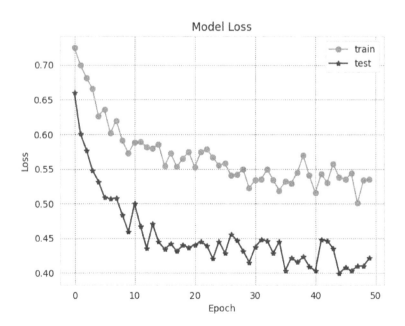

Fig. 7. Loss graph of VGG-16 model with fine-tuning

4.3 Confusion Matrix

The confusion matrix (CM) is a technique for quantifying the effectiveness of a classification system. It identifies the general errors the classifier is committing and details the individual errors. The CM helps the restriction by relying solely on classification precision. The CM for the VGG-16 model without and with parameter fine-tuning is depicted in Fig. 8 and Fig. 9, respectively. The conclusion drawn from the results is that pre-processing and parameter fine-tuning are some strategies that may be used to prevent overfitting in TL caused by a limited number of samples. Additionally, results demonstrate that fine-tuning in TL may be applied to improve a DL system's performance considerably. These osteoporosis indicators are crucial from the perspective of medicine.

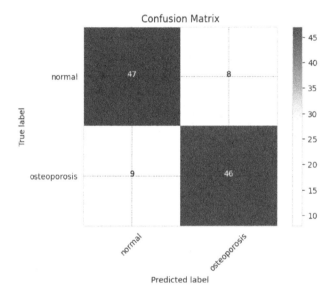

Fig. 8. Confusion Matrix of VGG-16 model without fine-tuning

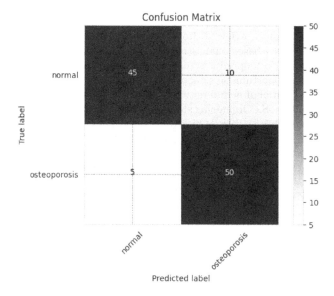

Fig. 9. Confusion Matrix of VGG-16 model with fine-tuning

5   Conclusion

It is exceedingly challenging to categorize osteoporosis using X-rays since the images produced from normal and osteoporotic patients are comparable. Numerous conventional characteristics are currently being used to distinguish osteoporotic patients from normal individuals. CNNs are now often used for feature extraction and classification. This work illustrates the effectiveness of CNN tuning and TL for diagnosing osteoporosis in knee X-rays under a limited training sample. The authors applied the VGG-16 TL method to systems previously trained on another dataset to classify osteoporosis. The tests showed that the fine-tuning approach helped TL reach an accuracy of 86.36%, which is better than the 84.54% attained by TL without fine-tuning. The findings demonstrate that component fine-tuning in TL may be implemented to improve a DL model's performance considerably. Future research will see us developing an ensemble strategy for identifying osteoporosis using VGG-16 on a knee X-ray by incorporating individual qualitative variables.

References

1. International Osteoporosis Foundation. Key Statistics For Europe. https://www. osteoporosis.foundation. Accessed 4 June 2023
2. Camacho, P.M., Petak, S.M., Binkley, N.: American college of endocrinology clinical practice guidelines for the diagnosis and treatment of postmenopausal osteoporosis-2016. Endocr. Pract. **22**(Suppl. 4), 1–42 (2016)

3. Smets, J., Shevroja, E., Hügle, T., Leslie, W.D., Hans, D.: Machine learning solutions for osteoporosis-a review. J. Bone Miner. Res. **36**(5), 833–851 (2021)
4. Tang, C., et al.: CNN-based qualitative detection of bone mineral density via diagnostic CT slices for osteoporosis screening. Journal **32**, 971–979 (2021)
5. Fang, Y., et al.: Opportunistic osteoporosis screening in multi-detector CT images using deep convolutional neural networks. Eur. Radiol. **31**, 1831–1842 (2021)
6. Batra, S., Sachdeva, S.: Organizing standardized electronic healthcare records data for mining. Journal **5**(3), 226–242 (2016)
7. Batra, S., Sachdeva, S.: Pre-processing highly sparse and frequently evolving standardized electronic health records for mining. In: Handbook of Research on Disease Prediction Through Data Analytics and Machine Learning, pp. 8–21. IGI Global (2021)
8. Janiesch, C., Zschech, P., Heinrich, K.: Machine learning and deep learning. Electron. Mark. **31**(3), 685–695 (2021)
9. Tang, D., et al.: A novel model based on deep convolutional neural network improves diagnostic accuracy of intramucosal gastric cancer (with video). Front. Oncol. **11**, 622827 (2021)
10. Singh, V., Asari, V.K., Rajasekaran, R.: A deep neural network for early detection and prediction of chronic kidney disease. Diagnostics **12**(1), 116 (2022)
11. Lei, Y., Belkacem, A.N., Wang, X., Sha, S., Wang, C., Chen, C.: A convolutional neural network-based diagnostic method using resting-state electroencephalograph signals for major depressive and bipolar disorders. Biomed. Signal Process. Control **72**, 103370 (2022)
12. Sachdeva, S.: Standard based personalized healthcare delivery for kidney illness using deep learning. Physiol. Measur. (2023)
13. Pawar, V., Sachdeva, S.: CovidBChain: framework for access-control, authentication, and integrity of Covid-19 data. Concurr. Comput. Pract. Experience **34**(28), e7397 (2022)
14. Tassoker, M., Öziç, M.Ü., Yuce, F.: Comparison of five convolutional neural networks for predicting osteoporosis based on mandibular cortical index on panoramic radiographs. Dentomaxillofacial Radiol. **51**(6), 20220108 (2022)
15. Batra, S., et al.: An intelligent sensor based decision support system for diagnosing pulmonary ailment through standardized chest X-ray scans. Sensors **22**(19), 7474 (2022)
16. Khan, A., Sohail, A., Zahoora, U., Qureshi, A.S.: A survey of the recent architectures of deep convolutional neural networks. Artif. Intell. Rev. **53**, 5455–5516 (2020)
17. Batra, S., Khurana, R., Khan, M.Z., Boulila, W., Koubaa, A., Srivastava, P.: A pragmatic ensemble strategy for missing values imputation in health records. Entropy **24**(4), 533 (2022)
18. Alzubaidi, L., et al.: Review of deep learning: concepts, CNN architectures, challenges, applications, future directions. J. Big Data **8**, 1–74 (2021)
19. Alafif, T., Tehame, A.M., Bajaba, S., Barnawi, A., Zia, S.: Machine and deep learning towards COVID-19 diagnosis and treatment: survey, challenges, and future directions. Int. J. Environ. Res. Public Health **18**(3), 1117 (2021)
20. Nayak, S.R., Nayak, D.R., Sinha, U., Arora, V., Pachori, R.B.: Application of deep learning techniques for detection of COVID-19 cases using chest X-ray images: a comprehensive study. Biomed. Signal Process. Control **64**, 102365 (2021)
21. Gatto, A., Accarino, G., Aloisi, V., Immorlano, F., Donato, F., Aloisio, G.: Limits of compartmental models and new opportunities for machine learning: a case

study to forecast the second wave of COVID-19 hospitalizations in Lombardy, Italy. Informatics **8**(3), 57 (2021)

22. Paul, S.G., et al.: Combating Covid-19 using machine learning and deep learning: applications, challenges, and future perspectives. Array **17**, 100271 (2023)

23. Chen, H., et al.: Automatic localization and identification of vertebrae in spine CT via a joint learning model with deep neural networks. In: Navab, N., Hornegger, J., Wells, W.M., Frangi, A.F. (eds.) MICCAI 2015. LNCS, vol. 9349, pp. 515–522. Springer, Cham (2015). https://doi.org/10.1007/978-3-319-24553-9_63

24. Yang, D., et al.: Automatic vertebra labeling in large-scale 3D CT using deep image-to-image network with message passing and sparsity regularization. In: Niethammer, M., et al. (eds.) IPMI 2017. LNCS, vol. 10265, pp. 633–644. Springer, Cham (2017). https://doi.org/10.1007/978-3-319-59050-9_50

25. Zhao, S., Wu, X., Chen, B., Li, S.: Automatic vertebrae recognition from arbitrary spine MRI images by a category-Consistent self-calibration detection framework. Med. Image Anal. **67**, 101826 (2021)

26. Yoo, T.K., Kim, S.K., Oh, E., Kim, D.W.: Risk prediction of femoral neck osteoporosis using machine learning and conventional methods. In: Rojas, I., Joya, G., Cabestany, J. (eds.) IWANN 2013. LNCS, vol. 7903, pp. 181–188. Springer, Heidelberg (2013). https://doi.org/10.1007/978-3-642-38682-4_21

27. de Lira, C.P., et al.: Use of data mining to predict the risk factors associated with osteoporosis and osteopenia in women. CIN: Comput. Inform. Nurs. **34**(8), 369–375 (2016)

28. Tafraouti, A., El Hassouni, M., Toumi, H., Lespessailles, E., Jennane, R.: Osteoporosis diagnosis using fractal analysis and support vector machine. In: 2014 Tenth International Conference on Signal-Image Technology and Internet-Based Systems, Marrakech, Morocco, pp. 73–77. IEEE (2014)

29. Kilic, N., Hosgormez, E.: Automatic estimation of osteoporotic fracture cases by using ensemble learning approaches. J. Med. Syst. **40**, 1–10 (2016)

30. Jang, M., Kim, M., Bae, S.J., Lee, S.H., Koh, J.M., Kim, N.: Opportunistic osteoporosis screening using chest radiographs with deep learning: development and external validation with a cohort dataset. J. Bone Miner. Res. **37**(2), 369–377 (2022)

31. Xue, L., et al.: A dual-selective channel attention network for osteoporosis prediction in computed tomography images of lumbar spine. Acadlore Trans. AI Mach. Learn. **1**(1), 30–39 (2022)

32. Dzierżak, R., Omiotek, Z.: Application of deep convolutional neural networks in the diagnosis of osteoporosis. Sensors **22**(21), 8189 (2022)

33. Yosinski, J., Clune, J., Bengio, Y., Lipson, H.: How transferable are features in deep neural networks? In: Advances in Neural Information Processing Systems, vol. 27 (2014)

34. Osteoporosis Knee X-ray Dataset. https://www.kaggle.com/datasets/stevepython/osteoporosis-knee-xray-dataset. Accessed 4 June 2023

VLSI Implementation of Reconfigurable Canny Edge Detection Algorithm

K. K. Senthilkumar[1] , E. Avantika[1], B. Gayathri[1],
and Vaithiyanathan Dhandapani[2(✉)]

[1] Prince Shri Venkateshwara Padmavathy Engineering College, Chennai, Tamilnadu, India
[2] National Institute of Technology Delhi, New Delhi, India
`dvaithiyanathan@nitdelhi.ac.in`

Abstract. Real-time video and image processing are used in various industrial, medical, consumer electronics and embedded device applications. These applications typically demonstrate an increasing demand for computing power and system complexity. Hence, edge detection is the most common and widely used technique in image or video processing applications. Several traditional canny edge detection methods use fixed thresholding techniques to compare the pixel values. This sacrifices the edge detection performance and increases the computational complexity. Hence, the Canny Edge detection algorithm is preferred to enhance the image quality with reduced complexity. They adjust the quality of the image by manipulating the Sigma and Threshold parameters and detect the edges accurately by eliminating the noise. The reconfigurable canny edge detection algorithm presents a procedure for detecting edges without multipliers. The new algorithm uses a low-complex, non-uniform histogram gradient to compute thresholds and variable sigma values that replace the add and shift operator instead of multipliers to reduce the area and sigma. The simulation is done in the Model-Sim platform using VHDL code which results in the output of bit sequences. By comparing the results of the reconfigurable canny edge detection and traditional algorithm, the new algorithm's performance can be observed with improvements of around 21% and 80% for consumed power and delay parameters respectively.

Keywords: Image Processing · Edge Detection · Canny Edge Detection · VLSI

1 Introduction

1.1 Image Processing

Edge detection is one of the significant steps in image processing algorithms which is used in many applications like image morphing, pattern recognition, image segmentation and image extraction etc. Edge detection is defined as a set of mathematical methods from those methods detecting the edges of the image, particularly at edges where the pixel value changes more sharply and has more discontinuities. Thus, in the ideal case by applying the edge detector to an image gives the different edges that are connected to form the outline of the object. Edges are fundamentally portrayed in four sorts in

S. Sachdeva and Y. Watanobe (Eds.): BDA 2023, LNCS 14516, pp. 110–119, 2024.
https://doi.org/10.1007/978-3-031-58502-9_7

any picture. They are step edge, incline edge, rooftop edge and line edge. In our edge detection process, first, the object is separated from the background then all the edges are detected to get the outline of the object. This is the explanation, the edge discovery become significant in PC vision and picture handling. Image processing applications like image quality enhancement, and video surveillance mainly require information about changes in the pixel value of an image. As in the picture division and upgrade applications, the significant step is picture understanding. The edge-identified picture shows just a blueprint of the item shape, which eliminates the foundation and keeps just the significant data. The edge map of an image has the outline of the objects present in that image. Thus, image processing algorithms have more focus due to their wide applications in many fields one such application is edge detection. Also, the VLSI implementation gives better results while considering the delay, latency and look-up table and also the platform supports proposing edge detection with minimal complication.

Canny edge detection is a method used to retrieve useful local information from the image which is converted into a grayscale image by separating the image object and the. He has found that the requirements for the application of edge detection on diverse vision systems are similar. Among the edge recognition strategies that grew up to this point, the shrewd edge identification calculation is one of the most rigorously characterized techniques that give great and dependable discovery.

The Canny edge identifier is dominatingly utilized in some true applications because of its capacity to separate huge edges with great discovery and great confinement execution. Tragically, the shrewd edge location calculation contains broad pre-handling and post-handling steps and is more computationally perplexing than other edge discovery calculations like Roberts, Prewitt and Sobel calculations. Furthermore, it performs hysteresis thresholding which requires computing high and low thresholds based on the entire image statistics which prevents the processing of individual blocks independently. This puts weighty necessities on memory and results in huge idleness preventing continuous execution of the watchful edge identification calculation. The external disturbance like noise occurrence in image preprocessing steps is also considered to be a main cause for decreased accuracy and high complexity.

2 Related Works

In [1], the Image division is the division of a picture into locales or classifications that compare to various articles or portions of items. The traditional Otsu method segments and detects the pixel edges without involving threshold values. But while segmenting an image without using threshold parameters, there is a certain delay in computational time in the processor used. To reduce the high computational complexity of the 2D Otsu method, a fast algorithm is used. In [2], a new method for the detection of cracks with a grey colour-based histogram and Otsu's Thresholding method covers the whole pavement image instead of implementing it in a two-dimensional region. This method divides the input image into four independent equally sized sub-images. Finally, all sub-images are assembled into the resulting image and tested on the dataset which contains different pavement images that consist of different cracks. The result indicates that the method can be used for rough estimation of cracks on asphalt pavement surface, hence it does not require the existence of a great amount of data. The poorly illuminated images cannot be processed using the traditional Otsu method since it results in less accuracy. The present work proposes a novel scheme for performing binarization in poorly illuminated images, often found in scanned collections of printed and handwritten texts. The methodology reconfigurable canny edge detection here is an adaptive region-wise histogram correction technique capable of enhancing the contrast of images automatically for further processing. The result shows the clean binarized version of a very poorly illuminated text image as output [3–7]. In [8], binarization is an important preprocessing technique for documented images. It is the process of segmenting the image into foreground and background pixels. This paper presents an improved new method for blurring and uneven light QR code image binarization. The method is based on the local threshold of the Bernsen method. After handling the picture with grayscale and Gaussian smoothing channel, it presents the worldwide edge in light of the difference between classes of the Otsu technique and the neighbourhood's window dim value mean square error. The results show that this method can get more complete images and less noise, and effectively overcomes the effects of blurring and uneven light. These papers [4, 7], insist on Image segmentation which is the process of partitioning a digital image into multiple image segments, also known as image regions or image objects. The aim is to study the anatomical structure, Identify the region of interest i.e., locate the tumor and other abnormalities, Measure the tissue volume to measure the growth of the tumor, and help in treatment planning before the radiation therapy in radiation dose calculation. The presented CS-L algorithm is tested on a set of lip images and results are validated under several aspects this reconfigurable canny edge detection method shows more efficient performance in segmenting the lip images than other algorithms. In [10], they insist on the fractal analysis by the box-counting method which is used to estimate the streamer discharge characteristics. The image processing and its hardware implementation are explained along with features in [11–13]. This is the process of assessing the factual characteristics. This paper focuses on enhancing the fractal analysis by developing a dynamic grayscale threshold algorithm which is the binarization process that converts the image from grayscale value to binary. The reconfigurable canny edge detection paper results show that the streamers in ester liquids have large streamer areas, more branched structures and stronger branching tendencies than in hydrocarbon liquids with reduced background noise.

3   Reconstructed Canny Edge Detection Algorithm

In this paper, a reconstructed canny edge algorithm implemented using a multi-threshold concept and eliminating the multipliers for threshold calculation and image segmentation steps is analyzed. This method uses a gradient-based edge detection procedure where the image is segmented into pixels and the local information available in each pixel is used to calculate the gradient value for comparing them with the nearest threshold values for the respected pixel to qualify as a valid edge. This algorithm includes a novel method for the hysteresis thresholds computation based on a non-uniform quantized 8-bit gradient magnitude histogram which removes the inherent dependency between the various blocks so that the image can be divided into blocks and each block can be processed in parallel.

The proposed system considerably reduces the area, increases delay and decreases the processing speed. To obtain better efficiency and accuracy, changes are made in the pre-processing steps of the image which reduces the noise penetration in the input image. In threshold calculation and kernel observations, the ASA (add shift add) operator is used instead of the multiplier to reduce the required gates count and the memory requirements of the system. Field Programmable Gate Arrays (FPGAs) have been extensively used in accelerating applications in many digital domains, examples include image and signal processing [9]. The VLSI synthesis environment dedicated to the design of image pro-cessing architectures is a simulation environment that includes the front-end data-flow emulator for both the validation of the algorithms and the RTL-synthesis system. The latest advancements in program logic related to custom software, in-built parallelism and dedicated multiply-accumulate units have resulted in better simulation results while proceeding with technology in the VLSI platform. Hence the proposed algorithm is implemented with less complexity than that of other implementations.

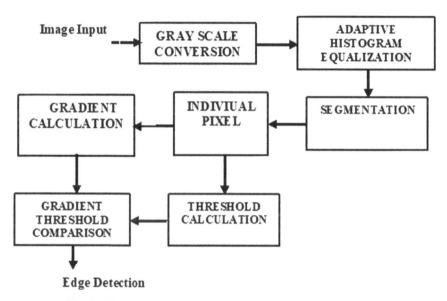

Fig. 1. Block Diagram of the Reconstructed Canny Edge Detection

Figure 1 is the proposed canny detection algorithm which uses adaptive or multi-threshold concepts to find the edges in the input image. The input image is primarily subjected to greyscale conversion where the noise or external disturbance contained in the image is filtered and colour converted into the grey image. Then it undergoes adaptive histogram equalization where the blurred gray scale image is converted into high contrast image which enhances the detection of edges. The high-contrast image is segmented into individual pixels using the image segmentation technique. Each pixel is processed to calculate the gradient magnitude using the local information available to the respective pixel. The threshold value is calculated using the multi-threshold concept where the threshold value is selected by the input image from a threshold range calculated from the kernel matrix. Here, the threshold value will be changed for different input images by finding the average gradient value of the particular image. Then the threshold and gradient are compared. If the gradient magnitude is greater than the threshold, the particular pixel containing that gradient value will be considered a strong edge and is displayed in the bit file. If the gradient value is equal to or slightly lesser than the threshold, that pixel is considered a blurred edge and is displayed in the simulation. If the gradient is way too small than the threshold, then that particular pixel gets rejected as an edge. The selected threshold will always be a close value to the average pixel value to get more detected edges to improve the accuracy. The final simulated bit file consists of pixel values that are qualified as the blurred or strong edge. By comparing simulations of existing and proposed algorithms, the accuracy can be determined by observing the detected pixels in both simulations. The threshold values are obtained by ASA operations using a 3×3 kernel matrix and according to each gradient value of a pixel, the nearest best threshold value gets compared and the edge is detected when the gradient is higher than the threshold. The process is done in modelsim software in individual modules and a simulated bit file is obtained.

4 Results and Discussion

The results obtained for the proposed Reconfigurable Canny Edge Algorithm using VHDL code implemented and executed in ModelSim software are discussed in this section concerning the performance comparison of design parameters observed using the Xilinx platform. Additionally, the algorithm is implemented using Matlab with the reconstructed code appropriate to modelsim execution for the visual understanding of the accuracy of detected edges.

4.1 Experimental Setup

In this section, we estimate the performances of the proposed method in Modelsim Altera 6.3g, Xilinx ISE 8.1i and Matlab 2018a are the three software tools used for the synthesis and the verification. The wave simulations and the obtained results of the fed pixel image in each step are discussed.

4.2 Simulation of Traditional Canny Algorithm

The wave simulation of the traditional canny edge detection algorithm is displayed and observed. Figure 2 displays the bit file obtained after processing the VHDL code developed for the traditional canny edge detection algorithm.

The observations of the simulation results display that only a few pixels are detected as the stronger edge and that are etched in the simulation output. These pixels are selected by comparing the gradient value calculated using a multiplier with the threshold and sigma values (that range above 5). So only when the gradient value is greater or equal to 5, it is considered a visual edge which is not obtained accurately in the traditional algorithm.

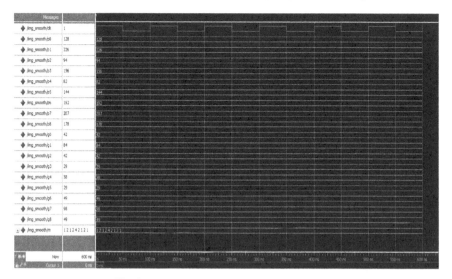

Fig. 2. Simulation Traditional Canny Algorithm

4.3 Simulation of Reconfigurable Canny Edge Detection Algorithm

The wave simulation of the modified and reconstructed canny edge detection algorithm is displayed and observed.

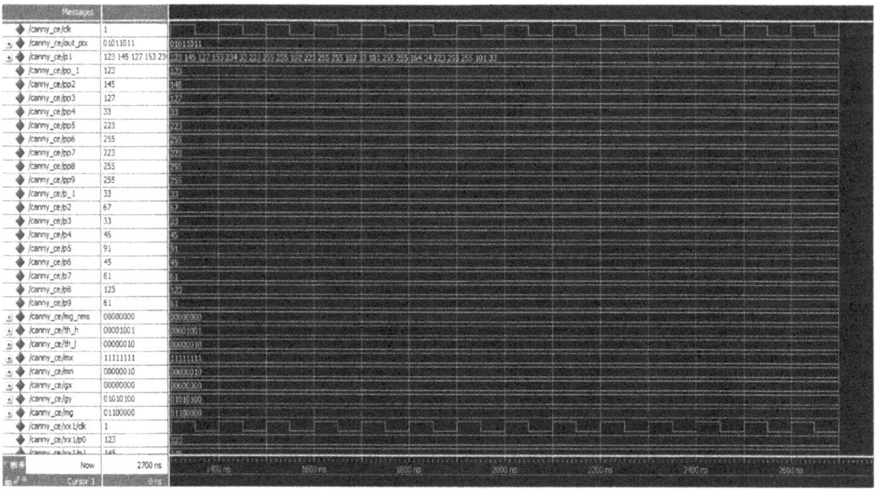

Fig. 3. Simulation of the Reconstructed Canny Algorithm

Figure 3 shows the result of the reconfigurable canny edge detection algorithm which includes the noise-robust effects in the edge-detected bit file. By analyzing this with the output of the traditional canny edge detection system, we can observe that the pixel detected as an edge is visually higher than the traditional canny edge detection algorithm. Also, the system is constructed using adders and shifters instead of the multiplier design. So the memory or area utilized by the new algorithm reflects the level of accuracy obtained in the reconfigurable canny edge detection technique.

4.4 Edge Detected Results

The result of the Reconfigurable Canny Detection Algorithm that is obtained using the MATLAB software by providing an input image for execution is displayed.

Fig. 4. Input Image

Figure 4 displays the original input image which is to be processed by the edge detection algorithms.

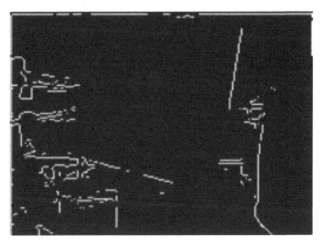

Fig. 5. Edge Detected Output of the Traditional Canny Edge Detection Algorithm

Figure 5 displays the edge-detected output obtained by processing the traditional canny edge detection algorithm.

Fig. 6. Edge Detected Output of the Reconfigurable Canny Edge Detection Algorithm

Figure 6 displays the edge-detected output obtained by processing the reconfigurable canny edge detection algorithm.

Additionally, the algorithm is implemented using Matlab with the reconstructed code appropriate to modelsim execution for the visual understanding of the accuracy of detected edges. The input image is fed to the Matlab software and after execution, the output of both traditional and reconstructed algorithm results is obtained. The edge-detected images are then displayed as the Matlab output. By analyzing both images, we can observe the accuracy of the detected edges where the reconfigurable canny edge detection algorithm detects more pixel edges than the traditional canny edge detection one. This enhances the efficiency of the reconfigurable canny edge detection project.

4.5 Comparison of the Design Characteristics

Table 1 specifies the comparison of the Xilinx design parameters of both the traditional canny edge detection and the reconfigurable canny edge detection algorithm. These parameters are analyzed and obtained by processing the VHDL code under the design characteristics in the Xilinx ISE version 8.1.

When observing the parameters like the area, no of occupied and utilized slices, the delay, required gates and consumed power, it is clear that the reconfigurable canny edge detection algorithm is more efficient and accountable than the traditional canny edge detection system. By using the table, the improvements obtained for each of the design parameters can be calculated and analyzed individually. In terms of consumed power, the proposed canny algorithm shows a 7% improvement over the existing canny edge detection procedure.

Table 1. Comparison of design parameters

Parameters	Traditional canny edge detection system	Reconfigurable canny edge detection system
Total Gates Required (area)	6,743	5,224
Delay (ns)	22.644	20.986
Power Consumption (mW)	173	147
4-input Lookup Table	3642	3534
No. of Occupied Slices	2349	2272

5 Conclusion

In this paper, the software implementation of the Reconfigurable Canny Edge Detection algorithm is proposed. It is the modified, reconstructed and noise-robust canny edge detection technique derived from the existing algorithm. Also, it is a multiplier-less algorithm and is suitable for low-cost devices. This paper focuses on the canny edge detection algorithm which is configured, reconstructed and split into different stages and the system can process the data stream directly. The detail of each module is discussed briefly. The input image is subjected to get processed and implemented using VHDL ModelSim and synthesized using the target device as spartan 6 using Xilinx ISE to analyze the design characteristics. This project displays both the synthesized or simulated output and the edge-detected image output using the ModelSim and MATLAB software respectively. The input image is given as pixel values in the VHDL code for simulation. Here both the traditional algorithm which is in use and the proposed reconstructed canny algorithm results are obtained. Also, the comparison between the current technology and the reconfigurable canny edge detection algorithm is analyzed and the differences are observed. The design parameters like power consumption, gate count and speed show 15%, 7% and 22% improvements respectively. Since the LUT count required is less, it enhances the possibility of implementing additional functions such as the Harris feature which can be added to the device to improve the additional features in this proposed algorithm.

References

1. Akagic, A., Buza, E., Omanovic, S., Karabegovic, A.: Pavement crack detection using Otsu thresholding for image segmentation. In: 41st International Convention on Information and Communication Technology, Electronics and Microelectronics (MIPRO), pp. 1092–1097 (2018). https://doi.org/10.23919/MIPRO.2018.8400199
2. Draper, B.A., Bruce, A., et al.: Accelerated image processing on FPGAs. IEEE Trans. Image Process. **XII**(12), 1543–1551 (2018)
3. Gourab, A., Rohan, M., et al.: Adaptive region-wise histogram correction using local thresholding technique for very poorly illuminated images. In: ICIP, India (2018)
4. Hema Rajini, N.: Modified cuckoo search algorithm based optimal thresholding for color lip image segmentation. In: ICECA, India (2019)

5. Janardhan, C., Ramanaiah, V., et al.: A novel approach for solving medical image segmentation problems with ACM. Int. J. Eng. Res. Appl. **VII**(11), 40–47 (2017)
6. Jianjia, P., Li-Na, Y., et al.: Image segmentation based on 2D OTSU and simplified swarm optimization. In: International Conference on Machine Learning and Cybernetics, South Korea (2016)
7. Jiangwa, X., Yang, P., et al.: Automatic thresholding using modified valley emphasis. IET Image Process. (2019)
8. Lingxiao, Y., Qingxiu, F., et al.: An improvement using Bernsen binarization algorithm for QR code image detection. In: 5th IEEE International Conference on Cloud Computing and Intelligence Systems, China (2019)
9. Mishra, Agarwal, M.: Hardware and software performance of image processing applications on reconfigurable systems. In: Annual IEEE India Conference (INDICON), India (2015)
10. Wan Azani, M., Nurushah Mohd, S., et al.: Overview of X-ray medical images segmented using image processing technique. In: JICETS, Malaysia (2022)
11. Senthilkumar, K.K., Kumarasamy, K., Dhandapani, V.: Approximate multipliers using bio-inspired algorithm. J. Electr. Eng. Technol. **16**, 559–568 (2021). https://doi.org/10.1007/s42835-020-00564-w
12. Harshini, V.S., Kumar, K.K.S.: Design of hybrid sorting unit. In: 2019 International Conference on Smart Structures and Systems (ICSSS), pp. 1–6 (2019). https://doi.org/10.1109/ICSSS.2019.8882866
13. Senthilkumar, K.K., Kunaraj, K., Seshasayanan, R.: Implementation of computation-reduced DCT using a novel method. EURASIP J. Image Video Process. **2015**(1), 1–18 (2015). https://doi.org/10.1186/s13640-015-0088-z

DMC Approach for Modeling Viral Transmission over Respiratory System

Raghevendra Jaiswal[1], Masood Asim[1], Urvashi Chugh[2], Prabhakar Agrawal[3](✉),
and S. Pratap Singh[4]

[1] Department of Electronics and Communication Engineering, GCET, Greater Noida, India
[2] IT-Department, KIET Group of Institutions, Ghaziabad, India
[3] Department of Electrical, Electronics and Communication Engineering, Galgotias University,
Greater Noida, India
`prabhakar.agarwal@galgotiasuniversity.edu.in`
[4] Department of Computer Science & Engineering, Symbiosis Institute of Technology Nagpur
Campus, Nagpur, India

Abstract. Diffusive Molecular Communication (DMC) is a widely accepted technique for modeling biological environments. Within DMC, information is conveyed from transmitting nanomachines to a receiving nano-machine by utilizing molecules that disperse through the medium. This Paper uses the DMC Approach for Modeling Viral Transmission over Respiratory System. It is noticeable that the complete respiratory tract is responsible to grade the severity of the disease. And therefore, literatures present propagation of CoVID-29 in the respiratory tract. Further, it is most important to mention that the impulse response of the system which characterizes ACE2 (Angiotensin-converting enzyme 2) concentration per unit area (f(y)) plays a major role in modeling viral transmission over the respiratory tract. The Author in [8] describes the propagation of SARS-COV2 bacteria over the respiratory tract and its binding with the ACE2 receptor however we present a generalized approach which can be applied to any type of bacteria and its binding with any receptor kind. In particular, analytical expressions of binding probability P_b, probability of the virus evading $P_e(y)$ and probability of binding rate y $P_b(y)$ under certain impulse responses are presented in this work. Also, the effect of different physical parameters on P_b, P_{nb} and $P_b(y)$ have been quantified with the help of numerical simulation. This work presents a mathematical model describing the concentration of virus and its distribution throughout the respiratory tract. Presented analysis shows perfect agreement with the theoretical background.

Keywords: Diffusive Molecular Communication · ACE2 · binding probability P_b · non- binding probability P_{nb} and respiratory tract

1 Introduction

Over the last decade, an interdisciplinary research field called molecular communications has emerged, bridging communication engineering, networking, molecular biology, and bioengineering [1–3]. This area is dedicated to developing innovative technology for

S. Sachdeva and Y. Watanobe (Eds.): BDA 2023, LNCS 14516, pp. 120–127, 2024.
https://doi.org/10.1007/978-3-031-58502-9_8

subtle sensing and actuation capabilities within the human body using a network of micro- and nanoscale devices [4, 5]. These devices can leverage natural cellular and tissue signaling for interaction and communication with the human body. An important advantage is the potential to enhance the compatibility of implantable systems, achieved by integrating communication system engineering with systems and synthetic biology [4, 5]. This emerging field could play a pivotal role in addressing current and future pandemics, offering insights into viral properties and characteristics as well as novel treatments. Molecular communications can aid in (a) understanding how viruses spread within the body, (b) comprehending the mechanisms used by viruses to enter or exit the human body, and (c) shedding light on the transmission of airborne viruses.

Further inside the realm of MC we have Diffusive molecular communication (DMC) emerging as an exceptionally advantageous technique for facilitating nano-scale communication in healthcare-related biological environments [6]. Within DMC, information is conveyed from transmitting nanomachines to a receiving nano-machine by utilizing molecules that disperse through the medium. The data is encoded through the concentration, variety, and timing of molecule releases [1]. In the context of biological scenarios, the DMC system may encounter various environmental influences, including limited spatial confines and degradation reactions.

Further DMC can be applied to develop various effective systems in order to fight worldwide respiratory infections, often caused by viruses, which continue to pose a significant and persistent public health challenge. Effectively combating these diseases hinges on our understanding of how viruses infiltrate and navigate the complex terrain of the human respiratory system. This study focuses on unraveling the dynamics of viral transmission within a simplified model that traces the route from the nasal cavity to the alveoli.

In the comprehensive work by [7], the integration of molecular communications into the context of viral infectious diseases is explored in detail. This research delves into the potential use of molecules as carriers of information to develop treatments and vaccines. The author conducts a thorough literature review covering molecular communication models for viral infections, both intra-body and extra-body. The study also includes a profound analysis of their impact on immune responses, along with considerations of practical experimental applications.

In a recent publication [8], the author introduced an innovative model of the human respiratory tract. This model simplifies the complexities of the original system and offers calculations for receptor density across various respiratory tract regions. Importantly, this work marks the first instance in the literature of determining the impulse response of the SARS-CoV2 infection process. Furthermore, the research explores the impact of variables such as mucus layer thickness, mucus flow rate, and ACE2 receptor density on the distribution of the virus within different respiratory tract regions and its influence on disease progression.

Our approach leverages the unique principles of molecular communication. While we acknowledge the intricate interconnection of organs in the human respiratory system, encompassing the pharynx, larynx, trachea, and alveoli, our investigation hones in on the fundamental path directly from the nose to the alveoli. This simplified perspective allows us to create a straightforward yet insightful model for assessing the dynamics of viral inhalation. At the heart of our research lies the development of a mathematical model describing the concentration of virus and its distribution throughout the respiratory tract.

The objective is to provide a solid foundation for researchers, healthcare practitioners, and epidemiologists to explore viral transmission dynamics in a controlled and straightforward manner. In the subsequent sections, we will delve into the mathematical intricacies of our model, the underlying assumptions of the simplified pathway, and the implications of our findings. We aim to advance the understanding of viral respiratory infections and stimulate further research into the applications of molecular communication in both public health and biomedical research, specifically focusing on the fundamental dynamics of viral inhalation from the nose to the alveoli.

This model enables us to quantify the volume of viruses entering the body through nasal inhalation. Molecular communication principles offer a novel framework for understanding viral transmission within this specific segment of the respiratory system, relying on the exchange of molecules for information transfer [8–10]. This study deviates from comprehensive models of viral inhalation dynamics, providing a relevant yet simplified viewpoint, particularly beneficial for early-stage monitoring and understanding of respiratory infections.

2 System Model

The human respiratory system has a very complicated and advanced architecture that perfectly controls the flow of oxygen and carbon dioxide from our nasal cavity to various parts of the body. Its various components involving pharynx, salivary glands, larynx, trachea, lungs, bronchi and alveoli are responsible for carrying out different complex tasks. The whole system is covered with a thin layer of mucus that helps to trap the foreign substances and prevent them from binding with the receptors present in our cells (Fig. 1).

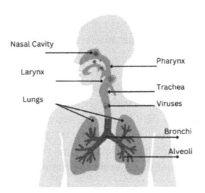

Fig. 1. Viral Transmission over Respiratory System

The Trachea plays a crucial role in providing a rigid structure for the airway to keep open and the Alveoli have balloon-like structures responsible for the diffusion of inhaled oxygen into the blood. The whole respiratory system is very complex to analyze and thus we prefer to have a simplified model to represent it thus we make the assumption that the rate of mucus production, denoted as "v," remains constant throughout the medium, spanning from the nasal cavity to the alveoli. Within this mucus layer, viruses undergo diffusion with a diffusion coefficient represented as "DA" To determine the concentration of viruses, we account for the effects of Brownian motion with drift. This mathematical framework, derived from Brownian motion with drift, takes into account three spatial dimensions: the y-axis, representing the distance from the entrance of the nasal cavity; the x-axis, denoting the distance from a longitudinal reference point; and the z-axis, representing the thickness or width of the mucus layer.

In the event that a droplet containing "N" viruses comes into contact with the mucus layer, the overall virus concentration can be calculated as follows [8]

$$C = \frac{2e^{[-\frac{y^2}{4D_A t}]}}{(4D_A t)^{\frac{3}{2}}} \tag{1}$$

where y is the distance along which the virus travels, D_A is the diffusion coefficient and t is the time virus takes in the along the length y

In our model, the impact of diffusion on virus concentration primarily becomes significant for larger values of time, "t". Consequently, in the context of our proposed model, the duration it takes for a virus to traverse a small segment, represented by "delta y," is exceedingly brief, rendering the effect of diffusion negligible. To comprehend the process of virus binding to the mucus layer, we initiate our analysis by creating a model that describes the distribution of the total virus population within the respiratory tract. This involves simulating the dynamics of a single virus as it attaches to the mucus layer.

Proceeding, we take into account the mucus layer thickness h(y) and the respiratory tract radius, which changes with distance as r(y), where y corresponds to the respiratory tract's path from the nasal cavity to the alveoli.

3   Proposed Probabilistic Measures for Viral Transmission

A First we find the expression for Binding probability to a single receptor i.e. P_b as follows [8]

$$P_b = 1 - e^{(-\lambda^1 C_1 \Delta t)} \tag{2}$$

To expand the exponential term we assume that x has a small value such that $= e^x$ $1 + x$

$$P_b = \frac{\lambda}{N_A} \frac{1}{\upsilon} \frac{2e^{[-\frac{y^2}{4D_A t}]}}{(4D_A t)^{\frac{3}{2}}} \tag{3}$$

where λ represents the receptor-virus binding rate and is a molar association constant NA is the Avogadro's constant and λ^1 is the association constant for a single virus. If the receptor concentration per unit area at y is f(y), then number of receptors, n(y), in the patch of length Δy becomes [1].

$$n(y) = 2\pi r(y)f(y)\Delta y \tag{4}$$

where r(y) is the tract radius and f(y) is the receptor concentration

The probability of the virus evading all the receptors in same patch, $P_e(y)$ is as follows [8]

$$P_e(y) = (1 - P_b)^{n(y)} \tag{5}$$

On further calculations and taking the assumption that $(1 - x)^n = (1 - nx)$ for $|nx| << 1$, which holds due to NA being much larger and $\Delta y \to dy$

$$P_e(y) = 1 - \frac{S\lambda}{4\pi \upsilon y^3} \frac{e^{\left[-\frac{y^2}{4D_A t}\right]}}{D_A^{\frac{5}{2}} t)^{\frac{3}{2}}} . erfc\left(\frac{y}{2\sqrt{D_A t}}\right) dy \tag{6}$$

As the total probability of binding and not binding with the receptor will be 1 hence we can write probability of binding as

$$P_b(y) = 1 - P_e(y) \tag{7}$$

When we expresss

$$f(y) = \frac{N_A}{2\pi D_A y} erfc(\frac{y}{2\sqrt{D_A t}}) \tag{8}$$

We get

$$P_b(y) = \frac{e^{\left[-\frac{y^2}{4D_A t}\right]}}{8\left(D_A^{\frac{5}{2}}\right)(t)^{\frac{3}{2}}} . \frac{S}{\pi y^2} erfc(\frac{y}{2\sqrt{D_A t}}) \tag{9}$$

4   Numerical Analysis

In this section we present the Numerical analysis and discussion for DMC Approach for Modeling Viral Transmission over Respiratory System. From the Mathematical demonstration we got different equation for different expression that is P_b, P_{nb} and $P_b(y)$, by considering the various values expectancy for this expression under different parameters that is virus Binding rate (λ), Mucus flow rate (v) and time (t).

In Fig. 2, we conducted an analysis of the Binding Probability of a Single Receptor (P_b) while considering various values of the Virus Binding Rate (λ), specifically, $\lambda = 0.5$, 1, 1.5, 2, and 2.5. Our findings indicate that as the value of λ increases, P_b also increases. The physical representation illustrates that when we increase the Virus Binding Rate for a specific duration, it signifies an increase in P_b.

In Fig. 3, we consider for different values of v = 0.4, 0.8, 1.2, 1.6, and 2.2, where v represents the mucus flow rate, our analysis reveals that as the values of v increase,

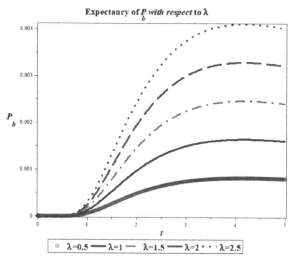

Fig. 2. Expectancy of P_b with respect to λ keeping v as a constant.

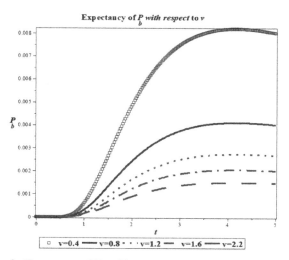

Fig. 3. Expectancy of P_b with respect to v keeping λ as a constant

P_b decreases. When we increment the mucus flow rate (v) for various scenarios, the physical representation demonstrates a notable trend. Specifically, it shows that as the mucus flow rate increases, the concentration of virus in the mucus decreases over time. This decrease in virus concentration is associated with a corresponding decrease in the Binding Probability of a Single Receptor (P_b).

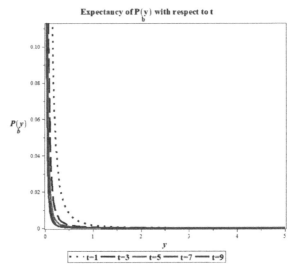

Fig. 4. Expectancy of $P_b(y)$ with respect to v keeping λ as a constant

In Fig. 4, we examine various values of t (1, 3, 5, 7, and 9) representing time. Our analysis of the Binding rate at y ($P_b(y)$) indicates a decrease after a certain threshold time period. The physical representation illustrates that the mucus has an impact on virus concentration, preventing it from reaching the final segment at distance y. As a result, the Binding rate at y distance becomes constant after a certain distance.

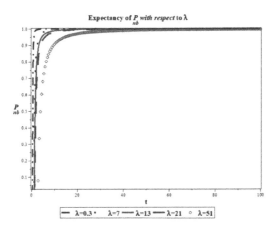

Fig. 5. Expectancy of P_{nb} with respect to λ.

In Fig. 5, we conducted an analysis of the Not Binding Probability of a Single Receptor (P_{nb}) while considering various values of the Virus Binding Rate (λ), specifically, λ = 0.3, 7, 13, 21, and 51. Our findings indicate that as the value of λ increases, the P_{nb} for some particular value of time increases exponentially after that when the threshold value reaches it decreases. The physical representation illustrates that when we increase the Virus Binding Rate for a specific duration, it signifies diseases in P_{nb}.

5 Conclusions

This work presents the use of Diffusive Molecular Communication for Modeling Viral Transmission over Respiratory System. Paper presents analytical expressions of binding probability P_b, probability of the virus evading $P_e(y)$ and probability of binding rate y $P_b(y)$. Also, the effect of different physical parameters v and λ on P_b and $P_b(y)$ have been quantified with the help of numerical simulation. In [8] the author considers propagation of SARS-COV2 bacteria over the respiratory tract whereas we have presented the similar results for a more generalized scenario which can be considered for any type of bacteria and receptors. We have also provided the variation of bacteria concentration as temporal variable time intervals in the respiratory tract in addition to spatial variables presented in [8]. Inclusion of different types of receptors and diffusion channels can be a future scope of this work.

References

1. Singh, S.P., Yadav, S., Singh, R.K., Kansal, V., Singh, G.: Secrecy capacity of diffusive molecular communication under different deployments. IEEE Access **10**, 21670–21683 (2022)
2. Mishra, S., Thakur, P., Singh, S P., Singh, G.: Impairment modeling of diffusive molecular communication system: the vision, potential and challenges. In: AIP Conference Proceedings (2023)
3. Singh, S.P., Dwivedi, V.K., Singh, G.: Multimedia nano communication for healthcare–noise analysis. In: Internet of Multimedia Things (IoMT), Academic Press. 2495, No. 1). AIP Publishing pp. 99–132 (2022)
4. Singh, R.K., Singh, S.P., Tiwari, S.: Performance evaluation of wireless nanosensor networks under interference. Nano Commun. Netw. **25**, 100311 (2020)
5. Singh, R.K., Singh, S.P., Tiwari, S.: Performance of electromagnetic nanonetwork under relaying for plant monitoring. Phys. Commun. **47**, 101316 (2021)
6. Jamali, V., Ahmadzadeh, A., Wicke, W., Noel, A., Schober, R.: Channel modeling for diffusive molecular communication—a tutorial review. Proc. IEEE **107**(7), 1256–1301 (2019)
7. Barros, M.T., et al.: Molecular communications in viral infections research: modeling, experimental data, and future directions. IEEE Trans. Mol. Biol. Multi-Scale Commun. **7**(3), 121–141 (2021)
8. Koca, C., Civas, M., Sahin, S.M., Ergonul, O., Akan, O.B.: Molecular communication theoretical modeling and analysis of SARS-CoV2 transmission in the human respiratory system. IEEE Trans. Mol. Biol. Multi-Scale Commun. **7**(3), 153–164 (2021)
9. Nakano, T.: Molecular communication: a 10 year retrospective. IEEE Trans. Mol. Biol. Multi-Scale Commun. **3**(2), 71–78 (2017)
10. Kantelis, K., Papadimitriou, G., Nikopolitidis, P., Kavakiotis, I., Tsave, O., Salifoglou, A.: Fick's law model revisited: a new approach to modeling multiple sources message dissemination in bacterial communication nanosystems. IEEE Trans. Mol. Biol. Multi-Scale Commun. **3**(2), 89–105 (2017)

Machine Learning in Particle Physics

Milind V. Purohit$^{(\boxtimes)}$ 🆔

Department of Physics and Astronomy, University of South Carolina,
Columbia, SC 29208, USA
purohit@sc.edu

Abstract. This note surveys developments in particle physics due to advances made in the fields of statistics, machine learning, and artificial intelligence. With the aid of examples and recent work, this article attempts to give a flavor of the effect of these advances on particle physics, including brief mention of cloud computing, classic machine learning techniques, statistics applications, new ML/AI techniques, reinforcement learning, and other advances. Suggestions are made regarding the future.

Keywords: particle physics · machine learning · statistics · simulation · optimal transport · physics

1 Introduction

Due to its data-heavy nature, particle physics, also known as High Energy Physics or HEP (also known as particle physics) due to the extreme energies per particle, has always had a great need for assistance from the field of statistics. In the late 1980's and early 1990's this was extended to include what seemed to us to be the nascent field of Machine Learning (ML), mostly limited to "Artificial Neural Networks" at that time.

Being outside the world of computing, and mostly ignorant of the strides already made in the 1950's, 60's, and 70's, we did not anticipate the explosion of interest and research in the "new" fields which have taken the world by storm. So much so that today many students who would have been attracted by the fundamental nature of particle physics are now lured by the promise of exciting research in the rapidly mushrooming fields of ML, Artificial Intelligence (AI), and their intersections with many areas of science.

This article explores a part of this story: how the booming areas of ML/AI are affecting our corner of the world of physics, by examining what has happened and what may be around the corner.

2 Early Days and the Engine of Change

At work in the 1970's, mainframes evolved from punched card machines such as the IBM 360, the ICL 1909, and others that devoured stacks of cards (sometimes

S. Sachdeva and Y. Watanobe (Eds.): BDA 2023, LNCS 14516, pp. 128–138, 2024.
https://doi.org/10.1007/978-3-031-58502-9_9

literally) to the PDP-11, the VAX 780 and similar mainframes. Languages like FORTRAN and COBOL flourished, while Algol and Unix were the leading edge of change. The CRAY was the "supercomputer" to get your hands on.

By the late 1970's kit computers and other small machines were available to be purchased by individuals and used at home. I recall one professor claiming that "once a personal machine can match the power of our VAX 780, I will buy one." But the power of laptops kept rising at an exponential rate fueled by Moore's Law and other business dynamics.

By the late 1980's the concept of "a farm of computers" to process the volumes of data being produced by experiments in particle physics became possible. Many university groups and national labs had such farms, and experimental physicists went from the hunter-gatherer stage of discovering electrons, then protons, then neutrons, and so on, to being farmers. We were an agricultural society! An example is provided by the E791 computing farm of the Univ. of Mississippi Department of Physics [1].

At the Univ. of Mississippi a 2800 MIP Data Reconstruction "Farm" was first set up in 1991. This "farm" was actually comprised of four separate machine groups, each with its own server and approximately 3.5 GB scratch disk plus server disk. It had a full-time system manager and was accessible via the Internet (@higgs1.phy.olemiss.edu). Some details of this early High Performance Computing (HPC) effort are available at [1] and are reproduced below:

- 66 DECstation 5000s; 49 MIPS R3000 CPUs; 17 MIPS 50 MHz R4000 CPUs.
- 36 Exabyte 8200 Tape Drives; 4 Tape Autoloaders (10 tape capacity each).
- 25 GB Total Disk Capacity; $400K Approximate Cost for Hardware/Software.
- UMiss VAXstation 4000, which served as our primary mail node and VMS platform.
- Was accessible via the Internet (@umsphy.phy.olemiss.edu) and BITNET (@umsphy).

Today, we have taken wing and everyone computes in the sky. Our data resides in "clouds", while AWS, Google, and others have made high-performance computing easily available. The trend of open-source software has really caught on, bringing humans close to an ideal of cooperation and sharing, at least in intellectual endeavors. Large data repositories are available for free or at small cost, creating an egalitarian computing society.

3   Computing in Particle Physics Today

A look at the computing structures of major HEP experiments reveals however that commercial solutions have not caught on. As illustrations some of the major computing centers in HEP are listed below:

- The Belle II experiment in Japan might need 1/3 Exabyte in all and 4-5 MHS06 CPU [2].
- The FermiGrid compute facility features 40,000 cores [3].

- The ATLAS experiment/CERN provides 1 Exabyte of storage and 1 million cores [4].
- The large DUNE effort at Fermilab uses part of the FermiGrid compute facility [3].

Will HEP soon be going commercial? On the one hand, commercial solutions are more expensive. On the other hand, they free up physicist and engineer time, and require no capital costs. Currently, the ideal solution seems to be to use commercial solutions for peak demand times [4].

4   Early Machine Learning: Classification, Regression, and Density Estimation

The classic data analysis in particle physics consists of fitting experimental data with a "mixture model" of signal and background distributions. In such an analysis of data, the signal density is frequently known from an underlying physics process, while the background density has to be guessed at and/or derived from data.

There are several issues that arise:

- Improving the signal to background ratios.
- Fitting data using some sort of regression, typically non-linear.
- Estimating densities, especially of backgrounds which arise from multiple and typically poorly understood sources.

These problems are very often multidimensional, and thus when first introduced Artificial Neural Networks were very attractive with their promise to solve some of these problems with little or no supervision. Clearly their use has caught on (see Fig. 1) and has improved signal to background ratios enormously during the last couple of decades.

The ATLAS experiment now uses several Higgs decay channels and states that "A detailed classification of selected events into 101 separate categories based on multi-class machine learning techniques is used . . . " [6]

5   An Example of ML: Detector Simulation

The Belle II experiment in KEK, Japan, needs to identify particles produced in the experiment. For this purpose, a sub-detector known as the "Time of Propagation", or "TOP" detector, [7,8] uses the time taken by photons to traverse the quartz bar in which they are produced via Cherenkov radiation from a charged particle to classify the charged particle as one of: electron (e), muon (μ), pion (π), kaon (K), proton (p), or deuteron(d). This detector is shown in Fig. 2.

The concept of charged particle identification is as follows. Photons are detected by modern photomultiplier tubes (PMT's) at the front face of the quartz bars. These tubes detect the x- and y-positions of the arriving photons, as well as

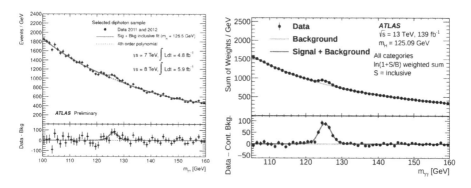

Fig. 1. Diphoton decays of the Higgs boson, i.e., $H \to \gamma\gamma$ from the original Discovery in 2012 and from the full data set from LHC Run 2 in 2023, as published by the ATLAS collaboration [5,6].

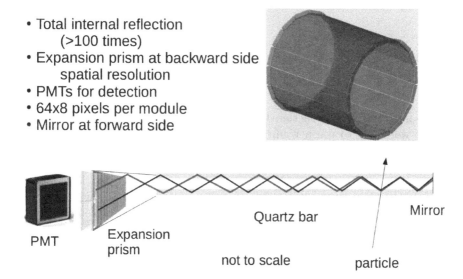

- Total internal reflection
    (>100 times)
- Expansion prism at backward side
    spatial resolution
- PMTs for detection
- 64x8 pixels per module
- Mirror at forward side

Fig. 2. The Time-of-Propagation sub-detector of the Belle II detector at KEK in Japan [9].

the arrival time (to within 40 ps or so). Let us call these photon "hits". Since the momentum and position of the incoming charged particle is known from separate tracking detectors, it is possible to simulate the expected photon distribution for each hypothesis and find which particle type most closely matches the observed hits. The problem is illustrated in Fig. 3 which shows the hit pattern for two of the observed variables (t and x) for three different hypotheses as well as the actual hits.

- Channel: $D^{*+} \rightarrow D^0 \pi_s^+$ with $D^0 \rightarrow K^- \pi^+$
   Tagging from π_s^+
- Position vs. time diagram
- Kaon flying away from prism
- PID from pattern of photons

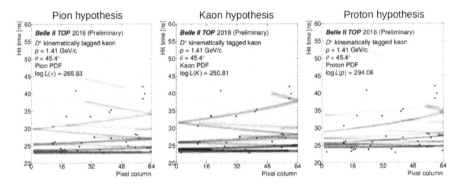

Fig. 3. An illustration of the complexities in particle type classification in the Belle II detector at KEK in Japan [9].

How may this reconstruction benefit from Machine Learning? The classic response would be to use a traditional or deep neural network as a classifier, with a logistic loss function, since the problem is one of classifying the observed hits as arising from one of 6 different hypotheses: e, μ, π, K, p, or d. However, this approach would require nine inputs (the three charged particle momenta, its three quartz bar entrance coordinates, and the PMT locations and time bins) for which we wish to get the probability of firing. Accurate representation with this approach is a tall order, since the number of dimensions is high.

Another approach is that the t vs. x images could be fed to a Convolutional Neural Network (CNN) which can then report the ID. This is the modern approach to image recognition which can utilize the recurrent structures visible in Fig. 3.

A third approach is to use density estimation in which we estimate the hit density at the (x, y) locations of the PMT's and the hit times, i.e., the full (x, y, t) vector of outcomes for each hypothesis. This can be followed by use of standard statistical methods to determine which hypothesis fits the data the best.

Of course, such an approach begs the question of how should one estimate the density. This is a vexing problem in many dimensions. In this approach the 9 inputs mentioned above could be regarded as 6 inputs: position and momentum of the charged particle that traverses the quartz, and 3 outputs: the observed hit patterns of (x, y, t) vectors. Needless to add, accuracy of the result is important. The detector has time resolution of less than 50 ps, and there are 512 pixels for each quartz bar. It is likely that the number of points needed for training is too high. An analytical approach can also be used.

Regardless of the approach used, some measures and questions remain. How does the result degrade as more particles traverse the bar? And as the time resolution is varied? All of these questions can be answered by a good estimator. A measure of effectiveness that can be used to compare the various approaches is, for instance, the TPR/FPR rate, i.e., the ratio of the True Positive Rate (TPR) to the total False Positive Rate (FPR) from all the incorrect hypotheses. Such studies have been done and more are underway within the collaboration.

6   Recent Methods in ML

Consider the image in Fig. 4. What's in this image: a cat or a dog? A pion or a kaon? Apart from CNN's, can we use template matching to classify our particles? Or Fourier or wavelet transforms?

Fig. 4. An illustration of the image classification problem [10].

Statisticians are interested in serious issues such as the generalization error. We would be satisfied with a good likelihood ratio (LR) to compare True and False positive rates. The LR was invented by Neyman and Pearson in 1928 [11] and was later proven by the same duo to be optimal in 1933 [12], and is widely used in particle physics as a solid, reliable result to base decisions on. Now particle physicists are paying more attention to issues of accuracy and generalization as the need for accurate ML increases.

The important thing is to approximate the true density as closely as possible so that MC estimates are accurate approximations to experimental data. Estimates must also be rapidly obtained because of immense data sizes. These twin demands of accuracy and speed are familiar, but pose questions at implementation time. In our problem with the particle classification, the VC dimension is known, but unfortunately generalization gap theory using this quantity is notoriously unreliable and not of much use in predicting the true generalization.

We need to develop enough expertise in ML to have a prescription ready for all data challenges as we encounter them. There is currently too much experimentation needed for each individual problem.

Finally, there are interesting new possibilities involving assignment of causality, and in sequential decision making using reinforcement learning.

7   Newer Methods from ML Used in Particle Physics

A relatively recently popular development is the method of Optimal Transport (OT). This technique has a storied history after its initial proposal and solutions (see e.g., [13,14]) and more recent work ([15–17]). In this method, one can simulate (for instance), the "optimal" transportation of vectors from a uniform distribution to a given distribution. Once trained, it can simulate other such transformations starting with a uniform random distribution of vectors in a d-dimensional space. Apart from enabling MC sample generation, it can also be used to estimate densities, estimate the "distance" between distributions via the concept of Wasserstein/Earth Mover Distance ([18]). Such methods as OT and others such as Normalizing Flows may also provide advantages in speed.

Other new statistical investigations include goodness-of-fit tests, including identifying regions where there is significant discrepancy between the data and the model.

"Explainable" and "Interpretable" ML are beginning to make an impact [19]. In business applications of AI, such as loan application decisions, we may worry about bias against subsets of customers. Similar considerations apply to the likelihood of an accident if a driverless car is not trained to be careful of oncoming pedestrians. In experimental physics, we want to know *why* the background was reduced. What aspect of the detector can we improve? Is the NN artificially cutting out background near the signal? There are issues of interpreting the vast number of parameters and architecture of NN's building sparse models, (e.g., what is the meaning of each of many the selections in a big decision tree?), and incorporating physics constraints. Other considerations, akin to the problem of figuring out which of thousands of pieces of data collected from consumers is most likely to predict their next purchasing decision, the general problem of dimension reduction is also significant in some HEP analyses.

We should mention exciting new areas such as Reinforcement Learning (RL) which are being applied to experiment design, accelerators, triggers, and other areas where instantaneous feedback from physicists is not possible but is needed to optimize the running of an experiment. Of course, techniques such as Kalman filters have been used for a long time in charged particle tracking, and these are commonly used in Markov Decision Processes (MDP's) such as RL.

Another new area is Generative AI. This technique can be used, for instance, in simulating large detectors as well as their individual sub-detectors [20–23]. There are questions that remain to be answered to everyone's satisfaction, such as "Can we use this to go beyond training data?" If the answer is confirmed in the affirmative, detector processes with unknown mechanisms and corresponding equations can be fruitfully simulated using ML. A recent publication, by Matchev *et al.* claims that [24] "data generated by a GAN cannot statistically be better than the data it was trained on". They state that "GAN generated data cannot contain any more information (for the purpose of an experimental analysis) than the data it was trained on ... while the focus of this paper has been on the usage of GANs for performing collider Monte Carlo, our arguments are also pertinent to other machine-learning-based generative models that learn from simulated training data, including Variational Auto Encoder based approaches. Likewise, our arguments could potentially affect the application of machine learning techniques for simulations outside high energy physics as well."

This seems like dismal news for applications of GANs and VAEs for simulation. On the other hand, others have recognized that neural nets do more than duplicate data distributions since they also interpolate between points. Indeed, in a recent publication [25] the response was "... there are reasons to think that a generative model actually contains more statistical power than the original data set. The key property of neural networks in particle physics is their powerful interpolation in sparse and high-dimensional spaces ... this advanced interpolation should provide GANs with additional statistical power." In this publication, the authors show that while a GAN cannot be expected to do better than knowing the true multi-dimensional distribution of variables, it can and does do better than the training sample. They go on to quantify the "amplification factor" which is the effective number of training samples the GAN is worth (in dimensions ranging up to 10). This is a significant and heartening conclusion for GANs, VAEs, etc.

The renaissance, if you will, of powerful statistical methods entering physics via AI has brought renewed attention to statistical uncertainties and their quantification. For instance, we see new emphasis on types of uncertainties. We are familiar with "statistical" and "systematic" uncertainties. Now, we are learning about "aleatoric" and "epistemic" uncertainties. Aleatoric means "depending on the throw of a dice", while Epistemic uncertainties relate to "knowledge or to the degree of its validation" [26]. How uncertainties may be quantified is not as straightforward as one might expect.

Perhaps these issues also contribute to the heightened need for "interpretable" or "explainable" AI, which refer to understanding the inner workings of neural nets and being able to explain simple terms (to executives, say) what the network is doing.

Finally, it is worth mentioning in passing that ML/AI is being used in understanding the physics itself in areas such as Nuclear Physics (QCD), Quantum entanglement etc.

8   New Paths in ML for Particle Physics

The American Association of Physics Teachers (AAPT) has issued a policy statement [27] which reads "...Computational physics has become a third way of doing physics and complements traditional modes of theoretical and experimental physics ...Computer simulations allow us to develop models that are not solvable analytically, to test theories where traditional experiments are too difficult or expensive, to ask "what-if" questions, and to visualize the time development of dynamical systems. As a result simulations provide different insights, which may not be possible to obtain through the use of traditional theoretical and experimental methods." This is a statement that resonates with many physics professors, and drives us to the conclusion that undergraduate and graduate students should be trained in solving these problems as an integral part of their experimental HEP courses in grad school. Studies have shown the importance of teaching computation as part of physics; ML/AI is a perfect interdisciplinary tool to introduce students to such activity.

An aspect of the recent revolution in ML/AI that has been emphasized by Hardt and Recht [28] is that datasets have been deliberately created to test and valildate various approaches to problems. Some of these, such as MNIST for image classification, have become very popular. The HEP community should similarly create datasets which feature problems in classification (typical Signal to Background ratio improvement problems), image classification (particle ID), detector simulation, triggers, and more. Some steps have already been taken, for instance by "The LHC Olympics 2020" challenge [29].

In addition, we need to develop, in the HEP community, enough expertise in ML to have a prescription ready for all data challenges as we encounter them. In the short term, this will mean emphasis on learning all the available options for NNs, interpretable models, feature selection, etc. In the longer term, we may even have AI assistance in tool selection. We have to extend GANs for simulation, and get interpretable AI to help us understand all this!

9   Conclusion

How should we balance legacy code with increasingly diverse and powerful new techniques available as open source code? HEP should celebrate the availability of not only open source code, but also new, powerful, and useful techniques from the ML community. We applaud the efforts of the ML/AI community and thank them for their contributions, as well as those of statisticians, to advance our science.

Acknowledgments. Many thanks to the organizers Profs. Bhalla, Sachdeva, and Watanobe, and the crew of BASE23 at NIT Delhi, India and at the University of Aizu, Japan.

References

1. https://www.phy.olemiss.edu/HEP/comp.html & parallel_comp.html
2. Hara, T.: Belle II Computing Update: KEK, 2020 May GDB
3. Khan, F.: HTCondor at Fermilab: Fermilab (2023)
4. De, K., Klimentov, A.: Future Data-Intensive Experiment Computing ...: Computing in High Energy and Nuclear Physics (2023)
5. The ATLAS Collaboration: Observation of a new particle in the search for the Standard Model Higgs boson with the ATLAS detector at the LHC: Phys. Lett. B716, 1–29 (2012)
6. The ATLAS Collaboration, Measurement of the properties of Higgs boson production at $\sqrt{s} = 13$ TeV in the $H \to \gamma\gamma$ channel using 139 fb^{-1} of pp collision data with the ATLAS experiment: EP 07 (2023). 088
7. Inami, K.: TOP counter for particle identification at the Belle II experiment. Nucl. Instrum. Methods Phys. Res. A **766**, 5–8 (2014)
8. Sandilya, S., Schwartz, A.: Kaon and Pion Identification Performances in Phase III data for TOP detector: BELLE2-NOTE-PL-2019-014
9. Bessner, M.: The Belle II imaging Time-Of-Propagation (iTOP) detector in first collisions: VCI Vienna, b 22 (2019)
10. Image from Wikimedia Commons, Creative Commons license
11. Neyman, J., Pearson, E.S.: On the use and interpretation of certain test criteria for purposes of statistical inference. Biometrika 20A, 175–240, 263–294
12. Neyman, J., Pearson, E.S.: IX. On the problem of the most efficient tests of statistical hypotheses. Phil. Trans. R. Soc. Lond. A. **231**(694–706), 289–337 (1933)
13. Mémoire sur la théorie des déblais et des remblais: G. Monge, De l'Imprimerie Royale (1781)
14. Kantorovich, L.V.: On the Translocation of Masses: J Math Sci 133, 1381-1382 (2006). Originally published in Dokl. Akad. Nauk SSSR, 37, No. 7–8, 227–229 (1942)
15. Brenier, Y.: Polar factorization and monotone rearrangement of vector-valued functions. Commun. Pure Appl. Math. **44**(4), 375–417 (1991)
16. Villani, C.: Topics in Optimal Transportation: American Mathematical Society (2003). in the Graduate Studies in Mathematics Series
17. Figalli, A.: The Monge problem on non-compact manifolds: Rend. Sem. Mat. Univ. Padova **117**, 147–166 (2007)
18. Vaserstein, L.N.: Markov processes over denumerable products of spaces, describing large systems of automata. Problemy Peredači Informacii. **5**(3), 64–72 (1969)
19. Rudin, C., et al.: Interpretable machine learning: fundamental principles and 10 grand challenges. Stat. Surv. **16**, 1–85 (2022)
20. Alanazi, Y., et al.: A survey of machine learning-based physics event generation. In: The Proceedings of the Thirtieth International Joint Conference on Artificial Intelligence (IJCAI-21) Survey Track
21. Butter, A., et al.: Ganplifying event samples. arXiv, 2008.06545 (2020)
22. Matchev, K.T., Shyamsundar, P.: Uncertainties associated with GAN-generated datasets in high energy physics: arXiV 2002.06307v2 (2020)

23. Kansal, R., et al.: Evaluating generative models in high energy physics. Phys. Rev. D **107**, 076017 (2023)

24. Matchev, K.T., Roman, A., Shyamsundar, P.: Uncertainties associated with GAN-generated datasets in high energy physics. SciPost Phys. **12**(3), 104 (2022)

25. Butter, A., et al.: GANplifying Event Samples. arXiv:2008.06545 [hep-ph] (2022)

26. "OxfordLanguages". https://languages.oup.com/google-dictionary-en/

27. The American Association of Physics Teachers (AAPT): Statement on Computational Physics (2023). https://www.aapt.org/Resources/policy/Statement-on-Computational-Physics.cfm

28. Hardt, M., Recht, B.: Patterns, Predictions, and Actions. Princeton University Press, Princeton (2022)

29. Kasieczka, G., Nachman, B., Shih, D., et al.: The LHC Olympics 2020. Rep. Prog. Phys. **84**, 12 IOP Publishing (2021). arXiv:2101.08320 [hep-ph]

Data Science and Applications

A Robust Ensemble Machine Learning Model with Advanced Voting Techniques for Comment Classification

Ariful Islam Shiplu[1]📷, Md. Mostafizer Rahman[1,2]($\boxtimes$)📷, and Yutaka Watanobe[2]📷

[1] Dhaka University of Engineering & Technology, Gazipur, Bangladesh
mostafiz26@gmail.com, mostafiz@duet.ac.bd
[2] The University of Aizu, Aizuwakamatsu, Japan
yutaka@u-aizu.ac.jp

Abstract. In the modern era, we find ourselves immersed in an ever-expanding flow of data where data is increasing exponentially. Data is generated from different platforms like Education, Business, E-commerce, and predominantly, social media platforms such as Twitter, YouTube, Facebook, and Instagram. Amidst this proliferation of content, user comments have emerged as a crucial element, serving as a platform for expressions of opinions, commendations, and critiques. However, within the abundance of user feedback lies a persistent issue: the presence of undesirable comments that elicit negative emotional responses and prove to be tedious and irrelevant. Effectively identifying and removing such comments poses a major challenge. This research addresses the imperative need for a robust comment classification model. To tackle this issue, a comprehensive investigation is conducted, employing a variety of machine learning models, including Decision Trees, Random Forests (RF), Naive Bayes, K-Nearest Neighbors, Gradient Boosting, AdaBoost, Logistic Regression, and Support Vector Machines (SVM) for comment classification. Furthermore, fundamental voting techniques such as Hard-Voting, Averaging, and Soft-Voting are incorporated with machine learning models to improve the classification performance. The objective is to discern the characteristics of text comments, classifying them, with the aim of achieving superior accuracy compared to prior research. In this paper, we propose a robust ensemble model, *RF+AdaBoost+SVM+Soft-Voting*, specifically designed for comment classification. The results obtained indicate that the proposed ensemble model achieved an impressive accuracy of approximately 98% for comment classification on YouTube dataset.

Keywords: Ensemble Model · Machine Learning · Voting Techniques · Comment Classification · Soft-Voting · Hard-Voting · Averaging

A. I. Shiplu and M. M. Rahman—Contributed Equally to this Research.

1 Introduction

In the contemporary digital landscape, the proliferation of comments across diverse online platforms, ranging from social media to e-commerce, education, and news, has become a ubiquitous phenomenon. These user-generated comments hold significant sway, influencing crucial decisions such as online purchasing choices, assessing the informational value of educational content, and gauging the sentiment, whether positive or negative, on social media posts. Additionally, in the context of news consumption, comments serve as a critical lens for discerning the authenticity of information, distinguishing between factual reporting and the propagation of rumors. Similarly, within the realm of online video content, comments offer insights into the perceived value of the material, whether it is regarded as informative or merely a superfluous diversion. Moreover, comments wield substantial influence in shaping public opinion, particularly in the political domain, where the sentiments expressed by ordinary citizens towards governmental figures can indicate levels of support or opposition. Thus, leveraging comments effectively becomes pivotal in optimizing time utilization, curbing the spread of misinformation, and fostering the dissemination of accurate and relevant information.

YouTube, recognized as the foremost video-sharing platform, has attained remarkable success in the digital realm for its ability to deliver information quickly and easily through video [21]. With a staggering user base of 2.7 billion individuals, it stands as the second most popular online platform, offering an extensive array of content categories, including educational videos, vlogs, news, unboxing presentations, gaming content, and more. Wattenhofer et al. investigate YouTube's social network dynamics, analyzing its subscription graph, comment graph, and video content corpus, revealing deviations from traditional online social networks and striking similarities to Twitter [47]. Tufekci [45] highlights the problem with YouTube's recommendation algorithm that leads users to extremist content regardless of their initial viewing preferences, thereby potentially increasing political polarization and promoting divisive ideologies. As the platform continues to evolve, the volume of videos uploaded to YouTube is escalating steadily, paralleled by a commensurate increase in user-generated comments on these videos. Regrettably, among these comments lurk undesired and intrusive remarks, often referred to as spam. The proliferation of such spam comments poses a formidable challenge for YouTube's administrative authorities. Despite the platform's efforts to implement its own spam classifying system, it remains susceptible to the persistence of spam in various instances.

Machine learning (ML), as a subset of artificial intelligence (AI) [19], empowers systems to autonomously learn and enhance their performance based on experiences [4], without explicit programming. It offers new solutions to complex problems that traditional methods might struggle to solve [8]. It involves the development of computer programs capable of accessing, analyzing, and learning from data independently. The primary objective of ML is to facilitate automatic learning and adjustment of computer systems without direct human intervention [9]. This field encompasses the construction of algorithms that receive and analyze input data, utilizing statistical analysis to predict output values within an acceptable range [20]. By enabling computers to learn from data, recognize patterns [11], and make decisions with minimal human intervention, ML has garnered significant attention across various fields. Usman et al. [1] employed Naive Bayes and Support Vector Machine (SVM) algorithms for comment classification from Twitter, and compared the precision, recall, and F-1 scores of the two algorithms. Hayoung Oh et al. [29] applied an Ensemble Machine Learning model for spam comment detection from YouTube, achieving approximately 95% accuracy based on their experimental analysis.

In the domain of comment classification, existing ML models demonstrate commendable performance; however, there remains significant scope for improvement. To address this gap, we propose an ensemble ML model with an advanced voting technique to improve the comment classification performance. In this paper, we leveraged a total of eight supervised ML algorithms and three powerful voting techniques: Hard-Voting (max voting), Averaging, and Soft-Voting (Weighted Averaging). Moreover, we crafted eight (08) ensemble models with various combinations of supervised ML algorithms and evaluated their accuracy. This paper makes the following contributions:

1. We propose a robust ensemble model (*Random Forest+AdaBoost+SVM+ Soft-Voting*) designed for text/comment classification, addressing the persistent need for improved performance in this domain.
2. We conducted experiments with the proposed ensemble model using a real-world dataset (YouTube Video Comments). Additionally, we compared the results obtained from the model with those of other state-of-the-art models.
3. The proposed ensemble model (*Random Forest+AdaBoost+SVM+Soft-Voting*) achieved Precision, Recall, F1-Score, and Accuracy scores of 98.00%, 97.96%, 97.96%, and 97.96%, respectively, for the comment classification task. Extensive experimentation and analysis highlight the superior efficacy of the proposed model compared to existing models. Notably, its performance surpasses that of prior models, representing a substantial advancement in the field of comment classification.

2 Background and Related Work

In this paper, we studied a wide range of literature from various application domains, encompassing text, comment, video, image, and program code classification.

2.1 Text Classification

Classify the text is more tricky that are generate from different sources like Social media [32], Business [17], and E-commerce [49]. Supervised ML algorithm and LSTM were utilized for text classification from Turkish language context [3]. For agriculture text classifications, a multi-sensor ML algorithm is used [38]. Canché et al. classify Big Textual Data by aggregating all texts and configuring each input file [15]. Belcastro et al. classify the social media text for analyzing the voter behavior in the presidential election campaign 2020 USA [7]. Allcott et al. showed how important media is in promoting election news in the 20th century and highlighted the impact of fake news in the 2016 USA election [2]. Aral et al. outline strategies for safeguarding elections from social media influence and give some solutions like hardening democracy [5].

2.2   Programming Code Classification

Watanobe et al. proposed a CNN model for code classification tasks by using the structural features of code [46]. Rahman et al. [35] proposed a sequential language model using LSTM for source code classification. A Bidirectional LSTM model is utilized for code evaluation and repair. In their work, the proposed Bidirectional LSTM model obtained a 97% F1-score for code classification task [36]. Tang et al. propose an innovative approach (CSGVD) and integrate sequence and graph embedding techniques to improve vulnerability detection in code [43]. Maiya et al. [26] proposed a low-code Python library, that contributes to the accessibility of ML by providing a unified interface for building, training, and applying sophisticated models to text, vision, graph, and tabular data.

2.3   Social Media Comment Classification

Madden et al. contribute significantly to the development of a comprehensive classification schema for YouTube comments, which provides a structured framework for organizing and understanding the multifaceted nature of user interactions and communications within the dynamic space of YouTube [24]. In study [29], an ensemble ML model was utilized for spam comment identification from YouTube. In their work, they found around 95% accuracy from the experimental analysis. Rodriguez et al. [39] employ various classifiers and deep learning techniques for comment classification. In their study, they present a comprehensive system that effectively detects spam tweets and evaluates their associated sentiments, offering an important contribution to mitigating spam-related challenges. Prasad et al. [34] introduced a stacked ensemble model and conducted a thorough analysis of YouTube comments.

2.4   Ensemble Techniques for Classification

Raza [37] used an ML algorithm and majority voting technique for accurate prediction of heart disease, which achieved a remarkable accuracy of 88.88%. Kumari et al. [23] focused on a combination of ML algorithms including RF, Logistic Regression, and Naive Bayes to predict diabetes mellitus with a high accuracy of 79.04% in the PIMA Indians diabetes dataset. This innovative method makes a significant contribution to the early detection and prediction of diabetes, demonstrating its potential to improve healthcare outcomes, and the method's effectiveness is further highlighted by applying it to a breast cancer dataset, where it achieves 97.02% accuracy. The study [28] provides an overview of the perspectives, concepts, algorithms and applications of ensemble learning.

3   Supervised Machine Learning Algorithms

Decision Tree: The decision tree algorithm is renowned for its simplicity and interpretability, making it a favored choice in data analysis, particularly when dealing with large datasets [25]. It inherently incorporates a built-in feature selection mechanism, allowing it to determine the most influential features for making accurate predictions. Represented in a tree-like structure, the decision tree efficiently classifies data elements based on a series of hierarchical decisions, enabling users to gain valuable insights into the underlying data patterns and decision-making processes [16]. The Gini Impurity is calculated as follows.

$$I_G(p) = \sum_{i=1}^{J} p_i(1 - p_i) \tag{1}$$

The Entropy can be written as follows.

$$\text{Entropy}(D) = -\sum_{i=1}^{C} p(i) \log_2 p(i) \tag{2}$$

The Information Gain is given by:

$$\text{Gain}(D, A) = \text{Entropy}(D) - \sum_{v \in \text{Values}(A)} \frac{|D_v|}{|D|} \text{Entropy}(D_v) \tag{3}$$

Here, $I_G(p)$ represents the Gini impurity for a set of samples at a node, Entropy(D) stands for the entropy of the data set D, and Gain(D, A) denotes the information gain for a specific attribute A with respect to the dataset D. The decision tree efficiently categorizes comments as *ham* or *spam* by traversing learned nodes during training, considering features like words, patterns, or linguistic cues. It assigns a class at the leaf node based on the majority label, ensuring accurate classification guided by learned decision criteria.

Random Forest Tree: The Random Forest (RF) classifier acts as a composite container of multiple decision trees trained on different subsets of the dataset [44], utilizing averaging to boost predictive accuracy. Known for its robustness, it efficiently handles various data complexities, including categorical data, imbalanced datasets, and missing values [31]. This method harnesses the collective strength of diverse decision trees, making it a powerful and dependable tool for accurate predictions, even in challenging data scenarios. For comment classification using RF, individual trees categorize the comment, and the final decision is made through aggregation, typically by voting or averaging, to determine whether it's *ham* or *spam*.

Naive Bayes: Bayes' theorem serves as an intuitive expression to quantify the extent of belief in a particular hypothesis given a specific piece of evidence [22]. It is a fundamental principle in probability theory that enables the calculation of conditional probabilities. The Naive Bayes algorithm, a prevalent classification technique in ML, is rooted in Bayes' theorem of conditional probabilities [16]. Here is the formula of Naive Bayes theorem: The product rule is given as:

$$P(H \cap E) = P(H|E) \cdot P(H) \tag{4}$$

$$P(H \cap E) = P(E \cap H) \tag{5}$$

$$P(H \cap E) \cdot P(E) = P(E|H) \cdot P(H) \tag{6}$$

Hence, the Bayes theorem is:

$$P(H|E) = \frac{P(E|H) \cdot P(H)}{P(E)} \tag{7}$$

where H = Hypothesis, E= Evidence. The Naive Bayes classification algorithm categorizes comments as *ham* or *spam* by calculating the probabilities of each class given the comment's features, assuming feature independence. This probabilistic framework allows the algorithm to make informed decisions, enhancing efficiency in tasks like email filtering and social media content moderation, where it assesses whether P(ham|feature) > P(spam|feature), to classify a comment as *ham*.

K-Nearest Neighbor: The K-nearest neighbor (K-NN) algorithm is renowned for its simplicity, interpretability, and effectiveness in classification tasks [42]. It stores all available cases and classifies new cases based on their similarity to existing cases, usually through distance metrics. By considering the k closest data points, it assigns class labels based on the most prevalent class among these neighbors. This intuitive approach aids in easy interpretation and facilitates its widespread application in diverse fields such as pattern recognition, recommendation systems, and data mining [16]. The similarity distance can be computed utilizing the following metrics. The Minkowski distance is given by:

$$D_p(X, Y) = \left(\sum_{i=1}^{n} |X_i - Y_i|^p \right)^{1/p} \tag{8}$$

where X and Y are vectors. The Manhattan distance (Taxicab distance) is expressed as follows:

$$d_T(x, y) = |x_1 - x_2| + |y_1 - y_2| \tag{9}$$

where (x_1, y_1) and (x_2, y_2) are points in a plane. The Euclidean distance is written as follows:

$$d = \sqrt{(x_2 - x_1)^2 + (y_2 - y_1)^2} \tag{10}$$

where (x_1, y_1) and (x_2, y_2) are points in a two-dimensional space. The formula for the K-NN algorithm is:

$$\hat{y} = \text{mode}(y_i)_{i \in \text{KNN}(x)} \tag{11}$$

where $\hat{y}$ is the predicted output for a new input x, KNN(x) represents the set of k nearest data points to x, and y_i is the output associated with the ith data point in the set. The function mode returns the most frequently occurring output in the set of outputs from the nearest neighbors. The K-NN algorithm can classify a new comment as *ham* or *spam* by examining the labels of its nearest neighbors in the numerical feature space, typically constructed using methodologies like TF-IDF. If the majority of these neighbors are labeled as *ham*, the algorithm assigns the same label to the new comment; conversely, if the majority are labeled as *spam*, the algorithm designates the new comment as *spam*, capitalizing on the premise that comments with similar numerical representations often belong to the same class.

Support Vector Machine: The Support Vector Machine (SVM) is recognized as a straightforward yet robust ML algorithm that yields accurate results while demanding relatively less computational power [48], adept at handling linear and nonlinear data separation by maximizing the margin between data points and a hyperplane, commonly a line. SVM effectively avoids overfitting [18]. By leveraging the kernel trick, SVM can address complex, non-linear problems [41]. SVM can classify comments as *ham* or *spam* by converting text into numerical feature vectors. Trained on labeled data, SVM efficiently assigns a new comment to a category based on its position relative to the established hyperplane, streamlining the classification process.

AdaBoost: AdaBoost is a clever technique in ML that teams up several *weak* learners to make better predictions [40]. By combining these less powerful models, AdaBoost boosts overall accuracy, creating a stronger and more reliable predictive system.

Gradient Boosting: Gradient Boosting is an ML technique for regression and classification problems. Gradient Boosting of regression trees yields effective and resilient models for both regression and classification, particularly suitable for handling noisy or incomplete data [13]. The final prediction is produced by the following formula,

$$y(pred) = y1 + (\eta * r1) + (\eta * r2) + \dots + (\eta * rN) \tag{12}$$

4   Ensemble Model

Ensemble methods have emerged as a powerful technique in the field of ML, aimed at mitigating the impact of noise, variance, and bias on the learning models [10]. These factors significantly contribute to the error in predictions and can impede the overall accuracy and stability of ML algorithms. By combining several base models [28,33], ensemble methods strive to create an optimal model that surpasses the limitations of individual weak learners. It is crucial to differentiate between strong and weak learners in this context. A strong learner exhibits a high accuracy in prediction, while a weak learner demonstrates relatively lower accuracy. The ensemble methods excel in transforming a system of these weak learners into a single robust learning system, thus capitalizing on the diverse capabilities of each individual model to achieve enhanced performance and predictive accuracy. Figure 1 shows a basic block diagram of the ensemble model.

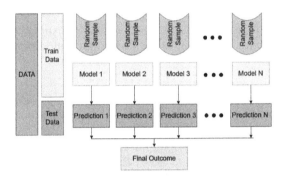

Fig. 1. A fundamental block diagram of ensemble model

4.1   Hard-Voting (Max-Voting)

Majority voting ensemble techniques involve combining predictions from multiple separate models to produce a final prediction [14]. The equation for Hard-Voting is given by:

$$\sum_{t=1}^{T} d_{t,j} = \max_{j} \sum_{t=1}^{T} d_{t,j} \tag{13}$$

where $j = 1, 2, 3, \cdots J$ and $t = 1, 2, 3, \cdots T$ are the number of classes and classifiers, respectively. $d_{t,j}$ is the decision function/classifier. $\max_j \sum_{t=1}^{T} d_{t,j}$ calculates the maximum number of predictions for a class j by the classifiers $d_{t,j}$.

4.2   Averaging

The ensemble averaging technique refers to a method used in ML and statistics to combine predictions from multiple models. The equation for Averaging is given by:

$$\hat{y} = \frac{1}{N} \sum_{i=1}^{N} f_i(x) \tag{14}$$

where $\hat{y}$ is the predicted output or label. N is the total number of individual models or base learners in the ensemble. $\sum_{i=1}^{N} f_i(x)$ is the sum of the predictions made by each base learner $f_i(x)$ for a given input x. $\frac{1}{N}$ is the reciprocal of the total number of models, representing the averaging process.

4.3   Soft-Voting (Weighted-Averaging)

Soft-Voting is a technique where the predicted probabilities of each class by individual models are averaged to determine the final class label [23]. The equation is given by:

$$\hat{y} = \frac{\sum_{i=1}^{N} w_i f_i(x)}{\sum_{i=1}^{N} w_i} \tag{15}$$

where $\hat{y}$ is the predicted output or label. N is the total number of individual models or base learners in the ensemble. w_i is the weight assigned to the prediction of the i-th base learner. Each base learner's prediction is multiplied by its corresponding weight. $\sum_{i=1}^{N} w_i f_i(x)$ is used for summing up the weighted predictions made by each base learner $f_i(x)$ for a given input x. $\sum_{i=1}^{N} w_i$ is the sum of the weights, representing the total weight assigned to all base learners. It's used to normalize the weighted sum of predictions.

5   Methodology

5.1   Text Preprocessing

The text preprocessing procedure begins with reading the data, followed by tokenization to break the text into individual words. Subsequently, punctuation is removed, and the text is converted to lowercase to standardize the input. Stopwords, commonly occurring words with minimal semantic meaning, are then removed. Finally, lemmatization or stemming is applied to further normalize the words by reducing them to their base or root form. Figure 2a shows the comprehensive preprocessing pipeline that enhances the quality and consistency of textual data for subsequent natural language processing tasks.

Figure 2b illustrates an example of text preprocessing. The process begins with data ingestion, followed by tokenization to segment the text into individual units. Punctuation is subsequently removed, and the text is converted to lowercase for standardization. Stopwords are then eliminated, and the words undergo lemmatization or stemming to enhance the overall quality and coherence of the textual data.

5.2   Proposed Ensemble Model

In this paper, we propose a robust ensemble ML model with advanced voting techniques to efficiently classify comments, as shown in Fig. 3. The fundamental comment preprocessing steps, as depicted in Fig. 2b, are executed prior to

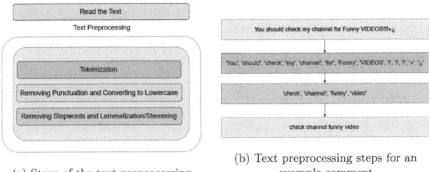

(a) Steps of the text preprocessing

(b) Text preprocessing steps for an example comment

Fig. 2. Text processing steps and an example of text processing

feeding the data into the ensemble model for training and testing. It is noted that lemmatization and stemming techniques are utilized to normalize the comments. Next, a Soft-Voting ensemble technique is employed to consolidate predictions from three baseline ML models (e.g., RF, AdaBoost, and SVM) with the aim of improving comment classification performance. The structure of the proposed ensemble model is *RF+AdaBoost+SVM+Soft-Voting*. Finally, the ensemble model is employed to classify the comments as either *Ham* or *Spam*.

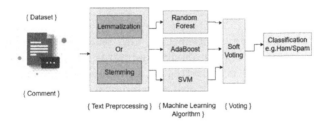

Fig. 3. Schematic diagram of the proposed ensemble model for comment classification

5.3 Evaluation Metrics

To assess the performance of the proposed ensemble comment classification model, the attributes such as True Positive (TP), True Negative (TN), False Positive (FP), and False Negative (FN) from the confusion matrix are used.

Accuracy: The accuracy metric is a pivotal performance indicator within the context of predictive modeling. It signifies the ratio of all correctly predicted samples, including both TP and TN, to the overall count of samples present in the dataset used for evaluation [6]. The accuracy of a model can be calculated using Eq. 16.

$$\text{Accuracy (A)} = \frac{TN + TP}{TN + FN + TP + FP} \tag{16}$$

Precision: Precision, denoting the ratio of TP to all samples classified as positive, serves as a measure of the model's accuracy in predicting positive instances [48]. This metric quantifies the model's capability to avoid FP by reflecting the proportion of correctly identified positive cases from the total predicted positive cases. The precision can be calculated using Eq. 17.

$$\text{Precision (P)} = \frac{TP}{TP + FP} \tag{17}$$

Recall: The recall, often referred to as sensitivity, represents the ratio between the number of tp and the total count of all samples whose true class is the positive category. It primarily emphasizes the proportion of all correct predictions for the positive class (TP) among all positive actual classes, encompassing the entire set of positive classes in the population or dataset [48]. Equation 18 uses for the Recall calculation.

$$\text{Recall (R)} = \frac{TP}{TP + FN} \tag{18}$$

F1-Score: The F1 score gauges how well a model performs by combining Precision and Recall into a single value. It calculates the harmonic mean of these two metrics to provide a comprehensive evaluation of accuracy [12,16].

$$\text{F1-Score} = 2 \times \frac{\text{precision} \times \text{recall}}{\text{precision} + \text{recall}} \tag{19}$$

5.4 Experimental Environment

We conducted experiments with supervised machine learning algorithms and basic ensemble techniques. All experiments were performed on a system running Windows 11, equipped with an AMD Ryzen 5 5600G processor (up to 4.4 GHz, 6 cores, 12 threads) and 8 GB DDR4 RAM.

6 Experimental Result

In this research, we use a YouTube dataset [29], which is a public dataset of comments collected on five popular music videos. The dataset includes a total of 1,956 authentic comments, as shown in Table 1. This dataset consists of two labels/classes: *Ham* and *Spam*. The comment content, along with the labeled class, is utilized for model training and testing.

Table 1. Dataset of YouTube video comments

Sl	Datasets	Ham	Spam	Total
1	Psy	175	175	350
2	KatyPerry	175	175	350
3	LMFAO	202	236	438
4	Eminen	203	245	448
5	Shakira	196	174	370
	Total	951	1005	1956

A comprehensive experiment is carried out in this research. First, we investigated the classification performances of various supervised ML models. Second, we carried out experiments on various ensemble models incorporating voting techniques. Table 2 presents the classification results of various supervised ML algorithms when the *stemming* method is employed for text processing. The decision tree exhibits the highest performance, achieving Precision, Recall, and F1-Score values of 0.969414, 0.969388, and 0.969390, respectively. In comparison, the second-best result is obtained by the RF tree, with Precision, Recall, and F1-Score values of 0.962793, 0.962585, and 0.962589, respectively.

Table 2. Quantitative results for comment classification while applying Stemming

Model	Precision	Recall	F1-Score
K-NN	0.806122	0.714286	0.693394
Decision Tree	0.969414	0.969388	0.969390
Random Forest	0.962793	0.962585	0.962589
Gradient Boosting	0.948282	0.942177	0.942052
AdaBoost	0.952600	0.948980	0.948926
Logistic Regression	0.938912	0.935374	0.935306
Naive Bayes	0.862245	0.857143	0.856424
SVM Linear	0.938690	0.931973	0.931803

When employing the *lemmatization* method for text processing, Table 3 displays the classification results. In this context, the RF tree yielded the highest classification results, achieving Precision, Recall, and F1-Score values of 0.969546, 0.959184, and 0.959187, respectively. The decision tree and Adaboost produced relatively better results, with Precision, Recall, and F1-Score values of 0.956860, 0.955782, and 0.955779, respectively. The text preprocessing methods, specifically *stemming* and *lemmatization*, have demonstrated a significant impact on comment classification results. The experimental findings reveal that supervised ML models yield better results when the *stemming* method is applied

Table 3. Quantitative results for comment classification while applying Lemmatization

Model	Precision	Recall	F1-Score
K-NN	0.827910	0.734694	0.716356
Decision Tree	0.956860	0.955782	0.955779
Random Forest	0.969546	0.959184	0.959187
Gradient Boosting	0.948282	0.942177	0.942052
AdaBoost	0.956860	0.955782	0.955779
Logistic Regression	0.945756	0.942177	0.942116
Naive Bayes	0.861123	0.857143	0.856558
SVM Linear	0.941404	0.935374	0.935234

for text processing compared to *lemmatization*, as illustrated in Tables 2 and 3. The Decision Tree algorithm achieved an F1-score of approximately 97% with *stemming*, while the RF tree attained an F1-score of approximately 96% with *lemmatization*. With the exception of the Naive Bayes algorithm, other models demonstrated relatively good results for both *stemming* and *lemmatization*.

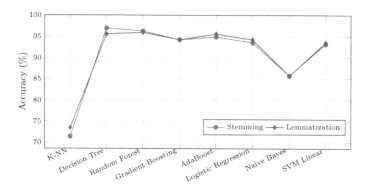

Fig. 4. Comment classification accuracy of the ML models for *stemming* and *lemmatization*

Moreover, the classification accuracy of the supervised ML models is calculated, as depicted in Fig. 4. It is evident that the Decision Tree achieved the highest classification accuracy of approximately 97% when employing the *stemming* method for text processing. On the other hand, the Naive Bayes algorithm yields lower accuracy compared to the other models.

To determine the optimal ensemble model, we designed eight (08) ensemble models using supervised ML algorithms, as outlined in Table 4. Subsequently, we conducted experiments on these ensemble models employing various voting techniques. Table 5 presents the classification results of the ensemble models with the *Soft-Voting* technique. Model-1 attains the highest Precision, Recall, and F1-Score values of 0.979958, 0.979592, and 0.979594, respectively. Additionally, Model-4 achieves relatively better Precision, Recall, and F1-Score values of 0.976758, 0.97619, and 0.976192, respectively. Table 6 displays the comment classification results of the ensemble models with the *Averaging* technique. Model-1 stands out with the highest Precision, Recall, and F1-Score, which are 0.9736, 0.972789, and 0.972789, respectively, compared to the other ensemble models.

Table 4. List of ensemble models for analysis and experiments

Model	Algorithm
Model-1	Random Forest + AdaBoost + Support Vector Machine
Model-2	Random Forest + GradientBoosting + AdaBoost + Support Vector Machine
Model-3	Decision Tree + Random Forest + Support Vector Machine
Model-4	Random Forest + Support Vector Machine
Model-5	Random Forest + Logistic Regression + Support Vector Machine
Model-6	Random Forest + GradientBoosting + Logistic Regression + Support Vector Machine
Model-7	Decision Trees + Random Forests + Naive Bayes + Gradient Boosting + AdaBoost + Logistic Regression + Linear Support Vector Machines
Model-8	Decision Trees + Random Forests + Naive Bayes + K-NN + Gradient Boosting + AdaBoost + Logistic Regression + Linear Support Vector Machines

Table 5. Quantitative results for comment classification using Soft-Voting

Model	Precision	Recall	F1-Score
Model-1	**0.979958**	**0.979592**	**0.979594**
Model-2	0.967406	0.965986	0.96598
Model-3	0.969596	0.969388	0.969391
Model-4	0.976758	0.97619	0.976192
Model-5	0.967406	0.965986	0.96598
Model-6	0.970483	0.969388	0.969385
Model-7	0.967406	0.965986	0.96598
Model-8	0.967406	0.965986	0.96598

Table 7 displays the classification results of the ensemble models using the *Hard-Voting* technique. In this scenario, Model-1 achieved the highest Precision, Recall, and F1-Score, with values of 0.970483, 0.969388, and 0.969385, respectively, surpassing the other seven (07) ensemble models. Although all the ensemble models achieved credible classification results across the three voting techniques, Model-1 outperformed the other models. Specifically, Model-1 obtained

Table 6. Quantitative results for comment classification using Averaging

Model	Precision	Recall	F1-Score
Model-1	**0.9736**	**0.972789**	**0.972789**
Model-2	0.9526	0.94898	0.948926
Model-3	0.959546	0.959184	0.959187
Model-4	0.933358	0.92517	0.924927
Model-5	0.949749	0.945578	0.945508
Model-6	0.944152	0.938776	0.938662
Model-7	0.970483	0.969388	0.969385
Model-8	0.93869	0.931973	0.931803

the best results when employing the *Soft-Voting* technique, clearly establishing itself as the superior ensemble model. Additionally, we calculated the accuracy of the ensemble models to determine the optimal model, as illustrated in Fig. 5. Model-1 achieved the highest accuracy, approximately 98%, when utilizing the *Soft-Voting* technique, which is notably superior to the other models.

Table 7. Quantitative results for comment classification using Hard-Voting

Model	Precision	Recall	F1-Score
Model-1	**0.970483**	**0.969388**	**0.969385**
Model-2	0.941404	0.935374	0.935234
Model-3	0.959546	0.959184	0.959187
Model-4	0.933358	0.92517	0.924927
Model-5	0.949749	0.945578	0.945508
Model-6	0.945756	0.942177	0.942116
Model-7	0.970483	0.969388	0.969385
Model-8	0.93869	0.931973	0.931803

In the domain of comment classification, various methods have been explored to enhance accuracy. In prior studies, Mehmood et al. [27] demonstrated a promising accuracy of 92.19% using methods such as Gradient Boosted Trees (GBT) and RF, combined with tokenization and stemming techniques. Othman et al. [30] achieved a mentionable accuracy of 87% employing methods like Naive Bayes, logistic regression, K-NN, and SVM. Hayoung Oh [29] introduced an ensemble model utilizing the *Soft-Voting* technique, achieving a high accuracy of 95.06%. However, our proposed ensemble model with the *Soft-Voting* technique surpasses the results of prior research, achieving an impressive accuracy of approximately 98%. This improvement underscores the potential of our proposed ensemble model to significantly elevate comment classification accuracy.

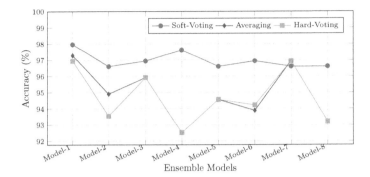

Fig. 5. Comment classification accuracy of ensemble models using different voting techniques

7 Conclusion

The classification of comments has emerged as a crucial research area due to the proliferation of comments from diverse sources, including social media, education, business, programming, and medical platforms. Effectively filtering out toxic comments from this vast sea of user-generated content has become a focal point for researchers. In this paper, we designed eight (08) ensemble ML models utilizing advanced voting techniques to determine the most suitable ensemble model for comment classification. The experiments are conducted using the YouTube dataset, which consists of two classes: *ham* or *spam*. According to the experimental results, the ensemble model *RF+AdaBoost+SVM+Soft-Voting* achieved the highest classification accuracy of 98% compared to other models. Therefore, in this paper, we propose the adoption of the best-fit ensemble model *RF+AdaBoost+SVM+Soft-Voting* for classifying comments. Furthermore, we conducted a comparative analysis with previous research. To the best of our knowledge, a study [29] reported the highest accuracy of approximately 95.06% for comment classification on the YouTube dataset. In contrast, our proposed ensemble model achieved a classification accuracy of approximately 98% on the same dataset, surpassing the previous results.

For future work, we aim to explore the performance of other ensemble models, such as Stacking and Blending, on diverse datasets from platforms like YouTube, Twitter, and Programming Learning.

References

1. Abubakar, U.B.U.: A comparison analysis of twitter based support vector machine and Bayes comment classification algorithms. Artif. Comput. Intell. (2020)
2. Allcott, H., Gentzkow, M.: Social media and fake news in the 2016 election. J. Econ. Perspect. **31**(2), 211–236 (2017)
3. Alzoubi, Y.I., Topcu, A.E., Erkaya, A.E.: Machine learning-based text classification comparison: Turkish language context. Appl. Sci. **13**(16), 9428 (2023)

4. Alzubi, J., Nayyar, A., Kumar, A.: Machine learning from theory to algorithms: an overview. In: Journal of Physics: Conference Series, vol. 1142, p. 012012. IOP Publishing (2018)
5. Aral, S., Eckles, D.: Protecting elections from social media manipulation. Science **365**(6456), 858–861 (2019)
6. Asthana, P., Hazela, B.: Applications of machine learning in improving learning environment. In: Tanwar, S., Tyagi, S., Kumar, N. (eds.) Multimedia Big Data Computing for IoT Applications. Intelligent Systems Reference Library, vol. 163, pp. 417–433. Springer, Singapore (2020). https://doi.org/10.1007/978-981-13-8759-3_16
7. Belcastro, L., Branda, F., Cantini, R., Marozzo, F., Talia, D., Trunfio, P.: Analyzing voter behavior on social media during the 2020 us presidential election campaign. Soc. Netw. Anal. Min. **12**(1), 83 (2022)
8. Bi, Q., Goodman, K.E., Kaminsky, J., Lessler, J.: What is machine learning? A primer for the epidemiologist. Am. J. Epidemiol. **188**(12), 2222–2239 (2019)
9. Carbonell, J.G., Michalski, R.S., Mitchell, T.M.: An overview of machine learning. Mach. Learn., 3–23 (1983)
10. Dietterich, T.G., et al.: Ensemble learning. Handb. Brain Theory Neural Netw. **2**(1), 110–125 (2002)
11. El Naqa, I., Murphy, M.J.: What is Machine Learning? Springer, Cham (2015)
12. Flach, P., Kull, M.: Precision-recall-gain curves: PR analysis done right. In: Advances in Neural Information Processing Systems, vol. 28 (2015)
13. Friedman, J.H.: Greedy function approximation: a gradient boosting machine. Ann. Statist., 1189–1232 (2001)
14. Gandhi, I., Pandey, M.: Hybrid ensemble of classifiers using voting. In: 2015 International Conference on Green Computing and Internet of Things (ICGCIoT), pp. 399–404. IEEE (2015)
15. González Canché, M.S.: Latent code identification (LACOID): a machine learning-based integrative framework [and open-source software] to classify big textual data, rebuild contextualized/unaltered meanings, and avoid aggregation bias. Int J Qual Methods **22**, 16094069221144940 (2023)
16. Gudivada, V.N., Rao, C.R.: Computational analysis and understanding of natural languages: principles, methods and applications. (No Title) (2018)
17. Halibas, A.S., Shaffi, A.S., Mohamed, M.A.K.V.: Application of text classification and clustering of twitter data for business analytics. In: 2018 Majan International Conference (MIC), pp. 1–7. IEEE (2018)
18. Han, H., Jiang, X.: Overcome support vector machine diagnosis overfitting. Cancer Inform. **13**, CIN–S13875 (2014)
19. Helm, J.M., et al.: Machine learning and artificial intelligence: definitions, applications, and future directions. Curr. Rev. Musculoskelet. Med. **13**, 69–76 (2020)
20. Jordan, M.I., Mitchell, T.M.: Machine learning: trends, perspectives, and prospects. Science **349**(6245), 255–260 (2015)
21. Joseph, A.M., et al.: COVID-19 misinformation on social media: a scoping review. Cureus **14**(4) (2022)
22. Joyce, J.: Bayes' theorem (2003)
23. Kumari, S., Kumar, D., Mittal, M.: An ensemble approach for classification and prediction of diabetes mellitus using soft voting classifier. Int. J. Cogn. Comput. Eng. **2**, 40–46 (2021)
24. Madden, A., Ruthven, I., McMenemy, D.: A classification scheme for content analyses of Youtube video comments. J. Document. **69**(5), 693–714 (2013)

25. Maimon, O.Z., Rokach, L.: Data mining with decision trees: theory and applications, vol. 81. World scientific (2014)

26. Maiya, A.S.: ktrain: a low-code library for augmented machine learning. J. Mach. Learn. Res. **23**(1), 7070–7075 (2022)

27. Mehmood, A., On, B.W., Lee, I., Ashraf, I., Sang Choi, G.: Spam comments prediction using stacking with ensemble learning. In: Journal of Physics: Conference Series, vol. 933, p. 012012. IOP Publishing (2018)

28. Mienye, I.D., Sun, Y.: A survey of ensemble learning: concepts, algorithms, applications, and prospects. IEEE Access **10**, 99129–99149 (2022). https://doi.org/10.1109/ACCESS.2022.3207287

29. Oh, H.: A Youtube spam comments detection scheme using cascaded ensemble machine learning model. IEEE Access **9**, 144121–144128 (2021)

30. Othman, N.F., Din, W.: Youtube spam detection framework using naïve bayes and logistic regression. Indonesian J. Electr. Eng. Comput. Sci. **14**(3), 1508–1517 (2019)

31. Pal, M.: Random forest classifier for remote sensing classification. Int. J. Remote Sens. **26**(1), 217–222 (2005)

32. Patel, P., Mistry, K.: A review: text classification on social media data. IOSR J. Comput. Eng. **17**(1), 80–84 (2015)

33. Polikar, R.: Ensemble learning. Ensemble machine learning: methods and applications, pp. 1–34 (2012)

34. Prasad, G., et al.: Sentiment analysis on cryptocurrency using Youtube comments. In: 2022 6th International Conference on Computing Methodologies and Communication (ICCMC), pp. 730–733. IEEE (2022)

35. Rahman, M.M., Watanobe, Y., Nakamura, K.: Source code assessment and classification based on estimated error probability using attentive LSTM language model and its application in programming education. Appl. Sci. **10**(8), 2973 (2020)

36. Rahman, M.M., Watanobe, Y., Nakamura, K.: A bidirectional LSTM language model for code evaluation and repair. Symmetry **13**(2), 247 (2021)

37. Raza, K.: Improving the prediction accuracy of heart disease with ensemble learning and majority voting rule. In: U-Healthcare Monitoring Systems, pp. 179–196. Elsevier (2019)

38. Reyana, A., Kautish, S., Karthik, P.S., Al-Baltah, I.A., Jasser, M.B., Mohamed, A.W.: Accelerating crop yield: multisensor data fusion and machine learning for agriculture text classification. IEEE Access **11**, 20795–20805 (2023)

39. Rodrigues, A.P., et al.: Real-time twitter spam detection and sentiment analysis using machine learning and deep learning techniques. Comput. Intell. Neurosci. **2022** (2022)

40. Schapire, R.E., Singer, Y.: Improved boosting algorithms using confidence-rated predictions. In: Proceedings of the Eleventh Annual Conference on Computational Learning Theory, pp. 80–91 (1998)

41. Sharma, G., Jurie, F., Pérez, P.: Learning non-linear SVM in input space for image classification. Ph.D. thesis, GREYC CNRS UMR 6072, Universite de Caen (2014)

42. Sun, Y., Ming, Y., Zhu, X., Li, Y.: Out-of-distribution detection with deep nearest neighbors. In: International Conference on Machine Learning, pp. 20827–20840. PMLR (2022)

43. Tang, W., Tang, M., Ban, M., Zhao, Z., Feng, M.: CSGVD: a deep learning approach combining sequence and graph embedding for source code vulnerability detection. J. Syst. Softw. **199**, 111623 (2023)

44. Tani, F.Y., Farid, D.M., Zahidur, M.: Ensemble of decision tree classifiers for mining web data streams. Commun. Appl. Electron. **1**(1), 26–32 (2014)

45. Tufekci, Z.: Youtube, the great radicalizer. N.Y. Times **10**(3), 2018 (2018)
46. Watanobe, Y., Rahman, M.M., Amin, M.F.I., Kabir, R.: Identifying algorithm in program code based on structural features using CNN classification model. Appl. Intell. **53**(10), 12210–12236 (2023)
47. Wattenhofer, M., Wattenhofer, R., Zhu, Z.: The youtube social network. In: Proceedings of the International AAAI Conference on Web and Social Media, vol. 6, pp. 354–361 (2012)
48. Yeturu, K.: Machine learning algorithms, applications, and practices in data science. In: Handbook of Statistics, vol. 43, pp. 81–206. Elsevier (2020)
49. Yıldırım, F.M., Kaya, A., Öztürk, S.N., Kılınç, D.: A real-world text classification application for an e-commerce platform. In: 2019 Innovations in Intelligent Systems and Applications Conference (ASYU), pp. 1–5. IEEE (2019)

Vector-Based Semantic Scenario Search for Vehicular Traffic

A. P. Bhoomika[1]([✉])[ID], Srinath Srinivasa[1][ID], Vijaya Sarathi Indla[2], and Saikat Mukherjee[2]

[1] International Institute of Information Technology, Bengaluru, India
{bhoomika.ap,sri}@iiitb.ac.in
[2] Siemens Technology and Services Private Limited, Bengaluru, India
{indla.vijayasarathi,mukherjee.saikat}@siemens.com

Abstract. Autonomous Vehicles (AVs) are expected to have the potential to impact urban mobility by providing increased safety, reducing traffic congestion, mitigating accidents and reducing emissions. Since AVs operate with little or no human intervention, it is very essential to perceive the external world and understand different objects and their relationships in the scene, and respond appropriately. For doing this effectively, AVs need to be trained on a variety of traffic situations and appropriate responses to them. Behaviour of vehicular traffic varies widely from one part of the world to another. An AV trained for traffic conditions in one part of the world may not be effective, or worse, even be risky in some other part of the world. There is hence a need to create datasets of vehicular traffic scenarios and design mechanisms to query, retrieve and reason about dynamic traffic scenarios. This paper discusses a method for vector based scenario search using a natural language interface for describing traffic scenarios. We first generate textual descriptions of snapshots of traffic scenarios captured from instrumenting vehicles using image captioning libraries. Next, we create vector embeddings of the captions, store them in a vector database to enable semantic scenario search using natural language based queries. This is an ongoing work where different other modalities of scenarios data are planned to be supported over an underlying image captioning and natural language search interface. Experimental results on the image captioning core, show encouraging results.

Keywords: Autonomous Vehicles · Image Captioning · Vector Embeddings · Semantic Scenario search

1 Introduction

In urban areas, where the conventional transportation system is becoming more disorganized and ineffective, technological advancements and automation in vehicle networks will improve road safety and reduce congestion [1]. Hence, there

This work is supported by Siemens Technology and Services Private Limited, Bengaluru, India.

is a need to build the Intelligent Transport Systems (ITS) with the goal of enhancing traffic safety and offering different services to its users. In this regard, Autonomous Vehicles (AVs) hold great potential for enhancing the safety and efficiency of transportation system by their ability to operate and perform all necessary functions with little or no human intervention. AVs have the potential to revolutionize the transportation system by reducing emissions, attenuating fatal crashes, expanding road capacity, and conserving fuel.

The Society of Automotive Engineers (SAE)[1] provide standards for levels of autonomy in AVs graded into five levels, with level 5 being the highest level of autonomy where the AV is expected to perform all driving tasks in all conditions without human attention. To aid this, AVs are typically equipped with multiple sensors of different kinds- including, Camera, LiDAR, Radar, IMU, and GPS sensors. Training AV models for different levels of autonomy requires collection and curation of driving data collected over several test runs called "campaigns". Campaign datasets are typically multi-sensor, multi-modal data extending to petabytes of storage. From this dataset, several scenarios need to be extracted, that represent trainable situations for the AV model. Such scenarios are segments of campaign that contain important events and are made up of a combination of different sensor modalities. For instance, an example scenario might be a segment where the vehicle being driven (also called the *ego vehicle*) made a turn and was immediately encountered by a crossing pedestrian.

It is necessary to understand such traffic scenarios to identify different objects involved in the scene to aid the AV in making major driving decisions. However, traffic scenarios can be arbitrarily complex, comprising of several objects of interest, and several kinds of interactions among them. Describing them formally in order to enable query and retrieval, will require an elaborate language design and formalism.

Given the recent advances in cross-modal embeddings and retrieval, in this paper, we explore the use of natural language constructs to describe complex traffic scenarios and different events occurring in the scene. For this, we rely on image captioning as the core element of our model, which has been shown to be effective in describing traffic situations and scene understanding [8,13,21].

Recently, vector databases have gained popularity for their ability to support semantic search over massive datasets. These databases store vector embeddings of objects and enable users to perform fast similarity for the query. The main goal of our work is to develop a framework to aid semantic scenario search based on natural language queries. Since the traffic scenes are described by captions, we create vector embeddings for them to encapsulate their semantic essence. The vector embeddings corresponding to the different scenes are stored in the vector database and we retrieve the top n similar results based on our query.

Our main contributions are as follows:

– We propose a framework for semantic scenario search wherein, firstly we generate captions for describing the traffic scene using the image captioning

---

[1] https://www.sae.org/.

model. Then, we create embeddings for the captions and perform semantic similarity search on them based on the natural language query.
- We create an image captioning dataset based on nuImages dataset [2] and perform our experiments on the dataset.

The rest of this paper is organized as follows: Sect. 2 explains some related work about image captioning and vector databases. In Sect. 3 the overall system architecture is discussed. The experimental results are described in Sect. 4. At last, conclusions and future work are discussed in Sect. 5.

2   Related Work

2.1   Image Captioning

Image captioning refers to the generation of textual description of images. It involves image understanding, which deals with identifying all the important objects, attributes and their relationships within the image. Then, a language model is employed to generate the image's textual description. Image captioning approaches can be broadly categorized into: 1) Template based approaches, 2) Retrieval-based approaches, and 3) Novel image captioning approaches. Template-based approaches generate the captions using a fixed template that has a number of blank slots in it. The blank slots in the templates are filled with different objects, attributes and actions identified by the captioning model. Though these approaches can generate syntactically correct captions, the templates are predefined and hence they cannot generate variable length captions. In the retrieval based approaches, captions are retrieved from existing set of captions. The images that are visually similar and their corresponding captions are obtained from the training set. These captions form the candidate captions set. The caption for a query image is retrieved from the candidate captions set. These methods can generate syntactically correct captions but they fail to generate semantically correct and image specific captions. Novel image captioning approaches–primarily based on cross-modal deep neural network models–analyze the visual content of the image and then use a language model to generate the captions. The captions generated using this method are more accurate and semantically correct compared to the other approaches [5,15].

Recently, extensive work has been carried out in the field of deep learning based image captioning. Li et al. [7] propose Bootstrapping Language-Image Pre-training for Unified Vision-Language Understanding and Generation (BLIP) image captioning model, which efficiently utilizes the noisy web data by bootstrapping the captions and generates the synthetic captions by filtering the noisy ones. The authors also propose BLIP-2 [6], a new vision-language pertaining method that bootstraps from frozen pre-trained unimodel models. This model also shows the emerging capabilities of zero-shot instructed image-to-text generation. Wang et al. [17] present Generative Image-to-text Transformer (GIT) captioning model which has a simplified architecture with a single image encoder and a single text decoder, and it is designed for a single language modeling task.

Dense captioning provides more descriptive captions of an image. This technique obtains the information about various objects in the scene using different regions in the image. Shaoet et al. [14] present a transformer based dense captioner which learns a mapping between the dense captions and their images using a transformer, thereby focusing on more informative regions in the image. Image captioning requires large number of annotated image-captions pair to train the models. Unsupervised image captioning utilizes unpaired image caption pairs for training the models wherein the text can come from various sources apart from the image. The work proposed by Yang et al. [20] demonstrate several improvements to the training cycle and performance of the existing captioning model. Attention based image captioning techniques dynamically focus on different regions of the image while the textual description is generated [5]. Attention based LSTM image captioning methods produce high quality textual descriptions for the images by combining sequence context and relations [19].

There are quite a few recent works where image captioning has been employed to generate captions for the snapshots of traffic scenes. Li et al. [9] propose an image captioning network to generate more reasonable captions of scenes by integrating element attention into an encoder-decoder mechanism. Seifi et al. [13] present a deep learning based image captioning method to convert traffic images to their descriptions. Li et al. [8] introduce image captioning to Intelligent Transportation System(ITS) inorder to describe traffic scenes and generate high-level semantic information for driving suggestions or strategies. Inorder to provide a comprehensive and reasonable description of complex traffic scenes, Zhang et al. [21] present a traffic scene semantic captioning model with multistage feature enhancement.

2.2   Vector Databases

Semantic information is carried within a particular kind of vector data representation called vector embedding. It is a way of representing semantics of data points in an n-dimensional space, also called as vector space, in which semantically similar data points lie closer with each other. Vector databases [11,16] store and index vector embeddings for fast retrieval and similarity search[2]. They have the capability of traditional databases which is absent in the standalone vector indices like FIASS and are able to handle the vector embeddings which is lacking in scalable traditional databases. As a result, vector databases offer unique support for storing the vector embeddings together with the combined capabilities of standalone vector indexes and traditional databases.

The most popular application of vector databases is semantic similarity search. In contrast to traditional methods of querying the database based on exact match, semantic similarity search retrieves the vectors that are most similar to the query based on semantic similarity metrics like cosine similarity, dot product, euclidean distance and so on.

---

[2] https://www.pinecone.io/.

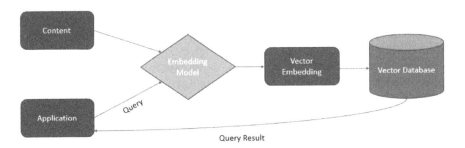

Fig. 1. Vector Similarity Search

Figure 1 depicts the semantic similarity search with vector databases. First, vector embeddings are created for the content using a vector embedding model. Then, the embeddings are indexed and stored in the vector database with a reference to their original content. Next, the same embedding model is used to create the query embedding for the given query. Finally the query embedding is compared with the vector embeddings stored in the database to retrieve the most similar embeddings.

In K-Nearest Neighbor (K-NN) search distance between the query vector and each and every vector in the database is computed to find the similar vectors. It is an exhaustive and inefficient process if the semantic similarity calculation involves millions of vectors. Approximate Nearest Neighbor (ANN) search circumvents this problem by approximating and retrieving the best possible similar results by the losing accuracy in favour of performance gain [4]. Thereby, it provides high speed search with near-perfect accuracy. A combination of different algorithms that facilitate the creation of vector indexes based on hashing, quantization and graph based search are being used for optimizing the query process. All of these algorithms transform the original vector representations into a compressed form for achieving the super fast search and retrieval.

3   Methodology

3.1   Dataset Description

nuImages[3] [2] is a large-scale dataset for autonomous driving with 2D image annotations. The dataset consists of 93000 annotated and 1.1M un-annotated images. The annotated images include rain, snow and night time driving conditions, which are essential for autonomous driving applications. Additionally 6 past and 6 future camera images at 2 Hz for are provided for each annotated image to study the temporal dynamics.

---

[3] https://www.nuscenes.org/nuimages.

3.2   System Architecture

The basic architecture for vector-based semantic scenario search is schematically depicted by Fig. 2. The image captioning model takes the snapshots of the traffic scenarios as the input and generates captions for them. Then, the captions are provided as the input to an embedding model to create vector embeddings and the embeddings are stored in a vector database along with a reference to the original images.

When a text query is submitted by the user, the same embedding model is used to create corresponding query embedding. Finally, the query embedding is compared with all the vector embeddings using the Nearest Neighbor Search (NN Search) and top 'n' semantically similar results are retrieved along with their similarity scores.

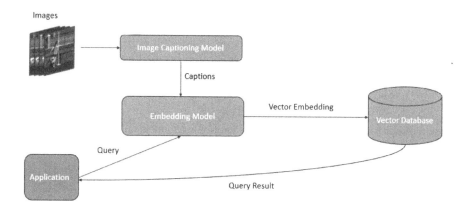

Fig. 2. The Overall System Architecture for Semantic Scenario Search

4   Experimental Setup

4.1   Data Preparation

We created an image captioning dataset based on nuImages dataset, wherein we randomly selected 1000 images and annotated them with text descriptions. The annotated images include vehicles, pedestrians, traffic lights, intersections, rain, snow, and night time which are essential for autonomous driving applications. From the image captioning dataset, we created train set and test set in the ratio 85:15.

4.2   Experimental Results

We considered the pre-trained image captioning models viz., BLIP [7], BLIP-2 [6] and GIT [17] and fine-tuned them using the train dataset for generating relevant captions for the nuImages data. The following metrics are used to evaluate the results of the fine-tuned models:

A. Bilingual Evaluation Understudy (BLEU): This metric counts the percentage of n-grams in the machine translation that overlap with the references to determine how well a translation matches a set of human-generated translations (reference translations) [12].

B. Recall Oriented Understudy of Gisting Evaluation (ROUGE): This metric compares system-generated summaries with reference summaries to measure the quality of a summary. It considers n-gram matching, word pairs between the ideal summaries framed by human subjects and the machine-generated summary [10].

C. Metric for Evaluation of Translation with Explicit Ordering (METEOR): This metric measures the quality of generated captions by considering the exact word matches and the semantic similarities [3].

Table 1 and Table 2 illustrate the aggregated BLEU, ROUGE, and METEOR scores for fine-tuned captioning models. It can be observed that the BLIP model fine-tuned on our image captioning dataset shows better performance compared to the other two models. Hence, we selected fine-tuned BLIP model for caption generation. Figure 3 shows the captions generated by the fine-tuned BLIP model for the test images. It can be observed that captions include the potential objects like traffic lights, pedestrians, vehicles, rain, night time and so on.

Table 1. Performance of fine-tuned image captioning models on our dataset in terms of aggregated ROUGE scores

Model	ROUGE-1	ROUGE-2	ROUGE-L
GIT	63	39	60
BLIP	69	46	65
BLIP-2	65	44	61

Table 2. Performance of fine-tuned image captioning models on our dataset in terms of aggregated BLEU and METEOR scores

Model	BLEU-1	BLEU-2	BLEU-3	BLEU-L	METEOR
GIT	46	36	29	23	55
BLIP	52	41	34	26	64
BLIP-2	55	44	36	29	57

Sentence embedding models are intended to capture a sentence's semantic content in a fixed-length vector. We created vector embeddings for the captions using all-MiniLM-L6-v2 sentence transformer model[4] which embeds the entire caption into a fixed length vector. A total of 93,472 vector embeddings, each of dimension 384, are created. The vectors are stored in the Milvus

---

[4] https://www.sbert.net/.

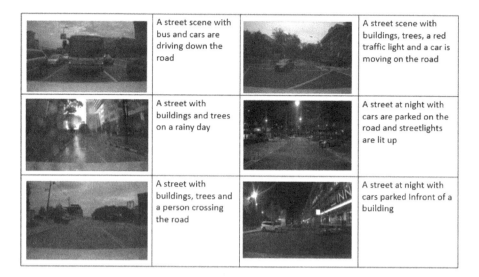

Fig. 3. Image captions generated by fine-tuned BLIP model

vector database [18] and indexed for faster similarity search. Milvus supports indexing techniques[5] that are based on Approximate Nearest Neighbor Search (ANNS) such as HNSW, FLAT, IVF_FLAT, IVF_PQ, IVF_SQ8, ANNOY, and SCANN. In general, a suitable indexing technique is selected to index the vectors based on the scenario. For example, FLAT indexing technique is best suitable in the scenario where accurate and exact search results are required on small, million scale dataset. While HNSW indexing technique is best preferred when there is a high demand for search efficiency.

A text query is embedded by using the same sentence embedding model that is used to create the vector embeddings for the captions. The query embedding is compared with the embeddings stored in the database and top 5 similar results are retrieved based on their similarity. The similarity metrics[6] considered for computing the distance between the vectors are Cosine distance, L2 distance, and Inner Product(IP). The results are finally mapped back to the original images. The Fig. 4 shows the top 5 similar results along with their similarity scores for the query "A street scene with traffic light, cars, and a bus".

Figure 5 shows the comparison of different indexes based on cosine similarity metric. It can be observed that, during the initial runs of the query, there is a significant variation in the search time as the query actually hits the indexes. Almost after 30 iterations of the query, the search time becomes comparably constant across all the indexes. We considered different combinations of similarity metrics and the indexing techniques for optimising the search time for the

---

[5] https://milvus.io/docs/index.md.
[6] https://milvus.io/docs/metric.md.

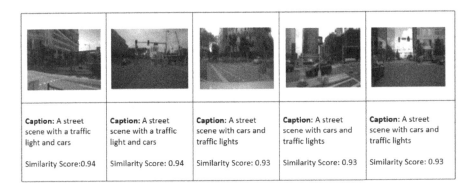

Caption: A street scene with a traffic light and cars	**Caption:** A street scene with a traffic light and cars	**Caption:** A street scene with cars and traffic lights	**Caption:** A street scene with cars and traffic lights	**Caption:** A street scene with cars and traffic lights
Similarity Score:0.94	Similarity Score: 0.94	Similarity Score: 0.93	Similarity Score: 0.93	Similarity Score: 0.93

Fig. 4. Top 5 similar images along with the similarity score for the query: "A street scene with traffic light, cars and a bus"

queries. Tables 3, 4, 5, 6, 7 summarize the performance statistics of five different queries for 30 iterations. It can be observed that the combination of the HSNW index and the cosine distance has best mean search time across all the queries.

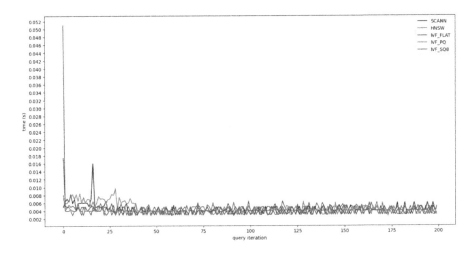

Fig. 5. Comparison of indexes based on Cosine similarity metric

Table 3. Performance statistics for the Query (in seconds): "A street scene with traffic lights"

Index	HSNW			IVF_FLAT			IVF_PQ			IVF_SQ8			SCANN		
Distance Metric	Cosine	L2	IP	Cosine	L2	IP	Cosine	L2	IP	Cosine	L2	IP	Cosine	L2	IP
Count	30	30	30	30	30	30	30	30	30	30	30	30	30	30	30
Mean	0.006927	0.007239	0.006975	0.010405	0.007258	0.008725	0.007192	0.007272	0.006789	0.007002	0.008754	0.008904	0.008177	0.008007	0.006928
Std	0.001284	0.001409	0.001376	0.013712	0.00136	0.008597	0.00147	0.001271	0.001224	0.00157	0.00146	0.001358	0.001931	0.009347	0.001421
Min	0.004998	0.004984	0.004986	0.006	0.005001	0.005883	0.003969	0.004951	0.004	0.004997	0.005991	0.006005	0.00526	0.004991	0.004983
25%	0.006021	0.006014	0.005553	0.007106	0.006003	0.006209	0.006401	0.006362	0.005991	0.005996	0.007987	0.008003	0.007348	0.005997	0.006001
50%	0.006927	0.007163	0.007024	0.008005	0.007085	0.007009	0.007002	0.007309	0.006765	0.007005	0.009017	0.008819	0.007912	0.006303	0.006997
75%	0.007501	0.008004	0.0081	0.008635	0.008133	0.00798	0.008006	0.008104	0.008	0.007962	0.009818	0.009506	0.008603	0.007001	0.00723
Max	0.011002	0.010645	0.009095	0.082855	0.00989	0.053939	0.010538	0.00927	0.008566	0.010901	0.011997	0.01276	0.016659	0.05732	0.012325

Table 4. Performance statistics for the Query (in seconds): "A pedestrian standing next to a vehicle parked on the road"

Index	HSNW			IVF_FLAT			IVF_PQ			IVF_SQ8			SCANN		
Distance Metric	Cosine	L2	IP	Cosine	L2	IP	Cosine	L2	IP	Cosine	L2	IP	Cosine	L2	IP
Count	30	30	30	30	30	30	30	30	30	30	30	30	30	30	30
Mean	0.007641	0.007022	0.006954	0.007384	0.00708	0.00707	0.006691	0.006361	0.007119	0.00632	0.008177	0.007763	0.006829	0.007169	0.00732
Std	0.001184	0.001367	0.001303	0.001323	0.001149	0.001166	0.000971	0.001011	0.001518	0.00136	0.001058	0.001348	0.001318	0.001038	0.001322
Min	0.004994	0.004999	0.004993	0.004979	0.004997	0.005002	0.005995	0.004971	0.004972	0.004004	0.00589	0.004979	0.004005	0.004999	0.005001
25%	0.006905	0.006	0.006026	0.006162	0.006066	0.006012	0.005995	0.005979	0.005997	0.005	0.007638	0.007005	0.006	0.006371	0.006128
50%	0.007658	0.007001	0.006769	0.007017	0.007005	0.006999	0.006757	0.006129	0.007262	0.006517	0.008063	0.007999	0.00677	0.007008	0.006993
75%	0.008111	0.007504	0.007971	0.008493	0.007928	0.008	0.00727	0.007001	0.00823	0.007001	0.008989	0.008659	0.007937	0.008008	0.008375
Max	0.01064	0.010126	0.010005	0.009786	0.009415	0.009429	0.008526	0.008243	0.009999	0.009742	0.010028	0.010209	0.009485	0.009425	0.01021

Table 5. Performance statistics for the Query (in seconds): "Pedestrian standing next to a car parked on the road"

Index	HSNW			IVF_FLAT			IVF_PQ			IVF_SQ8			SCANN		
Distance Metric	Cosine	L2	IP	Cosine	L2	IP	Cosine	L2	IP	Cosine	L2	IP	Cosine	L2	IP
Count	30	30	30	30	30	30	30	30	30	30	30	30	30	30	30
Mean	0.006835	0.007822	0.007749	0.008296	0.007843	0.007293	0.007773	0.006704	0.00831	0.006713	0.008444	0.006943	0.007252	0.007085	0.006686
Std	0.001214	0.00111	0.000987	0.001176	0.001327	0.001399	0.001379	0.001327	0.00169	0.001109	0.00118	0.001103	0.001501	0.001168	0.001088
Min	0.004961	0.005082	0.00601	0.005993	0.004998	0.005169	0.004979	0.004978	0.005413	0.005	0.006458	0.004999	0.004004	0.004998	0.004987
25%	0.005999	0.007068	0.007016	0.00755	0.007005	0.006142	0.007009	0.005569	0.007251	0.005999	0.007411	0.006016	0.006654	0.006064	0.005998
50%	0.006546	0.006797	0.007845	0.008513	0.007549	0.00705	0.00726	0.00651	0.008241	0.006793	0.00825	0.006997	0.007639	0.007048	0.006989
75%	0.007418	0.008671	0.008305	0.008988	0.008835	0.007922	0.008818	0.008	0.009367	0.00737	0.009211	0.007482	0.008169	0.007998	0.007183
Max	0.009578	0.009531	0.009768	0.010139	0.010463	0.011681	0.01049	0.009239	0.012256	0.008548	0.011638	0.010021	0.010198	0.009523	0.009088

Table 6. Performance statistics for the Query (in seconds): "A city street scene with motorcycle parked next to a bus and pedestrian crossing the road"

Index	HSNW			IVF_FLAT			IVF_PQ			IVF_SQ8			SCANN		
Distance Metric	Cosine	L2	IP	Cosine	L2	IP	Cosine	L2	IP	Cosine	L2	IP	Cosine	L2	IP
Count	30	30	30	30	30	30	30	30	30	30	30	30	30	30	30
Mean	0.006855	0.008188	0.00981	0.008247	0.007567	0.008234	0.007662	0.006742	0.007283	0.007992	0.008872	0.008133	0.006633	0.007511	0.010107
Std	0.001138	0.001147	0.007343	0.000957	0.001311	0.001132	0.001268	0.001392	0.001614	0.001756	0.001301	0.002107	0.001077	0.001089	0.002346
Min	0.004983	0.005904	0.006655	0.006002	0.005003	0.006139	0.005617	0.004518	0.004997	0.005527	0.006008	0.004999	0.004999	0.00497	0.006521
25%	0.006012	0.00749	0.007637	0.00751	0.006323	0.007328	0.006716	0.00598	0.006008	0.006998	0.008034	0.007011	0.005998	0.007005	0.008664
50%	0.006797	0.008258	0.008614	0.008227	0.007757	0.008242	0.007536	0.00651	0.006994	0.007628	0.00906	0.007672	0.00602	0.00769	0.009567
75%	0.007534	0.008884	0.009326	0.00894	0.008257	0.008917	0.008643	0.007663	0.008331	0.008941	0.009813	0.00875	0.007501	0.0084	0.011421
Max	0.009739	0.010329	0.048321	0.010067	0.010053	0.010295	0.010175	0.010098	0.011884	0.013687	0.011187	0.016856	0.008552	0.009241	0.015782

Table 7. Performance statistics for the Query (in seconds): "A street scene with a traffic light and street sign and car parked in front of a building and a bike driving down the street"

Index	HSNW			IVF_FLAT			IVF_PQ			IVF_SQ8			SCANN		
Distance Metric	Cosine	L2	IP	Cosine	L2	IP	Cosine	L2	IP	Cosine	L2	IP	Cosine	L2	IP
Count	30	30	30	30	30	30	30	30	30	30	30	30	30	30	30
Mean	0.006463	0.007373	0.009673	0.008905	0.008046	0.007742	0.007215	0.006716	0.008075	0.010043	0.009204	0.008589	0.00677	0.006652	0.008306
Std	0.000909	0.001147	0.001897	0.001247	0.001344	0.001132	0.001188	0.00115	0.001128	0.001291	0.001284	0.001153	0.001054	0.001024	0.000919
Min	0.004952	0.004996	0.007899	0.006652	0.005999	0.005908	0.004998	0.004975	0.006017	0.00712	0.006998	0.006398	0.004989	0.004519	0.006753
25%	0.005995	0.00668	0.008605	0.008057	0.007001	0.006931	0.006024	0.005998	0.007232	0.009007	0.008324	0.007704	0.006002	0.006004	0.007514
50%	0.00611	0.007208	0.009389	0.008975	0.008064	0.007546	0.007014	0.007	0.008387	0.010051	0.009143	0.008536	0.006761	0.006763	0.008475
75%	0.007005	0.008113	0.010274	0.009897	0.008967	0.008445	0.008009	0.007556	0.008775	0.011088	0.010093	0.009399	0.007305	0.007262	0.008835
Max	0.0086	0.010291	0.018476	0.01114	0.011542	0.009896	0.009752	0.009159	0.010266	0.012023	0.011758	0.0111	0.009046	0.008985	0.01002

5 Conclusions and Future Work

AVs need to be trained on specific scenarios extracted from the vehicular traffic dataset for making driving decisions in the autonomous driving scenario. In this paper, we proposed a method for vector based scenario search using a natural language interface for describing traffic scenarios. We employed image captioning technique to generate textual description for the snapshots of traffic scenarios and then we created vector embeddings of the captions. Then, the vector embeddings are stored in the vector database and scenario search is performed to retrieve most similar scenarios in optimal time. We created an image captioning dataset based on nuImages dataset and fine-tuned the image captioning model to generate relevant captions. The experimental results on the fine-tuned captioning model show promising results. We also experimented with different combinations of indexing techniques and semantic similarity search and inferred that the combination of the HSNW index and the Cosine distance has best mean search time across all the queries.

The image captioning model can generate relevant captions for traffic scene image data based on the visual features. However, this method is only capable to recognise the objects in the image and fails to identify the important events like vehicle turns, cut-in maneuvers and so on thereby greatly impacting the driving decisions. As a next step, we want to extend this work to video captioning for captioning the entire traffic scene video data to identify all the important events in the traffic scenario and optimise the query time for the scenario search.

References

1. Ahangar, M.N., Ahmed, Q.Z., Khan, F.A., Hafeez, M.: A survey of autonomous vehicles: enabling communication technologies and challenges. Sensors **21**(3), 706 (2021)
2. Caesar, H., et al.: nuscenes: a multimodal dataset for autonomous driving. In: Proceedings of the IEEE/CVF Conference on Computer Vision and Pattern Recognition, pp. 11621–11631 (2020)
3. Denkowski, M., Lavie, A.: Meteor universal: language specific translation evaluation for any target language. In: Proceedings of the Ninth Workshop on Statistical Machine Translation, pp. 376–380 (2014)
4. Han, Y., Liu, C., Wang, P.: A comprehensive survey on vector database: storage and retrieval technique, challenge. arXiv preprint arXiv:2310.11703 (2023)
5. Hossain, M.Z., Sohel, F., Shiratuddin, M.F., Laga, H.: A comprehensive survey of deep learning for image captioning. ACM Comput. Surv. (CsUR) **51**(6), 1–36 (2019)
6. Li, J., Li, D., Savarese, S., Hoi, S.: BLIP-2: bootstrapping language-image pre-training with frozen image encoders and large language models. arXiv preprint arXiv:2301.12597 (2023)
7. Li, J., Li, D., Xiong, C., Hoi, S.: BLIP: bootstrapping language-image pre-training for unified vision-language understanding and generation. In: International Conference on Machine Learning, pp. 12888–12900. PMLR (2022)

8. Li, W., Qu, Z., Song, H., Wang, P., Xue, B.: The traffic scene understanding and prediction based on image captioning. IEEE Access **9**, 1420–1427 (2020)
9. Li, Y., Wu, C., Li, L., Liu, Y., Zhu, J.: Caption generation from road images for traffic scene modeling. IEEE Trans. Intell. Transp. Syst. **23**(7), 7805–7816 (2021)
10. Lin, C.Y.: ROUGE: a package for automatic evaluation of summaries. In: Text Summarization Branches Out, pp. 74–81 (2004)
11. Pan, J.J., Wang, J., Li, G.: Survey of vector database management systems (2023)
12. Papineni, K., Roukos, S., Ward, T., Zhu, W.J.: BLEU: a method for automatic evaluation of machine translation. In: Proceedings of the 40th Annual Meeting of the Association for Computational Linguistics, pp. 311–318 (2002)
13. Seifi, P., Chalechale, A.: Traffic captioning: deep learning-based method to understand and describe traffic images. In: 2022 8th Iranian Conference on Signal Processing and Intelligent Systems (ICSPIS), pp. 1–6. IEEE (2022)
14. Shao, Z., Han, J., Marnerides, D., Debattista, K.: Region-object relation-aware dense captioning via transformer. IEEE Trans. Neural Netw. Learn. Syst., 1–12 (2022)
15. Sharma, H., Agrahari, M., Singh, S.K., Firoj, M., Mishra, R.K.: Image captioning: a comprehensive survey. In: 2020 International Conference on Power Electronics & IoT Applications in Renewable Energy and Its Control (PARC), pp. 325–328. IEEE (2020)
16. Taipalus, T.: Vector database management systems: fundamental concepts, use-cases, and current challenges. Cogn. Syst. Res. **85**, 101216 (2024)
17. Wang, J., et al.: GIT: a generative image-to-text transformer for vision and language. arXiv preprint arXiv:2205.14100 (2022)
18. Wang, J., et al.: Milvus: a purpose-built vector data management system. In: Proceedings of the 2021 International Conference on Management of Data, pp. 2614–2627 (2021)
19. Xiao, F., Xue, W., Shen, Y., Gao, X.: A new attention-based LSTM for image captioning. Neural Process. Lett. **54**(4), 3157–3171 (2022)
20. Yang, R., Cui, X., Qin, Q., Deng, Z., Lan, R., Luo, X.: Fast RF-UIC: a fast unsupervised image captioning model. Displays **79**, 102490 (2023)
21. Zhang, D., Ma, Y., Liu, Q., Wang, H., Ren, A., Liang, J.: Traffic scene captioning with multi-stage feature enhancement. Comput. Mater. Continua **76**(3), 2901–2920 (2023)

Searching for Short M-Dwarf Flares by Machine Learning Method

Hanchun Jiang$^{(\boxtimes)}$ (ID)

The University of Tokyo, 7-3-1 Hongo, Bunkyo, Tokyo, Japan
`hanchun.jiang@phys.s.u-tokyo.ac.jp`

Abstract. We propose a machine learning method to identify M-dwarf flares in astronomical observation data. A flare is a sudden increase of luminosity of a star's surface, and is thought to be the result of magnetic reconnection. Observations of the stellar flares play a crucial role in understanding stellar magnetic activity. In particular, analyzing flare time evolution (light curve) is essential. We use the data from Tomo-e Gozen camera, mounted on the Kiso Schmit telescope, with a cadence of approximately one second, which is shorter than the cadence of other telescopes such as NASA's Kepler space telescope and the Transiting Exoplanet Survey Satellite. The dataset is ideal for identifying fast flares. We develop a one-dimensional convolutional neural network (CNN) to detect fast and faint flares in optical light curves. We train the model on a limited number of real flares identified by human experts, augmented with a large number of artificially generated flares to detect sub-minute flare candidates within the light curves captured by Tomo-e Gozen camera, and subsequently fit these candidates to make the selections. Our novel CNN model has successfully identified potential flares characterized by a rise time in the range of $4\,\mathrm{s} \lesssim t_{\mathrm{rise}} \lesssim 88\,\mathrm{s}$, and energy levels spanning $10^{30}\,\mathrm{erg} \lesssim E_{\mathrm{flare}} \lesssim 10^{33}\,\mathrm{erg}$. Notably these potential flares exhibit shorter duration and lower energy compared to those detected by human experts, who typically identify flares with a rise time of $5\,\mathrm{s} \lesssim t_{\mathrm{rise}} \lesssim 100\,\mathrm{s}$ and energy of $10^{31}\,\mathrm{erg} \lesssim E_{\mathrm{flare}} \lesssim 10^{34}\,\mathrm{erg}$.

Keywords: M dwarf star · Stellar flare · Photometric · One-dimensional convolutional neural network

1 Introduction

1.1 Background and Motivation

Time-domain astronomy focuses on the study of how the brightness of an astronomical object such as a star varies over time, particularly on short-time scales. The brightness variation can be attributed to physical processes such as the surface motion or inherent changes within the object. By capturing the observational signatures, astronomers can gain insights into the nature of the objects and the physical processes governing their evolution. For example, detailed analysis

S. Sachdeva and Y. Watanobe (Eds.): BDA 2023, LNCS 14516, pp. 172–183, 2024.
https://doi.org/10.1007/978-3-031-58502-9_12

of brightness fluctuations can help us understand a star's characteristic density and temperature and the internal structure.

Flare is sudden increase in the brightness of a star, which is thought to result from magnetic reconnection [24] that triggers the release of energy. Flares affect all layers of the stellar atmosphere, heating plasma to tens of millions of Kelvins, accelerating electrons and protons to very high velocities, and generating electromagnetic radiation spanning a wide range of wavelengths. Flares can even affect the accretion disks of newly born stars by causing heating and ionization of the outer planetary atmospheres, thereby shaping the chemical evolution and atmosphere of stars [2]. Among these, the low-energy flares, which are fairly fast flares searched in this paper, can increase the ozone column by a fractional percentage on the atmosphere of an Earth-like planet [28]. Consequently, stellar flares constitute a crucial facet of stellar magnetic activity.

Flares are most common in low-mass stars that have a deep convective zone near the surface, such as M dwarfs [5], which are known to be magnetically active. Given that M dwarfs are considerably fainter than stars with ordinary masses like the Sun, the flares originating from M dwarfs result in a significantly larger *fractional* change in luminosity [1]. This unique feature allows us to detect even very faint signals. We thus focus on M dwarf flares in this study.

It is known that the flare frequency distribution (FFD) follows a power law relationship with a negative exponent, meaning that small flares are more frequent than larger flares [21]. Flare frequency distribution is closely related to a deeper question on what mechanism is responsible for heating the stellar corona. Theoretically, it has been suggested that smaller flares may dominate the corona heating process if the frequency is sufficiently high [3]. Identifying fast flares is crucial not only for detecting small flares, which play a significant role in the study of flare frequency distribution, but also for unraveling the physical mechanisms underlying the primary occurrence of magnetic energy release on smaller scales. For instance, fast flares can serve as indicators of individual magnetic reconnection and/or particle acceleration events, and their temporal characteristics may depend on the characteristic size of the elementary flux tube or the turbulent dynamics of the reconnecting current sheets [19]. However, previous studies are based on data from photometric surveys, such as Kepler [4] and Transiting Exoplanet Survey Satellite (TESS) [20], which have cadences of over 20 s. Due to the designed cadence for each space mission, fast flares remain unresolved and cannot be identified.

A wide-field survey with cadence as short as one second can significantly enhance our understanding of stellar flares. For this purpose, we utilize light curves by performing aperture photometry measurement using six different settings on data from Tomo-e Gozen, capturing frames at 1 or 2 frames per second (fps), over a 2 deg^2 region of the sky. The region was observed using 84 CMOS image sensors [14] from the Tomo-e Gozen camera mounted on the 1.05 m Kiso Schmit telescope with around 1-s cadence [22].

1.2 Related Works

Machine Learning Techniques. Flares occur at unpredictable intervals and thus it is necessary to perform long-term observations continuously [10]. Such observations generate an overwhelming amount of data, making it hard for us to analyze manually. As such, the machine learning method is efficient in extracting valuable information and knowledge from big data. Among many available methods, Convolutional Neural Networks (CNNs) stand out as an efficient tool for processing structured arrays of data. CNNs utilize layers of filters to autonomously learn and identify patterns and features within data (often images), showcasing their crucial role in the analysis of astronocal observation data. For example, CNNs find applications in image classification tasks, such as accurately and quickly classifying photometric galaxy images [9]. CNNs are used to capture characteristic features, such as elongated images of gravitationally lensed galaxies [18]. Yet another usage is eliminating noise, as demonstrated in denoising weak lensing convergence maps [25] (see more examples in review articles, such as [17, 26]).

Flare Detecting Methods. A number of approaches have been put forth for identifying flare signals from observational light curves. Leveraging data sets from missions like Kepler and Transiting Exoplanet Survey Satellite, some methods rely on light curve smoothing and outlier detection based on specific criteria, while others involve estimating the moments of apparent systematic changes in brightness to determine flare occurrences. Unfortunately, these techniques have inherent challenges, including misclassification of other astronomical events as flares and potential oversight of low-energy flare events. One still needs continued reliance on significant human effort. Some researchers have turned to machine learning methods in order to enhance objectivity and reduce the workload of flare detection. Recurrent Neural Networks (RNNs), which are well suited for handling time series data, were employed by [29] to detect flares. However, configuring RNNs to provide adequate coverage consumes a long time, making the training process itself challenging. Other studies use 1D convolutional neural networks (CNNs) for flare detection [8]. Since the 1D CNNs are robust, flare identification can be also done. Clearly, CNNs have the capabilities detecting fast flare events.

2   Method

In this study, we develop 1D CNNs to detect the flare signals within optical light curves. The input consists of segmented light curves of equal length, and the output is a label within the range of -1 to 1. We will explain the method through three sequential stages: pretreatment, training, and fitting of the flares.

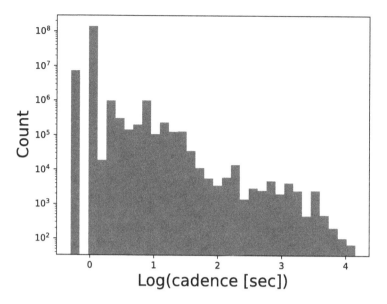

Fig. 1. The distribution of cadences. Most of the cadences are one second. Note the logarithmic sacle of the vertical axis.

2.1 Pretreatment

In this initial stage, we prepare the cut-outs of light curves for the input. We began by filtering out low-quality light curves that exhibit negative fluxes, potentially arising from system errors, or have excessively short or highly variable temporal sampling. Following this, we addressed gaps in the data. As depicted in Fig. 1, the most common cadences of a Tomo-e Gozen light curve are 1 s, but there are some time intervals longer than 1 s, due to the readout time or bad weather conditions, referred to as 'gaps'. Since CNNs require equidistant time intervals, they will consider the time interval between the start and the end of the gap as one second. To avoid this, we added new sampling points following the Gaussian distribution in the gaps, aiming to bring the time intervals in the gaps as close to 1 s as possible.

Subsequent to this preprocessing, we injected artificial flares into the light curves to generate the mock observational data. To model these artificial flares, we applied a mathematical model from Ref. [6], where the authors utilized 885 flare light curves observed by the Kepler telescope, as described in the following formula:

$$\bar{f}\left(t_{1/2}\right) = \begin{cases} 1 + 1.941t_{1/2} - 0.175t_{1/2}^2 \\ -2.246t_{1/2}^3 - 1.125t_{1/2}^4, & -1 < t_{1/2} < 0 \\ 0.689\exp\left(-1.6t_{1/2}\right) + \\ 0.303\exp\left(-0.2783t_{1/2}\right), & 0 < t_{1/2} \end{cases} \tag{1}$$

This describes flares as rise $(-1 < t_{1/2} < 0)$ and decay $(t_{1/2} > 0)$ phases. $\bar{f}$ is the relative flux defined as:

$$\bar{f}(\bar{t}_{1/2}) \equiv \frac{f(\bar{t}_{1/2})}{f_{\text{peak}}} \qquad (2)$$

and $t_{1/2}$ is defined as follows:

$$t_{1/2} \equiv \frac{t - t_{\text{peak}}}{t_{\text{FWHM}}} \qquad (3)$$

t_{peak} represents the time at which a flare reaches its peak flux, and t_{FWHM} denotes the full width at half maximum (FWHM) duration of a flare. Based on the results in the latter section, showing the sensibility of our model, we injected flare with specific characteristics. These characteristics include a proportion of 1%, the full width at half maximum values ranging from 1 to 60 s, and amplitudes between 0.2 and 1.0. These choices represent a balanced trade-off between accuracy and recall while maintaining the capacity to detect faint flares effectively. Following the injection of flares, we assigned a label of 1 to the data points within a flare, and a label of −1 to the remaining data points.

With the injection of flares completed, we proceeded to segment the light curves into 180-s cut-outs, assigning each cut-out a label based on the labels of the data points contained within it. This segmentation was necessary due to the variations in the lengths of the light curves, while the CNN requires uniform input shapes. Furthermore, our target flares are sub-minute, and this segmentation can help CNNs concentrate on flare detection while preventing the loss of flares. The segmentation was shifted every 30 s to ensure that no flares were overlooked.

2.2   CNN Network Architecture

The architectural design of our CNN network is depicted in Fig. 2. It consisted of 4 one-dimensional convolutional layers [16], aimed at recognizing the flare's shape from the 180-s segmented light curves. Batch normalization [12] is applied to address internal covariate shifts, ensuring high accuracy. All these layers employ ReLu activation functions. To reduce the number of parameters and keep the recall high, we introduced a max-pooling layer [23] between the second and third convolutional layers.

For classification, we flattened the results after the convolutional layers, including the features identified by convolutional layers, into a vector. This vector was then connected to two dense layers, which also contributed to maintaining high accuracy. In these two dense layers, we used Dropout [27], randomly disabling a fraction of the neurons. We set the rate as 0.1 to prevent model overfitting. The final output, falling within the range $[-1, 1]$, is generated using the hyperbolic tangent (Tanh) activation function.

Our optimization process utilized a mean square error loss function and the NAdam optimizer [7,13]. We also weighted the cut-outs containing flare signals based on their proportion relative to the total number of data points. This adjustment was necessary due to the significant data imbalance, with only 1% of the data containing flares.

2.3   Fitting Flares

Since each data point appears in around 6 cut-outs, after obtaining the label for each cut-out through the prediction by the CNN model, we calculated the average of these 6 labels to assign a label to each data point. An illustrative example is presented in Fig. 3. Subsequently, we identified flare candidates among clusters of data points with high labels that do not correspond to artificially injected flares. To be more specific, when we find the value of a label for a point exceeding 0.7 and that point does not belong to an injected flare, we will regard it as a flare candidate. The identified flare candidate initiates at the first data point within the cluster with a label exceeding 0, and the data point with the highest flux is designated as the flare's peak.

To differentiate the potential flares from those with peaks caused by systematic noise, we employed a fitting code from [1], which is based on the Hamiltonian Monte Carlo (HMC) method. This fitting code applied the function shown in Eq. 4 and provided us with the distribution of the parameter samples.

$$\frac{F_{\text{flare}}(t)}{\bar{F}} \equiv f(t) = \begin{cases} f_{\text{peak}} \left[\sum_{i=1}^4 a_i \left(\frac{t-t_{\text{peak}}}{t_{\text{rise}}} \right)^i + 1 \right] \\ \quad (t_{\text{start}} < t < t_{\text{peak}}), \\ f_{\text{peak}} \\ \quad (t_{\text{peak}} < t < t_{\text{peak}} + \Delta t_{\text{peak}}), \\ C f_{\text{peak}} \exp \left[-\frac{(t-t_{\text{peak}}-\Delta t_{\text{peak}})}{\tau_{\text{fast}}} \right] \\ + (1 - C) f_{\text{peak}} \exp \left[-\frac{(t-t_{\text{peak}}-\Delta t_{\text{peak}})}{\tau_{\text{slow}}} \right] \\ \quad (t_{\text{peak}} + \Delta t_{\text{peak}} < t). \end{cases} \quad (4)$$

Three of these parameters play a crucial role in our final selection of potential flares:

- **The mean of** t_{peak}: This represents the average value of t_{peak} samples obtained from the Hamiltonian Monte Carlo fitting code. A larger t_{peak} indicates a greater disparity in the predicted peak times between the CNN model and the fitting code.
- **The standard deviation of** t_{peak}: This indicates the degree of variation in t_{peak} samples obtained from the Hamiltonian Monte Carlo fitting code. A higher standard deviation suggests increased uncertainty in t_{peak}, which also means the t_{peak} of this candidate is hard to find.
- **The** β^2: We define a parameter $\beta^2 \equiv \chi^2_{\text{CNN}}/\chi^2_{\text{horizontal}}$, where χ^2_{CNN} is the χ^2 calculated when we use the fitting result, and $\chi^2_{\text{horizontal}}$ is the χ^2 derived when fitting the candidate with a horizontal line. If the peak of a candidate is due to a systematic error, it is likely that the light curve can only be adequately fitted by a horizontal line.

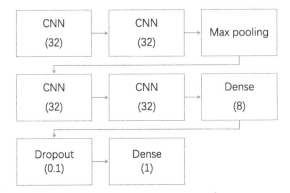

Fig. 2. The architecture of our CNN model. We used 4 one-dimensional convolutional layers with a kernel size of 32. We added a max-pooling layer between the second and third layers. These layers are connected to two dense layers with sizes 8 and 1, respectively. Between these two dense layers, we used Dropout with a rate of 0.1.

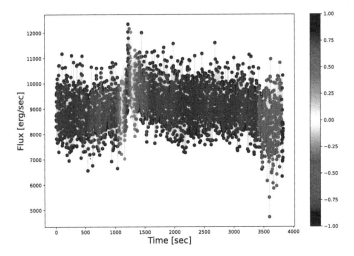

Fig. 3. An example of assigning labels to data. Points marked in red have a high possibility of belonging to a flare, while blue points indicate a lower probability of belonging to a flare. (Color figure online)

We constructed distributions of candidates based on these three parameters, enabling us to select potential flares from the candidate set by focusing on those with low mean t_{peak} values, low standard deviation of t_{peak}, and low β^2 values.

3   Results

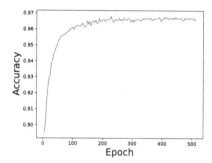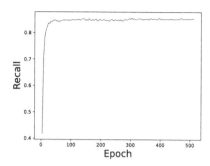

Fig. 4. (left) Accuracy on the validation set as a function of the training epoch. (right) Recall on the validation set as a function of the training epoch. Both the accuracy and the recall converge. The accuracy converges towards 97% and the recall converges towards 85%.

Following the pretreatment steps detailed in the previous section, we conducted cleaning of the original light curves, injected artificial flares, and used the cutouts after segmentation to train our CNNs network. Due to the highly imbalanced nature of our dataset, we used both accuracy and recall to evaluate the performance of our network. As depicted in Fig. 4, the accuracy and recall functions for the validation set were tracked during training over multiple epochs. We got high values in both accuracy and recall. The accuracy converges towards 97% and the recall approaches a convergence at around 85%.

After completing the training process, we got the flare candidates as explained in the previous section, and subsequently performed fitting. An example of the fitting result is illustrated in Fig. 5. In total, we identified 118 potential flares through the fitting process. In Fig. 6 and Fig. 7, we show flares previously detected by Tomo-e Gozen, Transiting Exoplanet Survey Satellite, and ULTRA-CAM. The Tomo-e Gozen flares identified by human observers are sourced from [1], the Transiting Exoplanet Survey Satellite flares are from [11], and the ULTRACAM flares are detailed in [15].

In Fig. 6, we plot our sample, human-detected Tomo-e flares, and Transiting Exoplanet Survey Satellite flares. This figure displays the relationship between flare energy and rise time, as well as histograms depicting the distribution of rise times and the total emitted energy. According to [1], the total emitted energy is expressed as follows:

$$E_{\mathrm{bol}} = \sigma_{\mathrm{SB}} T_{\mathrm{flare}}^4 \int A_{\mathrm{flare}}(t)\, dt$$

$$= \pi R_{\star}^2 \sigma_{\mathrm{SB}} T_{\mathrm{flare}}^4 \int \frac{\int d\lambda\, B(\lambda, T_{\star}) S(\lambda)}{\int d\lambda\, B(\lambda, T_{\mathrm{flare}}) S(\lambda)} f(t) dt. \qquad (5)$$

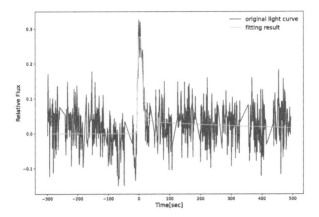

Fig. 5. One example of the fitting result.

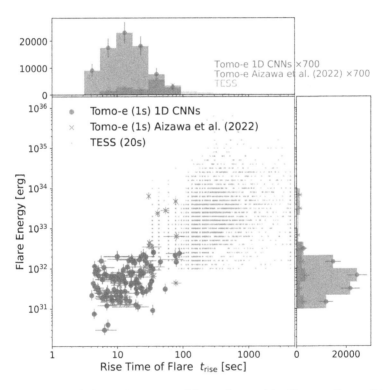

Fig. 6. Rise time vs bolometric energy of flares detected by Tomo-e Gozen (blue circles). Pink squares indicate flares detected by the Transiting Exoplanet Survey Satellite [11]. The upper and right panels show the histograms with respect to rise time and bolometric energy, respectively, where a factor of 700 is multiplied by the number of the Tomo-e Gozen flares given the difference of the effective total observation time for active M dwarfs. (Color figure online)

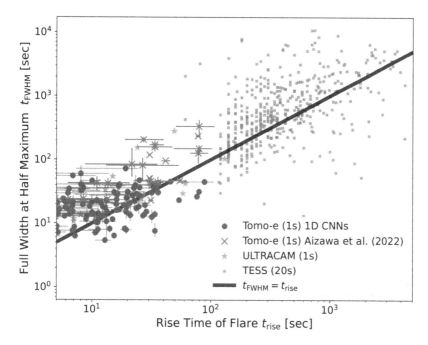

Fig. 7. Rise time and full width at half maximum (FWHM) of optical flares from M dwarfs. Orange stars indicate flares detected by ULTRACAM [15]. The grey solid line corresponds to $t_{\text{FWHM}} = t_{\text{rise}}$. (Color figure online)

We adjusted the Tomo-e flare data by multiplying it by a factor of 700. This correction was necessary because the total observation time by [11] is 700–1000 times longer than the survey conducted by [1]. We see that our model can successfully detect flares with shorter rise time with $4\,\text{s} \lesssim t_{\text{rise}} \lesssim 88\,\text{s}$ and lower energy range with $10^{30}\,\text{erg} \lesssim E_{\text{flare}} \lesssim 10^{33}\,\text{erg}$, which reaches a lower energy limitation than human eyes, detecting flares with time range $5\,\text{s} \lesssim t_{\text{rise}} \lesssim 100\,\text{s}$ and energy range $10^{31}\,\text{erg} \lesssim E_{\text{flare}} \lesssim 10^{34}\,\text{erg}$. Furthermore, as shown in Fig. 7, the potential flares identified by our model exhibit shorter rise times and full width at half maximum values, which shows again the capability of our machine learning model to detect short-duration flares that may be overlooked by human observers.

4   Summary and Conclusion

The flare frequency distribution is a crucial element in the study of stellar corona heating mechanisms. Challenges arise when dealing with low-energy flares with faint and short in duration. The short flares are often undetected due to the relatively long cadence of observations and also by the limitations of human visual check. To enable efficient flare detection, we propose to use machine learning to detect flares from high-time-resolution datasets. Through the implementation of one-dimensional CNNs, we have successfully detected lower-energy and faster flares, mitigating the limitations posed by cadence and human sensitivity.

We used real observational data from Tomo-e Gozen camera mounted on the Kiso Schmit telescope whose cadence is approximately one second. Following a set of data cleaning process and injection of artificial flares, we employed segmented cut-outs to train our network to identify flare candidates. Then we used the Hamiltonian Monte Carlo method to fit the candidates and select potential flares. Our model can successfully detect flares with shorter duration and lower energy, pushing beyond the limit of previous studies.

An important future task is to further enhance the sensitivity of our CNNs. To achieve this, we plan to examine the impact of the additional elements introduced during the gap-filling step on the CNN network. It is possible that these procedures may introduce artificial patterns into the light curves in the training data. We will also investigate the potential benefits of employing iterative training methods to enhance the overall performance of our model.

References

1. Aizawa, M., et al.: Fast optical flares from M dwarfs detected by a one-second-cadence survey with Tomo-e Gozen. Publ. Astron. Soc. Jpn. **74**(5), 1069–1094 (2022)
2. Benz, A.O., Güdel, M.: Physical processes in magnetically driven flares on the sun, stars, and young stellar objects. Ann. Rev. Astron. Astrophys. **48**, 241–287 (2010)
3. Bingert, S., Peter, H.: Nanoflare statistics in an active region 3D MHD coronal model. Astron. Astrophys. **550**, A30 (2013)
4. Borucki, W.J., et al.: Kepler planet-detection mission: introduction and first results. Science **327**(5968), 977–980 (2010)
5. Davenport, J.R.: The Kepler catalog of stellar flares. Astrophys. J. **829**(1), 23 (2016)
6. Davenport, J.R., et al.: Kepler flares. II. The temporal morphology of white-light flares on GJ 1243. Astrophys. J. **797**(2), 122 (2014)
7. Dozat, T.: Incorporating nesterov momentum into adam technical report (2015)
8. Feinstein, A.D., et al.: Flare statistics for young stars from a convolutional neural network analysis of TESS data. Astron. J. **160**(5), 219 (2020)
9. Gravet, R., et al.: A catalog of visual-like morphologies in the 5 candels fields using deep learning. Astrophys. J. Suppl. Ser. **221**(1), 8 (2015)
10. Hawley, S.L., et al.: Kepler flares. I. Active and inactive M dwarfs. Astrophys. J. **797**(2), 121 (2014)
11. Howard, W.S., MacGregor, M.A.: No such thing as a simple flare: substructure and quasi-periodic pulsations observed in a statistical sample of 20 s cadence TESS flares. Astrophys. J. **926**(2), 204 (2022)
12. Ioffe, S., Szegedy, C.: Batch normalization: accelerating deep network training by reducing internal covariate shift. In: International Conference on Machine Learning, pp. 448–456. PMLR (2015)
13. Kingma, D.P., Ba, J.: Adam: a method for stochastic optimization. arXiv preprint arXiv:1412.6980 (2014)
14. Kojima, Y., et al.: Evaluation of large pixel CMOS image sensors for the Tomo-e Gozen wide field camera. In: High Energy, Optical, and Infrared Detectors for Astronomy VIII, vol. 10709, pp. 456–465. SPIE (2018)

15. Kowalski, A.F., et al.: M dwarf flare continuum variations on one-second timescales: calibrating and modeling of ULTRACAM flare color indices. Astrophys. J. **820**(2), 95 (2016)
16. LeCun, Y., Kavukcuoglu, K., Farabet, C.: Convolutional networks and applications in vision. In: Proceedings of 2010 IEEE International Symposium on Circuits and Systems, pp. 253–256. IEEE (2010)
17. Moriwaki, K., Nishimichi, T., Yoshida, N.: Machine learning for observational cosmology. Rep. Prog. Phys. **86**, 076901 (2023)
18. Petrillo, C.E., et al.: Finding strong gravitational lenses in the kilo degree survey with convolutional neural networks. Mon. Not. R. Astron. Soc. **472**(1), 1129–1150 (2017)
19. Qiu, J., Cheng, J., Hurford, G., Xu, Y., Wang, H.: Solar flare hard X-ray spikes observed by RHESSI: a case study. Astron. Astrophys. **547**, A72 (2012)
20. Ricker, G.R., et al.: Transiting exoplanet survey satellite. J. Astron. Telescopes Instrum. Syst. **1**(1), 014003–014003 (2015)
21. Rosner, R., Vaiana, G.: Cosmic flare transients-constraints upon models for energy storage and release derived from the event frequency distribution. Astrophys. J. Part 1 **222**, 1104–1108 (1978). Research supported by the Langley-Abbot Program
22. Sako, S., et al.: The Tomo-e Gozen wide field CMOS camera for the Kiso Schmidt telescope. In: Ground-Based and Airborne Instrumentation for Astronomy VII, vol. 10702, pp. 140–156. SPIE (2018)
23. Scherer, D., Müller, A., Behnke, S.: Evaluation of pooling operations in convolutional architectures for object recognition. In: Diamantaras, K., Duch, W., Iliadis, L.S. (eds.) ICANN 2010. LNCS, vol. 6354, pp. 92–101. Springer, Heidelberg (2010). https://doi.org/10.1007/978-3-642-15825-4_10
24. Shibata, K., Magara, T.: Solar flares: magnetohydrodynamic processes. Living Rev. Sol. Phys. **8**(1), 1–99 (2011)
25. Shirasaki, M., Moriwaki, K., Oogi, T., Yoshida, N., Ikeda, S., Nishimichi, T.: Noise reduction for weak lensing mass mapping: an application of generative adversarial networks to Subaru Hyper Suprime-Cam first-year data. Mon. Not. R. Astron. Soc. **504**(2), 1825–1839 (2021)
26. Smith, M.J., Geach, J.E.: Astronomia ex machina: a history, primer and outlook on neural networks in astronomy. Roy. Soc. Open Sci. **10**(5), 221454 (2023)
27. Srivastava, N., Hinton, G., Krizhevsky, A., Sutskever, I., Salakhutdinov, R.: Dropout: a simple way to prevent neural networks from overfitting. J. Mach. Learn. Res. **15**(1), 1929–1958 (2014)
28. Tilley, M.A., Segura, A., Meadows, V., Hawley, S., Davenport, J.: Modeling repeated M dwarf flaring at an earth-like planet in the habitable zone: atmospheric effects for an unmagnetized planet. Astrobiology **19**(1), 64–86 (2019)
29. Vida, K., Bódi, A., Szklenár, T., Seli, B.: Finding flares in Kepler and TESS data with recurrent deep neural networks. Astron. Astrophys. **652**, A107 (2021)

Vayu Vishleshan: AQI Monitoring and Reduction Analysis

Mayank Deep Khare$^{(\boxtimes)}$ ⓘ, Shelly Sachdeva ⓘ, Divyam Dubey ⓘ,
Rohit Singh Rajpoot ⓘ, and Saurav Kumar ⓘ

National Institute of Technology, Delhi, New Delhi, India
{Mayankdeep,shellysachdeva,201210016,201210037,
201210040}@nitdelhi.ac.in

Abstract. In today's life, humans compromise with nature while evolving into a more advanced species. One of the main effects of that advancement is air pollution. Air pollution seriously threatens human health, the environment, and the general quality of life worldwide. A quantitative analysis of air quality was the purpose of developing the Air Quality Index (AQI), an indexing approach. The air quality index is computed using measurements for particulate matter (PM), PM2.5, PM10, NO2, CO, CO2, NH3, and other contaminants. Agnihotra (Yagya) is a method of environmental purification mentioned in the Hindu sculpture (The Book Yagya Vimarsh, written by Dr. Ramprakash, talks about the air pollution reduction method). This paper discusses the Vayu Vishleshan framework for monitoring air quality in the presence of Agnihotra (Yagya). This study is divided into two processes. The first one is AQI monitoring, and the second is AQI reduction. AQI Monitoring covers sensing particulate matter (PM), PM2.5, PM10, NO2, and CO and performing analysis over the AQI data before, during, and following Agnihotra (Yagya). According to analysis, there is an approximate 6–7% decrease in CO levels and an approximate 10–12% decrease in PM levels following Agnihotra.

Keywords: AQI · Particulate matter (PM) · Agnihotra · Air Quality Index · Vedic Science

1 Introduction

1.1 Air Pollution

Air pollution is a primary global concern that endangers human health, the environment, and overall quality of life. Rapid urbanization, industrialization, and increased automobile emissions have increased dangerous atmospheric pollutants, putting the air quality of many regions at risk. As air quality has become worse, robust monitoring systems have been developed to quantify pollution levels precisely and guide governmental policies and remedies. According to WHO data, almost all of the world's population (99%) breathes air that exceeds WHO guideline limits and contains high levels of pollutants, with low- and middle-income nations bearing the burden [1]. The Air Quality Index

© The Author(s), under exclusive license to Springer Nature Switzerland AG 2024
S. Sachdeva and Y. Watanobe (Eds.): BDA 2023, LNCS 14516, pp. 184–197, 2024.
https://doi.org/10.1007/978-3-031-58502-9_13

(AQI), which gives a standardized numerical representation of air quality and enables efficient communication of potential health hazards to the public population, is a critical statistic for quantifying air pollution [13]. Integrating the Internet of Things within emerging technologies like cloud computing artificial intelligence provides a promising opportunity for the development of air quality systems [3].

1.2 Air Quality Index (AQI)

An indexing technique designed for quantitative analysis of air quality is the Air Quality Index (AQI). One way to measure and track air quality is with the air quality index (AQI). Values for particle matter (PM), PM2.5, PM10, NO2, CO, CO2, NH3, and other contaminants are used to calculate the air quality index. To determine how to reduce pollution and what steps we can take to improve our air quality, the main focus of our project is to analyze the air quality index at various locations.

1.3 AQI Calculation

Using the Greater Vancouver Air Quality Index algorithm, the first sub-index for each gas is calculated.

$$I_p = ((I_{Hi} - I_{Lo}) / (BP_{Hi} - BP_{Lo})) * (C_p - BP_{Lo}) + I_{Lo}$$

where

I_p = the index for pollutant p
C_p = the truncated concentration of pollutant p
BP_{Hi} = the concentration breakpoint that is greater than or equal to Cp
BP_{Lo} = the concentration breakpoint that is less than or equal to C_p
I_{Hi} = the AQI value corresponding to BPHi
I^{Lo} = the AQI value corresponding to BPLo

1.4 Reducing Air Pollution

There are various ways to reduce air pollution, but not many people are very concerned about this in today's era. We need to put in some effort to purify our atmosphere. The ways to reduce Air pollution are as follows:-

- Smoking and forest fire reduction [5]
- iSpray: Using Intelligent Water Spraying to Reduce Air Pollution in Urban Areas [4]
- Negative Ion Generator:- Negative ion generators can improve indoor air quality. These ions attach to positively charged particles, such as dust, pollen, pet dander, and smoke, causing them to become heavier and fall to the ground. As a result, these particles are removed from the air, leading to potential benefits for individuals with respiratory conditions or allergies.
- Agnihotra: It is a Vedic practice involving the ritualistic burning of cow dung and ghee at sunrise and sunset. Advocates believe that Agnihotra reduces air pollution by purifying the atmosphere. However, scientific evidence supporting its effectiveness is limited, and its impact on AQI reduction may vary.

The contributions of this paper can be summarised as follows:-

1. This paper presents "Vayu Vishleshana," which aligns with its literal meaning of monitoring and analyzing the Air Quality Index (AQI) through the implementation of the Internet of Things (IoT) based AQI monitoring system.
2. The proposed research encompasses three essential modules: the Monitoring System, Communication and storage, and Reduction System. The Monitoring System is equipped with an array of specialized sensors meticulously designed to gather comprehensive data. The second module, the Connection System, integrates a microcontroller, Wi-Fi connectivity, and a dedicated power source, facilitating computational tasks, seamless power management, and efficient connectivity. The third module is dedicated to examining the reduction technique of environmental purification.
3. This study distinguishes itself by employing an IoT setup to monitor AQI and examine the effect of Agnihotra on environmental purification.
4. Following the collection of sensor data, subsequent analysis, and graph creation, our findings indicate a noteworthy reduction of approximately 6–7% in carbon monoxide (CO) levels and 10–11% in particulate matter (PM) levels post-implementation of the reduction measures, exemplified by the use of Agnihotra.

2 Literature Survey

This section includes a literature review of several air quality monitoring technologies and reduction technologies. The driving factors of the air quality index in China are discussed by Dongsheng Zhan, Mei-Po Kwan, and Wenzhong Zhang [13] for a study in spatiotemporal patterns of air pollution in China and used the geographical detector model to identify the effect intensity and interactions between the driving elements based on data from the Air Quality Index for 2015 across 338 Chinese cities. The impact of high-speed rail on air quality in counties: Econometric study with data from southern Beijing-Tianjin-Hebei, China by Luyang Zhao, Xiaoqiang Zhang, Fan Zhao [14] and According to research, High-Speed Rails (HSR) have both direct and indirect effects on county air quality. HSR directly impacts it due to the way long-distance travel has changed. HSR also indirectly influences. The paper The Effect of environmental regulation on Population Migration: Evidence from China's New Ambient Air Quality Standards by Baoxi Li, Tiantian Gui, Guo Chen, and Shixiong Cheng [15] shows that the new ambient air quality standard (NAAQS)S has a considerable negative impact on population migration in cities that rigorously monitor air quality. The paper Air Pollution and indoor work efficiency: Evidence from professional basketball players in China, written by Wendi Ni, Xiurong Hu, Yi Ju, and Qunwei Wang [16], also studied that younger players are more sensitive to the adverse effects of air pollution. The estimated reduction in work efficiency is around 0.422% for each 10% increase in AQI. This literature review also includes the reduction of Air Quality Index; the paper Vishagan Dhoop, Nano-Scale Particles with Detoxifying Medicinal Fume written by Balkrishna, Acharya & Yagyadev, Swami & Vipradev [12] talks about the evidence establishing the antimicrobial efficacy of Vishagan Dhoop/ Dhoopan combination was generated. Further studies in healthcare settings are needed to develop this combination into a disinfection technique with no potential harmful effects. The paper A Scientific Research

[17] by Shailee Bhatia and Shelly Sachdeva discusses methods of reducing air pollution using Agnihotra. Witzel et al. gave insights into agnihotra rituals and their impact in Nepal [17]. The paper Analytical Study of Effect of Agnihotra [19], written by Dhamija, Luv & Singh, Madhulika & Garg, talks about the analytical study of the effectiveness of Agnihotra in effective natural approach for the treatment of any pollution, heavy PM 2.5 and PM 10 particles and the use of Mango and Cow dung wood in the cure of ailment, depression, pollution control. Xinyuan Liu, Chaoyi Guo, and Yazhen Wu talk in the paper Evaluating the Cost and Benefit of Air Pollution [20] about how China has taken steps to improve air quality and the benefits and costs of implementing these policies.

3   Problem Statement

The primary goal is to examine air quality indexes in various locations, including homes, businesses, and temples. Data must be collected from devices via sensors and then analyzed to determine how to reduce pollution. We must go to locations conducting Vedic agnihotra to gather data, collect data at home, and examine the data using a graph to analyze the behavior of the Air quality index in various locations to determine what we can do to reduce pollution. So, In this project, we will see how Agnihotra (Yagya) affects our environment in a good or bad way. We will determine if Agnihotra (Yagya) purifies our environment by analyzing the air quality data in homes, temples, etc. We have to see the effect of agnihotra on our environment.

4   Proposed Vayu Vishleshan Framework

This section includes the proposed Vayu Vishleshan framework for AQI monitoring and reduction. In Hindi, Vayu stands for air, and Vishleshan means to analyze. This framework will first monitor the AQI before, at the time, and after some time of the agnihotra. Then, the comparative analysis will be done. Based on Agnihotra, the effect of Agnihotra on air Quality Fig. 1. The proposed Vayu Vishleshan framework structure is as follows. Figure 1 is the architecture diagram of the proposed system, which consists of three modules: monitoring system, communication system, and reduction System. The Monitoring System is equipped with an array of specialized sensors meticulously designed to gather comprehensive data. The second module, the communication system, integrates a microcontroller, Wi-Fi connectivity, and a dedicated power source, facilitating computational tasks, seamless power management, and efficient connectivity. The third module is dedicated to examining the reduction technique of environmental purification.

4.1   Monitoring of AQI

First, we must monitor the AQI in different places to analyze its behavior. For monitoring AQI, we considered only the primary pollutants which significantly affect the calculation of AQI. These Major pollutants are CO and PM 2.5. So, We take the readings of these two in different places at the same time so we can accurately monitor the behavior of AQI. We use Arduino devices, which have sensors that take the readings of these

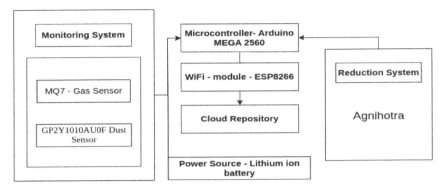

Fig. 1. Proposed Vayu Vishleshan Framework

two pollutants. So, to monitor these primary pollutants (CO and PM 2.5), there are the following sensor array requirements.

Array of Sensors
Gas sensors detect various contaminants that exist as gasses. The types of sensors used in the proposed framework system are listed in Table 1.

Table 1. Array of Sensors

Type	Sensor	Use
Gas	MQ6	for LPG, CO, and Smoke detection
Gas	MQ7	For CO gas detection
Dust	GP2Y1010AU0F	PM 2.5 to PM 10
GPS	NEO-6M	sensing the geographical coordinates

4.2 Communication System

This module communicates the sensor data over the cloud. It consists of Arduino Mega and ESP 8266 for storing and transmitting sensor data with the cloud database.

Arduino MEGA 2560
For processors to produce conclusions, they need help digesting the data gathered from multiple sensors. There are many types of processors, each with a unique set of character-istics. We'll use the Arduino MEGA 2560 in this study because it's based on the ESP8266, as opposed to, for instance, the Arduino Nano ATMEGA328P and the ESP8266-based NodeMCU-12E. Because it is based on the Atmega-2560 CPU and has more memory storage and input/output pins than other boards that are more accessible, we will use the Arduino MEGA 2560 in this study.

Module for WiFi: ESP8266

Wi-Fi is an internet-based technology for establishing connections between computers and web servers. The TCP/IP protocol layers in the ESP8266 Wi-Fi module are why we selected it; they enable microcontrollers to connect to any Wi-Fi network and access the internet [7].

After this system is set up, we have to see how AQI is calculated using these data so that we can monitor AQI. The Air Quality Index (AQI) categorizes air quality into color-coded levels. Green (0–50) signifies satisfactory air with little risk. Yellow (51–100) is acceptable but may pose risks for sensitive individuals. Orange (101–150) indicates unhealthy conditions for sensitive groups. Red (151–200) denotes unhealthy air for the general public, with higher risks for sensitive groups. Purple (201–300) signals a health alert, increasing chances for everyone. Maroon (301 and higher) signifies a hazardous level, warranting all health warnings and emergency precautions. The AQI is vital for concisely assessing and communicating air pollution's potential health impacts.

4.3 Reduction of AQI

Hindu scriptures mention Agnihotra (Yagya), a natural Agnihotra, for environmental purification. Yajur Veda Slokas details its benefits, including air purification. The elements required to perform agnihotra are discussed below [8–10].

Camphor

Some are directly diffused and smell good by capturing the foul odor. The remaining camphor produces oil consisting of pinene, dipentene, cineole, safrole, terpineol, etc.

Wood

Agnihotra, a fire-breathing medicine, primarily consists of wood, with cellulose and lignocellulose being the main components. Wood combustion produces hydrocarbons, which are oxidised and released as steam. The combustion process also produces aldehydes, ketones, acids, alcohols, phenols, carbon dioxide, and water. The produced alcohol and acid react to form an ester, which smells pleasant. After combustion, 0.2–4% of wood ash remains, which contains calcium, potassium, magnesium, aluminum, iron, manganese, sodium, and phosphorus, making it suitable for manure.

The chemical reaction of cellulose:

Cellulose in the presence of oxygen produces carbon dioxide and water (Eq. (1) and Eq. (2))

$$\underset{\text{Cellulose}}{(C_6H_{10}O_5)n} + \underset{\text{oxygen}}{6nO_2} \rightarrow \underset{\text{Carbon dioxide}}{6nCO_2} + \underset{\text{water}}{5nH_2O} \tag{1}$$

$$\underset{\text{Cellulose}}{(C_6H_{10}O_5)n} + \underset{\text{oxygen}}{3nO_2} \rightarrow \underset{\text{Carbon dioxide}}{6nCO_2} + \underset{\text{water}}{5nH_2O} \tag{2}$$

Cellulose breaks down into Carbon and water by the below reaction (Eq. (3))

$$\underset{\text{Cellulose}}{(C_6H_{10}O_5)n} \rightarrow \underset{\text{Carbon}}{6nC} + \underset{\text{water}}{5nH_2O} \tag{3}$$

Clarified Butter (Ghee From Cow Milk)

Ghee, composed of glycerol and carboxylic acid, is a safe and healthy substance that can be combusted without harmful substances, as Dr. Fundarlal, MD demonstrated. The primary acid components include palmitic, oleic, myristic, stearic, butyric, caperic, and lauric acids.

Glycerol

Combustion of glycerol produces formaldehyde (Eq. (5)).

Oxidation of glycerol produces glyceraldehyde, glyceric acid, tartaric acid, glycol aldehyde, glyoxal acid, and oxalic acid is produced.

Glycerol loses water to produce acrolein (Eq. (4)).

$$HOCH_2CH(OH)CH_2OH \rightarrow \underset{-H_2O}{H_2C} = \underset{acrolein}{CHCHO} \tag{4}$$
$$\underset{Glycerol}{}$$

Combustion of Glycerol (Eq. (5))

$$\underset{Glycerol}{HOCH_2CH(OH)CH_2OH} + O_2 \rightarrow H_2C = \underset{formaldehyde}{CHCHO} \tag{5}$$

Acid

Acid breaks down into aldehyde, and aldehyde reacts with oxygen to produce acid, and these acids further have hydrocarbons.

Complex acid in ghee breaks into simple acids, and then these simple acids produce hydrocarbons. The smell of ghee is due to the presence of caproic aldehyde, octalic aldehyde, nonalic aldehyde, and valeric aldehyde. Acetic acid converts to acetone and produces acetone with release of water and carbon dioxide (Eq. (6))

$$2\,\underset{Acetic\ acid}{CH_3COOH} \rightarrow \underset{acetone}{CH_3COCH_3} + \underset{carbon\ dioxide}{CO_2} + \underset{water}{H_2O} \tag{6}$$

Oleic acid in the presence of oxygen produces n-nonyl aldehyde (Eq. (7))

$$\underset{Oleic\ acid}{CH_3(CH_2)_7CH} = CH(CH_2)_7COOH + \underset{oxygen}{O_2} \rightarrow \underset{n-nonyl\ aldehyde}{CH_3(CH_2)_7CHO} + OHC(CH_2)_7COOH$$
$$\tag{7}$$

Now, oxidation of n-nonyl aldehyde produces nonanoic acid and is further converted to octane with the release of carbon dioxide (Eq. (8))

$$\underset{n\,-\,nonyl\ aldehyde}{CH_3(CH_2)_7CHO} + O_2 \rightarrow \underset{nonanoic\ acid}{CH_3(CH_2)_7COOH} \underset{-CO_2}{} \rightarrow \underset{octane}{CH_3(CH_2)_6CH_3} \tag{8}$$

All the equations are taken from the reference book Yagya Vimarsh [18]. In the combustion of ghee, some ghee is directly diffused into the air and makes the air pure for a longer period.

Havya Ingredients

Agnihotra is a method of oxidation of ingredients, using mantras to measure the time for each ingredient. It is mentioned in Vedic Granthas and has been proven to destroy germs, which are believed to cause diseases. Agnihotra is performed in sunlight, which is harmful to germs. When burned, the process emits a fragrance, killing germs and promoting good health. The Vedas also mention the Ragkiton species, which are associated with demons. The process is believed to destroy food poisons and promote good health effectively. Comparative analysis of AQI with or without Agnihotra is needed to understand its scientific effect.

5   Results and Findings

In Comparative analysis, we have first to collect our data in the proper software, then research and visualization will be done.

5.1   Data Collection

The study aims to understand the behavior of AQI with and without Agnihotra by collecting data on PM2.5 and CO levels at various sites using Arduino and IoT devices. The data was collected at multiple locations, including where Agnihotras are performed, residential areas, and daily Agnihotras. The data was collected at a rate of one reading every 10 minutes for three days, at home and in the same locations. The data was carefully gathered using IoT and Arduino sensors to ensure accuracy and quality. The data was saved in Excel sheets for better analysis and stored on Google Cloud for easy access. The data was then analyzed using Google Cloud for easy access.

5.2   Data Analysis and Visualization

The study collected data from hostel readings on three different days and near a temple, Aryasamaj Mandir Ashok Vihar (28.682377, 77.184347) on two occasions. An Excel sheet was created for better analysis, and daily graphs were created. The chart showed the difference between CO vs Time for separate days, allowing for a better conclusion on the level of AQI with and without Agnihotra.

Analysis of CO with Time in Both Places at the Same Time

Figure 2 explains that the level of CO before and after the Agnihotra is less in the places where Agnihotra is done than in the places where Agnihotra is not done, and in the time when Agnihotra is done, the level of CO increases in the areas where Agnihotra is done then the places where Agnihotra is not done. Table 2 shows that the average amount of CO level is decreasing in those places where Agnihotra is Performed.

Table 2. Comparison in CO level change

A place where Agnihotra is not done	A place where Agnihotra is done
Average CO level: - 381 ppm	Intermediate CO level when Agnihotra is performing: - 484 ppm Intermediate CO level when Agnihotra is not performing: - 355 ppm

CO vs Time (Day 1)

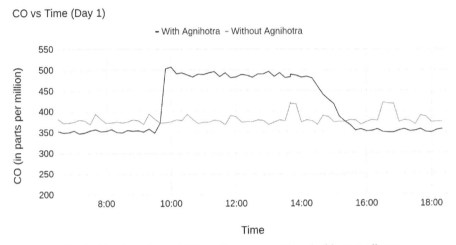

Fig. 2. Day 1 readings of CO vs. Time chart with and without agnihotra

Percentage Change in CO Level = (381-355)/388= 6.8 %

This means on day 1, we have 6.8 % less CO level at the place where Agnihotra is done than other places.

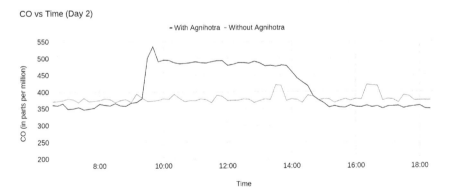

Fig. 3. Day 2 readings of CO vs. Time chart with and without agnihotra

According to Fig. 3 on Day 2, the level of CO before and after Agnihotra is also lower in the locations where Agnihotra is performed than in the areas where Agnihotra is not performed, and during the Agnihotra procedure, the level of CO is higher in the locations where Agnihotra is performed than in the places where Agnihotra is not performed. Based on the observations from day 2, the average CO level falls in the areas where Agnihotra is performed. 5.7 % less CO levels are observed where Agnihotra is done than in other places.

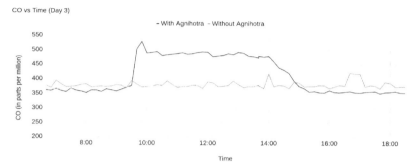

Fig. 4. Day 3 readings of CO vs. Time chart with and without agnihotra

According to Fig. 4 on Day 3, the level of CO is lower before and after Agnihotra in areas where it is performed than in areas where it is not performed, and the level of CO is higher in areas where Agnihotra is performed than in areas where it is not executed when it is completed.

Now, we will calculate the percentage of decrease in the average CO level in the areas where Agnihotra is performed. On day 3, we have 6.3 % less CO level at the place where Agnihotra is done than in other places.

Analysis of PM 2.5 with Time in Both Places at the Same Time

Figure 5 shows that on Day 1, the level of PM2.5 is higher in areas where Agnihotra is performed than in areas where it is not performed when it is performed. The level of PM2.5 is lower before and after Agnihotra in areas where it is performed than in areas where it is not performed. Table 3 shows that the average PM2.5 level decreases in those places where Agnihotra is performed.

PM 2.5 vs Time (Day 1)

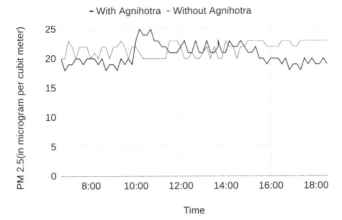

Fig. 5. Day 1 observation of PM 2.5 vs. Time chart with and without agnihotra

Table 3. Comparison in PM 2.5 level change

A place where Agnihotra is not done	A place where Agnihotra is done
Average PM 2.5 level = 21.5 μg/cubic meter	Average PM2.5 level when Agnihotra is performing = 22. Microgram/cubic meter When Agnihotra is not performing:- 19.3 μg/cubic meter

Percentage Change in PM 2.5 Level = (21.5−19.3)/21.5 = 10.2%

This means that on day 1, we have 10.2 % less PM2.5 level at the place where Agnihotra is done than other places.

PM 2.5 vs Time (Day 2)

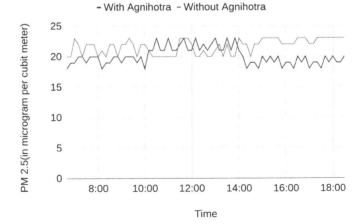

Fig. 6. Day 2 observations of PM 2.5 vs. Time chart with and without agnihotra

Figure 6 shows that on Day 2, the level of PM2.5 is lower in the regions where Agnihotra is performed than in the areas where it is not completed before and after. It is higher in the regions where Agnihotra is conducted when it is performed. This means that on day 2, we have 10.56 % less PM2.5 at where Agnihotra is done than other places.

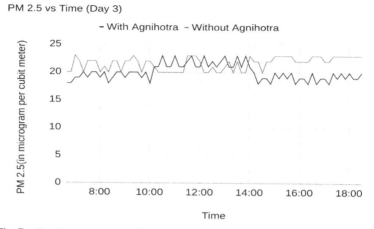

Fig. 7. Day 3 observations of PM 2.5 vs. Time chart with and without agnihotra

Figure 7 shows that on Day 3, the level of PM2.5 is lower in the areas where Agnihotra is performed than in the areas where it is not completed before and after. It is higher in the regions where Agnihotra is performed when completed. On day 3, we had 10.79 % less PM2.5 at the place where Agnihotra was done than other places.

After visualizing the graphs plotted by us, we can conclude that the AQI level doesn't change much in the daytime at the places where the Agnihotra is done. Only there is an increase in CO because of the combustion of wood, dried cow-dung cake, etc., but after some time, there is a significant drop in CO, and AQI is even better than AQI in residential areas.

In Residential Areas, CO almost remains constant at around 380 (referenced from the data collected), but in places where Agnihotri are performed continuously, the CO level increases to around 500 (due to the combustion of wood at the time of agnihotra) but in other time this level decreased up to 340-360 ppm(signifying the positive aspect of Agnihotra). Sacrificial fire breaks up the impurities of the air and reduces them to their parts, which, getting lighter, are expelled from the house and replaced by fresh air from outside. Similarly, The PM 2.5 level also gets to 18–20 micrograms per cubic meter in places where Agnihotra is done, but in other places, the PM 2.5 remains at 22-23 micrograms per cubic meter. After calculating the average of whole readings, we found:-

- In The places where Agnihotra is done, the level of CO is around 6–7% less than the amount of CO in other places
- The level of PM 2.5 is around 10–11% less than PM 2.5 in other places. This means that the significant pollutants of AQI (CO and PM 2.5) are less concentrated in the areas where Agnihotra are performed than in the regions where Agnihotra are not.

So, Agnihotra helps significantly in purifying the environment. In the study of the scientific perspective, we have also seen reactions that tell us how Agnihotra helps clarify the environment. Hence signifying that the Agnihotra helped significantly in controlling.

The pollution level of air.

6 Conclusion

Air pollution is one of the major concerns for human beings nowadays. Some studies are focused on air pollution reduction. Vedic sciences can be used to reduce the problem of air pollution, which has been scientifically proven. An IoT-enabled AQI monitoring kit helped monitor the AQI levels. With Agnihotra and without Agnihotra, effects were taken into consideration, and in conclusion, we saw a reduction in CO PPM of approximately 6–7%. In the case of PM, we received a 10–11% drop. Vedic science can help purify the air and remedy air pollution.

Disclosure of Interests. The authors have no competing interests to declare that are relevant to the content of this article.

References

1. WHO (World Health Organization), Air pollution. https://www.who.int/health-topics/air-pol lution#tab=tab_1
2. Sassi, M.S.H., Fourati, L.C.: Comprehensive air quality monitoring systems survey based on emerging computing and communication technologies. Comput. Netw. **209**, 108904 (2022). https://doi.org/10.1016/j.comnet.2022.108904
3. Abhang, P., Pathade, G.: Agnihotra technology in the perspectives of modern science - a review. Indian J. Tradit. Knowl. **16**(3), pp. 454–462 (2017). https://ssrn.com/abstract=301 9026
4. Cheng, Y., Zhou, Z., Thiele, L.: iSpray: reducing urban air pollution with intelligent water spraying. Proc. ACM Interact. Mob. Wearable Ubiquit. Technol. **6**(1), 29 (2022). Article 4. https://doi.org/10.1145/3517227
5. U.S. Environmental Protection Agency, Air Quality Index chart. https://www.epa.gov/wil dfire-smoke-course/wildfire-smoke-and-your-patients-health-air-quality-index
6. Met One Instruments, Inc. BAM 1020 AQI calculation formula. https://metone.com/how-to-calculate-aqi-and-nowcast-indices/
7. Arduino ESP8266 - Beginner Tutorial. https://create.arduino.cc/projecthub/Niv_the_anonym ous/esp8266-beginner-tutorial-project-6414c8
8. 'Does Yajna Add to the Prevalent Pollution?'—Article published in the proceedings of Ashwamedha Yajna held in Montreal, Canada (1996)
9. Mamta, S., Kumar, B., Matharu, S.: Impact of Yagya on particulate matters. Interdisc. J. Yagya Res. **1**, 01–08 (2018). https://doi.org/10.36018/ijyr.v1i1.5
10. Joshi, R.R.: "The Integrated Science of Yagya" compiled at Indian Institute of Technology, Bombay (2001)
11. Witzel, M.: Agnihotra Rituals in Nepal. In: Payne, R.K., Witzel, M. (eds.) Homa Variations: The Study of Ritual Change Across the Longue Durée, p. 371. Oxford University Press, Oxford (2015). https://doi.org/10.1093/acprof:oso/9780199351572.003.0014

12. Balkrishna, A., et al.: Vishaghn dhoop, nano-scale particles with detoxifying medicinal fume, exhibits robust anti-microbial activities: implications of disinfection potentials of a traditional ayurvedic air sterilization technique. J. Evid.-Based Integr. Med. **27**, 2515690X2110688 (2022). https://doi.org/10.1177/2515690X211068832

13. Zhan, D., Kwan, M.-P., Zhang, W., Yu, X., Meng, B., Liu, Q.: The driving factors of air quality index in China. J. Clean. Prod. **197**(Part 1), 1342–1351 (2018). ISSN: 0959-6526. https://doi.org/10.1016/j.jclepro.2018.06.108

14. Zhao, L., Zhang, X., Zhao, F.: The impact of high-speed rail on air quality in counties: econometric study with data from southern Beijing-Tianjin-Hebei, China. J. Clean. Prod. **278**, 123604 (2021). ISSN: 0959-6526. https://doi.org/10.1016/j.jclepro.2020.123604

15. Li, B., Gui, T., Chen, G., Cheng, S.: The effect of environmental regulation on population migration: evidence from China's new ambient air quality standards. J. Clean. Prod. **415**, 137786 (2023). ISSN: 0959-6526. https://doi.org/10.1016/j.jclepro.2023.137786

16. Ni, W., Hu, X., Ju, Y., Wang, Q.: Air pollution and indoor work efficiency: evidence from professional basketball players in China. J. Clean. Prod. **399**, 136644 (2023). ISSN: 0959-6526. https://doi.org/10.1016/j.jclepro.2023.136644

17. Bhatia, S., Sachdeva, S., Goswami, P.: A scientific perspective of agnihotra to curtail pollutants in the air. In: Sachdeva, S., Watanobe, Y., Bhalla, S. (eds.) Big Data Analytics in Astronomy, Science, and Engineering, BDA 2022, vol. 13830, pp. 211–219. Springer, Cham (2023). https://doi.org/10.1007/978-3-031-28350-5_17

18. Book Yagya Vimarsh by Dr. Ramprakash 2005 published by Anita Aarsh Publication (https://archive.org/details/YagyaVimarsh/page/n1/mode/2up)

19. Dhamija, L., et al.: Analytical study of effect of agnihotra on AQI and its psycho-social impacts: a perspective amidst second wave of pandemic challenges in national capital region of Indian subcontinents. Int. J. Indian Cult. Bus. Manag. **1**, 1 (2021). https://doi.org/10.1504/IJICBM.2021.10040589

20. Liu, X., et al.: Evaluating cost and benefit of air pollution control policies in China: a systematic review. J. Environ. Sci. **123**, 140–155 (2023). ISSN: 1001-0742. https://doi.org/10.1016/j.jes.2022.02.043

21. Rawat, N., Kumar, P.: Interventions for improving indoor and outdoor air quality in and around schools. Sci. Total Environ. **858**(Part 2), 159813 (2023). ISSN: 0048–9697. https://doi.org/10.1016/j.scitotenv.2022.159813

Efficient Knowledge Graph Embeddings via Kernelized Random Projections

Nidhi Goyal[1]($\boxtimes$) ⓘ, Anmol Goel[2] ⓘ, Tanuj Garg[2] ⓘ, Niharika Sachdeva[3] ⓘ, and Ponnurangam Kumaraguru[2] ⓘ

[1] Indraprastha Institute of Information Technology, Delhi (IIIT-D), New Delhi, India
nidhig@iiitd.ac.in
[2] International Institute of Information Technology, Hyderabad (IIIT-H), Hyderabad, India
pk.guru@iiit.ac.in
[3] InfoEdge India Limited, Noida, India
niharika.sachdeva@infoedge.com

Abstract. Knowledge Graph Completion (KGC) aims to predict missing entities or relations in knowledge graph but it becomes computationally expensive as KG scales. Existing research focuses on bilinear pooling-based factorization methods (LowFER, TuckER) to solve this problem. These approaches introduce too many trainable parameters which obstruct the deployment of these techniques in many real-world scenarios. In this paper, we introduce a novel parameter-efficient framework, KGRP which a) approximates bilinear pooling using Kernelized Random Projection matrix b) employs CNN for the better fusion of entities and relations to infer missing links. Our experimental results show that KGRP has 73% fewer parameters as compared to the state-of-the-art approaches (LowFER, TuckER) for the knowledge graph completion task while retaining 88% performance for the best baseline. Furthermore, we also provide novel insights on the interpretability of relation embeddings. We also test the effectiveness of KGRP on a large-scale recruitment knowledge graph of 0.25M entities.

Keywords: Knowledge Graph Completion · Kernelized Random projection · Link Prediction

1 Introduction

Knowledge Graphs (KGs) are structured graphs that store information in the form of triples (h, r, t). KGs are widely used in industrial applications ranging from recommendation to question answering. Despite the large utility of KGs in real-world applications, these suffer from the incompleteness of facts. For example, out of 3 million people in the Freebase Knowledge base, 94% of people have no known parents and 71% have no known place of birth [24]. To tackle

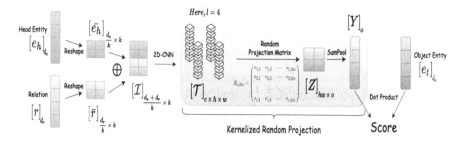

Fig. 1. An overview of our proposed framework, KGRP. The framework has two components a) Feature extraction using 2D-CNN b) Kernelized Random Projection for link prediction. The entity and relation embeddings are reshaped and converted to 2D matrices. The use of convolution layer captures the interactions between entities and relations effectively. Kernelization using a random projection matrix outputs the bilinear approximation of the embeddings.

this problem, [6] explores the task of adding new or missing links in KGs, known as Knowledge Graph Completion (KGC) task[1].

Existing works utilize translational (linear) and non-linear approaches for knowledge graph completion tasks. Additionally, bilinear models have proven effective for capturing features in literature [9]. The major limitation of bilinear pooling is quadratic growth with the number of parameters, thereby increasing computational complexity. To deal with this limitation, [2] use bilinear pooling-based factorization methods that project the outer product to lower-dimensional space using low-rank matrices. However, these methods introduce too many trainable parameters. Therefore, we need a method that further reduces parameters allowing us to project the bilinear pooling into lower-dimensional space. Random projection [10] is one of the popular dimensionality reduction methods that uses Johnson-Lindenstrauss lemma to preserve pairwise distances between the feature vectors. However, to deploy these methods, bilinear features need to be explicitly computed, and it also involves storing a large random projection matrix. Hence, [16] introduce an idea of using kernelized random projection which exploits Kronecker product and kernel-based methods to approximate bilinear pooling for fine-grained image categorization on low computational power devices like Raspberry Pi. This method eliminates the need to explicitly compute and store bilinear features. The underlying assumption is that features come from a single modality, i.e., image. We further extend and apply this idea to the KGs domain where we have multiple modalities (entities and relations). In this paper, we accomplish the Knowledge Graph Completion task by leveraging Kernelized Random Projection for parameter reduction jointly using 2D-convolution to capture the interactions between entities and relations. To

---

[1] We will use the terms '*Knowledge Graph Completion*' and '*Link Prediction*' interchangeably in the manuscript.

the best of our knowledge, this is the first work to utilize Kernelized Random Projection for the Knowledge Graph Completion task.

Our major contributions can be outlined as:

- We propose KGRP, a simple and parameter efficient framework that approximates bilinear pooling using kernelized random projection matrix for link prediction. We make use of convolutions to capture the interactions between entities and relations for the feature extraction task.
- We provide new insights and analysis of relations for KGRP on benchmark datasets. KGRP is able to model relationships well in comparison to baselines.
- We experiment on benchmark datasets, KGRP provides a reduction in parameters while maintaining on par performance against most of the prior works. We also validate the effectiveness of KGRP on a large-scale recruitment domain Knowledge Graph.

2   Related Works

2.1   Translational and Factorization-Based Models

Existing approaches on factorization focused on translational methods such as TransE [6], TransR [14], TransH [23], and TransD [11]. TransE [7] represents entities and relationships in the same space. It is a simple and efficient knowledge graph embedding technique but limited in capacity to deal with 1-to-1 relations and cannot handle 1-to-N, N-to-1, and N-to-N relations. TransH [23] introduces a mechanism where entities are projected onto relation-specific hyperplanes, allowing for distinct roles of an entity across various relations. TransR [14] introduces a projection matrix for every relation. TransD [11] simplifies TransR [14] by decomposing into product of two vectors instead of a single complex projection matrix. TuckER [4] is a simple linear model uses Tucker decomposition of the binary tensor formed by triples for link prediction on knowledge graphs.

2.2   Bilinear Models

Bilinear models were initially introduced by [20], employing them to represent image style and content individually. More recently, [13] investigated their potential within deep learning [16,19], particularly for fine-grained image categorization. Authors [16] adapted the concepts from [15] to enhance the computational efficiency of bilinear CNNs by approximating a Random Projection of the bilinear descriptors. LowFER [3] emphasize an approach free from constraints, leveraging the low-rank factorization of bilinear models. The major limitation of bilinear pooling is quadratic growth with the number of parameters, thereby increasing computational complexity. Additionally, large number of parameters obstruct the deployment of knowledge graph embedding techniques [3] in real-world scenarios. Our Work extends and applies the idea of Kernelized Random Projection to the Knowledge Graphs domain consisting of multiple modalities (entities and relations).

3 Proposed Approach

We name our framework Knowledge Graph embeddings using Kernelized Random Projection (KGRP). As illustrated in Fig. 1, our framework has two components: a) Feature extraction using 2D-CNN b) Kernelized Random Projection. In the following sections, we discuss our problem formulation and explain components in the architecture.

Given the set of entities $\mathcal{E}$ and relations $\mathcal{R}$ in a Knowledge Graph KG, the task of Knowledge Graph Completion is to assign a score to a triple (e_h, r, e_t), i.e., $\mathcal{F}(e_h, r, e_t)$ where $e_h \in \mathcal{E}$ is the head entity, $e_t \in \mathcal{E}$ is the object entity and $r \in \mathcal{R}$ is the relation between them.

3.1 Feature Extraction

Given an entity $e_h \in \mathcal{E}$, we represent its embedding vector e_h of dimension d_e as a look-up from entity embedding matrix $E \in \mathbb{R}^{n_h \times d_e}$, where $n_h = |\mathcal{E}|$. Similarly, for a relation $r \in \mathcal{R}$, we represent its embedding vector $\mathbf{r}$ of dimension d_r as look-up from relation embedding matrix $R \in \mathbb{R}^{n_r \times d_r}$, where $n_r = |\mathcal{R}|$. Both $\mathcal{E}$ and $\mathcal{R}$ are initialized randomly from a uniform distribution. First, we reshape the head entity embedding and relation embedding $e_h \in \mathbb{R}^{d_e}$ and $\mathbf{r} \in \mathbb{R}^{d_r}$, as $\bar{e}_h \in \mathbb{R}^{(d_e/k) \times k}$ & $\bar{r} \in \mathbb{R}^{(d_r/k) \times k}$ respectively where k is some common divisor of d_e and d_r. We then concatenate $\bar{e}_h$ & $\bar{r}$ to get a 2D tensor $\mathcal{I}$ of dimensions $[(d_e + d_r)/k \times k]$. This is done to map the head entity and relation to the common space. We apply a 2D convolutional layer on the resultant matrix to obtain a 3D tensor $\mathcal{T} \in \mathbb{R}^{c \times h \times w}$ i.e., c 2D feature maps of dimensions $h \times w$.

$$\mathcal{T} = CNN(\bar{e}_h \oplus \bar{r}) \tag{1}$$

The use of convolution layers captures the interactions between entities and relations in a better manner.

3.2 Kernelized Random Projection for Link Prediction

Once the features are extracted, we want to do Bilinear pooling over these features. Bilinear pooling works on the assumption that entities and relations belong to two different modalities. The goal of Bilinear pooling is to compute a global descriptor for a 3D tensor $(\mathcal{T})$ obtained from 2D-CNN by computing the outer product of local descriptors and then applying mean pooling over locations l. In Eq. 2, $\otimes$ defines the Kronecker product and $\mathcal{L}$ is the set of existing locations. Hence, there are hw locations in $\mathcal{L}$ and each local descriptor $\mathcal{T}(l)$ will be of size c, where c is the number of channels.

$$\Phi(\mathcal{T}) = \sum_{l \in \mathcal{L}} \mathcal{T}(l) \otimes \mathcal{T}(l) \tag{2}$$

Now, we want to approximate the bilinear pooling using kernelized random projection. We define a random projection matrix as $\bar{R}$ (Eq. 3), the entries of the random matrix are drawn from discrete or sparse distribution as defined by [1]. Here the sparsity is defined by $s = 1$ or $s = 3$. It has been suggested that greater sparsity levels can cause some loss in accuracy [12].

$$\bar{R}_{c,2to} = \sqrt{s} \begin{cases} 1 \text{ with prob. } 1/2\,s, \\ 0 \text{ with prob. } 1 - 1/s, \\ -1 \text{ with prob. } 1/2\,s \end{cases} \tag{3}$$

If we utilize the random projection vectors $\{r_1, r_2, r_3, r_4, \ldots\ldots r_{2t}\}$ as described by authors [16], then we will be performing valid random projection for some value of t (see Eq. 4).

$$\sum_{j=0}^{t-1} \left(\frac{r_{2j+1} \otimes r_{2j+2}}{\sqrt{t}} \right) \tag{4}$$

Equation 5 describes the property of the Kronecker product. Our task is to achieve RHS by approximating the bilinear pooling in the manner described in LHS of Eq. 5. We obtain Z of dimension $hw \times o$ using this property (See Fig. 1).

$$\langle x \otimes r_1 \rangle \langle x \otimes r_2 \rangle = \langle x \otimes x, r_1 \otimes r_2 \rangle \tag{5}$$

Furthermore, the same idea is extended to Eq. 6. In Eq. 7, the inner summation is equivalent to Z, the outer summation is the sum pooling, and the output obtained is y_i.

$$y_i = \frac{1}{\sqrt{o}} \left\langle \Phi(\mathcal{I}), \sum_{j=0}^{t-1} \left(\frac{r_{2j+1} \otimes r_{2j+2}}{\sqrt{t}} \right) \right\rangle_{R^{c2}} \tag{6}$$

$$\therefore y_i = \frac{1}{\sqrt{to}} \sum_{\mathcal{T} \in L} \sum_{j=0}^{t-1} \langle \mathcal{T}(l), r_{2j+1} \rangle \langle \mathcal{T}(l), r_{2j+2} \rangle \tag{7}$$

The above procedure is repeated o times to generate the complete output representation Y according to Eq. 8

$$Y = [y_1, ..., y_o] \tag{8}$$

The output Y is of dimension o such that $o = d_e$. To get the matching scores, we perform the inner product of this output with the object entity embedding $e_t \in \mathbb{R}^{d_e}$.

$$\mathcal{F}(e_h, r, \bar{e}_t) = \langle y_i, \bar{e}_t \rangle \tag{9}$$

We apply the sigmoid function after Eq. 9 to get the probability $p(\mathcal{F}(e_h, r, \bar{e}_t) = \sigma(\mathcal{F}(e_h, r, \bar{e}_t)$ of a triple belonging to a KG.

4   Experiments

4.1   Datasets

To evaluate our model, we perform experiments on two benchmark datasets, i.e., FB15k-237 [21] and WN18RR [8]. FB15k-237 is a subset of Freebase [5]

& WN18RR is a subset of WordNet [17]. Table 1 reports the entity, relation, train, test, and valid triples statistics on these two datasets. FB15k-237 [6] and WN18RR [6] are other benchmark datasets that were used previously in knowledge graph embeddings literature but deprecated due to the known test set leakage problem [8]. We evaluate in a filtered setting, i.e., during ranking, we remove corrupt triples which already exist in one of the training, validation, or test sets.

Table 1. Dataset Statistics for two benchmark datasets, FB15k-237 and WN18RR.

	FB15k-237	WN18RR
Entities	14,541	40,943
Relations	237	11
Train triples	272,115	86,835
Valid triples	17,535	3,034
Test triples	20,466	3,134

4.2 Experimental Setup

We perform coarse grid search to find the best set of hyperparameters for FB15k-237 and WN18RR. We utilize the given ranges i.e. $d_e = d_r \in \{30, 50, 100, 150, 200, 250\}$; learning rate $(lr) \in \{3*10^{-4}, 5*10^{-4}, 10^{-3}, 3*10^{-3}\}$; number of channels $(c) \in \{128, 256, 512, 1024, 2048\}$. We use $d_e = d_r = 200$, $lr = 5*10^{-4}$, dropouts= $\{0.2, 0.2, 0.3\}$, and $c = 2048$ for FB15k-237. We use the same hyperparameters and training settings for WN18RR except for $lr = 3*10^{-3}$ and $c = 1024$.

Baselines: We compare our model with several existing state-of-the-art approaches such as DistMult [25], ConvE [8], ComplEx [22], RotatE [18], TuckER [4], & LowFER [2].

4.3 Results and Analysis

Table 2 compares the parameter expression and number of trainable parameters for KGRP and baselines (TuckER, LowFER, ComplEx, ConvE). KGRP has 73% fewer parameters as compared to LowFER & TuckER on FB15K-237 whereas 14.6% fewer parameters on WN18RR. KGRP has 3M and 2M less parameters on FB15k-237 when compared to ComplEx and ConvE respectively. For WN18RR, decrease in parameters is 8M for ComplEx and 4M for ConvE. It is evident from Table 2 that KGRP introduces less number of trainable parameters and $n_e d_e + n_r d_r >> (wh+1)*c$. Table 3 reports the results (Hits@1, Hits@3, Hits@10, and MRR) of KGRP as compared to baselines. These metrics are well defined in the literature [8]. For FB15k-237, KGRP outperforms DistMult and ComplEx by +7% on the toughest Hits@1. KGRP also outperforms RotatE by 2% on MRR for FB15K-237. KGRP has an approximately 4.5% decrease in MRR as compared to LowFER and TucKER on both WN18RR and FB15K-237. Table 3 shows the drop in performance along with the reduced number of parameters as compared to the best baseline LowFER. We believe that KGRP captures multimodal (e_h, r) interactions using 2D-CNN and preserves the pairwise distances for most of the entities and relations using random projection.

Table 2. Comparison of parameters with baselines on FB15K-237 and WN18RR. † The parameters reported for ConvE are taken from their published paper for corresponding highest metrics.

Model	Number of parameters		
	Expression	FB15k-237	WN18RR
TuckER [4]	$(n_e + 4) * d_e + n_r d_r + d_e^2 d_r$	11M	9.4M
LowFER [2]	$(n_e + 4) * d_e + n_r d_r + (d_e + d_r) * k d_e$	11.3M	9.6M
ComplEx [22]	$2n_e d_e + 2n_r d_r$	6M	16.5M
ConvE [8]	$(n_e + n_r + 2) * d + (wh + 3) * c +$ $(2d_1 - w + 1) * (d_2 - h + 1) * cd + 2$	5.05M	10.14M
KGRP	$(n_e + 4) * d_e + n_r d_r + (wh + 1) * c$	**3M**	**8.2M**

Analysis of Relations: Figure 2 shows the 3D-PCA visualization of our relation embeddings trained on the WN18RR dataset. We use cosine distance to find the nearest neighbors for all the relations. We demonstrate that {*also_see_reverse, similar_to, similar_to_reverse*} are the closest relations to **also_see**. Hence, KGRP can incorporate semantic meaning (*also_see, similar_to*) and capture symmetric property (*also_see, also_see_reverse*) for all the relations. Table 4 reports the hits@10 metrics on WN18RR for individual relations. KGRP has similar (95.9%) performance for symmetric relations such as *derivationally_related_form*). We observe the performance increase on 8 out of 11 relations as compared to LowFER and TucKER. Furthermore, for relations such as *sysnet_domain_topic_of* and *hypernym*, there is a decrease in performance. The relation *hypernym* is present in 40% of the total number of triples which could be the possible reason for overall less Hits@10 as compared to LowFER.

Table 3. MRR, Hits @{1, 3, 10} results of link prediction on FB15k-237 and WN18RR. † The evaluation results for baselines are taken from literature. Missing scores not reported are denoted by "–".

Model	FB15k-237				WN18RR			
	MRR	Hits1	Hits3	Hits10	MRR	Hits1	Hits3	Hits10
DistMult [25]	0.241	0.155	0.263	0.419	0.430	0.390	0.440	0.490
ComplEx [22]	0.247	0.158	0.275	0.428	0.440	0.410	0.460	0.510
ConvE [8]	0.325	0.237	0.356	0.501	0.430	0.400	0.440	0.520
TuckER [4]	0.358	0.266	0.394	0.544	0.470	0.443	0.482	0.526
LowFER [2]	0.359	0.266	0.396	0.544	0.465	0.434	0.479	0.526
RotatE [18]	0.297	0.205	0.328	0.480	–	–	–	–
KGRP (Ours)	0.312	0.228	0.342	0.475	0.420	0.384	0.438	0.481
Performance (↓)	↓13%	↓14.2%	↓13.6%	↓12.6%	↓9.6%	↓11.5%	↓8.5%	↓8.5%
Parameters	↓ **73.4%**				**↓14.6%**			

4.4   Ablation Study

We demonstrate the effect of components and effect of dimensions for our KGRP framework.

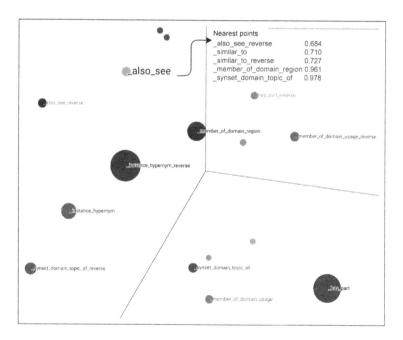

Fig. 2. 3-D PCA visualisation of relation embeddings using KGRP on WN18RR. *also_see, also_see_reverse, also_see,* and *similar_to* are correctly clustered together.

Effect of Components: One could argue that KGRP achieves substantial performance due to CNN module as compared to the baseline methods. We compensate for this by removing the 2D-CNN component from KGRP. We observe that removing 2D-CNN for FB15K-237, there is a performance drop of 1% across all the metrics whereas, for WN18RR, there is a performance drop of 7–10% for MRR and Hits@1 metrics. This is because WN18RR has less number of relations, i.e. 18 as compared to the number of entities in the dataset. Therefore, 2D-CNN assists the kernelized random projection by capturing better interactions among the entities and relations for these kinds of datasets. However, with similar parameter budgets, the baselines couldn't achieve the same accuracy.

Effect of Hyperparameters: We noticed a ±1% increase in MRR for each dimension in the hyperparameter range of d_e and d_r. We observe a similar trend with changing $c \in \{128, 256, 512, 1024, 2048\}$.

Table 4. Hits@10 of TuckER, LowFER, and KGRP for individual relations of WN18RR dataset.

Relations	# of triples	TuckER	LowFER	KGRP
also_see	112	0.614	0.627	**0.688**
derivationally_related_form	2148	0.957	0.957	**0.959**
has_part	344	0.129	0.138	**0.235**
hypernym	2502	0.189	0.189	0.128
instance_hypernym	244	0.591	0.576	0.447
member_meronym	506	0.131	0.155	**0.290**
member_of_domain_region	52	0.083	0.060	**0.481**
member_of_domain_usage	48	0.096	0.025	**0.396**
similar_to	6	1.0	1.0	**1.0**
synset_domain_topic_of	228	0.499	0.494	0.417
verb_group	78	0.974	0.974	**0.974**

4.5   Case Study on Large-Scale KG

We also experiment with real-world KG from one of the largest recruitment platforms in India. Our dataset consists of 2.6M train triples, 0.25M entities, and 13 relations. This large-scale dataset has 18× more entities than FB15K-237. For this, KGRP has 45.9M parameters and achieves 50% MRR and 45% Hits@1. Therefore, we validate that the KGRP model is scalable and parameter efficient for large-scale real-world datasets.

5   Conclusion

In this paper, we introduce a novel parameter-efficient framework called KGRP which uses CNN for feature extraction and approximates bilinear pooling using Kernelized Random Projection matrix to infer missing links. We carried out an ablation study of our framework. Our experimental results show that KGRP has 73% fewer parameters as compared to the state-of-the-art approaches (LowFER, TuckER) for the KGC task. We also validate and show the effectiveness of KGRP in a real-world scenario for large-scale recruitment domain KG. We provide an open-source code to ensure reproducibility. In the future, we want to deploy the proposed framework for large-scale enterprise KGs accomplishing the Knowledge Graph Completion task. We believe that our model is generalizable to other real-world datasets as well.

References

1. Achlioptas, D.: Database-friendly random projections: johnson-lindenstrauss with binary coins. J. Comput. Syst. Sci. **66**(4), 671–687 (2003)
2. Amin, S., Varanasi, S., Dunfield, K.A., Neumann, G.: LowFER: low-rank bilinear pooling for link prediction. In: III, H.D., Singh, A. (eds.) Proceedings of the 37th International Conference on Machine Learning. Proceedings of Machine Learning Research, vol. 119, pp. 257–268. PMLR, 13–18 July 2020. http://proceedings.mlr.press/v119/amin20a.html
3. Amin, S., Varanasi, S., Dunfield, K.A., Neumann, G.: Lowfer: low-rank bilinear pooling for link prediction. In: International Conference on Machine Learning, pp. 257–268. PMLR (2020)
4. Balazevic, I., Allen, C., Hospedales, T.: Tucker: tensor factorization for knowledge graph completion. In: Proceedings of the 2019 Conference on Empirical Methods in Natural Language Processing and the 9th International Joint Conference on Natural Language Processing (EMNLP-IJCNLP) (2019). https://doi.org/10.18653/v1/d19-1522, http://dx.doi.org/10.18653/v1/D19-1522
5. Bollacker, K., Evans, C., Paritosh, P., Sturge, T., Taylor, J.: Freebase: a collaboratively created graph database for structuring human knowledge. In: Proceedings of the 2008 ACM SIGMOD International Conference on Management of Data, pp. 1247–1250. SIGMOD '08, Association for Computing Machinery, New York, NY, USA (2008). https://doi.org/10.1145/1376616.1376746
6. Bordes, A., Usunier, N., Garcia-Duran, A., Weston, J., Yakhnenko, O.: Translating embeddings for modeling multi-relational data. In: Neural Information Processing Systems (NIPS), pp. 1–9. South Lake Tahoe, United States, December 2013. https://hal.archives-ouvertes.fr/hal-00920777
7. Bordes, A., Usunier, N., Garcia-Duran, A., Weston, J., Yakhnenko, O.: Translating embeddings for modeling multi-relational data. Adv. Neural Inf. Process. Syst. **26** (2013)
8. Dettmers, T., Minervini, P., Stenetorp, P., Riedel, S.: Convolutional 2d knowledge graph embeddings. In: Proceedings of the AAAI Conference on Artificial Intelligence, vol. 32, no. 1 (2018). https://ojs.aaai.org/index.php/AAAI/article/view/11573

9. Fukui, A., Park, D.H., Yang, D., Rohrbach, A., Darrell, T., Rohrbach, M.: Multi-modal compact bilinear pooling for visual question answering and visual grounding. In: Proceedings of the 2016 Conference on Empirical Methods in Natural Language Processing, pp. 457–468. Association for Computational Linguistics, Austin, Texas, November 2016. https://doi.org/10.18653/v1/D16-1044, https://www.aclweb.org/anthology/D16-1044

10. Gao, Y., Beijbom, O., Zhang, N., Darrell, T.: Compact bilinear pooling. In: Proceedings of the IEEE Conference on Computer Vision and Pattern Recognition, pp. 317–326 (2016)

11. Ji, G., He, S., Xu, L., Liu, K., Zhao, J.: Knowledge graph embedding via dynamic mapping matrix. In: Proceedings of the 53rd Annual Meeting of the Association for Computational Linguistics and the 7th International Joint Conference on Natural Language Processing (volume 1: Long papers), pp. 687–696 (2015)

12. Li, P., Hastie, T.J., Church, K.W.: Very sparse random projections. In: Proceedings of the 12th ACM SIGKDD International Conference on Knowledge Discovery and Data Mining, pp. 287–296. KDD '06, Association for Computing Machinery, New York, NY, USA (2006). https://doi.org/10.1145/1150402.1150436

13. Lin, T.Y., RoyChowdhury, A., Maji, S.: Bilinear CNN models for fine-grained visual recognition. In: Proceedings of the IEEE International Conference on Computer Vision, pp. 1449–1457 (2015)

14. Lin, Y., Liu, Z., Sun, M., Liu, Y., Zhu, X.: Learning entity and relation embeddings for knowledge graph completion. In: Proceedings of the AAAI Conference on Artificial Intelligence, vol. 29 (2015)

15. López-Sánchez, D., Arrieta, A.G., Corchado, J.M.: Data-independent random projections from the feature-space of the homogeneous polynomial kernel. Pattern Recognit. **82**, 130–146 (2018)

16. López-Sánchez, D., Arrieta, A.G., Corchado, J.M.: Compact bilinear pooling via kernelized random projection for fine-grained image categorization on low computational power devices. Neurocomputing **398**, 411–421 (2020)

17. Miller, G.A.: Wordnet: a lexical database for English. Commun. ACM **38**(11), 39–41 (1995). https://doi.org/10.1145/219717.219748

18. Sun, Z., Deng, Z.H., Nie, J.Y., Tang, J.: Rotate: knowledge graph embedding by relational rotation in complex space (2019)

19. Taheri, S., Toygar, Ö.: On the use of DAG-CNN architecture for age estimation with multi-stage features fusion. Neurocomputing **329**, 300–310 (2019)

20. Tenenbaum, J.B., Freeman, W.T.: Separating style and content with bilinear models. Neural Comput. **12**(6), 1247–1283 (2000)

21. Toutanova, K., Chen, D., Pantel, P., Poon, H., Choudhury, P., Gamon, M.: Representing text for joint embedding of text and knowledge bases. In: Proceedings of the 2015 Conference on Empirical Methods in Natural Language Processing, pp. 1499–1509. Association for Computational Linguistics, Lisbon, Portugal, September 2015. https://doi.org/10.18653/v1/D15-1174, https://www.aclweb.org/anthology/D15-1174

22. Trouillon, T., Welbl, J., Riedel, S., Gaussier, E., Bouchard, G.: Complex embeddings for simple link prediction. In: Balcan, M.F., Weinberger, K.Q. (eds.) Proceedings of The 33rd International Conference on Machine Learning. Proceedings of Machine Learning Research, vol. 48, pp. 2071–2080. PMLR, New York, New York, USA, 20–22 June 2016. http://proceedings.mlr.press/v48/trouillon16.html

23. Wang, Z., Zhang, J., Feng, J., Chen, Z.: Knowledge graph embedding by translating on hyperplanes. In: Proceedings of the AAAI Conference on Artificial Intelligence, vol. 28 (2014)

24. West, R., Gabrilovich, E., Murphy, K., Sun, S., Gupta, R., Lin, D.: Knowledge base completion via search-based question answering. In: Proceedings of the 23rd International Conference on World Wide Web, pp. 515–526. WWW '14, Association for Computing Machinery, New York, NY, USA (2014). https://doi.org/10.1145/2566486.2568032

25. Yang, B., Yih, S.W.t., He, X., Gao, J., Deng, L.: Embedding entities and relations for learning and inference in knowledge bases. In: Proceedings of the International Conference on Learning Representations (ICLR) 2015. ICLR (2015). https://www.microsoft.com/en-us/research/publication/embedding-entities-and-relations-for-learning-and-inference-in-knowledge-bases/

Cyber Systems and Information Security

From Silos to Unity: Seamless Cross-Platform Gaming by Leveraging Blockchain Technology

Rashmi P. Sarode[1]($\boxtimes$), Yutaka Watanobe[2], and Subhash Bhalla[2]

[1] Department of Computer Science and Engineering, IIT Madras, Chennai, India
rashmipsarode@gmail.com
[2] Department of Information Systems, University of Aizu, Aizuwakamatsu, Japan
yutaka@u-aizu.ac.jp

Abstract. By exploring the impact of blockchain technology within cross-platform gaming, this study confronts pivotal hurdles including asset ownership, player identity, and the interoperability within virtual economies. Through a blend of theoretical scrutiny and practical insights, the research illuminates blockchain's capacity to authenticate digital asset ownership, forge unified player profiles, and streamline interactions across various gaming platforms. Further, notwithstanding the solutions, the effective amalgamations of blockchain hinges on concerted efforts from game developers, platform operators, and additional key players. It emphasizes the criticality of norms, scalability, and user acceptance. Thus, this study advocates for a comprehensive approach to unlock blockchain's vast capabilities in enhancing cross-platform gaming experiences.

Keywords: Cross-platform gaming · blockchain technology · digital asset ownership · interoperability

1 Introduction

In recent years, the gaming industry has been transformed by a rising demand for cross-platform play. This shift has led to the evolving preferences of gamers who now seek a more interconnected and inclusive gaming experience. The appeal of cross-platform gaming is twofold: it is not just about bridging the technical divide between consoles, PCs, and mobile devices but also about fulfilling the innate human desire to connect, interact, and compete in a unified gaming community. Categorizing games is crucial for differentiating single-player from multiplayer experiences, competitive dynamics, skill significance, and a range of

---

Note: The work reported in this manuscript was carried out when one of the authors (Rashmi P. Sarode), was working in the University of Aizu, Japan with the other two authors of this paper.

genres like puzzles and RPGs. This distinction is key to refining cross-platform interoperability and understanding blockchain's impact in gaming.

Creating a seamless cross-platform experience presents challenges. Each gaming platform, with its unique capabilities, offers a distinct set of strengths and limitations. A game that is optimized for a high-end PC might not perform as effectively on a mobile device [1]. It prompts developers to adjust game elements for broad compatibility. Furthermore, disparities in game updates across platforms can introduce inconsistencies, impacting gameplay and user experience, particularly in multiplayer settings [2].

Besides the technical challenges, there are broader issues. Players invest significant time, and real money, in acquiring digital assets. They expect clear ownership rights. Since these assets span across platforms, questions about their validity and ownership emerge. Additionally, the task of managing player identities across platforms, each with its authentication systems, becomes complex [3].

Blockchain was originally developed for cryptocurrencies. Its decentralized ledger system presents a viable answer to numerous challenges in the gaming industry [4]. With attributes like transparency, security, and immutability, blockchain stands out as an instrument for standardizing in-game assets and player identities across platforms. Additionally, the implementation of smart contracts, self-executing agreements with terms embedded directly in the code, can guarantee uniform game mechanics, regardless of the platform in use [5].

The gaming industry stands to benefit by using Blockchain. Beginning with genuine ownership of in-game assets to the standardization of game mechanics, the possibilities are vast and transformative [6]. As this technology continues to evolve, it is anticipated that more game developers will harness its potential, leading to a more enriched gaming experience for players globally [7].

The objective of this paper is to navigate the intricate landscape of cross-platform gaming, shedding light on its challenges and exploring the transformative role of blockchain. Through this exploration, we aim to envision a future where cross-platform gaming, bolstered by blockchain, offers a harmonious and unified gaming ecosystem.

The manuscript continues from Sect. 2, which delves into the "Related Work," providing a backdrop of existing literature and studies in the domain. This is followed by Sect. 3, discussing the "Blockchain Fundamentals in Gaming," laying down the foundational principles of how blockchain integrates with the gaming world. In Sect. 4, we explore the "Transformation Potential of Blockchain in Gaming," highlighting the paradigm shifts this technology can bring about. Section 5 delves deeper into practical aspects, focusing on "Applying Blockchain to Gaming," elucidating the methodologies and techniques. Moving forward, Sect. 6 sheds light on the "Potential Benefits and Limitations" of this integration, offering a balanced perspective. Section 7, titled "The Road Ahead: Collaborative Efforts and Standardization," emphasizes the importance of collective endeavors and the need for industry standards to fully harness blockchain's potential in gaming. The manuscript culminates with Sect. 8, providing a comprehensive "Summary and Conclusions" of the research presented.

2   Related Work

The authors [8] discuss the transformative potential of cloud computing in the realm of online gaming. Moving away from traditional computation methods, there's an emphasis on computation as a service rather than a product. This shift allows users to bypass the need for expensive hardware and software, opting instead for cloud-based applications and infrastructures on a pay-per-use basis. Gamers often face challenges due to variations in computing platforms, which can limit their experiences. However, cross-platform online games deployed on the cloud allow players to engage with multiple participants using any device. This approach addresses the issue of game availability across different platforms and eliminates the need for new devices or multiple game licenses. The design for such games as a cloud computing service is further detailed, highlighting its benefits and addressing certain limitations, such as blurry graphics from inefficient graphic conversions between platforms.

The authors [9] present a comprehensive study on the potential of gaming platforms for telemedicine applications, focusing on a cross-platform comparison. The research evaluated the functionality of widely-used gaming platforms, including the Nintendo Wii, Microsoft Xbox 360, and Sony Playstation 3, for their applicability in telemedicine. A Home Automated Telemanagement (HAT) system was developed for patients with chronic diseases, such as congestive heart failure (CHF). This system aids patients in adhering to their treatment plans, monitoring symptoms, medication usage, and quality of life, while also providing disease-specific education. The HAT system was designed to operate on these gaming platforms, leveraging their internet-based application capabilities. The study found that all three platforms could effectively support a comprehensive telemedicine system, even for patients without prior computer or video game experience. However, each platform presented its own unique development and interface challenges.

The authors [10] introduce "CloudArcade," a novel cloud gaming system that integrates blockchain technology to address the challenges of traditional cloud gaming pricing models. By leveraging blockchain-empowered tokens, CloudArcade offers a unique payment method where players use cryptocurrency tokens, akin to coins in traditional arcades, to access gaming services. Instead of time-based pricing, CloudArcade's model is based on gaming content, such as limited lives in a game. This approach ensures transparency in transactions, as all are recorded on the blockchain, and allows for dynamic pricing that reflects market demand. The system is designed to enhance the gaming experience by eliminating concerns related to fluctuating prices and frequent payment requests. The paper also discusses the potential of blockchain in ensuring transparent, secure, and efficient transactions, and highlights the need for new business models that can optimize both player experience and resource consumption in cloud gaming.

3   Blockchain Fundamentals in Gaming

Blockchain technology has been making waves across various industries, and the gaming sector is no exception. One of the primary features of blockchain that resonates with the gaming community is decentralization. Unlike traditional gaming platforms where a central authority controls the game's assets and rules, blockchain allows for a decentralized system where players have true ownership of their in-game items. This means that items, once earned or purchased, belong to the player and can be traded, sold, or used across different games that recognize the blockchain.

The categorization of games is also a fundamental aspect that blockchain can support. By providing a framework for tagging and tracking different game types—whether they are competitive, cooperative, ability-based, item-centric, or character-driven—blockchain can facilitate a more organized and interoperable gaming ecosystem. This categorization extends to game genres, ensuring that assets and player achievements are relevant and transferable within similar game experiences

Another pivotal feature of blockchain in gaming is immutability. Once a transaction or an action is recorded on the blockchain, it cannot be altered or deleted. This ensures that players' achievements, scores, and in-game assets are permanently recorded, providing a tamper-proof history of their gaming journey. This immutability can also prevent cheating and ensure fairness in competitive gaming scenarios.

Lastly, transparency is a cornerstone of blockchain technology, and it plays a crucial role in gaming. With blockchain, all transactions and actions are recorded on a public ledger, ensuring that game developers and players can verify any transaction or event. This level of transparency can build trust among players, especially in games that involve monetary transactions or competitive rankings.

4   The Transformative Potential of Blockchain in Gaming

The integration of blockchain technology into the gaming industry is not just a technological advancement; it's a revolution. This shift promises to redefine the very fabric of gaming, from player interactions to game design. As we delve deeper into the transformative aspects, we will explore the broader implications and the future possibilities that blockchain brings to the gaming table.

4.1   True Ownership and Blockchain's Assurance of In-Game Assets

The concept of true ownership in the digital realm has always been elusive. Traditional gaming systems operate on a licensing model where players essentially "rent" digital assets. However, blockchain changes this perspective.

- **Transparency and Immutability:** At the heart of blockchain's promise is its transparent and immutable nature. Every transaction, once recorded, becomes a permanent part of the blockchain. This ensures that players have undeniable proof of their digital asset ownership.

- **Empowering Players:** With true ownership, players are no longer passive consumers. They become active participants, with the freedom to trade, sell, or utilize their assets across different gaming platforms. This not only enhances the gaming experience but also introduces new economic dynamics into the gaming world.
- **Benefits to Developers:** From a developer's perspective, blockchain opens up avenues for innovative game design. By creating unique, tradable assets, developers can foster deeper engagement, trust, and loyalty within the gaming community. Moreover, this model can lead to new monetization strategies, enhancing the profitability of gaming ventures.

Moreover, blockchain's assurance of in-game assets can be enriched by categorizing these assets according to the game's nature and genre. This categorization ensures that the value and utility of assets are preserved when transferred across games that share similar characteristics, thereby enhancing the player's investment in the gaming platform.

4.2 Unified Player Identity and Profile Management

The idea of a unified player identity transcends mere convenience. It's about creating a cohesive gaming universe where players' achievements, experiences, and assets are recognized universally.

- **Consistency Across Platforms:** Imagine a world where your achievements in one game are recognized and rewarded in another. With blockchain, this becomes a reality. Players can carry their identity across games, ensuring that their efforts and achievements are never lost.
- **Data Security and Privacy:** Storing player profiles on the blockchain ensures unparalleled security. Given the decentralized nature of blockchain, the risk of data breaches is minimized. Moreover, players have control over their data, ensuring privacy and consent.
- **Tailored Gaming Experiences:** For developers, unified profiles provide invaluable insights into player behaviors and preferences. This data can be harnessed to create personalized gaming experiences, enhancing player engagement and retention.

Figure 1 showcases the unified player profile's integration within a gaming platform, illustrating how user data and interactions flow seamlessly through various components to enhance the holistic gaming experience.

4.3 Seamless Interactions Across Platforms

The gaming industry has long been fragmented, with players confined to individual platforms. Blockchain promises to unify this fragmented landscape.

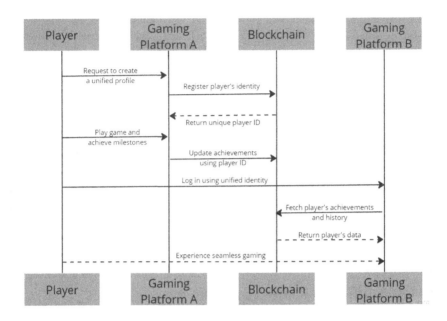

Fig. 1. Unified Gaming Profile Identity

- **Breaking Down Barriers:** With blockchain, the boundaries between different gaming platforms become porous. Players from diverse platforms can come together, compete, collaborate, and share experiences in a unified environment.
- **Enhanced Player Experience:** This seamless interaction ensures that players are no longer restricted by platform limitations. They can explore a broader gaming universe, enriching their overall experience.
- **Broadening Audience Reach:** For developers, cross-platform interactions mean a broader audience base. This can lead to increased game popularity, higher player engagement, and enhanced revenue opportunities.

4.4 Bridging Gaming Platforms and Economies with Blockchain

Blockchain's potential extends beyond interactions; it promises to redefine gaming economies.

- **Universal Gaming Currency:** Blockchain introduces the possibility of a universal gaming currency. Players can earn in one game and spend in another, creating a fluid and dynamic gaming economy.
- **Real-World Value:** With blockchain, in-game assets gain real-world value. They can be traded in decentralized marketplaces, leading to new economic opportunities for players.

– **Revolutionizing Game Design:** For developers, this interconnected economy offers a chance to design games that are not just entertaining but also economically rewarding. By integrating real-world value into game design, developers can create more engaging and immersive gaming ecosystems.

5 Applying Blockchain to Gaming

The application of blockchain technology to the gaming industry presents a myriad of solutions to existing challenges. Traditional gaming systems often grapple with issues related to asset ownership, security, and cross-platform limitations. Blockchain, with its decentralized, transparent, and immutable nature, can address these challenges head-on, offering a more secure and player-centric gaming environment.

5.1 Addressing Challenges with Blockchain

One of the primary challenges in the gaming industry is the lack of true ownership of digital assets. Players often spend significant time and resources acquiring in-game assets, only to find that they don't truly own them. Blockchain can rectify this by providing players with genuine ownership, backed by transparent and immutable transaction records. Additionally, security concerns, such as hacking and unauthorized asset transfers, can be mitigated using blockchain's robust encryption and consensus mechanisms. Furthermore, the siloed nature of gaming platforms can be overcome by leveraging blockchain's potential for cross-platform integration, allowing for seamless interactions and a unified gaming economy.

5.2 Registering a Digital Asset

In the process of registering a digital asset, it is crucial to incorporate the game's categorization—its type, genre, and the role of abilities, items, or characters. This categorization, recorded on the blockchain, will facilitate the asset's applicability and relevance across the gaming landscape, allowing for a more nuanced and meaningful asset transfer system.

Registering a digital asset involves creating a unique and verifiable record of that asset on the blockchain. This process ensures that the asset is authenticated and belongs to a specific player or entity. Once registered, the asset's details, ownership, and transaction history become immutable and transparent, providing genuine ownership and preventing unauthorized duplication or manipulation.

The pseudocode for registering a digital asset is as follows:

```
function registerAsset(playerID, assetDetails) {
    // Check if asset already exists
    if (blockchain.contains(assetDetails.assetID)) {
        return "Asset already registered";
    }

    // Create a new asset entry
    newAsset = {
        owner: playerID,
        details: assetDetails,
        timestamp: getCurrentTimestamp(),
        assetID: generateUniqueAssetID()
    };

    // Add the new asset to the blockchain
    blockchain.add(newAsset);
    return "Asset registered successfully";
}
```

5.3   Transferring an Asset Between Players

Transferring an asset between players entails updating the ownership record of a digital asset on the blockchain from one player to another. This process ensures a secure and verifiable change of ownership, maintaining the asset's integrity. Once transferred, the asset's new ownership is permanently recorded, providing transparency and preventing unauthorized transactions.

The pseudocode for transferring a digital asset is as follows:

```
function transferAsset(senderID, receiverID, assetID) {
    // Check if asset exists and belongs to the sender
    asset = blockchain.get(assetID);
    if (asset == null || asset.owner != senderID) {
        return "Invalid asset or unauthorized transfer";
    }

    // Update the asset's owner to the receiver
    asset.owner = receiverID;
    asset.timestamp = getCurrentTimestamp();

    // Record the transfer on the blockchain
    blockchain.update(assetID, asset);
    return "Asset transferred successfully";
}
```

The integration of blockchain into gaming can revolutionize the way players interact with games, ensuring a more secure, transparent, and interconnected gaming experience.

6   Potential Benefits and Limitations

The integration of blockchain technology with the gaming techniques brings forth many advantages. One of the most significant benefits is the assurance of true ownership of digital assets. Players can have genuine ownership of their in-game items, fostering a sense of achievement and value. This true ownership model, backed by the transparent and immutable nature of the blockchain, also paves the way for cross-game asset utilization, enhancing the overall gaming experience. Furthermore, the decentralized nature of blockchain ensures heightened security, reducing the risks of hacking and unauthorized transactions.

The categorization of games can significantly enhance the benefits of blockchain in gaming. It allows for targeted asset creation and transfer, aligning with players' preferences and gaming habits. However, this also introduces the challenge of developing a universally accepted categorization system that can be complex to implement and may require significant industry consensus.

However, while the benefits are substantial, there are also inherent limitations and challenges to consider. One of the primary technical challenges is the integration of blockchain into existing gaming infrastructures. Traditional gaming systems might not be readily compatible with blockchain, necessitating significant overhauls or the development of new platforms. Scalability is another concern. As games grow in popularity and user base, the blockchain must be able to handle an increasing number of transactions without compromising speed or efficiency.

User adoption presents its own set of challenges. While the gaming community is often receptive to technological advancements, the complexity of blockchain can be daunting for many. Ensuring user-friendly interfaces and seamless integration is crucial for widespread adoption. Educating players about the benefits and workings of blockchain can also play a pivotal role in its acceptance.

Lastly, the evolving landscape of regulatory and legal considerations cannot be overlooked. As blockchain ventures into the realm of real-world value and transactions, it attracts the attention of regulatory bodies. Developers and platforms must navigate these legal waters carefully, ensuring compliance while also advocating for regulations that support innovation.

7   The Road Ahead: Collaborative Efforts and Standardization

As the gaming industry embarks on the journey of integrating blockchain technology, collaboration emerges as a pivotal element. The vast and diverse landscape of the gaming world, with its myriad of developers, platform providers, and other stakeholders, necessitates a unified approach. Individual efforts, while commendable, might lead to fragmented solutions that lack interoperability. By fostering collaborative initiatives, the industry can ensure that blockchain integration is seamless, consistent, and maximally beneficial. Such collaborations can lead to the sharing of best practices, pooling of resources, and the development of joint solutions that cater to a broader audience.

Standardization is another crucial aspect of this integration. Without standardized protocols and practices, the risk of disjointed and incompatible systems increases. Standardization ensures that blockchain's implementation across different games and platforms adheres to a set of guidelines, promoting consistency and interoperability. This not only enhances the user experience but also simplifies the integration process for developers. Looking ahead, the potential for blockchain-enhanced cross-platform gaming is immense. As standardization and collaboration become industry norms, players can anticipate a future where they can seamlessly transition between games, carry over assets, and engage in a unified gaming ecosystem. This vision, while ambitious, is achievable with the concerted efforts of all industry stakeholders.

In the spirit of collaboration and standardization, it is essential to develop and agree upon a standardized taxonomy of games. This taxonomy would be integrated into the blockchain to facilitate clear definitions and categorizations, ensuring consistent recognition of assets and achievements across the gaming industry. Such standardization is key to unlocking the full potential of blockchain in creating a unified and diverse gaming ecosystem

8   Summary and Conclusions

This manuscript delves deep into the transformative potential of blockchain technology in the gaming domain, systematically addressing the challenges of asset ownership, player identity, and the interoperability of virtual economies. It highlights the necessity of a well-defined and categorized system of games within the blockchain to enhance asset ownership clarity and transfer, as well as to establish a unified player identity, and promoting seamless interactions across diverse gaming platforms.

Blockchain's decentralized nature not only guarantees true ownership of in-game assets and a unified player identity system but also promotes seamless interactions across diverse gaming platforms. The integration of intelligently categorized games is key to this process, reflecting the multifaceted nature of the gaming world and sharpening the focus on cross-platform interoperability.

For future work, optimizing blockchain architectures for enhanced gaming experiences and investigating user adoption dynamics within the gaming community are promising directions. Collaboration, standardization, and integration into existing gaming systems remain essential for realizing blockchain's full potential in this rapidly evolving landscape.

References

1. Feijoo, C., et al.: Mobile gaming: industry challenges and policy implications. Telecommun. Policy **36**(3), 212–221 (2012)
2. Patil, P.P., Alvares, R.: Cross-platform application development using unity game engine. Int. J. **3**(4) (2015)
3. Fahy, R., Krewer, L.: Using open source libraries in cross platform games development. In: 2012 IEEE International Games Innovation Conference, pp. 1–5. IEEE (2012)
4. Sarode, R.P., et al.: Blockchain for committing peer-to-peer transactions using distributed ledger technologies. Int. J. Comput. Sci. Eng. **24**(3), 215–227 (2021)
5. Min, T., Cai, W.: A security case study for blockchain games. In: 2019 IEEE Games, Entertainment, Media Conference (GEM), pp. 1–8. IEEE (2019)
6. Attaran, M., et al.: Blockchain for gaming. In: Applications of Blockchain Technology in Business: Challenges and Opportunities, pp. 85–88 (2019)
7. Muthe, K.B., Sharma, K., Sri, K.E.N.: A blockchain based decentralized computing and NFT infrastructure for game networks. In: 2020 Second International Conference on Blockchain Computing and Applications (BCCA), pp. 73–77. IEEE (2020)
8. Kangiwa, B.I.: Cross platform online gaming as a service: a cloud computing perspective. WATARI Multidiscip. J. Sci. Technol. Educ. **2**(1), 163–171 (2014)
9. Cha, E., Wood, J., Finkelstein, J.: Using gaming platforms for telemedicine applications: a cross-platform comparison. In: Proceedings of 2012 IEEE-EMBS International Conference on Biomedical and Health Informatics, pp. 918–921. IEEE (2012)
10. Zhao, J., et al.: Cloudarcade: a blockchain empowered cloud gaming system. In: Proceedings of the 2nd ACM International Symposium on Blockchain and Secure Critical Infrastructure, pp. 31–40 (2020)

Analysis of Job Processing Data – Towards Large Cloud Infrastructure Operation Simulation

Zofia Wrona[1] , Maria Ganzha[1] , Marcin Paprzycki[2]([⊠]) ,
and Stanisław Krzyżanowski[3]

[1] Faculty of Mathematics and Information Science, Warsaw University
of Technology, Warsaw, Poland
{zofia.wrona.stud,maria.ganzha}@pw.edu.pl
[2] Systems Research Institute Polish Academy of Sciences, Warsaw, Poland
marcin.paprzycki@ibspan.waw.pl
[3] CloudFerro Sp. z o. o., Warsaw, Poland
skrzyzanowski@cloudferro.com

Abstract. Cloud computing is the most popular way of delivering on-demand computational resources. Recently, the research in this area has started to focus on carbon-aware clouds. Here, the most challenging aspects are related to defining strategies for efficient task scheduling and resource allocation. These strategies can be simulated and assessed using dedicated tools. However, to perform their accurate evaluation, the tests should reproduce close-to-real conditions of the actual cloud center. In particular, they require running simulations with various mixtures of tasks that replicate the actual cloud center operation. Therefore, the main aim of this work was to prepare tools that will allow the generation of synthetic job streams, with mixes of realistic types of computational tasks. The core of this contribution is the analysis of actual job processing data from the CloudFerro cloud center. The proposed methodology is based on data clustering and includes a comparison between multiple algorithms. Furthermore, the resulting clusters have been categorized from the point of view of cloud center operation, in order to identify prototypical tasks' classes with respect to the resource demands. Finally, a tool that generates synthetic job streams, based on the Gaussian Mixture Model, which has been implemented, is summarized.

Keywords: carbon-aware computing · cloud-based processing · data clustering · data augmentation · K-Means

1 Introduction

Cloud computing facilitates the delivery of on-demand computational resources. Since the data centers, standing behind the cloud infrastructures, consume an enormous amount of electricity, a lot of recent research has been focused on investigating novel carbon-neutral alternatives. Among them, one can mention the Green Edge Processing (GEP)[1] project, initiated by the Warsaw-based company CloudFerro. In particular, it introduced a concept of cloud infrastructure with servers, encapsulated in physical containers, placed next to the green energy sources. One of the key challenges in implementing this system concept is the definition of efficient strategies, addressing aspects such as task scheduling or resource (re-)allocation, while capturing characteristics of the distributed infrastructure and the dynamic nature of green energy sources. Interestingly, these topics are also among the prevalent research areas in cloud computing, without direct relation to the use of distributed, heterogeneous, green energy sources.

The need to simulate the GEP ecosystem led to the development of the multi-agent – Extended Green Cloud Simulator (EGCS; for more details, see [22]). The EGCS is the digital twin of the envisioned infrastructure. It aims to facilitate modelling and assessment of system strategies against various quality metrics (e.g. amount of used power, generated costs, job execution success rate, etc.). In particular, the evaluation of strategies can be achieved by conducting simulations that test their efficiency in handling streams of jobs that match those actually processed by the infrastructure. In this context, note that in the current version of the EGCS, the characteristics of the tasks are generated randomly. Obviously, this does not provide a realistic representation of the environmental conditions since it is not likely to reflect the structure of real-life cloud processing tasks accurately.

Therefore, it is necessary to develop tools that will facilitate the generation of synthetic job streams, based on job processing data from the actual cloud center. Specifically, to perform tests in a controlled and repeatable manner, these generated samples should be composed of a mixture of different types of tasks, the general characteristics of which, are known in advance. To accomplish this, it is essential to analyze the real cloud center data, especially (but not only), in terms of their "trackable characteristics", and their correlations. Here, by trackable characteristics, we mean job execution parameters, collected in a real-life cloud center. While it could be possible to collect extra data, using dedicated software installed for this purpose, since such data is not being collected on a daily basis, it cannot be used for job characteristics modelling.

In this context, this contribution proposes the methodology and presents the results of the analysis of computational tasks, executed in CloudFerro's actual infrastructure. The core of the completed work concerns processing satellite images from the Copernicus data sets. In particular, the focus has been placed on examining the resource allocation patterns, the correlation between individual hardware requirements, and their impact on the final task execution status. After data preprocessing (primarily cleaning), the conducted analysis consisted of data clustering and categorizing individual clusters, by assigning distinct labels describing the observed computational demands (e.g. memory-intensive, CPU-intensive). Furthermore, the resulting clusters have been used as "task models" in the developed tool that allows the generation of synthetic job

---

[1] https://cloudferro.com/en/case-studies/green-edge-processing/.

streams by applying the augmentation algorithm based on the Gaussian Mixture Model (GMM).

Taking this into account, the remaining parts of this contribution are structured as follows. Section 2 describes the proposed data model, representing the client request, and outlines the results of the conducted exploratory analysis. Subsequently, Sect. 3 details the performed data cleaning and preprocessing, with particular emphasis on the applied dimensionality reduction methods. Then, Sect. 4 focuses on the data clustering, specifically, compares the results obtained when using different algorithms, and outlines the selected approach used to cluster and analyse the cloud center data. Following that, Sect. 5 presents and discusses the obtained clustering results, which have been used, later on, in the proposed synthetic data generation algorithm, described in Sect. 6. Finally, the conclusions from the conducted work are summarised in Sect. 7.

2   Shaping the Data Model

The data used in the reported analysis consisted of execution parameters collected for one month of task processing carried out in the actual CloudFerro infrastructure. In particular, the analyzed data was based on the execution of jobs, sent by the clients that are referred to as "client requests". In this context, each client request can contain one or more singular tasks, which constitute the processes that are to be executed in the cloud. Here, it should be pointed out that, in everyday practice, CloudFerro tasks are represented as the Argo Workflows [2]. This means that each individual task is divided into a sequence of consecutive steps, which are then "tracked" during their execution. From now on, when referring to a task and its steps, we will use the terms "workflow" and "workflow step".

The data set included information originating from two sources: 1) the Argo environment – with more detailed information including, among others, workflow progress, and 2) the CloudFerro's database – storing data concerning the overall execution of each workflow (i.e. without details that are available from Argo).

More specifically, the data obtained from the Argo environment has been stored in individual *.json* files, where each file corresponds to a single workflow. In particular, it provides information about the progress in workflow processing, including details regarding executed steps, duration of the workflow execution, and the amount of the requested storage and the consumed resources. Here, it should be pointed out, that besides the requested storage, the information about other initially requested resources is currently not being collected by CloudFerro, hence, it is not available in the analysed data set.

On the other hand, the information stored in the database provides details about completing the entire client request (i.e. the collection of executed workflows called, in this context, *request items*). Specifically, the information includes the final status of the request and its singular items, along with the assigned priorities and the deadline by which each item had to be completed.

The data from the Argo files was correlated with the "meta-information" from the database, using the unique workflow identifier –*workflowUID*. Based on the data collected from both sources, the data model of the workflow has been formulated and is presented in Fig. 1. The fields marked in red indicate information scrapped from the database, whereas the black ones were obtained from the Argo files. The model was divided into four main components: *Workflow*, *Metadata*, *Processing details* and *Workflow step*. Let us describe the information stored in each of these components individually.

Fig. 1. Data model of the workflow

The *Workflow* component is the main part of the data model. It contains information about all statuses that describe the final outcome of the workflow execution. In particular, five statuses were taken under consideration: *argo_status*, *argo_output_message*, *argo_detailed_message*, *request_item_status* and *request_status*. The *argo_status* provides the information about the final status of the processed workflow. It may take values *Succeeded*, *Failed*, or *Error*. Interestingly, the *Succeeded* status has two meanings: either that 1) no errors occurred during the workflow execution or that 2) the errors that occurred were successfully handled. In order to distinguish between these two states, an additional status *argo_output_message* has been introduced. It adds a detailed description to the final processing status, informing, among others, about a lack of required resources, the duplicated processing of the workflow, or the occurrence of processing errors. However, this status does not capture the cases when the workflow has been externally stopped, for instance, when the execution of the entire client request was cancelled. Since this information had a significant impact on the results of the performed clustering, causing, among others, increased variability inside the clusters, it was also necessary to include the third Argo status – *argo_detailed_message*. The *argo_detailed_message* differs from the *argo_output_status* by not originating from code but, instead, being automatically returned by Kubernetes (which is the environment where the workflows are actually executed). As such, it captures external events such as *request timed out, resource not found* or *stopped with strategy "stop"*.

The statuses described up to this moment are related strictly to the processing of the workflow "in Argo". However, they do not give information if the client's request has been completed successfully. Therefore, the model also includes two additional statuses, this time retrieved from the database: *request_item_status* and *request_status*, which correspondingly describe states of individual request items and of full client requests. Lastly, the *Workflow* component also includes the *priority* field, which is assigned by the system and indicates the importance of the given task in terms of its scheduling.

The information about the processing of the workflow is provided in the *Processing details*. Here, the type of the processed workflow is specified in the *workflowType* field. Furthermore, it contains details of the consumed resources, which were estimated by the Argo and are demarcated using default "duration units" [1]. Specifically, the Argo algorithm, which computes resource utilization, uses information about the resources requested by the client for processing a given workflow (information not available in the analysed data set), and the container's run time. Therefore, the resulting information about consumed resources includes the time, during which the resource was requested. For instance, it could be: 1 CPU core (*cpuTime*), 100Mi (mebibytes) of memory (*memoryTime*) and 10Gi (gibibytes) of temporary Kubernetes container's storage (*ephemeralStorageTime*). This means that value 6 of *cpuTime* corresponds to 6 min, during which the resource requested 1 CPU core.

Besides the consumed resources, *Processing details* also contains the "volume claim" (i.e. a client's request for a PersistentVolume (PV) [14] storage) represented by the field *storage*. Moreover, the remaining collected information contains the time frames of the workflow execution, the number of executed steps (with – *executedStepsNo*, or without – *initialStepsNo* repetition), and the size of the processed file (*processedSize*). The values stored in the *Processing details* describe the resources consumed by the entire workflow.

However, similar properties were also extracted for each individual step, and included in the *Workflow step* component. Apart from the fields that are common within the *Processing details*, each *Workflow step* contains information about the maximum number of possible retries (of this specific step; *retryLimit*), and the node (if such information was available), on which it has been executed.

The last component of the model is the *Metadata*. It contains the information used to identify individual workflows, and connect the Argo files with the entries from the database. Additionally, it was extended by the *requestName* field, which allows determining which workflows were executed as a part of which client request.

Let us now recall that this work aims to establish prototypical classes of client requests (and, possibly, workflows) that are regularly executed in the CloudFerro infrastructure. The obvious way to achieve this is through data clustering. In this context, based on the defined data model, it is easy to note that the clustering of collected data could be conducted at three different levels of granularity.

The most coarse level involves clustering the entire client requests. Such requests are identified by the *requestName*, whereas resources they consume, can be computed by aggregating the individual processing details of their underlying workflows.

The second level consists of the clustering of workflows. In such a case, the features of interest, include specifically the values stored in the *Processing details*, combined with workflow's statuses. Here, the information about the statuses is essential, since the amount of the consumed resources may depend on how the workflow processing was handled. For instance, if the Kubernetes error occurs in the early stages of the workflow execution (indicated by *Error argo_status*), it may impact the total resource utilization. Therefore, if the information about the status would not be included in the features, such cases may be included in the same clusters as the workflows that were executed without any errors. This, in fact, would not only increase the variability of the data, but also would not allow capturing the proper correlation of resource utilization with the given type of workflow.

Finally, the last level would involve clustering of individual workflow steps, including their resource consumption and the corresponding *names*. Essentially, the workflow steps can be interpreted as the consecutive phases, which handle each part of workflow processing. These steps can be, for instance, *create-product*, *process-product* or *download*. They are strictly correlated with a workflow type, namely, the set of steps is the same for all workflows within a given type. Therefore, their clustering may allow, among others, to examine which phases of a workflow execution are more resource-intensive. Subsequently, this information can be used to, for example, construct strategies that allocate nodes for the execution of individual workflow steps.

While each level of clustering can bring interesting results, let us recall that the goal of the work reported here was to generate synthetic streams of client requests. In this context, the "right" level of granularity is the clustering of workflows. Therefore, the features selected for further analysis included: *workflowType, storage, cpuTime, memoryTime, ephemeralDurationTime, processedSize, duration, initialStepsNo, priority, argo_status, argo_output_message, argo_detailed_message, request_item_status* and *request_status*.

The relationships between some of these features have been analyzed by computing the correlation matrix, represented in Fig. 2. The matrix was computed in Python using pandas [17], whereas the visualization was done in plotly [18].

It can be noted that most features have weak correlations. With regard to resource consumption, the strongest correlation was observed between the pairs *cpu* and *duration*, as well as, *cpu* and *memory*. This result is not surprising, since the executed workflows are, in this case, the "processing tasks". Therefore,

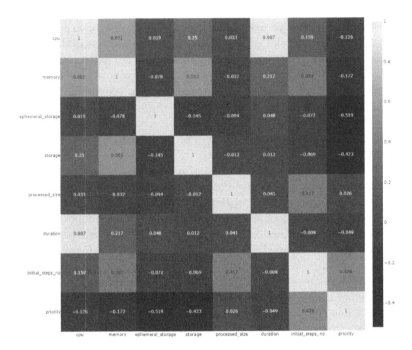

Fig. 2. Correlation matrix for multivariate analysis of workflow features

the data which is being processed by the CPU is actively manipulated (read and write) in the memory. Moreover, more CPU-intensive tasks usually require a longer time to be processed. Interestingly, a medium correlation was also captured between the *initialStepsNo* and the *processedSize*. It may indicate that workflows, which perform operations such as downloading, or processing, large (number of) images, require more steps to be completed.

These results were used to select combinations of features that were considered during the data clustering. However, before proceeding to the actual clustering, the data had to be cleaned and preprocessed, which is described in the next section.

3   Data Cleaning and Preprocessing

Let us begin with the description of the data set cleaning. It was primarily applied to handle the missing values and to remove the outlining observations.

In particular, during the exploratory analysis of the data set, it was discovered that not all Argo files had their corresponding entries in the database, and vice versa. Due to that, for some of the workflows, not all features, which were listed in the previous section, had their corresponding values. Moreover, in such cases, missing features comprised all consumed resources, or all completeness statuses, which made it impossible to impute them artificially. Upon further investigation, it was established that the underlying reason was that some of the workflows had been triggered manually by the developers and, therefore, were not registered in the database. On the other side, the database contained testing entries, for which Argo files were not created. All this information had been filtered out, and was not considered in further analysis.

Moreover, for some of the workflows, the values of collected features (i.e. final resource demands) differed significantly from those in the remaining observations. It was established that in these cases, the combination of execution and completeness statuses was also unclear, thereby not providing any explanation for the data deviations. After the consultation with the CloudFerro analysts, it was determined that, similarly to the previous case, these records correspond to testing entries, and therefore, they have been omitted. Table 1 summarises the size of the initial data set and the number of missing/testing data entries.

Table 1. Size of the initial data set, missing and testing data entries

Number of database entries	Number of Argo files	Missing Argo files	Missing database entries	Test database entries
52 653	41 445	10 715	287	584

After excluding the incomplete and testing information, the resulting data set contained 40 824 elements. Subsequently, before the actual clustering, this data had to be preprocessed.

Since the workflow model contained mixed types of features, the categorical nominal data has been encoded using one-hot encoding. Furthermore, for each workflow, for which the *argo_detailed_message* was other than *undefined* (i.e. some Kubernetes error was captured), the value of *argo_output_message* was substituted, with a corresponding value of *argo_detailed_message*. The reason for that, was to address the problem of uncaught Kubernetes events, as described in Sect. 2.

Afterwards, the obtained features were scaled by applying standardisation, and the overall dimensionality of the data was reduced using one of the selected methods: Principal Component Analysis (PCA) [12] or Uniform Manifold Approximation and Projection (UMAP) [16]. Both of these methods have been tested along with different clustering algorithms, as described in Sect. 4.1. During the testing, their hyperparameters were tuned by evaluating the results for different parameter combinations.

In the case of the PCA, the hyperparameter of interest was the number of components. It was selected based on the analysis of the Cumulative Explained Variance (CEV). In particular, the number of components, for which the CEV was above 95%, has been selected. In this case, the resulting number of components was 6 or 7, depending on the selected combination of features.

On the other hand, the hyperparameters of UMAP (e.g. minimum distance, number of neighbours, number of components) had to be selected individually for each considered clustering algorithm. That was caused by the differences in how the individual algorithms handled different density levels, shapes, and sizes of clusters. More specifically, it resulted from the fact that the changes in UMAP hyperparameters were causing modification of the shape of the reduced data space. For instance, by selecting a smaller number of neighbourhoods, clusters in the reduced space were more densely packed, while the larger minimum distance, resulted in their greater separation. The neighbourhood numbers, on which UMAP was tested, included 500, 700 and 1000, while the considered minimum distances were 0.1, 0.2 and 0.5. Moreover, the taken into account number of components ranged between 2 and 10.

The selection of the dimensionality method, that was to be used in the final clustering was based on the results obtained during the comparison of different clustering algorithms, described in the next section.

4   Clustering Cloud Center Data

The clustering has been performed on several combinations of features using different clustering algorithms. The goal, here, was to select the algorithm which would give the best results with regard to the selected evaluation metrics. The applied algorithms were obtained from the Python libraries scikit-learn [21] and hdbscan [11].

4.1   Comparison of Clustering Algorithms

The considered clustering algorithms were divided into three groups: 1) hard data clustering, 2) soft data clustering, and 3) combined data clustering (i.e. clustering that combines other multiple clustering algorithms). For all of these groups, the clustering was performed on two different sets of features.

The first, initial set, consisted of *cpuTime*, *memoryTime*, *ephemeralStorageTime*, *duration*, *storage*, *processedSize*, *argo_status* and *workflowType*. These features were selected based on the analysis described in Sect. 2. However, after performing initial tests, it was discovered that the variability inside the obtained clusters was high, and therefore, this set has been extended by adding two additional features: *executedStepsNo* and *argo_output_message*. These added features differentiate between workflows that were successfully processed and those that were affected by errors. In particular, the *executedStepsNo* gives the information on which workflows had to repeat the execution of some of their steps, due to their failure. The *argo_output_message*, on the other hand, provides more information about workflow processing (see Sect. 2).

For each of the clustering algorithms, different combinations of their individual hyperparameters were considered. Therefore, the results presented in this section correspond to the clustering attempt, for which the evaluation scores gave "the best outcomes".

For the hard data clustering, the selected algorithms included K-Means [10], Balanced Iterative Reducing and Clustering using Hierarchies (BIRCH) [24],

Hierarchical Density-Based Spatial Clustering (HDBSCAN) [15] and Imbalanced Clustering (IClust) [6]. The metrics used in the clustering evaluation consisted of the Silhouette score [20], Calinski-Harabasz score [7] and Davies-Bouldin index [9]. The combination of such performance metrics was selected in order to assess the clusters' separation, similarity and compactness, further used in the selection of the algorithm that could produce the most distinctive prototypical classes. In particular, (1) Silhouette score measures the cohesion and separation for each data point, thereby was selected to assess the separation between clusters from the perspective of individual point's relationship, (2) the Calinski-Harabasz score evaluates the ratio of between-cluster and within-cluster dispersion, allowing to determine the compactness of the clusters and (3) Davies-Bouldin index calculates the average similarity between clusters, which was used in identifying the clusters distinction. The collected results are presented in Table 2 (for the initial set of features) and Table 3 (for the modified set of features).

Table 2. Results of hard clustering for initial set of features

Features: CPU, memory, ephemeral storage, duration, storage processed size, argo status, workflow type

Clustering algorithm	Dim. reduction algorithm	Cluster no.	Silhouette	Calinski Harabasz	Davies Bouldin
K-Means	PCA	10	0.6992	105571.358	0.329
K-Means	UMAP	11	0.4471	60499.5218	0.673
BIRCH	PCA	8	0.6939	7918.5240	0.226
BIRCH	UMAP	12	0.4993	52283.1567	0.604
HDBSCAN	PCA	11	0.6496	9929.4708	1.190
IClust	PCA	8	0.4531	7958.5517	0.647

Table 3. Results of hard clustering for modified set of features

Features: CPU, memory, ephemeral storage, duration, storage executed steps no., processed size, argo status, argo output message, workflow type

Clustering algorithm	Dim. reduction algorithm	Cluster no.	Silhouette	Calinski Harabasz	Davies Bouldin
K-Means	PCA	11	0.7684	69606.488	0.332
K-Means	UMAP	11	0.4748	39829.599	0.715
BIRCH	PCA	8	0.6284	5616.482	0.279
BIRCH	UMAP	10	0.4887	49938.652	0.643
HDBSCAN	PCA	11	0.7801	10564.537	0.961
IClust	PCA	13	0.6923	23427.121	0.630

In the case of both sets of features, the optimal number of clusters ranged between 8–12. Furthermore, it can be noticed, that in terms of the final evaluation scores, the clustering performed with prior PCA dimensionality reduction gave significantly better results than when UMAP was used. Both UMAP and PCA were reducing the data to 6 dimensions. In terms of the compactness and separation of the clusters (indicated by the Davies-Bouldin index), the best-performing algorithm, in both cases, was BIRCH, while HDBSCAN achieved the highest Silhouette score. On the other hand, K-Means gave the best outcomes with regard to the between-cluster dispersion. Furthermore, notably, the extended set of features resulted in more accurate clustering. The overall best result, by considering all of the computed scores, was achieved by K-Means, for which the Silhouette score was 0.768, the Calinski-Harabasz score was 69606.488, and the Devies-Bouldin index was 0.332.

The next considered group of clustering algorithms were the soft (fuzzy) clustering algorithms. These algorithms can assign a given data point to more than one cluster. In this context, the used algorithms were Gaussian Mixture Model (GMM) clustering and Fuzzy C-Means (FCM) [5] combined with prior computation of the membership matrix using GMM. In this case, apart from the evaluation scores used in hard clustering, for the FCM, two additional indicators were also taken into account, namely the Xie-Beni index [23] and the Partition Coefficient (PC) [4]. The Xie-Beni index allows measuring the compactness and separation of the clusters in fuzzy settings (i.e. in the case when data points may belong to multiple clusters with varying degrees of membership), whereas PC quantifies the degree of fuzziness that can be used to assess the overlap in the cluster memberships. The obtained results are presented in Table 4 (for the initial set of features) and in Table 5 (for a modified set of features).

Table 4. Results of soft clustering for initial set of features

Features: CPU, memory, ephemeral storage, duration, storage processed size, argo status, workflow type

Clustering algorithm	Dim. reduction algorithm	Cluster no.	Silhouette	Calinski Harabasz	Davies Bouldin	Xie Beni	PC
GMM	PCA	9	0.6535	26677.739	1.327	–	–
GMM	UMAP	10	0.3993	44144.643	0.794	–	–
FCM	PCA	12	0.7031	91713.327	0.546	0.146	0.815
FCM	UMAP	12	0.4403	31828.880	0.787	0.188	0.502

Similarly to the previous results, the clustering performed with prior PCA dimensionality reduction resulted in better evaluation scores than when UMAP was used. The FCM, with prior GMM, delivered the best scores for both sets of features. However, compared with previous results, the K-Means algorithm still outperformed the FCM regarding the dispersion between clusters. Nonetheless, since K-Means and FCM gave the most promising results, the next set of tests investigated whether their combination would increase the clustering accuracy. Additionally, since BIRCH and HDBSCAN achieved the best *Davies-Bouldin* and *Silhouette* scores, they were added to the examined combinations.

Table 5. Results of soft clustering for modified set of features

Features: CPU, memory, ephemeral storage, duration, storage executed steps no., processed size, argo status, argo output message, processor

Clustering algorithm	Dim. reduction algorithm	Cluster no.	Silhouette	Calinski Harabasz	Davies Bouldin	Xie Beni	PC
GMM	PCA	10	0.7238	27131.852	0.963	–	–
GMM	UMAP	12	0.4446	37233.170	0.746	–	–
FCM	PCA	10	0.7532	64922.044	0.354	0.052	0.808
FCM	UMAP	11	0.4345	28606.029	0.774	0.331	0.532

To perform the combined clustering, the Iterative Combining Clusterings Method (ICCM), with a voting process, has been implemented [13]. The obtained results are summarized in Table 6 (for the initial set of features) and in Table 7 (for a modified set of features). Throughout all cases, the PCA dimensionality reduction method was applied, since in both soft and hard clustering, it resulted in higher evaluation scores. Moreover, for the second step of clustering (i.e. clustering centers of sub-clusters), the K-Means algorithm was used.

Table 6. Results of ICCM clustering for initial set of features

Features: CPU, memory, ephemeral storage, duration, storage processed size, argo status, workflow type

Clustering algorithms	Cluster no.	Silhouette	Calinski Harabasz	Davies Bouldin
K-Means, BIRCH, FCM	10	0.6813	85244.530	0.311
K-Means, HDBSCAN, FCM	9	0.6965	11225.954	0.209
HDBASCAN, BIRCH, FCM	9	0.6938	6931.991	0.251

Table 7. Results of ICCM clustering for modified set of features

Features: CPU, memory, ephemeral storage, duration, storage
executed steps no., processed size, argo status, argo output message,
workflow type

Clustering algorithms	Cluster no.	Silhouette	Calinski Harabasz	Davies Bouldin
K-Means, BIRCH, FCM	10	0.7532	64922.350	0.354
K-Means, HDBSCAN, FCM	10	0.7532	64901.290	0.354
HDBASCAN, BIRCH, FCM	10	0.6282	4372.680	0.394

For all combinations of algorithms, the evaluation scores were close to the results obtained for the K-Means clustering alone. However, since none of them outperformed it significantly, it was decided that standard K-Means could be used for the ultimate clustering of the cloud data. The results obtained using this approach are reported in what follows. Obviously, one can try to further explore other approaches. This may be particularly valuable if a larger dataset (e.g. collected during 6–12 month) will be available.

4.2 Clustering Workflow Data Using K-Means

Recall that the main point of the cluster analysis was to gain knowledge about the characteristics of individual workflows, specifically, to be able to generate synthetic, mixed, samples addressing the particular simulation scenarios. Therefore, the proposed clustering approach aimed at facilitating examining whether there exists a correlation between the types of individual workflows and their estimated resource consumption. Moreover, an important question was: can specific/distinct classes of workflows be captured? Finally, if this is the case, it was to be examined whether the obtained clusters will make sense from the perspective of CloudFerro (the infrastructure owner and operator).

As outlined in Sect. 2, the clustering algorithm should include, among its features, information about workflow execution statuses. However, in this context, the proposed workflow model contains two independent (in terms of interpretation) types of statuses: 1) describing the state of workflow processing, and 2) informing about the final status of the client request. As has been established, by running initial tests, attempting to "combine" these two statuses in a single clustering process resulted in a high variability inside the clusters, creating difficulties in their interpretation. Therefore, it was decided that the clustering should, in fact, be performed twice, by separately taking into account *argo_status* and *argo_output_message* (i.e. "argo-status-based" clustering), and then *request_item_status* and *argo_detailed_message* (i.e. "client-status-based" clustering). In the latter one, the *argo_detailed_message* was included to capture, for example, cancellation events (see Sect. 2).

The remaining features that were considered initially, included: *cpuTime*, *memoryTime*, *duration*, *ephemeralStorageTime*, *processedSize*, *executedStepsNo* and *workflowType*. However, since the correlation between *cpuTime*, *memory-Time*, and *duration* was high, it was examined if excluding one of these properties would improve (or worsen) the clustering accuracy. The comparison of the obtained clusters, for each tested combination of features, in the case of "argo-status-based" clustering, is presented in Fig. 3.

It can be observed that the best separation between the clusters was achieved for the combination of *memory* and *duration*. In order to verify (numerically) how each tested set of features impacts the clustering accuracy, the Silhouette score, the Calinski-Harabasz score and the Davies-Bouldin index were computed. Obtained results are reported in Table 8.

As can be seen, the best scores were achieved for the combination of *memory* and *duration*, therefore, this pair of features was used in further experiments with the "argo-status-based" clustering. Afterwards, the same evaluation was conducted for the "client-status-based" clustering. The resulting clusters are presented in Fig. 4.

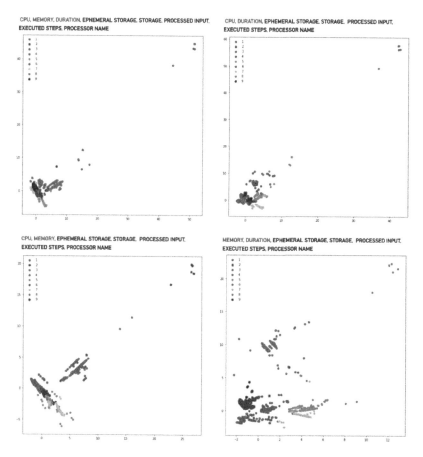

Fig. 3. Comparison of clustering results for different features in argo-status-based clustering

Table 8. Results of K-Means "argo-status-based" clustering with different combinations of CPU, memory and duration features

Features	Silhouette	Calinski Harabasz	Davies Bouldin
cpuTime, memoryTime, duration	0.7684	69606.488	0.332
cpuTime, memoryTime	0.7940	**74068.832**	0.268
cpuTime, duration	0.7919	67278.470	0.267
memoryTime, duration	**0.748**	70316.059	**0.265**

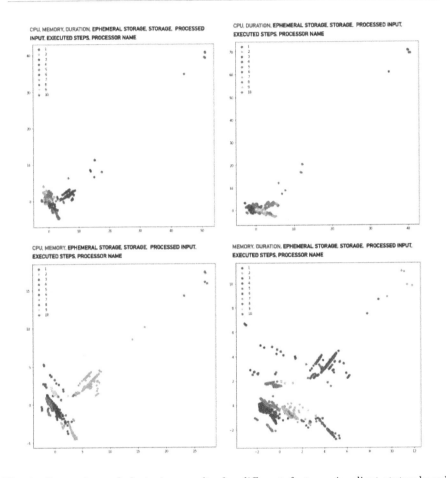

Fig. 4. Comparison of clustering results for different features in client-status-based clustering

Similarly to the previous case, the clusters obtained for the feature combination of *memory* and *duration* were most separated. Interestingly, the differences between the distribution of clusters for both "argo-status-based" and "client-status-based" clusterings were minimal, which is also particularly visible in their further analysis. Table 9 presents the comparison of computed evaluation scores.

Table 9. Results of K-Means "client-status-based" clustering with different combinations of CPU, memory and duration features

Features	Silhouette	Calinski Harabasz	Davies Bouldin
cpuTime, memoryTime, duration	0.7736	54429.868	0.332
cpuTime, memoryTime	0.7770	55297.692	0.3556
cpuTime, duration	**0.7747**	53483.433	0.346
memoryTime, duration	0.7740	**57536.319**	**0.328**

Based on the obtained results, it was decided that the final combination of features, used in clustering, will include *memoryTime* and *duration*, excluding the *cpuTime*. Moreover, the tests performed on this set of features indicated that the optimal number of clusters, in both cases, was 10. The results of both final clusterings are discussed in the next section.

5   Analysis of Clustering Results

Let us begin by introducing the approach used for naming (describing) the clusters. Since the total number of clusters was relatively high, and each contained multiple features, based on which independent labels could be assigned, it was difficult to determine a single name for each individual cluster. Therefore, the main concept, used to simplify the interpretation of the clusters was by, first, dividing them into groups, seen as "general categories". These groups were separately defined for "argo-status-based" and "client-status-based" clustering. Afterwards, each cluster inside a given group has been uniquely named, depending on its content.

The results of the first clustering, which included argo statuses, are presented in Table 10. Upon inspection, the clusters have been divided into three groups: "processed without errors", "processed with handled errors", and "processed with unhandled errors".

The first group, named "processed without errors", consists of 5 clusters, for which the *argo_status*, of the underlying workflows, is always *Succeeded* and the majority of *argo_output_messages* had value *product processed successfully*. As such, this group contains only workflows, the execution of which was "undisturbed". Interestingly, for each cluster in this group, almost all of its workflows belong to a single type, allowing the creation of unique clusters' names. The major exceptions were the workflows of type **download**, whose resource consumption was highly variable, causing them to be spread across multiple clusters. Such an outcome is not surprising since these workflows involve downloading data from, among others, third-party services, so their processing depends on

Table 10. Results of "argo-status-based" clustering

Cluster name	Cluster Size	Avg. CPU	Avg. memory	Avg. duration	Avg. storage	Avg. ephemeral storage	Avg. processed size
PROCESSED WITHOUT ERRORS							
grd_cog	18.5K	1K	30K	13 min	5	38	1 BLN
card_bs	1.1K	6K	250K	16 min	80	16	5 BLN
sen2cor	10.7K	7K	173K	44 min	20	1K	0.8 BLN
card_coh	1.6K	91K	11M	1 h	200	52	0.75 BLN
download	6	1M	12MM	6 D	0	0	3 BLN
PROCESSED WITH HANDLED ERRORS							
Already processed SEN2COR	5.7k	40	103	2 min	20	0	1 BLN
Already processed COH	1.7K	62	143	3 min	200	0	0.7 BLN
Not enough base product	848	24	60	1 min	200	0	0
Mixed errors	305	81	840	3 min	20	4	0
PROCESSED WITH UNHANDLED ERRORS							
Unhandled errors	296	7K	161K	3 h	27	1K	0.05 BLN

a number of "external factors" (e.g. network traffic). Nevertheless, since their presence in other clusters, had an impact on the data variability, they have been excluded from the analysis. By that, the achieved variability inside each cluster was "small enough", allowing interpretation of the average values of consumed resources as the resource utilization that may be expected from each type of workflow. For example, it can be stated that **card_bs** workflows require a low-to-medium amount of CPU and memory, whereas the consumption of the **card_cog** workflows is more resource-intensive. This information can be particularly useful, when designing the scheduling algorithms and/or prioritizing the client workflows.

Let us now consider the second group, named "processed with handled errors". Similarly to the first group, the *argo_statuses* of data, in these clusters, always have value *Succeeded*. However, the *argo_output_messages* indicate the occurrence of errors (e.g. *not enough base product*). As such, the workflows combined in these clusters were executed with exceptions, which were captured and properly handled. Indicated errors, combined with the dominating workflow type, were used to name the corresponding clusters. It can be observed that the resource consumption of all these clusters is low, suggesting that proper recognition of the errors may allow for minimizing resource utilization. In particular, this statement can be assessed by comparing clusters from this group to the ones from the last group.

The cluster, in the group, "processed with unhandled errors" contains workflows that combine different *argo_output_messages*, which indicate exceptions that led to the final *argo_status Failed*, or *Error*. Notable, the resource consumption of workflows, in this cluster, is much higher than in the case of clusters from the second group. The most common *argo_output_message* is *critical workflow error*, which does not provide any descriptive details about the nature of the actual error. Interestingly, this cluster also contains a few data records with *argo_output_message product processed successfully* that may have been misclassified. However, the latter is just a hypothesis which has not been verified.

Table 11 presents the results of clustering performed on the basis of the final status of the client request item. Here, the clusters also have been divided into three groups, which include "items completed successfully", "items completed successfully with workflow errors", and "items executed with failure".

Table 11. Results of "client-status-based" clustering

Cluster name	Cluster Size	Avg. CPU	Avg. memory	Avg. duration	Avg. storage	Avg. ephemeral storage	Avg. processed size
ITEMS COMPLETED SUCCESSFULLY							
grd_cog	18.4K	1K	30K	13 min	5	38	1 BLN
card_bs	1.1K	6K	247K	14 min	80	16	5 BLN
sen2cor	10.7K	7K	173K	43 min	20	1K	0.8 BLN
card_coh	1.6K	90K	11M	1 h	200	52	0.7 BLN
download	6	1M	12M	6 D	0	0	3 BLN
ITEMS COMPLETED SUCCESSFULLY WITH WORKFLOW ERRORS							
Already processed SEN2COR	5.7k	40	103	2 min	20	0	0.8 BLN
Already processed COH	1.7K	62	143	3 min	200	0	0.7 BLN
Cancelled	19	1K	22K	51 min	30	13	0.7
ITEMS EXECUTED WITH FAILURE							
Recognized errors	1.1K	40	268	2 min	150	1	2 MLN
Unrecognized errors	271	14K	237K	4 h	20	1K	0.05 BLN

The first group of clusters is similar to the first group from the "argo-status-based" clustering. In particular, it gathers all clusters, for which the final status of the client request item was *done*, and the *argo_detailed_message* did not indicate any errors. Interestingly, even though the "client-status-based" clustering was performed on a slightly different set of features than the "argo-status-based" one, both of them captured almost identical clusters, in terms of their distribution and structure.

A similar situation happened also for the first two clusters of the second group. The clusters *already processed sen2cor* and *already processed coh* have identical representatives in the "argo-status-based" clustering. However, the third cluster, named *cancelled*, does not correspond directly to any cluster from the previously obtained results. It gathers all client request items, the execution of which has been stopped. Compared to the remaining clusters from this group, the average resource utilization for this cluster is significantly higher. Moreover, all of the workflows, which belong to this cluster, in the "argo-status-based" clustering, have been assigned to the *unhandeled errors* cluster. This suggests that the cancellation requests were not caught by the error handling mechanism. This also explains the higher resource consumption.

Finally, the last group contains two clusters, for which the client request item execution has failed. In particular, the first cluster was named *recognized errors*, since the error messages of the *argo_detailed_message* of its underlying workflows are very specific. On the other hand, the second cluster, named *unrecognized errors*, contains more general errors. The comparison of the average values of their resource consumption, demonstrates directly how error handling may impact the amount of utilized resources. In particular, the pertinent values, in the cluster with unrecognized errors, are significantly higher than in these cases when the errors were properly recognized.

As a result of the conducted analysis, it was possible to establish and investigate the correlation between the individual types of workflows and their average resource utilization, as well as the impact of the exception handling. However, from the perspective of synthetic data generation, particularly significant were the results obtained in clusters with workflows completed without errors, since they provided information about the expected resource consumption of each individual workflow type. As such, they have been used in the proposed synthetic data generation algorithm, which is described in the next section.

6   Generation of the Synthetic Workflow Streams

The computed clusters represent the realistic mixture of different workflow types that actually materialize within the CloudFerro infrastructure. Let us name this mixture "default". Its composition has been represented in Fig. 5.

Note that this mixture has been captured on the basis of one month of data. Therefore, it is possible that if more data were available, a different cluster structure could materialize. Moreover, only on the basis of at least 12 consecutive months of data, it would be possible to try to understand annual variations in user-generated requests. Nevertheless, these potential limitations have no detrimental effect on what follows.

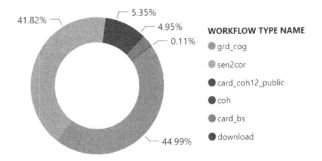

Fig. 5. Default mixture of workflows in CloudFerro data

First, let us assume that for the purpose of the development of strategies for the Extended Green Cloud, a stream of synthetic workflows, representing the default mix has to be instantiated. On the basis of the performed analysis, it can be stipulated that such stream would include mostly workflows of the type **grd_cog**, while, for instance, workflows of type **download** would appear very rarely. Obviously, focusing only on the default job stream would be rather restricting for the purpose of designing and testing a comprehensive strategy for a large scale EGC deployment.

However, knowing the actual types of workflows that CloudFerro is processing, allows also generation of custom workflow mixtures. Specifically, to achieve this goal, a "workflow stream generator", which allows specifying the desired mixture of workflows that is to be included in the generated sample workflow stream, has been developed. Here, the proposed approach is based on using the obtained clusters that separate workflows according to their types and support the generation of custom workflow stream mixes.

Based on the completed workflow clustering, the following clusters have been selected. Here, let us note that this is the preliminary decision made to run the initial simulations. However, it has to be stressed that the design of the developed generator is modular. Therefore, workflows with other characteristics can also be included as needed. In this way, if a larger data sample is available, and its clustering will result in clusters with different characteristics, corresponding workflow streams can be generated.

In the developed EGCS, first, clusters from the "argo-status-based" clustering, for which workflows finished without any errors, have been selected. Second, special clusters, individually computed for the workflows of type **download**, have been used. Note that such workflows were excluded from the results of the "argo-status-based" clustering, due to high variability of their data. This variability influenced the stability of other captured clusters (see Sect. 5). However, it should be noted that workflows of this type are very important for the types of client requests that are being regularly processed by CloudFerro. Moreover, a brief reflection on the nature of the GEP project reveals that workflows of type **download** will become even more prevalent and important. For instance, in the case of the Extended Green Cloud, data and/or jobs will have to be sent to the locations where the green energy-powered nodes are located (and the processing results will be transmitted "back"). Hence, it is necessary to be able to represent them in the workflow stream generator.

The method used to generate synthetic samples of workflows was based on the Gaussian Mixture Model (GMM) [3,19]. This was because, among others, GMM allows the representation of a given dataset by a mixture of Gaussian probabilistic distributions. As such, since it is a generative model, it can be used to randomly sample new data, the distribution of which resembles the original input. Moreover, it is naturally extendable and scalable, in the case when a richer mixture of synthetic workflow streams is to be generated.

The main algorithm, used in the workflow generator, is as follows. First, the user specifies the number of workflows to be generated from each cluster type. Next, the algorithm iterates through the clusters, treating their underlying workflows as individual input data sets. Before proceeding to the actual sampling, the dimensionality of the data is reduced using PCA. Next, the GMM hyperparameters (i.e., the number of GMM components) are tuned through the analysis of the Akaike Information Criterion (AIC) [8]. Afterwards, using the selected number of components, and input workflow data, the GMM is generated and trained. Finally, the sample of the selected size is drawn and appended to the common output dataset.

However, before returning the final sample, some of the workflow features are being filtered out since they are not important from the perspective of the simulations that are to be run. For example, information about final statuses (e.g. *argo_status*, *request_item_status*) is irrelevant, since generated workflow streams aim to serve as input data, hence, their execution outcomes are assumed to be a'priori unknown. Here, it should be noted that since features of interest are only numerical, the proposed algorithm has not been extended to also handle the categorical data. Specifically, the selected set of features includes *cpu*, *memory*, *duration*, *ephemenralStorage*, *storage*, *processedSize* and *deadline*, for both, that entire workflows and their individual steps. The type of workflow is selected from the cluster name and is also appended to the resulting features. Finally, the generated workflow stream set is stored in the *.json* file so that it can be easily injected into the simulator.

The developed generator has been validated using standard testing procedures. The comparison of the shapes of the synthetically generated sample and the original data has been conducted on the default mixture of the synthetic workflows. Table 12 presents the number of workflows generated per each cluster type. With respect to workflows of type **download**, three clusters have been used: *download_low*, *download_medium* and *download_high* that reflect the average resource demands of **download** workflows, identified after their individual clustering.

Table 12. Number of synthetic workflows generated per each cluster type

Cluster name	Number of generated workflows
card_bs	1130
card_coh	1615
grd_cog	18394
sen2cor	10686
download_low	19
download_medium	11
download_high	6
TOTAL	31861

Table 13. Comparison of differences in generated values between synthetic workflow stream and real data

Cluster name	Mean % error	Std. % error	Synthetic data range	Real data range
CPU				
card_bs	0.70%	23.9%	3879	5859
card_coh	0.04%	63.3%	87138	273084
grd_cog	0.09%	58.6%	1817	16064
sen2cor	0.15%	40.6%	6580	9908
download	0.72%	0.1%	1162721	1159889
MEMORY				
card_bs	0.71%	22.9%	182803	274809
card_coh	0.04%	63.2%	10491353	32767431
grd_cog	0.01%	59.6%	62696	562985
sen2cor	0.01%	40.6%	157772	236251
download	0.72%	0.1%	12278012	12247858
EPHEMERAL STORAGE				
card_bs	0.97%	39.4%	11	19
card_coh	0.11%	64.1%	49	152
grd_cog	0.08%	60.1%	85	769
sen2cor	0.31%	42.1%	1051	1630
download	0%	0%	0	0
DURATION				
card_bs	0.57%	81.3%	182	820
card_coh	0.46%	72.5%	5679	16499
grd_cog	3.6%	90.3%	986	173700
sen2cor	1.0%	51.9%	2308	11833
download	0.13%	0.1%	581951	581092
PROCESSED SIZE				
card_bs	0.01%	2.8%	182803	274809
card_coh	0.13%	4.7%	10491353	32767431
grd_cog	1.18%	4.1%	62696	562985
sen2cor	0.02%	0.1%	157772	236251
download	4.14%	5.7%	12278012	12247858

The statistical metrics, including the mean value, the standard deviation and the range, have been compared for each type of workflow and each of the features: *cpu, memory, duration, ephemenralStorage* and *processedSize*. The features *storage* and *deadline* were excluded from this comparison since, in the current state of the original data, they are constant for the majority of the workflows. In the case of the mean and the standard deviation, the differences between an original and synthetic sample were measured, using the percentage absolute error. The obtained results are summarized in Table 13.

It can be noted that the differences between the mean values of the synthetic and the real samples for each feature, and each generated type of workflow, are minimal. The percentage absolute mean error for almost all of the results is within 1%, whereas the largest error (obtained for the *processedSize* feature of generated workflows of type **download**) is about 4%. It proves that the average values of the generated samples adequately resemble the original data.

On the other hand, the analysis of the standard deviation and the range shows that the variability within a synthetic sample is significantly different. The percentage error of standard deviation, in the majority of the results, varies between 20% to 70%. The highest difference occurred for the workflows of the type **grd_cog** for their *duration* feature, whereas the lowest ones were obtained for the *processedSize* feature. The comparison of the ranges outlines that the differences between the maximal and minimal values are much higher for the real data. It is not surprising, considering that the synthetic workflows were generated based on the imprecise clustering results. For example, the cluster named **grd_cog** contained some of the workflows of type **sen2cor**. These workflows could possibly be outliers, thereby contributing to the variability within **sen2cor** workflows, in the original data. Moreover, in terms of the synthetic workflow generation, their inclusion affects the shape of the data, used in training the GMM. This, in turn, influences the values categorized as the **grd_cog** workflow type. Accordingly, it should be noted that the current generation algorithm may not capture some of the extremes that may appear in the original sample. Improving that would require better recognition of the outlying observations, which is to be investigated in the future.

In addition to the comparison of statistics of the individual features, their correlation has also been assessed. Figure 6 depicts the differences in correlation between the corresponding features in the real (top figure) and the synthetically generated (bottom figure) workflows.

For the features of the synthetically generated workflows, the correlation metrics appear to be nearly identical to those obtained from the original data. Even though the synthetic sample tends to yield slightly higher correlation measures than those of the original sample, the differences are negligibly small. As a result, it can be concluded that the generated workflow stream adequately represents the original characteristics of the data.

After the assessment of the synthetic mixture of workflows, it can be incorporated into the EGCS. In particular, the *.json* file, containing workflow stream mixture, can be injected into the resources of the EGCS *Engine*, responsible for running the simulations. In the configuration parameters, used to define how the simulation will be run, it is possible to specify the strategy of task generation. When the strategy called *FROM_SAMPLE* is selected, the *Engine* will look for the workflow stream file and load it while generating the client agents. Additionally, it is also possible to specify if the entire workflow stream will be used or only a part of it (by giving a specific number of workflows that are to be selected). The resulting system (EGCS + Simulator) has also been validated.

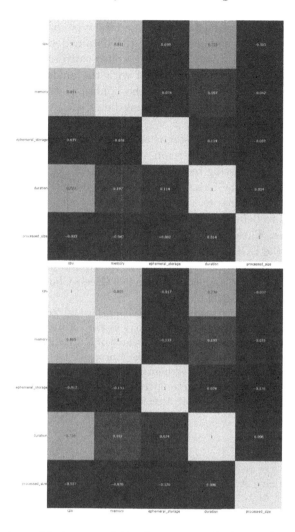

Fig. 6. Comparison of feature correlation between synthetic sample and real sample

It can be stated that it is ready to be used to run simulations and evaluate the quality of possible Extended Green Cloud infrastructure management strategies.

7   Concluding Remarks

This contribution describes the process leading to, and results of, analysis of workflow processing data, captured in the CloudFerro cloud center. As part of the research, after data had been reviewed and appropriately preprocessed, two clusterings were carried out, and the resulting clusters were categorized and named. The obtained results proved that there exists a direct correlation between the amount of consumed resources and the types of individual processing requests. Moreover, the characteristics of the obtained clusters indicate, that proper error handling positively impacts resource utilization. In this context, the discussed observations were consulted with the analysts from CloudFerro (including the co-author of this work), who confirmed that these findings (1) are explainable and consistent, and (2) may be of use in the company's task-processing strategy.

Separately, the computed cluster characteristics were used to develop and implement a synthetic workflow stream generator, which allows the creation of custom mixtures of processing requests. The obtained samples have been incorporated into the Extended Green Cloud Simulator and, as such, allow performing realistic simulations. Therefore, the next step in the conducted research will be to use the results to define, evaluate and tune the Extended Green Cloud management strategies. These strategies will be implemented, and their utility will be studied using the EGCS. The EGCS, along with the developed tools (including synthetic data generator), used to obtain the results presented in this work, can be found in https://github.com/Extended-Green-Cloud/green-cloud.

Acknowledgements. The research of Maria Ganzha and Zofia Wrona was funded in part by the Warsaw University of Technology as part of the Excellence Initiative – Research University (IDUB) Program. The research of Marcin Paprzycki and Stanisław Krzyżanowski has been funded in part by the European Union's "Horizon Europe" research and innovation funding programme as part of the "Autonomous, scalable, trustworthy, intelligent European meta operating system for the IoT edge-cloud continuum" (aerOS) project under Grant Agreement No. 101069732.

References

1. Argoproject: Argo resource duration. https://argoproj.github.io/argo-workflows/resource-duration/. Accessed 27 Sept 2023
2. Argoproject: Argo workflows. https://argoproj.github.io/argo-workflows/. Accessed 27 Sept 2023
3. Arora, A., Shoeibi, N., Sati, V., González-Briones, A., Chamoso, P., Corchado, E.: Data augmentation using gaussian mixture model on CSV files. In: Dong, Y., Herrera-Viedma, E., Matsui, K., Omatsu, S., González Briones, A., Rodríguez González, S. (eds.) DCAI 2020. AISC, vol. 1237, pp. 258–265. Springer, Cham (2021). https://doi.org/10.1007/978-3-030-53036-5_28
4. Bezdek, J.: Numerical taxonomy with fuzzy sets. J. Math. Biol. **1**, 57–71 (1974)
5. Bezdek, J.C., Ehrlich, R., Full, W.: FCM: the fuzzy C-means clustering algorithm. Comput. Geosci. **10**(2), 191–203 (1984)
6. Brodinova, S., Zaharieva, M., Filzmoser, P., Ortner, T., Breiteneder, C.: Clustering of imbalanced high-dimensional media data. Advances in Data Analysis and Classification (2017)
7. Caliński, T., Harabasz, J.: A dendrite method for cluster analysis. Commun. Stat.-Theory Methods **3**(1), 1–27 (1974)
8. Cavanaugh, J.E., Neath, A.A.: The Akaike information criterion: background, derivation, properties, application, interpretation, and refinements. WIREs Comput. Stat. **11**(3), e1460 (2019)

9. Davies, D.L., Bouldin, D.W.: A cluster separation measure. IEEE Trans. Pattern Anal. Mach. Intell. **PAMI-1**(2), 224–227 (1979)
10. Hartigan, J.A., Wong, M.A.: Algorithm as 136: a k-means clustering algorithm. J. R. Stat. Soc. Ser. C (Appl. Stat.) **28**(1), 100–108 (1979)
11. HDBSCAN: The HDBSCAN clustering library. https://hdbscan.readthedocs.io/en/latest/. Accessed 27 Sept 2023
12. Jolliffe, I.T.: Principal Component Analysis for Special Types of Data. Springer, Cham (2002)
13. Khedairia, S., Khadir, M.T.: A multiple clustering combination approach based on iterative voting process. J. King Saud Univ. - Comput. Inf. Sci. **34**(1), 1370–1380 (2022)
14. Kubernetes: Persistent volumes. https://kubernetes.io/docs/concepts/storage/persistent-volumes/. Accessed 28 Sept 2023
15. McInnes, L., Healy, J., Astels, S.: HDBSCAN: hierarchical density based clustering. J. Open Source Softw. **2** (2017)
16. McInnes, L., Healy, J., Melville, J.: UMAP: uniform manifold approximation and projection for dimension reduction (2020)
17. Pandas: Pandas documentation. https://pandas.pydata.org/docs/index.html. Accessed 27 Sept 2023
18. Plotly: Plotly open source graphing library for python. https://plotly.com/python/. Accessed 27 Sept 2023
19. Reynolds, D.: Gaussian mixture models. In: Li, S.Z., Jain, A. (eds.) Encyclopedia of Biometrics, pp. 659–663. Springer, Boston (2009)
20. Rousseeuw, P.J.: Silhouettes: a graphical aid to the interpretation and validation of cluster analysis. J. Comput. Appl. Math. **20**, 53–65 (1987)
21. Scikit-learn: machine learn in python. https://scikit-learn.org/stable/. Accessed 27 Sept 2023
22. Wrona, Z., Ganzha, M., Paprzycki, M., Krzyżanowski, S.: Extended green cloud - modeling cloud infrastructure with green energy sources. In: Mathieu, P., Dignum, F., Novais, P., De la Prieta, F. (eds.) PAAMS 2023. LNCS, vol. 13955, pp. 428–433. Springer, Cham (2023). https://doi.org/10.1007/978-3-031-37616-0_37
23. Xie, X., Beni, G.: A validity measure for fuzzy clustering. IEEE Trans. Pattern Anal. Mach. Intell. **13**(8), 841–847 (1991). https://doi.org/10.1109/34.85677
24. Zhang, T., Ramakrishnan, R., Livny, M.: Birch: a new data clustering algorithm and its applications. Data Min. Knowl. Disc. **1**, 141–182 (1997)

Exploring Approaches to Detection of Anomalies in Streaming Data

Damian Rakus[1], Maria Ganzha[1] (ID), Marcin Paprzycki[2](✉) (ID), and Artur Bicki[3]

[1] Faculty of Mathematics and Information Science, Warsaw University
of Technology, Warsaw, Poland
`maria.ganzha@pw.edu.pl`
[2] Systems Research Institute Polish Academy of Sciences, Warsaw, Poland
`marcin.paprzycki@ibspan.waw.pl`
[3] EMCA S.A., Warsaw, Poland
`artur.bicki@emca.pl`

Abstract. Numerous methods have been proposed to detect anomalies
in data streams. In this work, a comprehensive study of performance
of AutoEncoders and Predictive networks, applied to two datasets, is
presented. The first dataset (from the paper mill) is labeled, whereas
the second (from the server farm) is not. In this context, first, AutoEncoders and Predictive networks are applied to the labeled dataset and
tuned, to improve their performance. Moreover, chronological and random training data splitting is explored. Additionally, an industry expert's
suggested performance evaluation method is proposed. Effects of its use
are experimentally investigated. It is shown that the proposed approach
outperforms the state-of-the-art approaches. The best of breed model
and approach from the labeled paper mill dataset, is applied to the log
data from a server farm. Obtained results turned out to "make sense" to
the log data owners, and the developed method is going to be tried in a
real-life deployment.

Keywords: anomaly detection · AutoEncoders predictive networks ·
performance evaluation

1 Introduction

Recent developments, leading to actual realization of Internet of Things ecosystems, bring about new opportunities. One of the areas that can benefit from
availability of sensor generated data, is Industry 4.0. Here, analysis of incoming
data may allow detection of anomalies in the behavior of "machinery". This,
in turn, may support realization of predictive and preventive maintenance [8].
Similarly, it may support undertaking actions, which will prevent crash(es) in a
data center (see, also, [7]). Obviously, the open research question is, how to best
recognize an *actual anomaly* and to avoid either missing one, or raising a false
alarm, when the reasons for data fluctuations are "benign".

S. Sachdeva and Y. Watanobe (Eds.): BDA 2023, LNCS 14516, pp. 250–274, 2024.
https://doi.org/10.1007/978-3-031-58502-9_17

In the context of detecting anomalies in a server farm, we were contacted by a Polish company: EMCA. EMCA has its dedicated software called Energy LogServer that aggregates log data from multiple servers. Their solution warns about system malfunction if one of the specified parameters exceeds an established threshold. However, this approach is far from ideal as:

- a specific (single) parameter, exceeding a threshold, does not always mean that a system failure will actually happen,
- some malfunctions are not preceded by (one, or more) parameters exceeding a specific threshold value.

Therefore, the ultimate goal of reported work was to create a robust machine learning model capable of:

- detecting upcoming system failures, based on the multi-server log data,
- digesting and processing multivariate time series data,
- being based on unsupervised learning, as log data is not labeled.

Before addressing the problem of interest, investigation of numerous approaches, proposed for the anomaly detection, for both supervised an unsupervised learning, was performed. Moreover, measures of their success have been established. In this context, the aim of this work is, first, to compare the performance of two classes of anomaly detection methods, applied to the labeled multidimensional time series data from a paper mill. Moreover, an alternate, industry-needs-based, performance measure method is proposed. Its is argued that this evaluation method is more appropriate in the context of real-world industrial applications. Next, it is stipulated that the best resulting approach should deliver reasonable results when applied to the log data from a server farm. Here, since the "ground truth" is unknown, an opinion of the server farm log data owner is used to assess utility of the proposed approach.

Separately, this work is also based on a foundational belief that, while fine tuning a single method to work well for a specific dataset is important, commencing comparative studies, exploring and comparing multiple approaches (and their versions) is equally crucial. Moreover, only then, it will be possible to truly understand the landscape of the state-of-the-art in the field. Here, the field being anomaly detection in multivariate data streams.

2   Related Work

Realization of Industry 4.0 vision, facilitates application of machine learning to analysis of sensor-generated data streams. This allows, among others, detecting upcoming anomalies, with the goal off preventing catastrophic events [8]. However, it should be stressed that while different methods can be applied to anomaly detection, not all of them are useful in the case of the paper mill type data, as well as the server farm log data. Here, in the first case, for the generated data stream, in each measurement, more than 50 numerical values are present (representing sensor data). Similarly, each measurement in server farm log data is represented by multiple numerical values. This being the case, let us note that popular anomaly detection methods, like *SORAD*, *ARIMA* or *OARX*, do *not* work with multidimensional data (see, [7,16,17]). While variables, from subsequent measurements, could be split into separate time series, and these models could be trained on each one of them independently, actual relationships between variables would be lost. Next, *Shapelets* [1] also cannot be applied, as this method works only for the time series that always "starts and ends at the same place". Moreover, in Shapelets, the entire time series is classified as an anomaly, which makes it impossible to establish where/when the anomaly occurred (which is absolutely crucial in the real-world industrial scenarios). On the other hand, *PCA*-based methods are very sensitive to the selection of the number of principal components [2,6,9,10,13]. Moreover, they have problems with large number of components, due to the "pollution" of the normal space. Hence, their use, for instance for dimensionality reduction, is doubtful (see, also, [7]).

Therefore, deep learning methods, which work on the multidimensional data, and on selected section(s) of time series, seem to be the most natural choice for this problem. These methods can spot existence of anomalies, and indicate the moment of their occurrence. Therefore, in this contribution, performance of two popular deep learning approaches has been explored. (A) *AutoEncoder networks* – which combine data from several measurements into a compressed form, and then reconstruct the input data [14]. (B) *Predictive Networks* – based on measurements from several contiguous time steps, try to predict the value of the next measurement [4,5]. Moreover, standard Voting-based meta-classifiers can be applied, to "combine" suggestions provided by "base methods". Here, since the core aspects of these methods are not being modified, it is assumed that readers interested in details of each of them can easily find interesting details in the literature cited above, and in the Internet-based repositories.

3   Experimental Setup

In scope of the reported work, tests were conducted on two different datasets. The dataset of actual interest is an aggregation of logs from the EMCA's LogServer application. Here, the overarching intention is to train a model that could be "applicable" for EMCA daily activities. However, it would be extremely resource consuming to use that dataset itself, for the prototyping purposes. It is not labeled and, therefore, in order to evaluate each trained model, it would require for an expert, knowing intricate details of the EMCA system, to verify all potential anomalies detected by the model. This would be too time consuming and, separately, it is impossible to evaluate metrics such as F1-score or True Positive Rate, as the total number of actual anomalies, in the dataset, is unknown. The only metric that could be calculated would be precision. However, a reliable assessment of the best model cannot be performed using only precision. Therefore, a labeled dataset from the paper mill factory was used first, in order to study behavior of approaches that may be applied to the server farm dataset. Let us now describe both datasets in more detail.

3.1 Paper Mill Dataset

To realistically compare performance of anomaly detection methods, the paper mill dataset, used in [12], was selected. It contains measurements from a sheet-making machine, and consists of 18,398 records, collected every 2 min. There are 124 anomalies in the set. Each record consists of: (i) information if an anomaly occurred at a given moment; (ii) categorical variables – 2 columns and (iii) numeric variables – 59 columns (representing sensor data). Detailed information about meaning of each column has not been provided. Nevertheless, its "authors" suggested to divide the data into time windows containing 5 measurements each, and to discard columns with categorical variables. These suggestions have been applied in the reported experiments. Authors of the dataset published also the results of their best model (obtained using XGBoost and AdaBoost), which were: (1) $precision = 0.071$, (2) $F1 = 0.114$, and (3) False Positive Rate $FPR = 0.026$. Here, these results will be treated as the *ground truth performance*, against which other results will be compared.

3.2 EMCA's LogServer Dataset

Dataset provided by EMCA was an aggregation of logs, collected by the dedicated software. Obtained data covered time period between December 1, 2020 and March 31, 2021. It consists of logs from the *syslog* program, available on Unix based operating systems. The program collected 3 types of records.

- Firewall – records informing whether the firewall let the network packet through, or if it rejected it.
- System Health – records containing the system state related information, such as CPU or RAM usage.
- Event – records describing other system related events.

```
<30>device="SFW"
date=2021-02-13
time=00:15:38
timezone="CET"
device_name="SFV4C6"
device_id=C010012WDG4HY9D
log_id=127726618031
log_type="System Health"
log_component="Memory"
log_subtype="Usage"
priority=Information
unit=byte
total_memory=4145111040
free=2614394880
used=1530716160
```

Fig. 1. Content of the message field, for the example of the System Health record

Each record had a priority value assigned, equal to one of the following possibilities: Information, Notice, Warning, Error. The total volume of data was

107.7 GB and consisted of 86,917,534 records, written in CSV format. The most important column of the file was the *message* column that included the entire record information as a key-value dictionary. Since the message field could contain different keys, the file had 104 distinct columns, making it practically impossible to display the CSV file in a "human-readable" way.

Example content of the message field, for the System Health, can be found in Fig. 1. It can be determined that it's the System Health record, based on the value 'System Health' for the 'log_type' key. Log_component key's value equal to Memory, which informs that the record contains information regarding RAM memory. Total RAM memory is equal to 4,145,111 040 bytes (based on the content of total_memory and unit keys) and the current RAM usage is equal to 1,530,716,160 bytes (used key).

Example of the message field, for the Firewall record, is presented in Fig. 2. Allow value, under the status key, informs that the specific packet was allowed to go through the firewall. The packet came from the machine with IP 95.40.123.161 (src_ip key) and was sent to the machine with IP 31.179.270.196 (dst_ip key). The record itself does not contain important information regarding anomaly detection. However, the number of Firewall events in a specific time window can be useful. For example, the spike in the Firewall records number can be interpreted as a DDoS (Distributed Denial of Service) attack.

```
<30>device="SFW" date=2021-02-13 time=13:05:51
timezone="CET" device_name="SFV4C6" device_id=C010012WDG4HY9D
log_id=010101600001 log_type="Firewall" log_component="Firewall Rule"
log_subtype="Allowed" status="Allow" priority=Information
duration=0 fw_rule_id=39 policy_type=3
user_name="" user_gp="" iap=0
ips_policy_id=0 appfilter_policy_id=0 application=""
application_risk=0 application_technology="" application_category=""
in_interface="PortC" out_interface="PortA" src_mac=00:00:00:00:00:00
src_ip=95.40.123.161 src_country_code=POL dst_ip=31.179.250.196
dst_country_code=POL protocol="TCP" src_port=36670
dst_port=995 sent_pkts=0  recv_pkts=0
sent_bytes=0 recv_bytes=0 tran_src_ip=
tran_src_port=0 tran_dst_ip=10.4.4.1 tran_dst_port=0
srczonetype="WAN" srczone="WAN" dstzonetype="LOCAL"
dstzone="LOCAL" dir_disp="" connevent="Start"
connid="464289792" vconnid="" hb_health="No Heartbeat" |
message="" appresolvedby="Signature" app_is_cloud=0
```

Fig. 2. Content of message for the record of type Firewall.

In terms of anomaly detection, the most crucial information can be extracted from the System Health records, as their content describes the current system state. Those records are collected every 5 min. Based on them, a dataset called **Basic dataset** was created. This time series dataset consists of 5 min windows. Here, every window contains the following information:

– CPU usage by system processes (percentage),
– CPU usage by user processes (percentage),

- free CPU power (percentage),
- RAM usage (bytes),
- free RAM (bytes),
- disk usage – Configuration value (percentage),
- disk usage – Reports value (percentage),
- disk usage – Signature value (percentage)
- disk usage – Temp value (percentage).

Sometimes, the LogServer data was missing records. If a single time window was missing a record, then its values were interpolated, based on the two neighboring records. If more than one time window in a row was missing values then, the series was considered finished and time when data was available again marked the beginning of a new time series.

It is worth noting that the System Health records are only a fraction of all records in the log data. Despite the fact that the individual Event and Firewall records bring little value, it would be unwise to totally disregard their contribution to the "knowledge about the state of the server". That's why another dataset called **Extended dataset** was built. It was created by enriching the **Basic dataset** with the following parameters:

- count of Event type records in a 5 min window,
- count of Firewall type records in a 5 min window,
- count of System Health type records in a 5 min window,
- count of events with Information priority in a 5 min window,
- count of events with Notice priority in a 5 min window,
- count of events with Warning priority in a 5 min window,
- count of events with Error priority in a 5 min window,
- kilobits sent in a 5 min window,
- kilobits received in a 5 min window.

Here, based on expert knowledge of EMCA engineers, it was assumed that this record can deliver useful information as, for example, increased number of Firewall records could be interpreted as a DDoS attack, while a sudden spike of Warning records could notify about a system malfunction.

Both time series consisted of 26,588 records in total. Example records of the **Extended dataset** are shown in Table 1. This Table was divided into two parts, due to huge number of columns per record.

Analysing the first record shows that it describes 5 min time window starting at December 1, 2020; 00:00:00:00 (timestamp column). Moreover, it can be established that:

- no Event type records were reported (column event_count),
- 1,289 Firewall records were reported (column firewall_count),
- 10 System Health records were reported (column health_count),
- 215 records with Notice priority were reported (column notice_count),
- 1,084 records with Info priority were reported (column info_count),
- 0 records with Warning or Error priority were reported (columns warning_count and error_count),

Table 1. Sample records from the Extended dataset

timestamp	event_ count	firewall_ count	health_ count	notice_ count	info_ count	warning_ count	error_ count	mem_used	mem_free
2020-12-01 00:00:00	0	1289	10	215	1084	0	0	1.987613e+09	2.157568e+09
2020-12-01 00:05:00	7	1144	10	223	937	1	0	1.991729e+09	2.153452e+09
2020-12-01 00:10:00	2	1187	10	217	990	0	0	1.991115e+09	2.154066e+09
2020-12-01 00:15:00	8	1087	10	236	869	0	0	1.989059e+09	2.156122e+09
2020-12-01 00:20:00	0	1120	10	218	912	0	0	1.972785e+09	2.172396e+09

transmitted_kbits	received_ kbits	disk_ conf	disk_ temp	disk_ reports	disk_ signature	cpu_ user	cpu_ system	cpu_idle	contains_na
5996.90	6195.98	18.0	3.0	21.0	22.0	3.39	2.50	94.11	0
2827.39	2986.55	18.0	3.0	21.0	22.0	3.07	1.85	95.07	0
1536.67	1737.29	18.0	3.0	21.0	22.0	3.10	1.91	94.99	0
1379.36	1560.16	18.0	3.0	21.0	22.0	3.15	1.82	95.02	0
721.56	787.31	18.0	3.0	21.0	22.0	3.68	2.07	94.25	0

- average RAM usage was equal to 1 987 613 000 bytes (column mem_used) and free RAM usage was equal to 2 157 568 000 bytes (column mem_free)
- 5,996.90 kilobits were sent (column transmitted_kbits) and 6,195.98 kilobits were received (column received_kbits),
- disk usage for specific parts was equal: Configuration 18% (column disk_conf), Temp 3% (column disk_temp), Reports 21% (column disk_reports), Signature 22% (column disk_signature),
- user processes consumed 3.68% CPU (column cpu_user), 2.07% CPU handled system processes (column cpu_system), and 94.25% CPU was unused (column cpu_idle)
- all System Health related records were reported (column contains_na) – this information was not fed to the neural network

3.3 Data Splitting

Let consider how the available time series data can be used in model training. The *classic data splitting* divides the time series into chronological overlapping windows of a fixed length. Next, the first N (e.g. 80%) windows are used for training and the remaining ones for testing.

An *alternate data splitting*, was proposed in [12]. Here, part of the time series (e.g. 80%) is randomly selected from the time windows, and used for training, while the remaining ones are used for testing. Here, it is assumed that this approach can better deal with the situation when, over time, drift in characteristics of the time series occurs. In what follows, performance of models trained with both data splittings approaches will be compared.

3.4 Performance Assessment

The *Classic Evaluation method* approach distinguishes between (a) true positives – correctly detected anomalies, (b) false positives – anomalies falsely reported, (c) true negatives – correctly recognized lack of anomaly, and (d) false negatives

– anomalies that were not detected. Based on occurrences of each situation, standard metrics, i.e. *True Positive Rate* (*TPR*), *precision*, or *F1* score (*F1*), can then be calculated.

After consultation with the representatives of the industry (and with EMCA, in particular), an *Alternative Evaluation method* approach has been formulated. It's goal is to realistically capture the situation and the expectations, rooted in the actual industrial practice. Here:

- *True positive* – measurement is considered an anomaly (i) if the model correctly classified it, or (ii) if the model correctly classified anomalies in at least one of k previous, or k subsequent time windows (k is a small number, and $k = 5$ was used here). The idea is that if the model warned about the anomaly "k moments earlier", or "k moments later", the anomaly "was captured". Moreover, "capturing an anomaly", before a critical error, is highly desirable. Furthermore, recognizing an anomaly shortly after it happened may still allow prevention of a "major problem". It may also allow learning what actually caused given anomaly.
- False positive – a measurement reported as an anomaly is a false positive if and only if neither current measurement, nor k previous or k subsequent were marked as anomalies. Here, the goal is to avoid "raising flags" when the system behaves "normally".
- False negative – measurement has not been marked as an anomaly, despite being one. In addition, neither k previous nor k subsequent measurements were indicated as an anomaly.
- True negative – no anomaly occurred, and a measurement was not reported as an anomaly.

Here, we recognize that this approach to performance assessment, while anchored in the knowledge of the industrial experts, may seem rather controversial. Therefore, in what follows, both assessment methods have been reported. Nevertheless, it is our belief that the rationale behind the proposed modified performance measurement "makes sense". Moreover, it better captures the actual needs of those who deal with anomaly detection on daily basis.

Let us note that detecting anomalies is a binary classification problem. Hence, for each time step, *true* is assigned if the system proposes that an anomaly occurred, and *false* otherwise. However, it should be stressed that since anomalies are very rare, these two classes are extremely unbalanced. Therefore, the standard *accuracy* is worthless. Specifically, since anomalies appear in less than 1% of time steps. Hence, a model that always returns *false*, would achieve accuracy above 99%. Therefore, "composite" evaluation methods, based on the number of true positives, have been selected.

- *True Positive Rate* (TPR) represents percentage of anomalies detected by the model; in the production systems, it is important to maximize the number of detected anomalies.
- *Precision* captures the fraction of correctly reported anomalies; it matters as it is impossible to human-verify (too) frequently reported false alarms.
- *F1* reports fraction of the correctly detected anomalies in relation to the incorrect ones; it assess the overall performance of the model.

3.5 Models Used in Experiments

As noted, the performance of AutoEncoders and Predictive Networks (PN) has been explored. Moreover, the results from multiple versions of each architecture have been combined into Voting models. Specifically, the following network architectures have been used (and tuned). For AutoEncoders: CNN, LSTM, CNN with LSTM layer, CNN with 2 LSTM layers (CNN LSTM v2) and Voting meta-classifier. For Predictive networks: CNN, LSTM, CNN with LSTM layer and Voting meta-classifier. Their detailed descriptions can be found in [11], pages: 27–35 and 87–94; and in the literature cited there.

Neural networks were implemented using *Keras*, and *Keras Self-Attention* for the self-attention layers. *Pandas* and *NumPy* packages were used for the data processing, while *sklearn* was used to normalize the data and divide the dataset into the training and the test sets. Finally, *matplotlib* was used for result plotting. Networks were trained within Google Colab. Codes, and are available at [11].

3.6 Methodology

For AutoEncoders, as proposed in [12], windows consisting of five subsequent measurements have been used. After training, time windows from the test set were passed to the AutoEncoders that applied its operations (compression + reconstruction from the compressed format) on each time window. For each time window, the mapping error (from the input to the output) was calculated, as the Mean Squared Error, where a single error is the absolute difference between the original value of the categorical variable and its value after being processed by the AutoEncoder network. The threshold was set at the 98th percentile of the error value. If the mapping error exceeded the threshold, the time window (likely) contained an anomaly. However, it is not known which specific measurement (out of these in the window) is the actual anomaly. Here, it was stipulated that if a given measurement is an anomaly, then all time windows containing it will be also reported as anomalous. Thus, if M successive time windows are reported as anomalous, then the measurement that occurred in all of them was judged as being anomalous.

For the *Predictive Networks*, data was divided into windows consisting of six measurements. Here, the sixth one was to be predicted, based on the values of the first five measurements. After training, as previously, the threshold was set at the 98th percentile of the prediction errors. If the error of the prediction of the sixth value was above the threshold, an anomaly was reported.

During initial experiments, when the dataset was split chronologically, the "expected" problem materialized. Trained models worked well on the training set, but their effectiveness drastically decreased for the test set. While, usually, such behavior indicates model overtraining, changing hyperparameters did not help. It can be argued that because data was collected only for 25 days, it is not representative enough. However, since no other data was available, the observed behavior provided one more reason to explore the *alternate data split*.

4   Experimental Results

Since the paper mill data is labeled, it allows an accurate quality assessment of the applied methods. It also supports fair comparison, and understanding the differences, between the classic and the alternate performance evaluation.

4.1   Performance of Basic Models

Initially, performance of the basic versions of all models was evaluated. The results for the AutoEncoders have been summarized in Table 2. For the classic evaluation, the best *TPR* was obtained for the chronological split and LSTM. The remaining performance measures delivered best results for random data split and Voting. However, for *precision* and random split, CNN LSTM v2 was slightly better. Similar results occurred for the alternate evaluation, with LSTM having best *TPR* for the chronological split, while *precision* and *F1* being best for Voting and random split. Comparing evaluation approaches, as expected, all performance measures are higher for the alternative approach. This is because, in the classic approach the model must capture the "exact moment" when the anomaly occurred, whereas in the alternative approach, delivering a "precise estimate" is acceptable.

Table 2. AutoEncoders.

Model	Classic evaluation method					
	Random data split			Chronological split		
	TPR	*precision*	*F1*	*TPR*	*precision*	*F1*
CNN	0.1048	0.0570	0.0739	0.0882	0.0099	0.0179
LSTM	0.1129	0.0664	0.0836	**0.4118**	0.0157	0.0303
CNN LSTM	0.1129	0.0645	0.0821	0.3824	0.0181	0.0346
CNN LSTM v2	0.1210	**0.0698**	0.0885	0.3824	0.0187	0.0356
Voting	**0.1452**	0.0690	**0.0935**	0.3824	**0.0200**	**0.0380**
	Alternate evaluation method					
CNN	0.1613	0.0971	0.1212	0.1471	0.0170	0.0307
LSTM	**0.1935**	0.1403	**0.1627**	0.4706	0.0198	0.0380
CNN LSTM	**0.1935**	0.1311	0.1563	0.4117	0.0216	0.0410
CNN LSTM v2	0.1855	0.1329	0.1549	0.4412	0.0239	0.0454
Voting	0.1855	**0.1447**	0.1625	0.1855	**0.0241**	**0.0455**

The next set of results concerns performance of predictive networks. The results are summarized in Table 3. As previously, alternate evaluation delivers "better results". In some cases, an improvement of more than the order of two was reported (for example, for Voting, *precision* jumped from 0.1169 to 0.2899). In the classical evaluation, for the chronological split, CNN LSTM had the best

Table 3. Predictive Networks.

Model	Classic evaluation method					
	Random data split			Chronological split		
	TPR	precision	F1	TPR	precision	F1
CNN	0.3600	0.0968	0.1525	0.3824	0.0212	0.0403
LSTM	0.3600	0.1023	0.1593	0.4706	**0.0278**	**0.0524**
CNN LSTM	**0.4000**	0.1064	0.1681	**0.7059**	0.0213	0.0413
Voting	0.3600	**0.1169**	**0.1765**	0.3824	0.0246	0.0462
	Alternate evaluation method					
CNN	0.5714	0.2381	0.3361	0.5882	0.0356	0.0671
LSTM	0.6111	0.2750	0.3793	0.6471	**0.0416**	**0.0782**
CNN LSTM	**0.6389**	0.2706	0.3802	**0.8236**	0.0280	0.0542
Voting	0.5715	**0.2899**	**0.3846**	0.5882	0.0411	0.0768

TPR, while LSTM – the best *precision* and *F1* scores. For the random split, CNN LSTM had the best *TPR*, again, while Voting scored best for the remaining two measures. For the alternate evaluation, the same pattern followed. It is worth noting that Predictive Networks outperformed AutoEncodes in all categories. In some cases, the performance gain was (for both evaluation methods) of order of two or more. For instance, for AutoEncoders, Voting, for random data split and classic evaluation, had *TPR = 0.1452*, while CNN LSTM, for Predictive networks had *TPR = 0.4000*. Finally, the best obtained results outperform these reported in [12]. Therefore, since the ground truth results have been outperformed, and since a number of additional performance improving methods have been tried, this comparison will be further elaborated only after performance of all modified approaches have been reported.

4.2   Application of Gaussian Dropout and Self Attention

In the second set of experiments, the basic models have been modified by replacing the networks' dropout layers with the Gaussian dropout layers. In addition, a single layer, implementing the self attention mechanism [3], was added to each neural network. The results for the AutoEncoder models are presented in Table 4. Here, with just a few exceptions, a slight improvement over the base models can be observed. However, sometimes an almost two-fold improvement has also been observed. For instance, for the random data split, for the classic evaluation, the best *TPR* jumped from 0.1425 to 0.4000. Moreover, Voting and LSTM can be seen as the best models. For the classical evaluation, LSTM has best *TPR*, while Voting leads in *precision* and *F1* performance measures. For the alternate evaluation the pattern remains, with CNN LSTM v2 having the best *TPR*. Here, when comparing the random and the chronological data splitting, no clear conclusions can be drawn. Depending on the evaluation method and the model, either splitting method may be a "winner".

Table 4. AutoEncoders with Gaussian dropout and self-attention.

Model	Classic evaluation method					
	Random data split			Chronological split		
	TPR	precision	F1	TPR	precision	F1
CNN	0.1048	0.0631	0.0788	0.1176	0.0125	0.0227
LSTM	**0.1210**	0.0704	0.0890	**0.4706**	0.0142	0.0275
CNN LSTM	0.1129	0.0619	0.0800	0.3529	0.0173	0.0330
CNN LSTM v2	**0.1210**	0.0710	0.0893	0.3824	0.0158	0.0303
Voting	0.1048	**0.0844**	**0.0935**	0.3529	**0.0198**	**0.0374**
	Alternative evaluation method					
CNN	0.1694	0.1148	0.1368	0.1765	0.0195	0.0352
LSTM	0.1855	0.1322	0.1544	**0.5883**	0.0195	0.0378
CNN LSTM	0.1855	0.1211	0.1465	0.3824	0.0205	0.0389
CNN LSTM v2	**0.1935**	0.1404	0.1627	0.4412	0.0203	0.0388
Voting	0.1694	**0.1579**	**0.1634**	0.2941	**0.0287**	**0.0522**

Table 5. Predictive networks with Gaussian dropout and self-attention.

Model	Classic evaluation method					
	Random data split			Chronological split		
	TPR	precision	F1	TPR	precision	F1
CNN	0.3600	0.1034	0.1607	0.4706	**0.0274**	**0.0518**
LSTM	0.3600	0.1047	0.1622	0.2648	0.0183	0.0343
CNN LSTM	0.3600	0.0978	0.1538	**0.5882**	0.0185	0.0358
Voting	0.3600	**0.1169**	**0.1765**	0.4706	0.0258	0.0489
	Alternative evaluation method					
CNN	0.6111	0.2750	0.3793	0.5294	**0.0341**	**0.0641**
LSTM	0.6111	0.2821	0.3860	0.4412	0.0330	0.0613
CNN LSTM	**0.6216**	0.2771	0.3833	**0.7941**	0.0274	0.0529
Voting	0.6111	**0.3143**	**0.4151**	0.5588	0.0336	0.0635

Next, the same model modifications have been applied to the Predictive networks. The results are reported in Table 5. Interestingly, for the classic evaluation and the random data splitting, all models achieved the same TPR (0.3600). However, for the remaining criteria, Voting performed best. For the chronological data splitting, CNN LSTM delivered best TPR (0,5882, almost twice better than for the random data split), while CNN had best $precision$ and $F1$ measures.

For the alternative evaluation and the random data splitting, again, Voting had best $precision$ and $F1$ scores, while CNN LSTM had slightly better TPR (then Voting). For the chronological data splitting, the same overall pattern materialized, with CNN LSTM having the best TPR, while vanilla CNN having the best *precision* and *F1* scores. Interestingly, in all cases, the chronological splitting delivered better results than the random splitting. Finally, when comparing AutoEncoders and Predictive networks, no clear winner can be found.

4.3 Application of Active Learning

In the case of chronological data splitting, it is possible to apply an "active learning". Here, models, apart from making predictions about incoming data, can also learn from it. Again, after multiple preliminary tests it was established that, for the dataset in question, the greatest performance improvement occurs when models are given 100 time windows for prediction, and then they are trained, on this very data, for 10 epochs. This approach (as an upgrade of the approach from Sect. 4.2) was also tested for the scenario, when after k new time windows materialized, the oldest k time windows were discarded from training dataset, and an "updated dataset" was used for training. Here, some improvement in model quality was noted. However, re-training using *only* the new data achieved better results (which are thus reported in what follows). Nevertheless, it should be stressed that these results materialized for the paper mill data. Hence, no claim about their generalizability is made.

For the AutoEncoder networks, the results are presented in Table 6. For both evaluation methods, Voting achieved the best performance. These results are up to four times better than in the case of chronological splitting, without active learning. In general, in comparison with the basic models, majority of models improved their performance.

Table 6. Modified AutoEncoders + active learning.

	Classic evaluation method		
	TPR	precision	F1
CNN	0.0882	0.0131	0.0228
LSTM	0.2059	0.0162	0.0300
CNN LSTM	0.1176	0.0134	0.0241
CNN LSTM v2	0.1176	0.0119	0.0216
Voting	**0.2353**	**0.0211**	**0.0387**
	Alternative evaluation method		
CNN	0.1471	0.0227	0.0394
LSTM	**0.3529**	0.0302	0.0556
CNN LSTM	0.1765	0.0213	0.0380
CNN LSTM v2	0.2059	0.0223	0.0402
Voting	**0.3529**	**0.0895**	**0.0584**

Table 7. Modified predictive networks + active learning.

	Classic evaluation method		
	TPR	precision	F1
CNN	**0.2941**	**0.0260**	**0.0477**
LSTM	0.2059	0.0211	0.0384
CNN LSTM	0.2353	0.0151	0.0284
Voting	0.2059	0.0227	0.0408
	Alternate evaluation method		
CNN	**0.4118**	0.0403	0.0735
LSTM	0.3529	0.0385	0.0694
CNN LSTM	**0.4118**	0.0286	0.0534
Voting	0.3529	**0.0414**	**0.0741**

The results for the predictive networks have been presented in Table 7. Interestingly, for the classic evaluation, vanilla CNN achieved the best results among the models. For the alternative evaluation mode, CNN obtained best *TPR*, while Voting delivered best *precision* and *F1* scores. Interestingly, while for the classic evaluation method the best performance of AutoEncoders and Predictive networks is quite similar, for the alternate evaluation approach Predictive networks are clear winners. However, it is not possible to unequivocally state that active learning helps across the board (compared to base and, separately, to Gaussian dropout and self-learning). Here, the most fair statement would be "it depends". Moreover, the reasons for the observed dependencies are not clear.

4.4 Applying Change Statistics

In order for the models to be used in a production environment, they should *not alarm too often* about a "non-existent problems". Hence, it is important to focus on reducing the total number of false positives. Here, let us note that, for instance, in a 24-hour cycle, large changes in sensor-obtained data may be "natural". For example, this happens when a paper mill starts the work-day, or has a scheduled maintenance. Here, (sudden/large) changes in measurements are not anomalies, but they are "natural phenomena". In order to avoid reporting anomalies at these moments, the change statistics was used. It was created based on prediction/reproduction errors on the training set. This statistics can then be divided into k minute "baskets". If the model detects an anomaly, it checks to which basket the "suspicious" time window belongs. If the error value, for a given time window, does not exceed a certain percentile of the error value for the basket in the change statistics (multiplied by a selected factor), then it is stipulated that the model has not detected an actual anomaly, because larger changes are "allowed" in this time interval. After multiple experiments, it was established that the best results are achieved when the error value for the time window is compared to the 98th percentile of the error values from the basket in the change statistics, with the multiplication factor equal to 1 (no actual change to the obtained value). Moreover, the basket in the change statistics, should consist of 10-min time intervals. Again, it should be stressed that this approach is problem (dataset) dependent and that parameter tuning is going to be required for all cases when it is to be applied.

For chronological data split, active learning approach, from Sect. 4.3, was enriched, on the other hand for random data split, approach from Sect. 4.2 was modified (as active learning cannot be used for random data split). Both approaches, after modifications, used the change statistics mechanism, described above. The results for the AutoEncoder networks have been reported in Table 8, and in table Table 9 the results for the Predictive networks. For AutoEncoders, Voting performed best, in all but one case, for both evaluation methods, and for both data splits. The only difference is the *precision* for the random data split and the classic evaluation, where slightly better performance was obtained by CNN LSTM. Moreover, it can be seen that using change statistics improved the overall model quality. Although the *TPR* has slightly diminished, most models have achieved better *F1* scores. For Predictive networks, in majority of cases, the Voting model performed best, with the best results, in terms of the *precision* and *F1* scores. Only in terms of *TPR*, the CNN LSTM network fared better.

Table 8. Modified AutoEncoder + change statistics.

Model	Classic evaluation method					
	Random data split			Active learning (chronological split)		
	TPR	precision	F1	TPR	precision	F1
CNN	0.0484	0.1304	0.0706	0.0882	0.0135	0.0233
LSTM	0.0565	0.1228	0.0773	0.1471	0.0122	0.0226
CNN LSTM	0.0484	0.1579	0.0741	0.1176	0.0127	0.0230
CNN LSTM v2	**0.0726**	0.1636	0.1006	0.1176	0.0110	0.0202
Voting	0.1049	**0.1733**	**0.1307**	**0.2647**	**0.0211**	**0.0392**
	Alternate evaluation method					
CNN	0.1210	0.3659	0.1818	0.1176	0.0186	0.0321
LSTM	0.1290	0.3077	0.1818	0.2941	0.0265	0.0485
CNN LSTM	0.1210	**0.4286**	0.1887	0.1765	0.0205	0.0367
CNN LSTM v2	0.1452	0.3750	0.2093	0.2059	0.0208	0.0378
Voting	**0.1532**	0.4130	**0.2235**	**0.3236**	**0.0314**	**0.0573**

For the alternate evaluation and the random data split, the two models outperformed the remaining ones. First, CNN LSTM, with $TPR = 0.5882$, $precision = 0.3175$, and $F1 = 0.4124$. Second, Voting with $TPR = 0.5313$, $precision = 0.3696$, and $F1 = 0.4359$. Although the CNN LSTM network found

Table 9. Modified predictive networks + change statistics.

Model	Classic evaluation method					
	Random data split			Active learning (chronological split)		
	TPR	precision	F1	TPR	precision	F1
CNN	0.2800	0.1228	0.1707	**0.1765**	**0.0229**	**0.0405**
LSTM	0.2800	0.1045	0.1522	0.1765	0.0211	0.0376
CNN LSTM	**0.3200**	0.1212	0.1758	0.1471	0.0132	0.0242
Voting	0.2800	**0.1458**	**0.1918**	0.1471	0.0205	0.0360
	Alternate evaluation method					
CNN	0.5313	0.3091	0.3908	0.3529	**0.0490**	**0.0860**
LSTM	0.5588	0.2923	0.3838	0.3529	0.0455	0.0805
CNN LSTM	**0.5882**	0.3175	0.4124	0.3529	0.0337	0.0615
Voting	0.5313	**0.3696**	**0.4359**	0.3235	0.0480	0.0837

more anomalies (as evidenced by the higher *TPR*), Voting reported false positives less often (it reached greater *precision*). Here, recall that the purpose of introduction of the change statistics was to reduce the number of false positives. Hence, in this context, Voting can be considered a better model. Overall, all models improved their *precision* and *F1* scores, for both evaluation methods. However, the *TPR* indicator became slightly worse.

4.5 Piecewise Aggregate Approximation

The last, somewhat successful, method (based on the approach defined in Sect. 4.4) to improve quality of models, was application, to the dataset, of the Piecewise Aggregate Approximation. Specifically, time-series data is often affected by the noise that causes the values of the measurements to fluctuate. Here, the main goal was to reduce those fluctuations by converting the original time-series into a new one. The new time-series is created by dividing the original time-series into windows of k measurements. Next, each window is substituted with one measurement, equal to the average of measurements within the window. If the original time-series contained N measurement, then the size of new time-series depends on whether the windows are overlapping or not. If they do not overlap, then the resulting time-series contains N/k measurements, if the windows do overlap and 2 consecutive windows have l the same measurements, then the new time-series will contain $N/(k-l)$ measurements. During the tests, the best results were achieved by using the approach with the overlapping windows; each containing 2 measurements. However, as will be seen, the results of this experiment were inconclusive. Some of the architectures saw a slight improvement in performance, while others saw a slight decline. The results for AutoEncoders, for random data split and with extra active learning, can be found in Table 10. Here, once more, the choice of the best model is not

Table 10. Modified AutoEncoders + Active learning + Piecewise Aggregate Approximation.

Model	Classic evaluation method					
	Random data split			Active learning (chronological split)		
	TPR	precision	F1	TPR	precision	F1
CNN	**0.4032**	0.1471	0.0633	0.0882	0.0154	0.0262
LSTM	0.0565	**0.2258**	0.0903	0.1765	0.0143	0.0264
CNN LSTM	0.0565	**0.2258**	0.0903	0.1471	0.0167	0.0300
CNN LSTM v2	0.0645	0.2000	0.0976	0.2059	0.0190	0.0348
Voting	0.0806	0.1311	**0.1300**	**0.2941**	**0.0209**	**0.0390**
	Alternate evaluation method					
CNN	0.0968	0.3750	0.1538	0.1176	0.0214	0.0362
LSTM	0.1129	**0.5186**	0.1854	0.2941	0.0252	0.0465
CNN LSTM	0.1048	0.4483	0.1699	0.2059	0.0243	0.0435
CNN LSTM v2	0.1129	0.4242	0.1783	0.2941	0.0292	0.0532
Voting	**0.1694**	0.2500	**0.2019**	**0.3236**	**0.0311**	**0.0567**

trivial. However, recall that, as stated above, the greatest importance should be given to the *precision* metric, as the purpose of using the Piecewise Aggregate Approximation method (similarly to the application of change statistics) was to reduce the total number of reported false positives. From this perspective, LSTM and CNN LSTM models are "the best". They achieved exactly the same $TPR = 0.0565$, $precision = 0.2258$, and $F1 = 0.0903$. Overall, the LSTM model can be seen as the best. It had $TPR = 0.1129$, $precision = 0.5186$, and $F1 = 0.1854$. Here, Voting had better $TPR = 0.1694$, but had a low precision, of only 0.2500. In summary, *precision* of individual models has improved. Only Voting recorded a decrease in the *precision* and an increase of the *TPR*. However, the *F1* score deteriorated for all models.

For the predictive networks, the results are summarized in Table 11. In the classic evaluation mode, the CNN network turned out to be the best. It achieved $TPR = 0.3846$, $precision = 0.1754$, and $F1 = 0.2410$. The remaining models performed worse in all respects. For the alternate evaluation, LSTM achieved best results. It detected more than half of the anomalies, obtaining $TPR = 0.5429$, and every third reported anomaly was real, as evidenced by the $precision = 0.3220$. Overall, it can be observed that the predictive networks have also seen an increase in *precision*. However, unlike AutoEncoders, some models achieved also better *TPR* and *F1* scores. Interestingly, greater improvement can be observed in the case of the classic assessment method.

Table 11. Modified predictive networks + Active learning + Piecewise Aggregate Approximation.

Model	Classic evaluation method					
	Random data split			Active learning (chronological split)		
	TPR	precision	F1	TPR	precision	F1
CNN	**0.3846**	**0.1754**	**0.2410**	0.1765	0.0222	0.0395
LSTM	0.3333	0.1429	0.2000	0.2059	0.0199	0.0364
CNN LSTM	0.3704	0.1449	0.2083	**0.2647**	0.0224	0.0413
Voting	0.3077	0.1739	0.2222	0.1538	**0.0238**	0.0412
	Alternate evaluation method					
CNN	0.5313	0.3148	0.3953	0.2941	0.0397	0.0699
LSTM	0.5429	0.3220	**0.4043**	0.3824	**0.0410**	**0.0741**
CNN LSTM	**0.5588**	0.2969	0.3878	0.4118	0.0390	0.0712
Voting	0.4688	**0.3488**	0.4000	**0.4412**	0.0393	0.0721

4.6   Attempt to Remove Trends from the Data

Another attempted modification, which was considered as a way to improve the operation of the models, was to change the input data processing. Upon inspection, it was noticed that the feature values, for the measurements, change over time, so that the feature values occurring in the last 20% of time windows do not appear in the first 80% of time windows. This may have been the reason why the models performed poorly, when the time windows are split chronologically. To circumvent this issue, an attempt was made to remove the changing trend from the data. Hence, the following approach was proposed:

- for Predictive networks – try to predict how the measurement will change, at a given moment, based on information on how the measurement value changed in several previous steps,
- for AutoEncoders – to compress and reconstruct several successive values, representing the change in the measurement value for several successive time steps.

The change in the measurement value for the kth time step was calculated as the difference of the measurement values in the kth and the k-1st timesteps. However, as a result, the performance of both Predictive and AutoEncoder models worsened, so this approach was abandoned.

4.7   Summary of Experimental Results for the Paper Mill Dataset

On the basis of the performed tests, one can compare the obtained results with the results presented in [12]. In order for the comparison to be as credible (and fair) as possible, the best models evaluated from each approach were selected using the classic evaluation method. The comparison of the models is presented in

Table 12. Comparing performance of "best" models with results from [12]; classic evaluation.

Model	Network Type	Approach	TPR	precision	F1
[12]	XGBoost/AdaBoost	–	–	0.071	0.114
Voting	AutoEncoder	base	0.1452	0.0690	0.0935
Voting	Prediction	base	0.3600	0.1169	0.1765
CNN LSTM v2	AutoEncoder	Gaussian dropout and self attention	0.1210	0.0710	0.0893
Voting	AutoEncoder	Gaussian dropout and self attention	0.1048	0.0844	0.0935
Voting	Prediction	Gaussian dropout and self attention	0.3600	0.1169	0.1765
Voting	AutoEncoder	change statistics	0.1049	0.1733	0.1307
Voting	Prediction	change statistics	0.2800	0.1458	0.1918
LSTM	AutoEncoder	Piecewise Aggregate Approximation	0.0565	**0.2258**	0.0903
CNN LSTM	AutoEncoder	Piecewise Aggregate Approximation	0.0565	**0.2258**	0.0903
CNN	Prediction	Piecewise Aggregate Approximation	**0.3846**	0.1754	**0.2410**

the Table 12, and the CNN predictive model from the Table 11 can be considered the best, as it achieved a *TPR* of 0.3864, a *precision* of 0.1754 and an *F1* score of 0.2410. Comparing the model with the results reported in the original work, i.e. *False Positive Rate* (FPR) equal to 0.026, *precision* equal to 0.071 and *F1* equal to 0.114, it can be concluded that the model developed in this work is "twice as good". Higher precision translates into the fact that the model obtained fewer false positives, and a higher *F1* score indicates that the model is generally better in identifying anomalies than the approach from [12].

It is also worth noting that not only the "most tuned" model performs better than those from [12]. For Predictive Networks, even the basic approach results in better both, *precision* and *F1* scores. AutoEncoder networks, on the other hand, only surpass the results reported in [12] after applying the change statistics. Another conclusion drawn from the analysis of the Table 12 is the fact that, in the case of the classic evaluation mode, the Voting model was usually the best network. This has changed only in the final approach, where other network models such as CNN, LSTM, or CNN LSTM proved to be the most successful. In addition, it can be seen that using the same approach, better results have been obtained using Predictive Networks. They achieve a higher rate of *true positives* and an better *F1* score than the AutoEncoder networks. AutoEncoder networks, on the other hand, have a higher *precision*, but the difference in this metric is smaller than in the case of the *TPR* and *F1* scores.

Comparing the models in terms of the alternative method of evaluation, in the Table 13, the best model can be considered the predictive Voting model in the approach in which change statistics were used. It achieved a *TPR* of 0.5313, a *precision* of 0.3696, and an *F1* score of 0.4359. It can also be seen that also in the alternative evaluation method, Predictive Networks perform better than AutoEncoders. The former have higher *TPR* and *F1* scores, while AutoEncoders report a little better *precision*.

4.8   LogServer Dataset Experiments

After evaluating models on the labeled paper mill dataset, and finding best approaches, an attempt was made to use the obtained knowledge to study data

Table 13. Comparing performance of "best" models; alternate evaluation.

Model	Network type	Approach	TPR	precision	F1
LSTM	AutoEncoder	base	0.1935	0.1403	0.1627
CNN LSTM	Prediction	base	**0.6389**	0.2706	0.3802
Voting	Prediction	base	0.5716	0.2899	0.3846
CNN LSTM v2	AutoEncoder	Gaussian dropout and self attention	0.1935	0.1404	0.1627
Voting	AutoEncoder	Gaussian dropout and self attention	0.1694	0.1579	0.1634
Voting	Prediction	Gaussian dropout and self attention	0.6111	0.3143	0.4151
Voting	AutoEncoder	change statistics	0.1532	0.4130	0.2235
Voting	Predition	change statistics	0.5313	0.3696	**0.4359**
LSTM	AutoEncoder	Piecewise Aggregate Approximation	0.1129	**0.5186**	0.1854
Voting	AutoEncoder	Piecewise Aggregate Approximation	0.1694	0.2500	0.2019
LSTM	Prediction	Piecewise Aggregate Approximation	0.5429	0.3220	0.4043
Voting	Prediction	Piecewise Aggregate Approximation	0.4688	0.3488	0.4000

gathered by the EMCA's LogServer. Specifically, voting models of augmented AutoEncoders and voting models of augmented Predictive networks, described in Sect. 4.5, have been applied. Here, it should be recalled that the LogServer data was not labeled, since precise detection of all anomalies by human would have been too time consuming. This is why, in the first phase of the reported work, various approaches have been tried on labeled data and then the "best methodology" (in terms of results and overall robustness) have been applied to the unlabeled dataset. Obviously, it is possible that still different approaches could lead to the better results. However, as discussed in what follows, obtained results are quite reasonable and likely to be explored by EMCA (as confirmed by the co-author of this contribution).

Here, it is also worth noting that, since data is unlabeled, calculation of the True Positive Rate and the F1-score was not possible. Only model precision could have been calculated. All the remaining aspects of the experimental setup have been exactly as these reported for the paper mill dataset experiments. The precision, obtained for the two models is shown in Table 14.

Table 14. Experimental precision of voting models, using approach from Sect. 4.5, applied to the LogServer dataset

Precision for the LogServer data				
Voting model	Basic dataset		Extended dataset	
	# of reported anomalies	precision	# of reported anomalies	precision
of AutoEncoders	46	0.5435	77	0.5064
of prediction models	25	0.5600	37	0.8982

Surprisingly, models obtained better precision on the LogServer data than on the papermill dataset. The Voting model of Prediction networks, processing the extended dataset, can be considered to be the best model, as it achieved *precision* of 0.8982. Hence, only 1 out of 10 reported anomalies was a false positive. Therefore, this model could be considered as a candidate for a production environment, as a human expert would not "waste time" reacting to false alarms. In addition, the following conclusions can be formulated:

- regarding count of detected anomalies:
  - processing the extended dataset resulted in reporting more anomalies than in the case of the basic dataset,
  - Voting model of AutoEncoders reported more anomalies than Voting model of Prediction networks.
- regarding the *precision*:
  - Voting model of Prediction networks achieved better *precision* than voting model of AutoEncoders, on both the basic and on the extended dataset,
  - contrary to The Voting model of AutoEncoders, Voting model of Prediction networks achieved significantly better *precision* on the extended dataset compared to the basic dataset.

4.8.1 Detected Anomalies Analysing anomalies detected in the LogServer data, it can be concluded that two anomaly types have been identified. First type stands out by an occurrence of a sudden, short-term spike of CPU and RAM usage (as represented in Fig. 3, and Fig. 4). In Fig. 3 it can be observed that between 20:00, on December 6 2020 and 02:00 on December 7, 2020, the CPU was using fraction of its power on processing the system and user processes. However, around 22:00 and 23:00, two CPU usage spikes can be observed. Those spikes lasted around 10 min and, as marked by gray vertical line, and the models correctly interpreted an anomaly around 23:00. On the other hand, in Fig. 4 there is a sudden RAM usage spike that was probably correlated with the CPU usage spike, depicted in Fig. 3.

The second anomaly type involves on appearance of a Warning, or and Error, type records, in logs. That situation is captured in Fig. 5. On March 16, 2021, two spikes in the count of Warning records can be observed. The first spike started slightly before 07:00 and lasted until around 08:00. The second spike started around 08:40 and finished after 09:00. The gray vertical line showcases the moment when the models reported an anomaly.

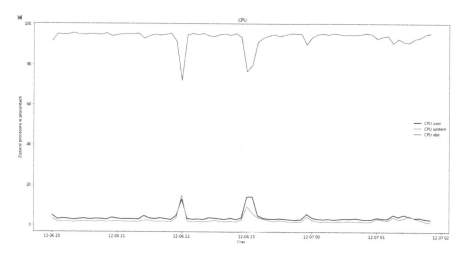

Fig. 3. Example of an anomaly, resulting in a sudden increase of CPU usage. The gray vertical line is the moment when model reported the anomaly.

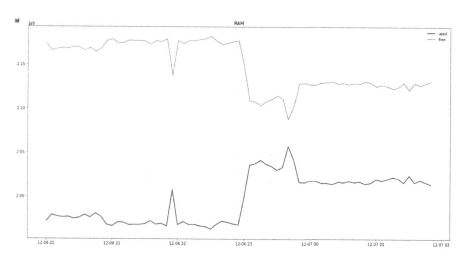

Fig. 4. Example of an anomaly, resulting in a sudden increase of RAM usage. The gray vertical line marks the moment when model reported the anomaly.

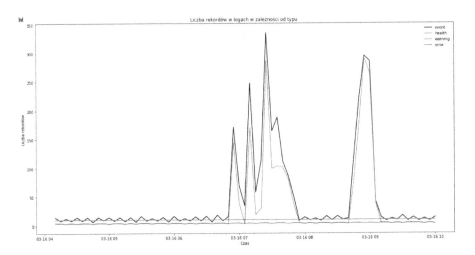

Fig. 5. Example of an anomaly related to the appearance of Warning type records. The gray vertical line showcases the moment when model reported the anomaly.

4.8.2 Comparison of the Final Approach with the Starting Approach

It is also interesting to compare used approach, from Sect. 4.5, with the basic approach, from Sect. 4.1. In order to do so, the voting models of base approaches were used to detect anomalies in LogServer data and the results have been verified by an expert from EMCA. Results of the experiment are showcased in Table 15.

Table 15. Precision of models from Sect. 4.1 applied to the LogServer data

Precision of models on LogServer data				
Voting model	Basic dataset		Extended dataset	
	# of reported anomalies	precision	# of reported anomalies	precision
of AutoEncoder	131	0.5038	146	0.5000
of prediction models	73	0.5479	95	0.5263

Here, it can be seen that the Voting models using basic approach reported more anomalies than voting models leveraging the final approach. Once again, Voting model of AutoEncoders reported more anomalies than voting model of Predictive networks. However, this time, both model classes achieved similar *precision*. Moreover, Voting model of basic AutoEncoders achieved slightly smaller *precision* than its tuned counterpart. It also reported more anomalies, thus (potentially) requiring more effort from human experts to verify them. When it comes to Voting model of Prediction networks, especially on the extended dataset, Voting model using basic approach achieved significantly smaller *precision* equal to 0.5263 compared to *precision* of 0.8982 for final approach Voting model.

It can be then concluded that, as is should be the case, the final approach that uses (1) self attention layers, (2) change statistics, and (3) Piecewise Aggregation Approximation, obtains results that are better than the basic approach.

5   Concluding Remarks

The aim of this work was to systematically compare two approaches to anomaly detection (AutoEncoders and Predictive networks), depending on (1) used architectures, (2) architecture modifications (mostly additions of extra modules and/or techniques), (3) the way that data is split into training and testing, and (4) the performance evaluation approach. As a result, it can be claimed that, as expected (see, also [15]), there is no silver bullet. Even the Voting-based meta-classifier does not(!) outperform all basic approaches in all cases. Nevertheless, for the paper mill dataset, it was possible to substantially outperform the baseline performance, reported in [12].

It is also worthy noting, that the "somewhat discouraging" results, reported in this contribution, have been obtained for a specific dataset. Hence, the results presented here should not be expected to generalize to other datasets. Overall, for each actual industrial problem, it will be necessary to adjust not only model hyperparameters, but also how the data is split, what additional information about he nature of the data should be used, and which model, with which modifications will deliver the best results for the case at hand.

Both model classes did quite well, when applied to the EMCA's LogServer data. AutoEncoder models achieved *precision* of over 50%, on both the basic and the extended dataset. That *precision* is higher than best *precision*, achieved on the labeled paper mill dataset. Predictive networks have reported smaller number of anomalies, but had much better *precision*, that was equal to 89%, on the extended dataset. This result should be "good enough" to attempt to apply this approach in the production environment.

Acknowledgments. Work of Maria Ganzha was funded in part by the Centre for Priority Research Area Artificial Intelligence and Robotics of Warsaw University of Technology within the Excellence Initiative: Research University (IDUB) programme. Work of Marcin Paprzycki and Artur Bicki was funded in part by the "Empowered AI in Energy Logserver - AI module for algorithmic discovery of knowledge collected in IT system events as a response to challenges in the field of Cybersecurity"; contract: POIR.01.01.01-00-0152/22.

References

1. Beggel, L., Kausler, B.X., Schiegg, M., Pfeiffer, M., Bischl, B.: Time series anomaly detection based on Shapelet learning. Comput. Stat. **34**(3), 945–976 (2019). https://doi.org/10.1007/s00180-018-0824-9. https://ideas.repec.org/a/spr/compst/v34y2019i3d10.1007_s00180-018-0824-9.html
2. Callegari, C., Gazzarrini, L., Giordano, S., Pagano, M., Pepe, T.: A novel PCA-based network anomaly detection. In: 2011 IEEE International Conference on Communications (ICC), pp. 1–5, July 2011. https://doi.org/10.1109/icc.2011.5962595

3. CyberZHG: Keras self-attention (2018). https://github.com/CyberZHG. gitHub repository

4. Davis, N., Raina, G., Jagannathan, K.P.: LSTM-based anomaly detection: detection rules from extreme value theory. CoRR abs/1909.06041 (2019). http://arxiv.org/abs/1909.06041

5. Eiteneuer, B., Niggemann, O.: LSTM for model-based anomaly detection in cyberphysical systems (2020)

6. Harrou, F., Kadri, F., Chaabane, S., Tahon, C., Sun, Y.: Improved principal component analysis for anomaly detection: application to an emergency department. Comput. Ind. Eng. **88**, 63–77 (2015). https://doi.org/10.1016/j.cie.2015.06.020. http://www.sciencedirect.com/science/article/pii/S036083521500279X

7. Janus, P., Ganzha, M., Bicki, A., Paprzycki, M.: Applying machine learning to study infrastructure anomalies in a mid-size data center – preliminary considerations. In: Proceedings of the 54th Hawaii International Conference on System Sciences, HICSS 2021, Kauai, Hawaii, USA, 5 January 2021, pp. 1–10. ScholarSpace (2021). http://hdl.handle.net/10125/70636

8. Kamat, P., Sugandhi, R.: Anomaly detection for predictive maintenance in industry 4.0 – a survey. E3S Web Conf. **170**, 02007 (2020). https://doi.org/10.1051/e3sconf/202017002007

9. Kudo, T., Morita, T., Matsuda, T., Takine, T.: PCA-based robust anomaly detection using periodic traffic behavior. In: 2013 IEEE International Conference on Communications Workshops (ICC), pp. 1330–1334 (2013). https://doi.org/10.1109/ICCW.2013.6649443

10. Paffenroth, R.C., Kay, K., Servi, L.: Robust PCA for anomaly detection in cyber networks. CoRR abs/1801.01571 (2018). http://arxiv.org/abs/1801.01571

11. Rakus, D.: Praca dyplomowa magisterska: Zastosowanie metod analityki danych do analizy zachowań zespołu serwerów – kody (2021)

12. Ranjan, C., Reddy, M., Mustonen, M., Paynabar, K., Pourak, K.: Dataset: rare event classification in multivariate time series (2019)

13. Ringberg, H., Soule, A., Rexford, J., Diot, C.: Sensitivity of PCA for traffic anomaly detection. ACM SIGMETRICS Perform. Eval. Rev. **35**, 109–120 (2007). https://doi.org/10.1145/1254882.1254895

14. Russo, S., Disch, A., Blumensaat, F., Villez, K.: Anomaly detection using deep autoencoders for in-situ wastewater systems monitoring data (2020)

15. Saad, E., et al.: Generalized zero-shot learning for image classification;comparing performance of popular approaches. Information **13**(12), (2022). https://doi.org/10.3390/info13120561. https://www.mdpi.com/2078-2489/13/12/561

16. Schmidt, F., Suri-Payer, F., Gulenko, A., Wallschläger, M., Acker, A., Kao, O.: Unsupervised anomaly event detection for cloud monitoring using online Arima. In: 2018 IEEE/ACM International Conference on Utility and Cloud Computing Companion (UCC Companion), pp. 71–76 (2018). https://doi.org/10.1109/UCC-Companion.2018.00037

17. Thill, M., Konen, W., Bäck, T.: Online anomaly detection on the Webscope S5 dataset: a comparative study. In: 2017 Evolving and Adaptive Intelligent Systems (EAIS), pp. 1–8 (2017). https://doi.org/10.1109/EAIS.2017.7954844

Blockchain-Based Framework for Healthcare 5.0

Vijayant Pawar[1], Shelly Sachdeva[1(✉)], and Subhash Bhalla[2]

[1] National Institute of Technology Delhi, New Delhi, India
{vijayantpawar,shellysachdeva}@nitdelhi.ac.in
[2] University of Aizu, Aizuwakamatsu, Japan

Abstract. This article presents a Blockchain-based data-sharing approach that offers reliability, integrity, and decentralization properties of Blockchain, making the system user-controllable. It contains the evolution of the healthcare industry with respect to other industries. We also discuss the impact of industry 5.0 technologies and Blockchain-enabled healthcare. The proposed system stores medical data off-chain with IPFS, and the reference of off-chain data is stored on Blockchain. Information flow is set up with the help of smart contracts deployed over Blockchain to ensure immutability and traceability. A prototype has been simulated on the Rinkeby test network using a Proof-of-Work consensus algorithm for various parameters such as upload time, retrieval time, and gas consumed for transaction execution.

Keywords: Covid-19 · Industry 5.0 · Blockchain

1 Introduction

Industry 5.0 is about orchestration between humans and machines, making work easier and faster. The aim of Industry 5.0 in various domains such as Cities and regions, Energy, Disaster prevention, Healthcare, Agriculture, Finance, and public services are discussed with the help of Table 1. The advent of mechanical manufacturing facilities first employing steam and water power ushered in the industrial revolution in the eighteenth century. Water and steam-powered machines were provided to help workers in the mass production of goods. Industry 1.0 is the beginning of the industry culture, which focuses equally on scale and efficiency. The end of the twentieth century marked the start of the second industrial revolution. The development of devices that run on electrical engineering was known as Industry 2.0. Running and maintaining are more cost-effective and cost-effective than water and steam-based devices, which were inefficient and resource-hungry. Industry 3.0 marked a significant advancement in the industrial environment with the introduction of computers and automation. It is also called the programmable logic controllers' era, but they just specialized computers for factory automation. The boom in the internet and telecommunication in the 1990s revolutionized how we connected and exchanged information. It resulted in paradigm changes in the manufacturing industry by merging the physical and the virtual world. Industry 5.0 uses the cyber-physical system to analyze, share and guide intelligent action for various processes in the industry to make the machine smarter.

S. Sachdeva and Y. Watanobe (Eds.): BDA 2023, LNCS 14516, pp. 275–288, 2024.
https://doi.org/10.1007/978-3-031-58502-9_18

Table 1. Aim of Industry 5.0 in different domains

Domains	Aim		
Cities and regions	Data will be shared to allow for more intelligent solutions	In the suburbs and rural areas, decentralized communities will emerge	Allow for a variety of lifestyles in civilizations
Energy	Reliable energy will be available to everyone	Local circumstances will be used to construct decentralized microgrids	Clean and sustainable energy will be supplied
Disaster prevention	Catastrophe information is shared across enterprises, allowing faster disaster response	Digital technology will be employed to help mitigate disasters	Even in the case of a calamity, medical services will be maintained
Healthcare	At the preventative stage, new techniques will deliver treatment to the individual	Individuals will utilize and manage data related to their life stages independently	Stakeholders' data will be accessed following fine-grained rules
Agriculture and Food	The food value chain will also be optimized using technology	Private enterprises and agritech start-ups will be among the participants	Data sharing on manufacturing, transportation, and sales to improve the whole supply chain
Finance	Diverse, custom-tailored financial services will be made available due to digital transformation	Financial systems will distribute assets across society efficiently and effectively	Improved financial services availability will lead to increased economic freedom and income equality
Public Services	Actors deliver more innovative public services by promptly exchanging data among many participants	Government-created safety nets will enable anybody to face a range of security issues	Public authorities shall make necessary preparations and offer services promptly and suitably

The benefits of Industry 4.0 are improved productivity and output, enhanced customization for flexible manufacturing, enhanced worker safety and production, and access to data across the supply chain for better decision-making. Industry 5.0 is a refinement, and an extensive version of Industry 4.0 improves the quality of life and facilitates human-machine interaction. Table 2. Depicts the evolution of Industry 5.0 and Healthcare 5.0.

In December 2019, a cluster of pneumonia cases was discovered in Wuhan, China. The sickness was determined to be caused by a newly identified coronavirus. Covid-19 was given to the illness after that. Covid-19 expanded throughout China and beyond the world. The WHO declared a worldwide significant public health emergency on January 30, 2020 [1]. History has seen many respiratory infections earlier, like severe acute respiratory syndrome (SARS-Cov), identified in China in 2003, and MERS-Cov, identified in Saudi Arabia in 2012. Still, the horrific effect of COVID-19 is above all these earlier setbacks.

Table 2. Industry and Healthcare 5.0

INDUSTRY		1.0	2.0	3.0	4.0	5.0
Aim		Production	Industrialization	Automation	Digitalization	Personalization
Focus	Industry	Mechanics	Electricals	Electronics and Computers	Cyber-physical Systems	Customer-centric
	Healthcare	Evidence-based treatment model	Value chain integration model	Operating model	Business model	Customer model
Differentiator	Industry	Mechanization	Mass Production	Mass Automation	Mass Customization	Mass Personalization
	Healthcare	Patient survivability	End-to-end service coverage	Cost to serve, efficiency	Mass Customization	Mass Personalization, Quality of life

The heavy usage and extension of IoT devices and instruments in hospitals [2] make it easy for hospitals and clinics to collect real-time and every bit of patient data. Therefore, there is a need to collect and store voluminous data to be analyzed efficiently and effectively. Big data tools like Hadoop, Kafka, and Hive are needed. Once the data is stored, various artificial intelligence and deep learning algorithms can find trends, model, and predict outcomes from the data. Once the trained model generates the final report, its hash/reference is stored on the Blockchain. Once stored on the Blockchain, it inherently follows Blockchain's various properties, such as reliability, security, and traceability. Figure 1 presents the use of Industry 5.0 technologies in the COVID-19 pandemic.

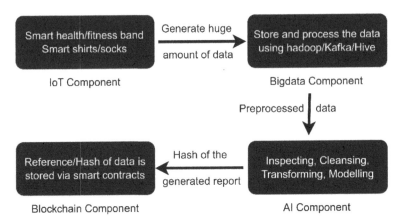

Fig. 1. Industry 5.0 technologies in Covid-19

1.1 Motivation

Today's healthcare system lacks a model that can store medical data so that the patient has ownership over it. The immutability and reliability of data in traditional systems are not guaranteed. Due to the current pandemic situation, the need for a patient-centric system and receiving reliable and immutable information is urgent. We can counter the situation by using industry 5.0 technologies like IoT, Bigdata, AI, and Blockchain. In adverse conditions like a pandemic, we can find out the current status of distributed geographic locations and predict the consequences of the disaster in a precise way.

1.2 Research Contributions

In this study, we have introduced a blockchain-enabled framework for healthcare 5.0, incorporating internet-of-things, big data, and artificial intelligence. In comparison to state-of-the-art findings, the contributions of the article are outlined below:

- A blockchain-based framework is proposed that allows the patient to fully control their data, give granular access to others, and preserve personal anonymity.
- It employs a decentralized file system, specifically the InterPlanetary File System (IPFS), to manage extensive healthcare data.
- We perform thorough experiments to assess the performance of the proposed frameworks across different aspects, such as throughput, response time, and gas consumption.

The rest of the paper is organized as follows. Section 2 reviews the related work. The design and implementation of the framework are discussed in Sect. 3. In Sect. 4, the effectiveness of the proposed framework is discussed with the help of a secure medical information exchange example and COVID-19 data analysis. Finally, Sect. 5 concludes the paper and discusses future work.

2   Related Work

This section is divided into two parts: In the first part, we discuss how industry 5.0 technologies are helpful in tracking, surveillance, identification, prevention, and alleviation against the Covid-19 pandemic, and in the second part, we cover how Blockchain can revolutionize the healthcare system. IoT provides a platform to track real-time data. For example, the Worldmeter (www.worldmeter.info) is one of the most popular Covid-19 tracking application provides a real-time update on the actual number of total infections, total deaths, recovered, and critical cases. In addition, Bigdata delivers tools for efficient data storage so that later on, information and knowledge can be extracted from it. In [3], a modelled study of forecasting Covid-19 within and outside China is done, which can be used by the health authorities for public health planning and control worldwide. Furthermore, AI and deep learning can enhance the detection and diagnosis of Covid-19 [4]. At the same time, Blockchain makes the report that is the outcome of AI and the deep learning phase secure and traceable. Table 3 shows the impact of industry 5.0 technologies on Covid-19.

Table 3. Impact of industries 5.0 technologies on Covid-19

Health-measures	IoT	Bigdata	AI	Blockchain
Tracking, surveillance, identification, and prevention	High	High	Average	Low
Examples	Real-time monitoring and live updates in different Asian, US, and European online databases	Efficiently get knowledge out of the humongous amount of data	Uncovering of Covid-19 symptoms through chest X-ray (IIT Gandhinagar, India)	Direct interaction between patient and final authority without needing intermediaries
	Live tracking of the risky zones in India (Aarogya Setu app, covid19india)	Extraction of association between data from various resources	Prediction of progression via digital imaging and clinical data	Use of manpower, in-kind, medical equipment's and monetary donations become transparent
Mitigation of impact	High	Average	High	Average
Examples	Virtual clinics (LiveHealth, USA)	Pharmaceutical supply modelling for a variety of drugs	Diagnose medical disorders associated with Covid-19 automatically (Zebra Medical AI, Apollo Hospital)	Distribution of patient medication to the pharmacy. So, that patient gets a doorstep service
	Information transmission via WhatsApp in India	Modelling of the utilities and equipment's for operation theatres	Medical chatbots for enquiry related to Covid-19(St. Joseph Hospital, Seattle)	

Healthcare data is regarded as highly sensitive and requires a safe and reliable means to protect it. Therefore, medical data should be collected, exchanged, and handled securely [5, 6]. There are already numerous frameworks proposed to resolve these issues; for example, the schemes set out in [7–9] to meet the need for safe and efficient accessibility, manageability, and other critical security criteria for medical data. These solutions help offer different safety requirements under desired healthcare scenarios. However, with the latest developments in healthcare technology, these strategies are not enough. The patient has been exploited through unfair means by various stakeholders, and they access patient data without their consent [10, 11]. Therefore, researchers are keen to find various security solutions in the context of blockchain-based approaches to healthcare. Numerous research studies have been carried out in [13, 14] regarding Blockchain's potential use in healthcare. Electronic medical treatment processes for manual and remote access to patient data and safeguarding healthcare data privacy are the most foregoing application areas where blockchain technology can create value [15].

SimplyVital Health [16] is a startup company founded in 2016 aiming to leverage blockchain technology in healthcare. Their publicly available web materials indicate that they are working on two products: "ConnectingCare" and "Health Nexus." Connecting-Care is a care coordination tool used by providers that leverage blockchain technology to create a secure audit trail. Health Nexus plans to be its healthcare-focused Blockchain with an underlying cryptocurrency token called "HLTH". Medrec has proposed the study in [17], in which a decentralized approach of using blockchain technology to handle the EHR/EMR (Electronic medical record) is adopted. The authors have presented a possible case study of blockchain usage in healthcare that offers an EHR/EMR prototype. The various challenges and opportunities like Clinical Health Data Exchange, Interoperability, Claims Adjudication, Patient Billing Management, and Drug Supply Chain Integrity that blockchain applications face in the healthcare industry are discussed [18]. The authors believe that blockchain technology will improve patient care, treatment efficacy, security, and reducing costs. They suggest that electronic medical record management will be made more efficient, disintermediated, and secured through blockchain technology.

Kuo et al. [19] provide a comprehensive overview of biomedical and healthcare applications that could be developed using blockchain technology. They view decentralized management of records, the immutability of audit trails, data provenance, data availability, security, and privacy as benefits from implementing blockchain technology over traditional distributed database management systems. The authors also discuss potential challenges that blockchain applications may face in a healthcare environment relating to transparency, confidentiality, speed, scalability, and resistance to malicious actors. Metrics can be used to evaluate the feasibility, intended capability, and compliance of a blockchain-based application in the healthcare space discussed in [20]. Dufel [21] discusses Blockchain, alongside other peer-to-peer technologies, and their application towards healthcare. BitTorrent, a peer-to-peer file-sharing system, is discussed, as well as distributed hash tables. The authors suggest that only a combination of Blockchain, distributed hash tables, and BitTorrent would effectively create a peer-to-peer health information exchange system.

Zhang [22] aims to fill the information gap regarding software architectural styles and recommendations for constructing blockchain-based healthcare applications. To do this, they discuss challenges in addressing healthcare interoperability, develop a case study of a blockchain-based healthcare application they are building, and suggest how using familiar software patterns can directly address some challenges.

The application developed by the authors uses the Ethereum test blockchain to provide a web portal that patients can use to access and update medical records and fulfill prescription requests. "Mercantis" [20] was a winning project proposed at the Distributed Health Hackathon during 2017 that leveraged Ethereum smart contracts to create a decentralized marketplace for healthcare data. The proposed system enables patients to control their medical information and monetize it if they chose to do so by selling it to researchers; researchers can have improved access to data by leveraging the decentralized data market. Esposito et al. [12] outlined the disadvantages of using cloud storage technology to set up a medical data-sharing system. They also brought up the potential problems of using blockchain technology to share medical data (such as privacy protection). MedicalChain [23] is a Hyperledger blockchain network with its cryptocurrency (i.e., Med-token) aiming to bind insurance companies, healthcare providers, and research institutions with predefined fees. Besides, [24] presents Medshare, which uses Blockchain to provide a trustless sharing of healthcare data between various service providers. The research community is now identifying various frameworks for the safe data accessibility of a blockchain-based healthcare system. It leads to an effective and improved data accessibility process through private/permissioned Blockchain for safer and faster access to healthcare data. Furthermore, it offers a patient-centric methodology, in which patient consent is needed by every stakeholder before processing and accessing his data.

3 Blockchain-Enabled Framework Architecture

In this section, we discuss the prototype and implementation of the proposed system to provide more ownership to the patient over his medical data in a secure way. Only authorized entities can access the medical records by the patient's consent while keeping their identity anonymous. An abstract view of the framework is shown with the help of Fig. 2. The main focus of the paper is on two things. First, a record audit trail of the health information exchange, and second is to perform analysis over Covid-19 data gathered from geographically distributed resources. To carry out both the tasks mentioned above, we store data on the Ethereum blockchain with smart contracts. With the help of transactions in the proposed framework, partial and complete access to health information can be controlled.

In more detail, the relationship between patient and healthcare provider can be recorded with Blockchain's help. Furthermore, as data is stored as a transaction in the Blockchain, the data stored inherently becomes transparent and immutable. Due to these characteristics of Blockchain integrity of stored and exchanged data is maintained.

As a result, audit traces of the information flow will be transparent and unaltered. Cryptographic hashes are used to ensure the integrity of the data being transferred. The result produced by the hashing algorithm is stored in Blockchain with the help of a smart contract named MedicalSC as shown in algorithm 1. Medical data collected from EHR is encrypted with the help of the open-source implementation of a Pretty Good Privacy encryption scheme, i.e., GPG encryption. To encrypt medical data, the proposed architecture employs asymmetric key cryptography. Where medical data is encrypted with the help of the recipient public key. The encryption process is performed on the client-side before putting the data on IPFS. The entire process of accessing medical data is done through smart contracts that maintain references to content identifiers. To preserve the privacy of individuals, identities are pseudonymous. The smart contract, on the other hand, can link Ethereum's public address to a generally acknowledged method of unique identity. The subsequent section presents the implementation details for each component of the framework.

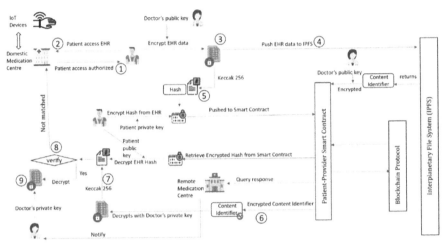

Fig. 2. Architecture of the Blockchain-enabled healthcare data framework

3.1 Blockchain

Initially, Blockchain technology was used to facilitate the exchange of digital money packaged as transactions that are recorded on an immutable, tamper-proof data structure (i.e., the ledger) and exchanged through a peer-to-peer network. Other protocols, such as Ethereum, have developed the concept of safeguarding state machines and algorithmic logic (via Smart Contracts) over a decentralized p2p network based on this concept [15]. A consensus algorithm [17] preserves the state of the data and agrees on it. In this paper, we use smart contracts, which can run on any blockchain platform and provide a tamper-resistant log of health information stored as a transaction in Blockchain. The smart contract allows patient healthcare data to be accessed and exchanged only after their permission. Particularly, our system broadcasts blockchain transactions that include cryptographically signed information on data ownership, access credentials, and data integrity.

To establish tamper-evident logs of health information exchange, we use smart contracts that can be deployed in any blockchain-based protocol that runs the EVM. The smart contract allows patient-driven healthcare data interchange that is only accessed with the permission of the patient. More particular, our system broadcasts blockchain transactions that include cryptographically signed metadata that provides data ownership, access privileges, and data integrity. Overall, the Blockchain acts as a historical log of recorded transactions on the blockchain state, providing a transparent, time-stamped sequence of every healthcare data exchange. The actual medical data is kept on an IPFS cluster at the user's request rather than on blockchain blocks. The smart contract keeps track of pointers to encrypted content identifiers for data stored on the IPFS cluster, as stated in the following sections.

3.2 Key Management

To facilitate the interaction between various system stakeholders, users (U_i) (either patient (P_i) or Medical Professionals (MP_i)) are assigned two pair of keys:

1. An Ethereum Public/Private key pair ($PubK_U$, $PriK_U$). The first private key is generated using SHA256. Then this public key is created using the Elliptic Curve Digital Signature Algorithm (ECDSA). Finally, Ethereum uses secp256k1 to generate a public key. This pair of ($PubK_U$, $PriK_U$) is used for authentication to interact with the Ethereum blockchain.
2. GPG key pair ($GPGPubK_U$, $GPGPriK_U$) for encrypting and decrypting the medical data is generated using GnuPG standard along with strong paraphrase to protect the keys.

Where U_i is either P_i or MP_i, two open-source JavaScript libraries are utilized to construct this component. The framework leverages the Web3.js package for the Ethereum key pair to build externally owned accounts for each P_i and MP_i accordingly. Similarly, the GnuPG.js package is used to encrypt and decrypt medical data sent between patients and medical providers. Figure 3 provides a code snippet for creating GPG keys for a patient, as well as a code sample for producing GPG keys for a medical practitioner.

Fig. 3. Generation of GPG keys for the patient

3.3 Encryption and Validation Scheme

The encryption and validation scheme ensures secure data transmission and verifies the integrity of the information are discussed as follows:

Encrypt & Sign: The framework encrypts a file or any other object that comprises medical data (e.g., JSON object) with the public key of the intended receiver, e.g., MP_i, to ensure the secrecy of the medical data transmission. This is necessary to ensure that the information requestor can only decrypt the medical data acquired via IPFS. The data is then encrypted and sent to IPFS using the PGP public key, $PGPPub_{MP}$. IPFS returns a content identification, which is encrypted using the recipient's public key $PubK_{MP}$ and sent to the smart contract. To confirm that the data has not been tampered with, the framework hashes the encrypted medical data and then signs the output message hash with the patient's private key (i.e., Pri_{KP}). It then sends this data to $Medical_{SC}$, which manages all of the metadata.

Validate & Decrypt: The metadata is requested from $Medical_{SC}$ by the intended receiver, such as MP_i. The intended recipient decrypts the IPFS content identification and locally retrieves the encrypted file from IPFS using its private key (i.e., $PriK_{MP}$) upon receipt. The recipient additionally uses the Pub_{KP} to decrypt the encrypted hash value of the patient's file from the metadata. The recipient then generates a message digest for the encrypted file using the same hashing algorithm and compares it to the metadata (previous decrypted). Validation is successful if the two hash values are the same. Only then may the recipient proceed to decode the file using the GPG private key, $GPGPriK_{MP}$, in a secure manner.

3.4 Smart Contract Layer

A distinct $Medical_{SC}$ smart contract is executed on the Blockchain for each patient-medical doctor interaction to ensure that medical data is always in the patient's hands (i.e., data owner) (shown in Algorithm 1). The data owner is the smart contract owner, who has the authority to write particular metadata to the Blockchain and allow access to medical data according to GDPR requirements.

The contract specifies a collection of data pointers and permissions to the medical data in further detail. Access to the medical data file is expressed at this tier as an IPFS content identifier reference. The data is indexed using the intended recipient's public key, which is stored on the Blockchain. The procedure of recording metadata on the Blockchain is performed by calling the addData() method. A call to the searchFile() method, on the other hand, returns the metadata for a specific medical data item.

3.5 Medical Data Storage

In essence, the Blockchain stores metadata for each encrypted medical record that is protected by a smart contract. Access permissions to the data, hashes to validate digital signatures, and encrypted copies of the references to the medical information are all stored in the smart contract. The accurate medical data is stored in an IPFS cluster, which collects data from various IPFS daemons (private or public) and provides a means for data replication over numerous peers.

4   Medical Information Exchange and Covid-19 Data Analysis

Beyond the secure storage of local healthcare providers, the Covid-19 epidemic has demonstrated an increased necessity for supporting health information exchange requests and prompt response for patient records. Because the existing healthcare system is unstable and changeable owing to a single point of failure. As a result, in the event of the Covid-19 epidemic, we require a more trustworthy method. So that we may more carefully and properly analyze the current situation and forecast the future. Furthermore, existing medical systems fail to simplify EHR successfully because of the complexity of internal data structures.

In light of the aforementioned issues, we believe that a more patient-centered approach to medical data collection is required. Medical practitioners will be able to start with a patient and audit trails of the patient's medical history, such as medical data, symptoms, diagnostic tests, past therapies. For each entity participating in the system, information is preserved through the smart contract. As a result, the odds of data tampering and non-repudiation are reduced.

In this section, the author discusses two things: An illustration of the proposed architecture depicting a patient-centered medical journey. First, the medical journey is broken down into steps, which are depicted in Fig. 2, and second, Covid-19 data analysis is done to calculate current and predict the future situation.

Execution Flow of the Proposed System
Patients (P_i) and medical professionals (MP_i) are the two sorts of Users (U_i) that the system can register. The registration takes place in a medical facility. With the Key Management component, a pair of keys is produced for each U_i. The registration and validation of the identity of each user are already discussed above in this paper.

Steps 1 to 2 – Includes registration and authentication process. So that medical data access (raw data or EHR) is provided to P_i.
Steps 3 to 4 – P_i, the patient, encrypts the file with $GPGPubK_{MP}$, and then pushes it to IPFS storage. This phase results in the creation of an encrypted file as well as a content identifier (i.e., URL) that links to that file. The IPFS URL is additionally encrypted with $PubK_{MP}$ before being uploaded to $Medical_{SC}$ as metadata.
Step 5 – P hashes the encrypted file with keccak256, which is subsequently encrypted using Pri_{KP} and uploaded to $Medical_{SC}$ as metadata. Later, as part of the digital signature validation procedure, this piece of information is employed.

Medical Professional Side. When a medical professional or healthcare provider MP_i gets an alert, he or she goes to the $Medical_{SC}$ smart contract, which P has shared and authorized.

Step 6 – MP_i, a medical specialist, uses $PriK_{MP}$ to decode the IPFS URL and get the encrypted file using information from the smart contract.
Step 7 – From $Medical_{SC}$ metadata, MP_i obtains the encrypted hash h_E of the encrypted file. MP_i also generates a hash h_L of the encrypted file obtained from IPFS using the keccak256 hash algorithm on the encrypted file.
Step 8 – MP_i decrypts h_E with Pub_{KP} and then compares the hash value to h_L.

Step 9 – If the hashes are identical ($h_E == h_L$), MP decrypts the file using GPGPriK$_{MP}$, otherwise notifying the patient or healthcare provider.

5 Results

The Ethereum official test network Rinkeby is used to implement results on various parameters such as upload and retrieval time and transaction cost parameters using the dataset https://ourworldindia.org/coronavirus-source-data. Figure 4 and Fig. 5 show the effect of file size vs upload time for IPFS storage and Blockchain storage. Figure 6 and Fig. 7 show the increase in retrieval time concerning file size. The gas consumed in the case of IPFS and Blockchain storage is shown in Fig. 8 and Fig. 9.

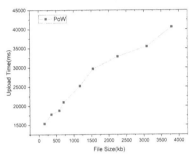

Fig. 4. File size vs IPFS upload time

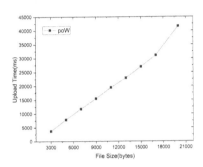

Fig. 5. File size vs blockchain upload time

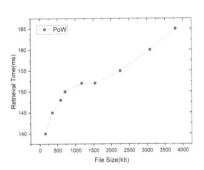

Fig. 6. File size vs IPFS retrieval time

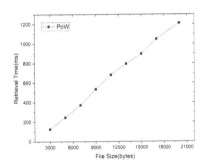

Fig. 7. File size vs blockchain retrieval time

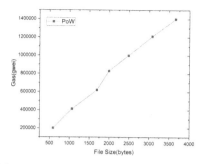
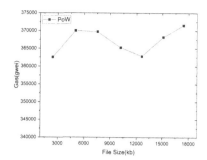

Fig. 8. File size vs gas in blockchain storage

Fig. 9. File size vs gas in IPFS storage

6 Conclusions

This article examines how we can improve the existing healthcare system with industry 5.0 technologies. It also introduces a blockchain-based architecture that allows users to access sensitive medical data in a user-centric manner. The proposed framework's effectiveness is demonstrated by deploying a medical user journey on the Ethereum blockchain. The extent of health information sharing should not be confined to a particular location, especially in pandemic scenarios, but should be transmitted rapidly and securely across borders. Furthermore, we believe that patients should be able to use micro-transactions to allow access to limited views of their data. Further to the above, we also perform analysis over Covid-19 data to estimate the pandemic's current impact and predict future effects. In future work, we'll look into ways to enable safe health data interchange among many IoT devices authorized via a blockchain network.

References

1. Chang, M.C., Park, D.: How should rehabilitative departments of hospitals prepare for coronavirus disease 2019. Am. J. Phys. Med. Rehab. (2020)
2. Catarinucci, L., De Donno, D., Mainetti, L., et al.: An IoT-aware architecture for smart healthcare systems. IEEE Internet Things J. (2012)
3. Roosa, K., et al.: Real-time forecasts of the COVID-19 epidemic in China from February 5th to February 24th, 2020. Infect. Disease Model. (2020)
4. Vaishya, R., Javaid, M., Khan, I.H., Haleem, A.: Artificial intelligence (AI) applications for COVID-19 pandemic. Diabetes Metab. Syndr. Clin. Res. Rev. **14**(4), 337–339 (2020)
5. Puppala, M., He, T., Yu, X., Chen, S., Ogunti, R., Wong, S.T.C.: Data security and privacy management in healthcare applications and clinical data warehouse environment. In: 2016 IEEE-EMBS International Conference on Biomedical and Health Informatics (BHI), February 2016, pp. 5–8 (2016)
6. Abouelmehdi, K., Beni-Hssane, A., Khaloufi, H., Saadi, M.: Big data security and privacy in healthcare: a review. Procedia Comput. Sci. **113**, 73–80 (2017). The 8th International Conference on Emerging Ubiquitous Systems and Pervasive Networks (EUSPN 2017)/The 7th International Conference on Current and Future Trends of Information and Communication Technologies in Healthcare (ICTH-2017)/Affiliated Workshops

7. Kahani, N., Elgazzar, K., Cordy, J.R.: Authentication and access control in e-health systems in the cloud. In: 2016 IEEE 2nd International Conference on Big Data Security on Cloud (BigDataSecurity), IEEE International Conference on High Performance and Smart Computing (HPSC), and IEEE International Conference on Intelligent Data and Security (IDS), April 2016, pp. 13–23 (2016)
8. Azeta, A.A., Iboroma, D.O.A., Azeta, V.I., Igbekele, E.O., Fatinikun, D.O., Ekpunobi, E.: Implementing a medical record system with biometrics authentication in e-health. In: 2017 IEEE AFRICON, September 2017, pp. 979–983 (2017)
9. Kumar, T., Braeken, A., Liyanage, M., Ylianttila, M.: Identity privacy preserving biometric based authentication scheme for naked healthcare environment. In: 2017 IEEE International Conference on Communications (ICC), May 2017, pp. 1–7 (2017)
10. Yksel, B., Kp, A., Zkasap, Z.: Research issues for privacy and security of electronic health services. Future Gen. Comput. Syst. **68**, 1–13 (2017). http://www.sciencedirect.com/science/article/pii/S0167739X16302667
11. Jabeen, F., Hamid, Z., Akhunzada, A., Abdul, W., Ghouzali, S.: Trust and reputation management in healthcare systems: taxonomy, requirements and open issues. IEEE Access **6**, 17 246–17 263 (2018)
12. Esposito, C., Santis, A.D., Tortora, G., Chang, H., Choo, K.K.R.: Blockchain: a panacea for healthcare cloud-based data security and privacy? IEEE Cloud Comput. **5**(1), 31–37 (2018)
13. Zhang, P., Walker, M.A., White, J., Schmidt, D.C., Lenz, G.: Metrics for assessing blockchain-based healthcare decentralized apps. In: 2017 IEEE 19th International Conference on e-Health Networking, Applications and Services (Healthcom), October 2017, pp. 1–4 (2017)
14. Mettler, M.: Blockchain technology in healthcare: the revolution starts here. In: 2016 IEEE 18th International Conference on e-Health Networking, Applications and Services (Healthcom), September 2016, pp. 1–3 (2016)
15. Liu, W., Zhu, S., Mundie, T., Krieger, U.: Advanced blockchain architecture for e-health systems. In: 2017 IEEE 19th International Conference on e-Health Networking, Applications and Services (Healthcom), pp. 1–6. IEEE (2017)
16. Damiani, J.: Simplyvital health is using blockchain to revolutionize healthcare (2017). https://www.forbes.com/sites/jessedamiani/2017/11/06/simplyvital-health-blockchainevolutionize-healthcare/#3777e022880a
17. Azaria, A., Ekblaw, A., Vieira, T., Lippman, A.: MedRec: using blockchain for medical data acess and permission management. In: 2016 2nd International Conference on Open and Big Data (OBD), August 2016, pp. 25–30 (2016)
18. Rabah, K.: Challenges & opportunities for blockchain powered healthcare systems: a review. Mara Res. J. Med. Health Sci. **1**(1), 45–52 (2017). ISSN 2523-5680. https://medicine.mrjournals.org/index.php/medicine/article/view/6
19. Kuo, T.-T., Kim, H.-E., Ohno-Machado, L.: Blockchain distributed ledger technologies for biomedical and health care applications. J. Am. Med. Inform. Assoc. JAMIA **24**(6), 1211–1220 (2017). https://doi.org/10.1093/jamia/ocx068
20. Mangosalad/mercantis-distributedhealth-2017-winner (2018). https://github.com/MangoSalad/Mercantis-DistributedHealth-2017-Winner
21. Dufel, M.: A new paradigm for health information exchange. Technical report, Peer Health (2016). http://peerhealth.io/download-whitepaper/
22. Zhang, P.: Design of blockchain-based apps using familiar software patterns to address interoperability challenges in healthcare. Ph.D. thesis, Vanderbilt University (2017). http://www.dre.vanderbilt.edu/~schmidt/PDF/PLoP-2017-blockchain.pdf
23. Albeyatti, A.: White paper: medicalchain. MedicalChain self-publication (2018)
24. Xia, Q., Sifah, E.B., Asamoah, K.O., Gao, J., Du, X., Guizani, M.: Medshare: trust-less medical data sharing among cloud service providers via blockchain. IEEE Access **5**, 14 757–14 767 (2017)

Semantics for Resource Selection in Next Generation Internet of Things Systems

Katarzyna Wasielewska-Michniewska(ID), Marcin Paprzycki(✉)(ID),
and Maria Ganzha(ID)

Systems Research Institute, Polish Academy of Sciences, Warsaw, Poland
{Katarzyna.Wasielewska,Marcin.Paprzycki,Maria.Ganzha}@ibspan.waw.pl

Abstract. Over the last two decades, the complexity and scale of computer systems radically increased. This is caused, mainly, by the proliferation of data to be processed, and the increasing number and heterogeneity of digital artifacts that can, and need, to be used for deployment of software components and for processing of data. Here, design paradigms, such as cloud/fog/edge processing, and construction of a computing continuum, are trends worth mentioning. Moreover, these changes should be seen also in the context of rapid acceptance of the Internet of Things, which combines very large numbers of sensors and actuators. These changes result also in new challenges that need to be tackled: dynamic environments, heterogeneous data models and processing elements, distributed execution of user workflows, etc. In this context, one of the crucial issues that needs to be addressed is the selection of the right resource(s) that can/should execute a given task/workflow. One of the approaches that can be considered to address such challenges is application of semantic data processing. In this contribution potential benefits and limitations of application of semantic technologies are discussed.

Keywords: semantic · matchmaking · IoT · resources · edge-cloud continuum

1 Introduction

With the proliferation of data sources, constantly generating streams of data that need to be processed and/or stored, and with increasing processing needs, observed in the last two decades [39], a shift towards a modularized architectures and distributed computing is clearly visible. Among others, this trend is realized by the concept of Internet of Things (IoT), which refers to a collective network of connected devices. These devices include not only "edge devices", i.e. sensors and actuators. Within IoT ecosystems, multitude of "computing-capable devices", with various characteristics and processing capabilities that can communicate between themselves and/or the "central cloud" can be found. Therefore, in (large) IoT-based applications, data processing and logic can be distributed among multiple interconnected "locations" [12].

© The Author(s), under exclusive license to Springer Nature Switzerland AG 2024
S. Sachdeva and Y. Watanobe (Eds.): BDA 2023, LNCS 14516, pp. 289–315, 2024.
https://doi.org/10.1007/978-3-031-58502-9_19

Recently, the concept of the *computing continuum* has been formulated and is often referenced within the Next Generation IoT (NGIoT) architectures [45]. The computing continuum means that a single logical ecosystem consists of edge devices, central cloud and numerous "resources" in between. This conceptualization enables creation of a new class of services, spanning across distributed infrastructures. Specifically, the original prevailing conceptual model of an IoT ecosystem, consisting of "edge devices" and a "central cloud" is being replaced by the vision of Edge-Cloud continuum (ECC; [31,37]). In the ECC additional "layer(s)" of connected devices materialize. For instance, in the case of an IoT-enabled construction company, each construction site may have its own server(s) that deal with information processing for that site, while the central cloud stores and processes (combined) information from all construction sites. Such ecosystem may be working jointly with IoT-enabled trucking and supplier companies. Here, complex interactions, between various "components" of such heterogeneous ecosystem may have to be realized.

Let us now assume that, for the remaining parts of this contribution, ECC-type, large, highly heterogeneous ecosystems (possibly, of the future) are considered. It is also assumed that, in such ecosystems, used-defined workflows, are to be efficiently executed, to deliver "business value". Here, efficiently may mean various things. For instance, it may mean, among many others that execution time will be minimized, or that use of green energy will be maximized. In order to realize efficient execution, the "right device" (from here on, called *resource*) should be selected, to best match the characteristics of (a) incoming workflow, (b) user requirements concerning parameters to be optimized, and (c) resource localization, ownership and availability. It should be also noted that in an open ecosystem, or in the ECC ecosystem that is "large enough", devices may appear and disappear dynamically, which makes the selection process even more difficult and important. Separately, as noted in earlier works [7,29], the expertise of the user can vary. Hence, she/he may either specify incorrect conditions for job execution (e.g. require that a specific resource will be used, while this resource is not "the best" for the workflow to be executed), or may be "confused" and could use some guidance/recommendation from the system.

Therefore, to effectively realize the vision of the continuum, it is necessary to provide an abstraction layer that will hide the technical complexities of underlying heterogeneous resources (servers, clusters, edge devices, etc.) and allow to reliably deploy services and execute jobs/workflows with agreed-on Service Level Agreement (SLA). Hence, some of the crucial open problems are: (a) how to model the resources and the underlying ECC architecture, (b) how to adaptively place and schedule services/jobs/workflows?

For example, let's consider a job that needs to be executed somewhere in the continuum, which is explicitly characterized by a specified job requirements description (e.g. software, RAM, CPU, disk space, etc.), as well as some business constraints (e.g. deadline for execution, maximum acceptable price, importance of use of green energy, etc.). The problem that is going to be addressed is as follows: how to select an appropriate resource in a way that is transparent to the user, while matching the user-specified requirements.

Similar research, but with different assumptions about the context, was undertaken years ago for Grid and, later, Cloud computing (see, [17,18]). The idea of the Grid is based on the distributed computing paradigm. Its goal was to create a highly available computing infrastructure, including heterogeneous, geographically distributed, multi-domain computer resources. Solutions based on computational Grids (and, later, also Clouds) gained popularity as tools for solving large scale problems in areas such as industrial design, petroleum engineering, aerospace industry, computational chemistry, etc [15,19,27]. They addressed the problem of distribution of data, and completion of large amounts of, often, similar/repeatable calculations. They provided architectures, and implemented tools, to access, modify and transfer geographically distributed data, often originating from multiple administrative domains. Here, a lot of work was focused on resource selection, to commission a job executing on a Grid infrastructure and on scheduling algorithms [26]. Contrary to the current scenarios, the considered infrastructures were mostly large Data Centres, with relatively stable architectures and a predefined set of nodes, with well-defined characteristics. Over time, the ideas behind Grid computing evolved, and stimulated work leading to conceptualization of Cloud computing, and later Edge computing (also called Fog computing or fogging) and Mist computing [9,28].

Edge and Mist computing have emerged as forms of Cloud computing closer to the "edge" of the ecosystem, and to the "things" that the ecosystem comprises. Here, note that Edge computing is based on ideas of non-centralized processing at the "edge of a network" (in close proximity to where the data originates). An example of this approach is an industrial Internet-of-Things, where peripheral devices, such as wristbands or weather stations, have some embedded computing capabilities, and intelligence to handle the incoming data. Noteworthy, some of the solutions proposed for the Grid (and Cloud) are still valid. Therefore, after necessary adjustments and adaptations one can attempt at applying them to the IoT scenarios. Hence, the research reported in what follows, can be naturally seen as having its roots in work completed, by the authors of this publications, between 2007 and 2015.

One of the ongoing challenges that has been recognized already in earlier work, is the need for flexibility in describing the available resources, and, on the other hand, user requirements. This is needed to facilitate mechanisms that will allow efficient matchmaking between "what a user wants" and "what is available". Such mechanisms should be applicable to different application domains and allow to represent "any level" of complexity of the resource description. Additional aspect, to be seriously considered, is the possibility to consider different requirements with different weights, e.g. speed of executions is less important than price, or execution start time is somewhat less important than use of green energy. Furthermore, matchmaking may need to be complimented with a recommendation mechanism, using some expert knowledge to support users that have a workflow to complete, but are not sure what are the best "conditions" for it's execution.

One of the possible ways to address the aforementioned needs is to use semantic data representation and semantic data processing. Even though, it has been recently established that semantics provides effective ways to manage data models and implement interoperability [20,33], the question is if semantics alone is enough to enable intelligent resource selection, or if it needs to be complimented with other technologies remains open. Such research problem was initially discussed in [47,49] for Grid computing. This contribution, is a follow-up investigating how semantics can help in resource selection and matchmaking with requirements for the computing continuum and in the context of IoT-based applications. Specifically, the aim of this work was to present limits of usability of "plain semantic technologies" and some ways in which semantic technologies can cooperate with other well-known approaches (e.g. existing methods for multicriterial decision support).

To achieve the outlined objectives, in Sect. 2 some concepts that constitute the context for the research are presented. In Sect. 3 approach to realize resource selection mechanisms using semantic technologies are presented. First, in Sect. 3.1 the required knowledge representation is presented. Then in Sects. 3.2, 3.3, 3.4 different variants are discussed, in which sole semantics or semantics enriched with other methods is used. Finally, in Sect. 4, the most important observations and guidelines are presented.

2 Related Work

In the following subsections basic concepts that are addressed in the proposed approach, including selected state-of-the-art contributions, are introduced.

2.1 Next Generation IoT Applications

As mentioned, the resource selection problem is typical for distributed environments that evolved from the Grid, Clouds, Edge, to IoT and ECC concepts. The matchmaking of requirements with available resources is present in all aforementioned paradigms. Currently, it is being considered also in the context of the Next Generation IoT (NGIoT). The NGIoT architecture is focused on user-awareness, self-awareness and semi-automation, which should enable to create human-centred systems.

In line with this direction is, and provides an example and a motivation for considerations presented in this paper, the Horizon Europe aerOS project[1]. The goal of aerOS is to provide autonomous, scalable, trustworthy, intelligent meta Operating System for the IoT edge-cloud continuum. Note that, a growing number of applications require a dynamic approach that intelligently utilises and leverages strengths of resources from all three computing layers (IoT devices, edge servers, and the Cloud) to achieve optimal performance while considering data sovereignty and privacy restrictions. Intelligent distribution of jobs across

---

[1] https://aeros-project.eu.

resources should allow to balance between real-time responsiveness, efficient data processing, and compliance with data regulations. This drives the innovative concept of IoT-Edge-Cloud Continuum – an architecture approach where the management of resources, and computing capabilities is performed with an overarching and unifying view across the three computing layers.

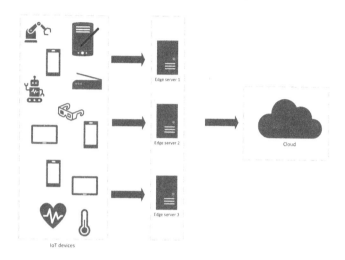

Fig. 1. Concept of Edge-Cloud Continuum.

In order to achieve its goals, an efficient solution for the selection of the "best place" in the continuum, in which the service should be deployed, or job should be executed, needs to be proposed. User should be able to use heterogeneous resources without the need of knowing the technicalities of the underlying infrastructure. To this aim, the decisions that need to be taken should be supported by automatic intelligent mechanisms. The attributes that should be taken into account during decision making, can come from: (i) requirements expressed by the user, and/or (ii) current state of the continuum, i.e. static and dynamic characteristics of available resources.

The aerOS project provides an interesting context to consider in what way and to what extend semantics can help in achieving the NGIoT objectives. Lets consider the following sequence of actions:

1. User specifies resource requirements (possibly with a job description - "job profile"), using an ontology-driven web interface that automatically transforms input information to an ontological representation. If expert knowledge is to be used, the user defines "job profile" that specifies, as much as possible, a problem – input data properties.
2. *Orchestrator* queries the current state of the continuum, for resources matching specified criteria. If beforehand required, one of the semantic analysis methods can be used enhance user specified requirements with expert knowledge available in the system (*Decision support - step 1*).

3. List of resources matching the criteria (or empty list) is returned.
4. User requirements regarding the contract (describing terms of collaboration with a resource provider), e.g. maximum acceptable price, penalty for delay, timeline, are analyzed to further narrow down on available resources.
5. *Orchestrator* evaluates collaboration terms from resource providers and selects one if the terms are acceptable (*Decision support - step 2*).

Note that, "job" can be of different nature, i.e. (1) it's goal may be to deploy a service, or (2) to commission job execution that may utilize an already deployed service(s).

In the above described sequence of actions there are two moments, in which decision support can be used. First, to improve/compliment user specified requirements, by proposing to fill the missing information based on the expert knowledge or propose alternative requirements if those specified are against expert recommendations. Second, to select the best resource for a job execution, based on its configuration and the SLA constraints.

2.2 Resource Selection

Historically, Grids were usually managed by dedicated middlewares that enabled sharing, managing and utilizing resources, based on their configuration and on the user requirements [5]. Cloud resource management was discussed in [32], while the related problem of service selection was considered in [42]. It can be observed that, even though Grid systems allowed to achieve "more" in terms of computation, their implementation was more complex, while efficient resource usage required technical knowledge. The user often needed to understand the infrastructure and decide how to use the Grid. With the evolution of the distributed architectures, the increasing importance of providing friendly and smooth user interface that does not require very advanced programming skills from the user, has been recognized. Specifically, in case of the computing continuum, to be utilized efficiently, an abstraction layer, facilitating transparent resource selection, has to be developed.

There are questions that need to be answered in such solutions, not necessarily by the user, but possibly also automatically by the orchestration/managing component: which resource configuration is the best for the job to be run? is such resource available? are the terms of usage acceptable compliant between what resource provider can offer and what the user requested? To be able to effectively answer these questions a knowledge representation scheme should be considered that allows to persist all necessary information and query it with respect to required conditions. Furthermore, the scheme used for knowledge representation should be resistant to context changes (e.g. different description standards), adaptable and allow flexible modelling of knowledge. These features are important because of a dynamic nature of the discussed distributed environments, where heterogeneous resources can change their configuration, and terms of collaboration can describe different aspects. On the other hand, the accompanying domain, providing the context for a solution deployment, can also undergo remodelling and extension with new concepts.

Lets consider a generalized situation when a user has a computational job to be executed in the continuum, which covers different resources, providing a unified entry point. The user may have knowledge about the problem itself, e.g. training of a ML model with a given architecture. However, (s)he is not certain which resource available in the infrastructure, will be most suitable to run such job, specifically what resource configuration is recommended to be used. On the other hand, another user may be certain that what (s)he specified, regarding resource configuration for a given problem, is correct and no recommendation is needed from the system. Selection mechanism should help users with different levels of expertise to choose optimal resources in the best place in the continuum to solve their problems (run their jobs), and to select the best terms of use of these resources. The mechanism should support optimizing the overall performance of the whole continuum, i.e. avoiding overutilizing and underutilizing resources.

2.3 Semantic Data Processing

Semantics is the study of interpretation of signs and symbols that depends on context (relationships with surrounding concepts) and pragmatics (intention by which the language is used). Semantics and semantic data processing is a research direction with a long history and several "reshapings" on the way. Early publications [16,35] claim that semantics and ontologies are the backbone technologies of the next web generation, as they enable effective and efficient access to heterogeneous and distributed information sources.

Semantic data processing is based on conceptualizing knowledge in the form of *ontologies*. Overall, ontologies can be found in fields such as knowledge management, information retrieval and integration, electronic commerce and Semantic Web, where they are intended to provide a common terminology and ensure shared understanding of semantic markup (semantic metadata encode the meaning that can be read and interpreted correctly by machines). Typically, an ontology is defined as a formal specification of shared conceptualization [21]. In practice, an ontology defines common terms and rules that are used to describe a given domain of knowledge, and is formally specified (machine-readable) using the following constructs:

- concepts describing domain elements (called classes that can have subclasses representing concepts that are more specific),
- properties describing concepts,
- restrictions on values that properties can take,
- relations between concepts,
- axioms and assertions.

An ontology can contain information about both (i) concrete data items representing entities (individuals), and (ii) structural information about data, usually in a given area of interest. An ontology, together with a set of individuals/instances of classes, constitutes a knowledge base.

In this context, semantic data representation provides: (i) common under-standing of the structure of information and its usage rules among people, or software agents, (ii) ability to analyze and reuse domain knowledge, and make its assumptions explicit, (iii) separation of the domain knowledge from the opera-tional knowledge, (iv) knowledge representation in the machine-readable manner. Moreover, semantics allows to process the meaning of information automatically, to relate and integrate heterogeneous data, to deduce implicit information from the existing explicit information in an automated way.

Ontologies can have different degree of formalization, (1) from the highly informal, expressed in a natural language, (2a) through semi-informal in a struc-tured form of a natural language, (2b) and semi-formal in an artificial and for-mally defined language, to (3) rigorously formal, expressed in a language with formal semantics. Ontologies can be built using various languages e.g. UML, ER, OWL/RDFS, WSML, etc. The vision of the Semantic Web [3] is to make the web resources easily interpreted by programs/agents by using a semantic markup, i.e. machine-understandable annotations to describe the resources. Here, RDF is intended to be a core language to support an effective creation, exchange and use of annotations.

A concept, related to an ontology, but with more practical perspective, is a knowledge graph [25]. Ontology and knowledge graphs can be used together to represent knowledge: ontology defines the domain knowledge in terms of con-cepts and relations, while the knowledge graph is more like a database, which is structured and targeted for a given application.

Semantic knowledge representation allows to model different aspects of the computing infrastructure depending on the specific needs. Contrary to the database schema and to the object-oriented programming that define structures to store data, ontology provides partial theory of a given domain that can be accepted and utilized by people and applications, at the same time ensuring clarity and expressiveness.

3   Proposed Approach

To support the selection of the best resource to deploy a service or to execute a job, several methods can be proposed.

Lets consider what kind of support using various techniques provided by semantic data processing can be deliver in this context. Here, we will recognize the following "levels" of semantic support: simple SPARQL-based selection of a resource on behalf of the user, class expression-based matching, graph-based matching, or the most advanced user support mechanism based on multi-criterial analysis and expert domain knowledge usage. All approaches use semantic data processing. They delineate where semantic analysis/use of semantic technologies can help and where it needs to be supplemented by other approaches.

3.1   Knowledge Representation

Lets assume that all data is semantically annotated and can be semantically processed. Ontologies allow to address the problem of matchmaking between heterogenous descriptions of resources and requirements that come from the same conceptual model (domain). The information that needed to be modelled covers:

– infrastructure/continuum description and resource configuration,
– jobs to be submitted by the user,
– terms of collaboration with service objectives and quality of service,
– economical aspects of collaboration e.g. payment, penalty,
– domain knowledge and expert recommendations that may be used if information provided by the user is insufficient to make a good choice.

The set of proposed ontologies to address these needs is depicted in Fig. 2). The decision to modularize ontologies, with respect to the domain of interest, was undertaken, in order to increase reusability, and to facilitate ease of maintenace. Each ontology has been additionally divided into two parts: conceptual model (T-Box) and instances (A-Box).

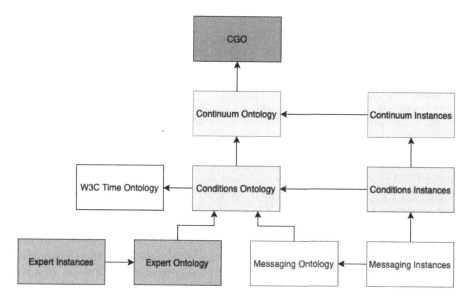

Fig. 2. Ontologies representing knowledge in the system.

First, the *Continuum Ontology* defines concepts for the description of a continuum structure and a resource configurations. Note that resource descriptions may vary depending on the layer of the continuum to which the resource is assigned, e.g. specification of a wristband may differ from specification of an edge server, or simply type of IoT devices that are connected to the continuum. The Continuum Ontology is based on the Core Grid Ontology (CGO; [50]) that, even though focused on Grids, already contains a multitude of concepts related to structure, configuration and organization of grid elements (see Fig. 3) and can be further extended as needed. In the Continuum Ontology some important properties and concepts had to be added to enable proper reasoning add adjust the model to the concept of the continuum.

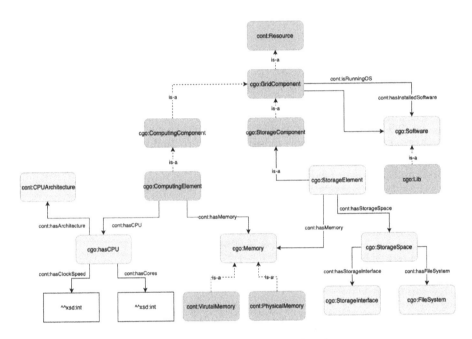

Fig. 3. Extract from Continuum Ontology.

Listing 1.1 presents a simplified sample of an ontologically-demarcated resource description, serialized as N3. The individual *Center1_EdgeSystem1* represents a node with Linux Mint operating system, AMD Opteron 6176 processor, 256 GB storage size, out of which 100 GB is available. All these characteristics are modelled with datatype and object properties that come from the Continuum Ontology. Individuals are also instances of classes from this ontology, besides *cgo:WorkerNode* class that was defined in CGO ontology [34].

Listing 1.1. Example of grid resource description in N3.

```
@prefix  : <http://example.com/ContinuumInstances#> .
@prefix cgo: <http://purl.org/NET/cgo#> .
@prefix cont: <http://example.com/ContinuumOntology#> .
@prefix owl: <http://www.w3.org/2002/07/owl#> .
@prefix rdf: <http://www.w3.org/1999/02/22-rdf-syntax-ns#> .
@prefix rdfs: <http://www.w3.org/2000/01/rdf-schema#> .
@prefix xml: <http://www.w3.org/XML/1998/namespace> .
@prefix xsd: <http://www.w3.org/2001/XMLSchema#> .
```

```
:Center1_EdgeSystem1 a cgo:WorkerNode,
        owl:NamedIndividual ;
    cont:hasCPU :AMD_Opteron_6176 ;
    cont:hasStorageSpace :NodeType1_StorageSpace ;
    cont:isRunningOS :LinuxMint_21 .

:AMD a cont:CPUVendor,
        owl:NamedIndividual .

:AMD64 a cont:X86_64,
        owl:NamedIndividual .

:AMD_Opteron_6176 a grid:CPU,
        owl:NamedIndividual ;
    cont:hasArchitecture :AMD64 ;
    cont:hasCores "12"^^xsd:int ;
    cont:hasVendor :AMD ;
    cgo:availableNum "8"^^xsd:int ;
    cgo:clockSpeed "2.3GHz"^^xsd:string .

:LinuxMint_21 a cont:Linux,
        owl:NamedIndividual ;
    cont:hasVersion "21.2"^^xsd:string .

:NodeType1_StorageSpace a cont:StorageSpace,
        owl:NamedIndividual ;
    cont:hasAvailableSize "102400"^^xsd:int ;
    cont:hasTotalSize "262144"^^xsd:int .
```

The Conditions Ontology (see Fig. 4) defines concepts for description of collaboration terms guiding as resource usage (SLA). It extends Continuum Ontology to relate the service objectives to the specific resources/configurations.

The collaboration terms can be referred to as job execution conditions. Listing 1.2 presents ontological description of such terms. Here, it is indicated that execution should end before 20th December 2022 with deadline penalty of 100. Usage of resource will be charged with pay as you go mechanisms with some additional pricing conditions. Naturally, such ontological description can be extended with any required terms and conditions. *SampleJobSLA.*

Listing 1.2. Example of cond:JobExecutionConditions instance.

```
@prefix : <http://example.com/ConditionsInstances#> .
@prefix cond: <http://example.com/ConditionsOntology#> .
@prefix owl: <http://www.w3.org/2002/07/owl#> .
@prefix rdf: <http://www.w3.org/1999/02/22-rdf-syntax-ns#> .
@prefix rdfs: <http://www.w3.org/2000/01/rdf-schema#> .
@prefix time: <http://www.w3.org/2006/time#> .
@prefix xml: <http://www.w3.org/XML/1998/namespace> .
@prefix xsd: <http://www.w3.org/2001/XMLSchema#> .

:SampleJobSLA a cond:JobExecutionConditions,
        owl:NamedIndividual ;
    cond:deadlinePenalty "100.0"^^xsd:float ;
    cond:jobExecutionTimeline :SampleExecutionTimeline ;
    cond:paymentConditions :SamplePayment .

:SampleExecutionTimeline a owl:NamedIndividual,
        time:DateTimeInterval ;
    time:hasEnd :Dec20 .

:SamplePayment a cond:PaymentConditions,
        owl:NamedIndividual ;
    cond:delayPenalty "50.0"^^xsd:float ;
```

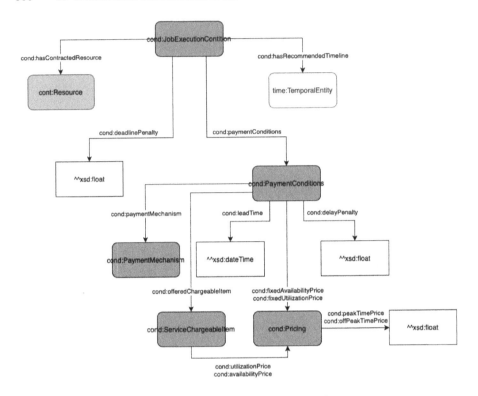

Fig. 4. Extract from Conditions Ontology.

```
    cond:fixedAvailabilityPrice  :SamplePricing ;
    cond:paymentMechanism  :payAsYouGo .

:Dec20 a owl:NamedIndividual ,
        time:Instant ;
    time:inXSDDateTime  "2022-12-20T23:59:59"^^xsd:dateTime .

:SamplePricing a cond:Pricing,
        owl:NamedIndividual ;
    cond:offPeakTimePrice "10.0"^^xsd:float ;
    cond:peakTimePrice "20.0"^^xsd:float .

:payAsYouGo a cond:PayAsYouGo,
        owl:NamedIndividual .
```

The Messaging Ontology defines concepts describing the content of messages exchanged in the system. The concepts have relations to the Conditions Ontology, and indirectly to the Continuum Ontology. This is an operational ontology not significant to the problem discussed in this paper.

The Expert Ontology defines concepts for modelling domain and expert knowledge (knowledge base) and proposes a structure, in which such knowledge can be captured. Such representation should enable intuitive definition of job profiles, and effective search among collected opinions/recommendations, which are used when resource requirements should be enhanced. For example, a job is to train an ML model using a GPU is to be commissioned to the continuum but no additional conditions are specified to narrow down on available resources, depending on, e.g. input data or algorithm to be used. Orchestrator may use expert recommendations to proposed specific GPU type or required amount of available memory needed. The knowledge representation schema should allow to store opinions/recommendations of multiple experts that will be semantically analyzed to select the most representative opinion/recommendation for the combination of problem and input data properties. Note that using expert recommendations should be optional as the resource selection can be performed without such "guidance". The result may be longer list of potential resources selected to be used and less precise matchmaking.

Figure 5 presents main concepts and relations in Expert Ontology that are used to model and persist expert and domain knowledge.

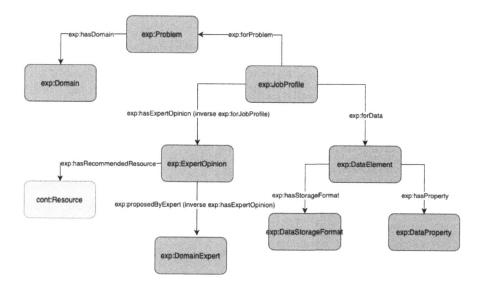

Fig. 5. Basic concepts and their relations in the Expert Ontology.

Here, one can find the basic terms that are common for different domains, which include:

- *Domain* – identifies the domain that is being modelled,
- *Problem* – concept that represents problem/type of job that is to be address using the resource(s),
- *Data Element* – type of data that serve as input,
- *Domain Expert* – concept representing an expert (human or system) that submits recommendations in domains of knowledge assigned to it,
- *Job Profile* – models job characteristics by combining instances of classes *Problem, Data Element, Expert Opinion,*

– *Expert Opinion* – concept representing expert recommendation that combines instances of classes representing expert, job profile and resource.

Job profile should relate problem/job from a given domain with possible input data characteristics and expert recommendations about resources that can be used. For example, lets consider a problem of running a FL training of a model that as an input requires medical ultrasound images and uses CNN.

Listing 1.3 presents a sample instance *Opinion1FLTrainingProblem* of an *exp:ExperOpinion* class. Expert opinion represents a recommendation that relates job profile instance to the description, or a specific instance of a recommended resource. In Listing 1.3 an expert *HPCExpert1* has recommended using *computingElement1* resource to solve a problem defined in *FLTrainingProblem-JobProfile*. The recommended resource is represented with a class expression that imposes some restrictions on the resource. The recommended resource should have Linux Mint operating system, NVIDIA GeForce GPU and at least 10 GB of available memory.

Listing 1.3. Example of an exp:ExpertOpinion instance.

```
@prefix : <http://example.com/ExpertInstances#> .
@prefix exp: <http://example.com/ExpertOntology#> .
@prefix cont: <http://example.com/ContinuumOntology#> .
@prefix cont_inst: <http://example.com/ContinuumInstances#> .
@prefix owl: <http://www.w3.org/2002/07/owl#> .
@prefix rdf: <http://www.w3.org/1999/02/22-rdf-syntax-ns#> .
@prefix rdfs: <http://www.w3.org/2000/01/rdf-schema#> .
@prefix xml: <http://www.w3.org/XML/1998/namespace> .
@prefix xsd: <http://www.w3.org/2001/XMLSchema#> .

:Opinion1ForFLTrainingProblem a exp:ExpertOpinion,
        owl:NamedIndividual ;
    exp:forJobProfile :FLTrainingProblemJobProfile ;
    exp:hasExpert :HPCExpert1 ;
    exp:hasRecommendedResource :computingElement1 .

:ExpertDefinedComputingElement1 a owl:Class ;
    owl:equivalentClass [ a owl:Class ;
        owl:intersectionOf ( cont:Resource
            [ a owl:Restriction ;
                owl:onProperty cont:hasMemory ;
                owl:someValuesFrom [ a owl:Class ;
                    owl:intersectionOf ( cont:PhysicalMemory
                        [ a owl:Restriction ;
                            owl:onProperty cont:hasAvailableSize ;
                            owl:someValuesFrom [ a rdfs:Datatype ;
                                owl:onDatatype xsd:integer ;
                                owl:withRestrictions ( [ xsd:
                                    minExclusive 10240 ] ) ]
                                ] ) ] ]
            [ a owl:Restriction ;
                owl:hasValue cont_inst:LinuxMint\
                _21 ;
                owl:onProperty cont:isRunningOS ]
            [ a owl:Restriction ;
                owl:hasValue cont_inst:NVIDIA_Geforce_RTX_30 ;
                owl:onProperty cont:hasGPU ] ) ] .

:computingElement1 a :ExpertDefinedComputingElement1,
        owl:NamedIndividual .
```

3.2 SPARQL Based Selection

In case the requirements for resource are well defined and do not require support in their formulation, a simple methods, based on SPARQL [1] can be applied. SPARQL is a set of specifications that provide languages and protocols to query and manipulate RDF graph contents on the web or in an RDF store. RDF is a directed, labeled graph data format for representing the semantic information.

Here, the SPARQL query will be used to support matchmaking between the requirements and the resource and the collaboration term specifications. SPARQL contains capabilities for querying required and optional graph patterns, along with their conjunctions and disjunctions. Moreover, it supports aggregation, subqueries, negation, creating values by expressions, extensible value testing, and constraining queries by source RDF graph.

The SPARQL query consists of:

1. Prefix declaration – used to abbreviate URIs,
2. Dataset definitions – states what RDF graphs/ontologies are used,
3. Result clause – states what information will be returned from the query,
4. Query pattern – states what to query for, in the underlying dataset,
5. Query modifiers – operations on query results.

Listing 1.4 contains a sample query for a computing resource with specific GPU and minimum size of available memory of 10 GB running Linux Mint OS.

Listing 1.4. Example of SPARQL query.

```
PREFIX cont: <http://example.com/ContinuumOntology#>
PREFIX cont: <http://example.com/ContinuumInstances#>
PREFIX cgo:  <http://purl.org/NET/cgo#>

select ?res
where {
?res a   cont:Resource .
         cont:isRunningOS cont_inst:LinuxMint\_21 .
         cont:hasGPU cont_inst:NVIDIA_GeForce_RTX40 .
         cgo:hasMemory ?memory .
    ?memory cgo:hasAvailableSize ?size .
filter ( ?size > 10240 )
}
```

Such query returns URIs of instances of *cont:Resource* class, matching the requirements, and the filter restricting memory size. SPARQL query is flexible when specifying conditions and filters, however the user needs to know the internal structure of the queried ontology. Moreover, there may exist a resource that is slightly "worse" and potentially could be used, but it would not be found and considered.

Similarly as in the case of an SPARQL based approach, a DL query (OWL class expression matching), with sematic reasoners can be used for resource matchmaking.

The resource requirements are transformed into a class expression. Note that, SPARQL was designed for RDF and there is no connection in its specification to OWL.

Therefore, SPARQL and OWL can be treated as two separate technologies, in a broad field of semantic analysis. SPARQL has syntax that can be argued to be more expressive that OWL. On the other hand, not every class expression can be transformed into a SPARQL query. There exists an extension to SPARQL, called SPARQL-DL [2] introduced as a query language for OWL-DL (subgroup of OWL that is computationally efficient). Having in mind these differences, those two querying methods are treated as distinct approaches in this paper.

Listing 1.5 presents a sample class expression (representing the same restrictions as a SPARQL example). All conditions are represented by restrictions on selected classes (analogically to where conditions in the SPARQL query from previous example).

Listing 1.5. Example of a class expression generated by the semantic web interface.

```
@prefix : <http://www.jadeOWL.org/queries/Conditions_3cdaaff9-cc9b-48f2-aa82-
    bbed54940c75#> .
@prefix owl: <http://www.w3.org/2002/07/owl#> .
@prefix rdf: <http://www.w3.org/1999/02/22-rdf-syntax-ns#> .
@prefix rdfs: <http://www.w3.org/2000/01/rdf-schema#> .
@prefix xml: <http://www.w3.org/XML/1998/namespace> .
@prefix xsd: <http://www.w3.org/2001/XMLSchema#> .
@prefix cgo: <http://purl.org/NET/cgo#> .
@prefix cont: <http://example.net/ContinuumOntology#> .
@prefix cont_inst: <http://example.com/ContinuumInstances#> .

:Condition_3cdaaff9-cc9b-48f2-aa82-bbed54940c75 a owl:Class ;
owl:equivalentClass [
  a owl:Class ;
    owl:intersectionOf (
    cont:Resource [
    a owl:Restriction ;
            owl:onProperty cont:hasMemory ;
        owl:someValuesFrom [
          a owl:Class ;
          owl:intersectionOf (
            cont:VirtualMemory [
              a owl:Restriction ;
              owl:onProperty cont:hasAvailableSize ;
              owl:someValuesFrom [
                a rdfs:Datatype ;
                owl:onDatatype xsd:integer ;
                            owl:withRestrictions (
                  [ xsd:minExclusive 10240 ]
                )
              ]
            ]
          )
        ]
  ]
  [
    a owl:Restriction ;
    owl:onProperty cont:hasGPU ;
            owl:someValuesFrom [
      a owl:Class ;
      owl:intersectionOf (
        cont:GPU
        [
          a owl:Restriction ;
                    owl:onProperty cont:hasCores ;
                    owl:someValuesFrom [
          a rdfs:Datatype ;
          owl:onDatatype xsd:integer ;
          owl:withRestrictions (
```

```
                [ xsd:minExclusive 2 ]
                )
            ]
          ]
        )
      ]
    ]
    [
      a owl:Restriction ;
      owl:hasValue cont_inst:LinuxMint_21 ;
            owl:onProperty cont:isRunningOS
    ]
    )
] .
```

The result will be URIs of all instances of *cont:Resource* class that match the restrictions. As in the case of SPARQL, if there is a resource that slightly misses what is specified to be required, it would not be returned. In both cases, class expression matching and the SPARQL approach, if no resource matches the requirements, the user has to modify the search criteria, e.g. relax the restrictions.

To sum up, after user specifies what (s)he needs, (s)he receives a list of resources that exactly match her/his request. This list is unordered and there is no way to express importance of individual criteria. If none of available resources matches the specified criteria exactly, the request will "fail". Moreover, if requirements such as minimum 16 GB of RAM are specified then resources with 16GB or 96GB will be treated as equally suitable since they both match the condition. This can be a problem in case of intelligent resource selection for the continuum since such open ended conditions or leaving too many options for GPU may very negatively influence the objective of optimizing performance for the continuum as a whole.

3.3 Graph-Based Selection

A graph-based ontological matchmaking algorithm described in [30,36] could be considered, (after some adaptations, needed to match the aerOS context) if there are some preferences that need to be considered, e.g. one requirement more important than the other. The algorithm uses the fact that, in a knowledge space, all information resources are connected, directly or not, to one another (instead of existing separately). Moreover, different relations between objects can have different strength. The existence and strength of such relations can be considered when assessing how two concepts/instances are relevant to each other. The concepts of measuring semantic closeness, and semantic relevance, were introduced to that aim. Semantic relevance is based on a variety of directed relations that can be found in the knowledge space, as well as indirect relations that are provided by the context. Note that, any ontology can be represented as a directed graph, where concepts/individuals are nodes, and edges represent properties. Moreover, properties can be interpreted as decision criteria in the selection process. Graph can be generated on both conceptual (T-Box) and instances (A-Box) levels. On the conceptual level, nodes are classes (concepts) and edges correspond to property axioms defined in the ontology (here instances are not considered).

On the instances level, nodes correspond to individuals and edges to properties asserted for considered individuals (here specific resources and context information are considered). In this approach, matchmaking is equivalent to measuring "distance" between instances of concepts (classes) in the ontology.

Each resource, with a corresponding node having paths to all nodes representing property values from the requirements individual, is included in the final ranking of matched resources (i.e. only resources with defined values for properties appearing in the restrictions are considered here). Resources, for which some of the paths can be constructed (they can address only part of the requirements) are considered in the ranking but as not fully matched resources.

When the graph-based method for semantic matchmaking is used, it is also possible to capture expert knowledge concerning importance of relations between concepts and importance of individual criteria to the user. The relevance and weights for properties (represented by graph edges) both on the conceptual and instances levels are means to express expert information, related to importance of selection criteria. Distance assignments, done by the experts, and weights assignment on instances level are both stored as ontology annotations. The resulting list of available resources is ordered, according to semantic closeness to the user request. Thus, this approach is not likely to "fail" (in the sense of giving no suggestion at all), as all individuals, in a common ontology are, almost always, linked to each-other.

Figure 6 shows part of a conceptual level model of the Continuum Ontology. Concepts (classes) are nodes and properties are directed associations. Each edge has assigned a sample distance value (the greater the value the less important is relation between objects; these values should be assigned by experts; they are applied across all executions of the algorithm). Note that, here, the software available on the resource is the most important – distance is 0.2, *cgo:Memory* is more important than *cgo:CPU* – distances 0.5 and 1 respectively. Distance values equal to 1 are default.

Figure 7 presents instances corresponding to classes from the part of the conceptual model from Fig. 6. The *requirements* instance is an example of an individual generated from user requirements. Individuals *resource1* and *resource2* (also of class *cont:Resource*) represent resources. The *resource1* has the required memory configuration and Linux Mint operating system but in version 20 instead of required 21.3. The *resource2* has the required operating system represented with instance *LinuxMint_21* and memory with higher available size than required.

The graph-based approach is dedicated to scenarios it which it is know which resource configuration to use, since no support is given in the form of answer to the question "how to specify constraints for resource configuration".

Noteworthy is the fact that, even though expert knowledge is considered in this approach, it is of different kind than that considered in the next discussed approach. It is not used to match problems/jobs and recommended resources. Instead it assesses, which aspects in semantic description of resource and collaboration conditions should influence the selection, and to what degree. It can be, however, claimed that specifying requirements in terms of one selected individ-

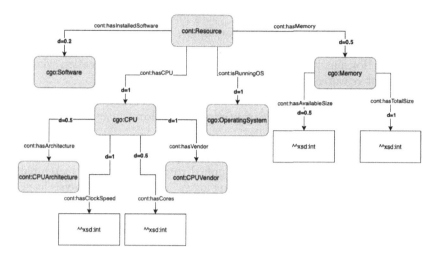

Fig. 6. Fragment of the conceptual model with assigned distances.

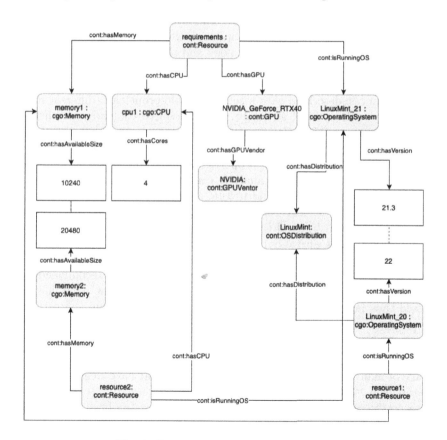

Fig. 7. Fragment of the instances model.

ual can be less intuitive than providing conditions, as in case of class expression (DL query) matching and SPARQL matching.

To sum up, this approach allows to express additional preferences related to resource selection but it does enhence the requirements specification when it is not clear what resource should be used.

3.4 Multicriteria Analysis Supported Selection

The last proposed approach to facilitate resource matchmaking is based, in part, on multicriterial analysis. In literature, there are numerous multicriteria analysis methods [13] that can potentially be applied to extend resource matchmaking and user support based on semantic technologies. Multicriterial analysis has been applied to many practical problems and has a long history of fruitful research. However, with an increasing interest in semantic technologies, a question has to be answered. Is it possible to apply existing multicriterial methods in a matchmaking scenario, in which data used in decision making is formally represented as an ontology? One of key challenges of designing an intelligent matchmaking that would combine semantic technologies with multicriterial analysis is the selection of a suitable MCDA technique. The main point, here, is to be able to use an existing MCDA approach (and its implementation), while taking advantage of knowledge captured in the ontology and provided in the user-generated job execution request.

As before, lets consider expert knowledge and requirements represented as ontology instances, described with a set of possible properties (different in each case) that have hierarchical structure. For a resource configuration there are properties describing CPU, GPU, memory, operating system, whereas for collaboration terms there are properties describing pricing, payment mechanisms, job execution timeline, etc. These properties can be interpreted as the decision criteria, therefore, multicriterial analysis can be used to analyze alternatives, with respect to both numerical and textual criteria.

The MCA can be used to select expert opinion that recommends resource configuration that can be used to run a job specified by the user. This can be useful when user is not sure about what kind of resource to use for a well-defined problem and how problem's input data influence resource selection. Therefore, the problem/job formulation can be analyzed, and appropriate recommendations based on expert opinions can be made. Taking into account what has been discussed thus far, the MCA method should have the following characteristics (that will guide the choice of a resource selection):

- usage of knowledge coming from many experts that can have different weights assigned,
- usage of many hierarchically structured criteria that have weights assigned,
- hierarchical structure of alternatives vary from case to case (i.e. different trees corresponding to different ranges of used properties from the ontology), however they all are based on the common ontology,
- a mechanism to handle hierarchical criteria structure in an easy and intuitive way.

During the initial research [46] methods that seemed to be appropriate for the job execution scenario were selected to be analyzed, according to the methodology introduced in [8]. They included: TOPSIS [10,41], PROMETHEE [6,22,23], GRIP [24,40], and Analytical Hierarchy Process (AHP; [4,14,38,43,44]). Additonally, weighted sum method (WSM), weighted product method (WPM), MAUT (multi-attribute utility theory; e.g. SMART, SMARTS, SMARTER) were considered. All these methods utilize weights assigned to decision criteria and perform an evalutation of alternatives' values for selected criteria, the difference is in the ways these data are aggregated and analyzed.

The following paragraphs briefly introduce methods that were considered.

The evaluation confirms that TOPSIS, PROMETHEE, GRIP and AHP constituted good candidates to choose from. First of all, their features match stated requirements (can be used/or adjusted to be used with ontologies and support multiple criteria with many decision makers), they are all well-founded and broadly used. Moreover each of the method represents a different approach to perform MCA. However, the natural support for ontologies (the hierarchical application of pairwise comparisons matched very well with the structure of ontologically formalized knowledge) and semantic data processing, as well as clear interaction with the decision maker (e.g. during preference specification) lead to the choice of AHP to be used in the proof-of-concept adaptation and implementation.

Noteworthy is also the fact that AHP has been applied in many fields, and there is an ongoing work to improve the method.

Additionally, the decision was based on the following observations: (i) in WSM, WPM, SMART (and derivative methods) weights of specific criteria are assigned by the user, which can be difficult in case of complex hierarchical structure of criteria (the problem of what values should be assigned, and their influence on the underlying mathematical model), additionally WSM requires attributes expressed in the same unit (it cannot be assumed in the context of discussed decision problem), (ii) outranking methods are dedicated rather to limiting the number of alternatives, and afterwards, other method can be applied to select the best alternative, (iii) in MAUT methods the definition of utility function requires from the user to posess an advanced knowledge of the problem, possible solutions and their influence on requirements (in the context of discussed decision problems it cannot be assumed that possible solutions are known).

Finally, given the fact that AHP works only in the case when the comparison matrices are consistent, and that other criticisms concerning the AHP have also been raised [11], it is not claimed that this is the best method that can be used in the proposed MCA based approach to provide support to users. AHP was selected to show how MCA methods can be combined with semantically represented expert knowledge in the context of user support. It should be stressed that any other method fulfilling the stated requirements can be adopted to be used along with semantic data representation and processing.

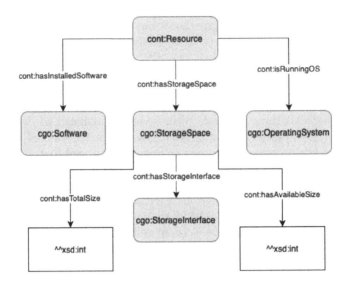

Fig. 8. Sample partial resource description structure.

As mentioned before, expert opinions and resources and collaboration conditions are ontologically demarcated, which allows to represent them as trees (edges correspond to properties, while nodes to individuals or literals). As a result, the MCA method should analyze alternatives that can be represented as a hierarchical structure (see Figs. 8, 9). Note that, in the ontology, there are defined many properties that can be used to describe a resource.

The AHP method specifies consecutive steps that lead to the selection of an optimal variant (alternative) taking into account opinions of many experts. AHP ca be adjusted to meet the requirements set in the task execution scenario by [48]: (i) proposing an innovative method to combine multicriteria analysis with ontologies by using the fact that ontologies can be represented as a directed graph (automatic generation of hierarchical problem structure), (ii) automatic assessment of values for criteria with translation to a scale proposed by Saaty.

Combining the multicriterial decision support methods with semantic technologies allows the system to "make suggestions". Considering multiple expert opinions, allows the decision support functionality to make the user request more detailed, or to suggest that a completely different method should be used. Here, the main problem is (as in many similar situations) how to capture and keep up-to-date the expert knowledge.

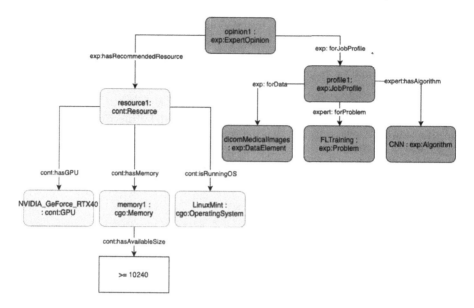

Fig. 9. Example of an expert opinion structure.

4   Concluding Remarks

In this contribution, an ontology-based method for representation of all aspects of knowledge needed to facilitate the use of computational infrastructures have been proposed. The research was initiated for the Grid systems. However, with modifications, it is applicable to Cloud, Fog, Mist and Edge computing paradigms. Applicability of the discussed ideas for Edge-cloud continuum is presented within the scope of the aerOS project. These approaches share a common core assumptions related to distributed computing. The areas that need to be modelled are: infrastructure configuration and state, job definition and collaboration conditions, domain knowledge related to how the system will be utilized, expert knowledge and recommendations.

SPARQL and class expression matching methods are simple and efficient to find some resources that can be used to run a job. However, they do not allow to rank the resources with respect to how well the requirements were met. If too many resources are returned job can be executed on a resource that in fact is not the best. This can hamper the idea of optimizing the continuum performance as a whole. Graph-based resource selection allows to express preferences with respect to requirements that may be more important than others. Based on that, resources can be ranked and the one matching the best the requirements can be selected. However, when user is not sure how to formulate the requirements, this method will not help in using the continuum. Moreover, the way of representing requirements is less intuitive than in case of other methods. Finally, the MCA-based approach gives as a result a ranked list of resources and allows to consider expert recommendations in specifying resource requirements. As a result, the matchmaking between needs and available resources should allow to utilize the continuum in the most efficient way. On the other hand, this approach is not based only on semantic technologies but requires application of a multicriterial analysis method.

Acknowledgments. This work was partially supported by the European Union's "Horizon Europe" research and innovation funding programme as part of the "Autonomous, scalable, trustworthy, intelligent European meta operating system for the IoT edge-cloud continuum" (aerOS) project under Grant Agreement No. 101069732.

References

1. SPARQL 1.1 Overview. https://www.w3.org/TR/sparql11-overview/
2. SPARQL-DL. https://www.w3.org/2001/sw/wiki/SPARQL-DL
3. W3C Semantic Web. https://www.w3.org/standards/semanticweb/
4. Ishizaka, A., Labib, A.: Review of the main developments in the Analytic Hierarchy Process. Expert Systems and Applications **38**(11), 14336–14345 (2011)
5. Asadzadeh, P., Buyya, R., Kei, C., Nayar, D., Venugopal, S.: Global grids and software toolkits: a study of four grid middleware technologies. In: High-Performance Computing: Paradigm and Infrastructure (2004). https://doi.org/10.1002/0471732710.ch22
6. Mareschal, B., Brans, J.P., Macharis, C.: The GDSS PROMETHEE procedure: a PROMETHEE-GAIA based procedure for group decision support. ULB Institutional Repository 2013/9373, ULB – Universite Libre de Bruxelles (1998)
7. Brennan, J., et al.: Scaling campus grids: implementing a modified ontology based emi-wms on campus grids (2013). https://api.semanticscholar.org/CorpusID:59852881
8. Roy, B., Slowinski, R.: Questions guiding the choice of a multicriteria decision aiding method. EURO J. Decis. Process. **1**(1–2), 69–97 (2013). https://doi.org/10.1007/s40070-013-0004-7
9. Buyya, R., Srirama, S.: Fog and edge computing: principles and paradigms. In: Wiley Series on Parallel and Distributed Computing. Wiley (2019). https://books.google.pl/books?id=cdSvtQEACAAJ
10. Hwang, C.L., Yoon, K.: Multiple Attribute Decision Making: Methods and Applications. Springer, Heidelberg (1981). https://doi.org/10.1007/978-3-642-48318-9
11. e Costa, C., Vansnick, J.-C.: A critical analysis of the eigenvalue method used to derive priorities in AHP. Eur. J. Oper. Res. **187**(3), 1422–1428 (2008)
12. Di Martino, B., Rak, M., Ficco, M., Esposito, A., Maisto, S., Nacchia, S.: Internet of things reference architectures, security and interoperability: a survey. Internet of Things **1–2**, 99–112 (2018). https://doi.org/10.1016/j.iot.2018.08.008. https://www.sciencedirect.com/science/article/pii/S2542660518300428
13. Dodgson, J., Spackman, M., Pearman, A., Phillips, L.: Multi-criteria analysis: a manual. Economic history working papers, London School of Economics and Political Science, Department of Economic History (2009)
14. Dyer, R.F., Forman, E.H.: Group decision support with the Analytic Hierarchy Process. Decis. Supp. Syst. **8**, 99–124 (1992)

15. Editor, T.: Design Patterns for SOA and Grid. Technical report, BEinGRID Meta-Deliverable AC1 (2007)
16. Fensel, D.: Ontologies: A Silver Bullet for Knowledge Management and Electronic Commerce, 2nd edn. Springer, New York (2003). https://doi.org/10.1007/978-3-662-09083-1
17. Foster, I.: What is the grid? a three point checklist. Grid Today **1**(6) (2002)
18. Foster, I., Kesselman, C. (eds.): The Grid 2, Second Edition: Blueprint for a New Computing Infrastructure. The Elsevier Series in Grid Computing. Elsevier (2004)
19. Gagliardi, F.: The EGEE European grid infrastructure project, pp. 194–203 (2004). https://doi.org/10.1007/11403937_16
20. Ganzha, M., et al.: Towards high throughput semantic translation. In: Third International Conference, InterIoT 2017, and Fourth International Conference, SaSeIot 2017, Valencia, Spain, 6–7 November 2017, Proceedings, pp. 67–74 (2011). https://doi.org/10.1007/978-3-319-93797-7_9
21. Gruber, T.R.: A translation approach to portable ontology specifications. Knowl. Acquis. **5**(2), 199–220 (1993) . https://doi.org/10.1006/knac.1993.1008
22. Brans, J.P., Vincke, P.: Note-a preference ranking organisation method. Manag. Sci. **31**(6), 647–656 (1985). https://doi.org/10.1287/mnsc.31.6.647
23. Brans, J.P., Vincke, P., Mareschal, B.: How to select and how to rank projects: the PROMETHEE method. Eur. J. Oper. Res. **24**, 228–238 (1986)
24. Figueira, J.R., Greco, S., Slowinski, R.: Building a set of additive value functions representing a reference preorder and intensities of preference: GRIP method. Eur. J. Oper. Res. **195**, 460–486 (2009)
25. Kejriwal, M.: Knowledge graphs: a practical review of the research landscape. Information **13**(4) (2022). https://www.mdpi.com/2078-2489/13/4/161
26. Krauter, K., Buyya, R., Maheswaran, M.: A taxonomy and survey of grid resource management systems for distributed computing. Softw. Pract. Exp. **32**(2), 135–164 (2002). https://doi.org/10.1002/spe.432
27. Laria, D.: D4.1.3 Final BREIN Architecture (2009)
28. López Escobar, J.J., Díaz Redondo, R.P., Gil-Castiñeira, F.: In-depth analysis and open challenges of mist computing. J. Cloud Comput. **11**(1) (2022). https://doi.org/10.1186/s13677-022-00354-x
29. Lysik, K., et al.: Combining aig agents with unicore grid for improvement of user support. In: Guerrero, J.E. (ed.) The First International Symposium on Computing and Networking - Across Practical Development and Theoretical Research, Dogo SPA Resort, Matsuyama, Japan, 4–6 December 2013, pp. 66–74. IEEE Computer Society (2013). https://doi.org/10.1109/CANDAR.2013.18
30. Mesjasz, M.M., Paprzycki, M., Ganzha, M.: Establishing semantic closeness in an agent-based travel support system. Scalable Comput. Pract. Exp. **14**(2), 111–130 (2013). http://www.scpe.org/index.php/scpe/article/view/844
31. Milojicic, D.: The edge-to-cloud continuum. Computer **53**(11), 16–25 (2020). https://doi.org/10.1109/MC.2020.3007297
32. Mimura Gonzalez, N., Carvalho, T., Miers, C.: Cloud resource management: towards efficient execution of large-scale scientific applications and workflows on complex infrastructures. J. Cloud Comput. **6**, 1–20 (2017). https://doi.org/10.1186/s13677-017-0081-4
33. Modoni, G.E., et al.: Integrating the aal casaware platform within an iot ecosystem, leveraging the inter-iot approach. In: Singh, P.K., Pawłowski, W., Tanwar, S., Kumar, N., Rodrigues, J.J.P.C., Obaidat, M.S. (eds.) Proceedings of First International Conference on Computing, Communications, and Cyber-Security (IC4S

2019), pp. 197–212. Springer, Singapore (2020). https://doi.org/10.1007/978-981-15-3369-3_15

34. Paprzycki, M., et al.: Utilization of modified coregrid ontology in an agent-based grid resource management system. In: Philips, T. (ed.) Proceedings of the ISCA 25th International Conference on Computers and Their Applications, CATA 2010, Sheraton Waikiki Hotel, Honolulu, Hawaii, USA, 24–26 March 2010, pp. 240–245. ISCA (2010)

35. Pileggi, S.F., Fernandez-Llatas, C.: Semantic Interoperability Issues, Solutions, Challenges. River Publishers, Wharton (2012)

36. Rhee, S.K., et al.: Measuring semantic closeness of ontologically demarcated resources. Fundam. Inf. **96**(4), 395–418 (2009)

37. Rosendo, D., Costan, A., Valduriez, P., Antoniu, G.: Distributed intelligence on the edge-to-cloud continuum: a systematic literature review. J. Parallel Distrib. Comput. **166**, 71–94 (2022). https://doi.org/10.1016/j.jpdc.2022.04.004. https://www.sciencedirect.com/science/article/pii/S0743731522000843

38. Saaty, T.: The Analytic Hierarchy Process. RWS Publications, Pittsburg (1990)

39. Sestino, A., Prete, M.I., Piper, L., Guido, G.: Internet of things and big data as enablers for business digitalization strategies. Technovation **98**, 102173 (2020). https://doi.org/10.1016/j.technovation.2020.102173. https://www.sciencedirect.com/science/article/pii/S0166497220300456

40. Greco, S., Slowinski, R., Figueira, J.R., Mousseau, V.: Robust ordinal regression. In: Ehrgott, M., Figueira, J.R., Greco, S. (eds.) Trends in Multiple Criteria Decision Analysis, International Series in Operations Research & Management Science, vol. 142, pp. 241–283. Springer, Heidelberg (2010).https://doi.org/10.1007/978-1-4419-5904-1_9

41. Shih, H.S., Shyur, H.J., Lee, E.S.: An extension of TOPSIS for group decision making. Mathematical and Computer Modelling **45**(7-8), 801 – 813 (2000). https://doi.org/10.1016/j.mcm.2006.03.023

42. Sun, L., Dong, H., Hussain, F.K., Hussain, O.K., Chang, E.: Cloud service selection: state-of-the-art and future research directions. J. Netw. Comput. Appl. **45**, 134–150 (2014). https://doi.org/10.1016/j.jnca.2014.07.019. https://www.sciencedirect.com/science/article/pii/S108480451400160X

43. Saaty, T.L.: How to make a decision: the analytic Hierarchy Process. Eur. J. Oper. Res. **48**, 9–26 (1990)

44. Saaty, T.L.: Decision making with the analytic hierarchy process. Int. J. Serv. Sci. **1**(1), 83–98 (2008)

45. Vermesan, O., Bacquet, J.: Next generation internet of things: distributed intelligence at the edge and human machine-to-machine cooperation. In: River Publishers Series in Communications. River Publishers (2019). https://books.google.pl/books?id=hunsvQEACAAJ

46. Wasielewska, K., Ganzha, M., Paprzycki, M., Badica, C., Ivanovic, M., Lirkov, I.: Multicriterial analysis of ontologically represented information. In: AIP Conference Proceedings. vol. 1629, pp. 281–295. American Institute of Physics (2014)

47. Wasielewska, K., Ganzha, M., Paprzycki, M., Badica, C., Ivanovic, M., Lirkov, I.: Semantic technologies in a decision support system. vol. 1684, p. 060002 (2015). https://doi.org/10.1063/1.4934301

48. Wasielewska, K., et al.: Applying saaty's multicriterial decision making approach in grid resource management. Inf. Technol. Control. **43**(1), 73–87 (2014). https://doi.org/10.5755/J01.ITC.43.1.4587

49. Wasielewska, K., et al.: Applying saaty's multicriterial decision making approach in grid resource management. Inf. Technol. Control **43** (2014). https://doi.org/10.5755/j01.itc.43.1.4587

50. Xing, W., Dikaiakos, M.D., Sakellariou, R., Orlando, S., Laforenza, D.: Design and development of a core grid ontology. In: Proceedings of the CoreGRID Workshop: Integrated research in Grid Computing, pp. 21–31 (2005)

Author Index

© The Editor(s) (if applicable) and The Author(s), under exclusive license
to Springer Nature Switzerland AG 2024
S. Sachdeva and Y. Watanobe (Eds.): BDA 2023, LNCS 14516, pp. 317–318, 2024.
https://doi.org/10.1007/978-3-031-58502-9

Printed in the United States
by Baker & Taylor Publisher Services